# DOCUMENTA FIFTEEN HANDBOOK

english

ruangrupa and
Artistic Team

A.K. Kaiza
Alvin Li
Andrew Maerkle
Ann Mbuti
Annie Jael Kwan
Ashraf Jamal
Wong Binghao
Camilo Jiménez Santofimio
Carine Zaayman
Carol Que
Chiara De Cesari
Dagara Dakin

Enos Nyamor
Farhiya Khalid
Ferdiansyah Thajib
Hera Chan
Joachim Ben Yakoub
Krzysztof Kościuczuk
Marta Fernández Campa
Max Kühlem
Nuraini Juliastuti
Övül Ö. Durmuşoğlu
Pablo Larios
Ralf Schlüter
Rayya Badran
Skye Arundhati Thomas
Tina Sherwell

HATJE CANTZ

# Jimmie Durham

## I Want You to Hear These Words About
## Jo Ann Yellowbird
## (Ars Poetica)

From what kind of yellow bird comes the name Yellowbird?
It must mean Kunh gwo, the sacred Yellowhammer.

Ka (But now), no more dreaming or explaining;
Jo Ann Yellowbird took rat poison and died.

A chorus was provided a year before in
A pamphlet concerning related events:
"STOP THE GENOCIDE OF INDIAN PEOPLE"
"Jo Ann Yellowbird, an activist in
the American Indian Movement, was seven months
pregnant when she was kicked in the stomach
by a police officer. Two weeks later her
baby, Zintkalazi, was born dead. Jo Ann
has filed suit against the officer who kicked her
and the authorities who refused her medical treatment."

And to show that I am a sophisticated poet and
Not a pamphleteer, I quote from the Vocabulary
Of a Lakota Primer printed to educate those children
Of the Pine Ridge who have not been kicked to death:

| | |
|---|---|
| Billy Boy said, | Billy eya |
| "I like the sheriff" | Canakaa wustuca lake |
| Overtake the night | A han he ju |
| Starve | Aki ran |
| Pneumonia | Caru na pere |
| Wash your face | Ete glu jajja |
| Your face is dirty | Ete nu sapa |
| Comb your hair | Glak ca yo |
| Wash your clothes | Ha klu ja ja pi |
| Supervisor | Igmu wa pa se |
| Always take a bath | Ye han nu wan po |
| Be silent! | Inila yanka yo |
| My eye hurts | Ista mayazan |
| Commissioner of Indian Affairs | Ta kal Tunkashile ya pi |
| Earth | Maka |
| Plow | Maka iyublic |
| 160 acres | Maka i yu ta pi sope la |
| Shovel | Ma ki pap te |
| Allotment | Makove owapi |
| My chest hurts | Maku mayazan |
| I have none | Manice |
| Heaven | Marpiya |
| The Pope | Oyublaye |
| Church | Owacekiye |
| Your ears are dirty | Nure ni sape |
| My ears ache | Nure opa mayazan |
| Wrong procedure | Ogna sni |
| Cut your hair | Pehin gla sla yo |

from: *Poems That Do Not Go Together*, Wiens Verlag, Berlin and Edition Hansjörg Mayer, London, 2012

# CONTENTS

# CONTENTS

# INTRODUCTION 8
# LUMBUNG 10
# WHAT IS HARVEST? 42
# A–Z INDEX 44



# KASSEL – VENUES 226

## MITTE 228



## FULDA 246



## BETTENHAUSEN 256



## NORDSTADT 262



# SUSTAINABILITY & ACCESSIBILITY 266
# VISITOR INFORMATION 270
# ENGAGEMENT 274
# APPENDIX 284

# INTRODUCTION

documenta fifteen
*publication plan*

**I — PRACTICAL**

① HANDBOOK
- German
- English

② CHILDREN'S BOOK
walking,
finding,
sharing

**II — COSMOLOGICAL**

① LUMBUNG STORIES
Literary book on
lumbung cosmology
( 8 publishers,
7 authors)

② MAJALAH LUMBUNG
Bound edition
- German

③ MAJALAH LUMBUNG
2 (two) editions
Vol 1 : Harvest
Vol 2 : Sharing
- English, Indonesian

**III — TOPICAL**

① MANUALS FOR THE LIVING

② MANUALS FOR THE DYING

**IV — PROCESSUAL**

● LUMBUNG PRES[S]

① ARTISTS' BOOK

② HARVEST BOOK BY THE ARTISTIC TEAM

③ HARVEST BOOK BY RURUHAUS

# ASSALAMUALAIKUM[1], DEAR READER

With this handbook you will get detailed insight into documenta fifteen. While still containing general information about the exhibition, it is also informative about the important collective processes that preceded it and that permeate the show without necessarily being visible to the naked eye. The following section, titled *lumbung*, is a collectively authored chronicle of our journey towards the 15th edition of documenta. It starts with the collective "us" of ruangrupa, the Artistic Directors, and our extension, the Artistic Team, and spirals out to include more and more individuals and collectives who have joined us on the lumbung journey.

lumbung is a term you will hear a lot throughout this book and the exhibition. It refers to a concept of collective sharing that lies at the heart of documenta fifteen, and its meaning will become apparent in the coming pages. The images and drawings accompanying this section are from the lumbung *harvest*. The harvest is an artistic recording of discussions and *majelis* assemblies meant for passing forward knowledge and experience. It will also be present in the different venues of the exhibition.

The handbook gives basic information about lumbung practice and the members' and artists' *translation* of their local practices to Kassel, as well as about the other artists to whom they have extended invitations. We see the three-year preparation period and associated processes as an important part of documenta fifteen. In addition, the handbook contains information about our open space, *ruruHaus*, and the local *ekosistem* in Kassel, as well as the public program *Meydan* and the mediation program *sobat-sobat*.

This can always be only a snapshot, because documenta fifteen is not a static exhibition. Many contributions by *lumbung artists* and members will continue to evolve and change during the exhibition period and after.

In addition to the handbook, there are other publications dedicated to specific aspects of lumbung as practice, cosmology, experimentation, and playfulness that are, in themselves, results of lumbung processes.

We hope you will have a great time reading and spending time in the exhibition and with the lumbung members and artists. And remember! "Make friends not art!"[2]

```
ruangrupa & Artistic Team
documenta fifteen
```

1 *Assalamualaikum* is a common greeting in Indonesia, used both formally and colloquially, meaning "peace be upon you."
2 *ruangrupa, siasat* a short tactical guide for artist run initiative, https://www.sculpture-center.org/files/siasat.pdf

# LU⌁BUNG

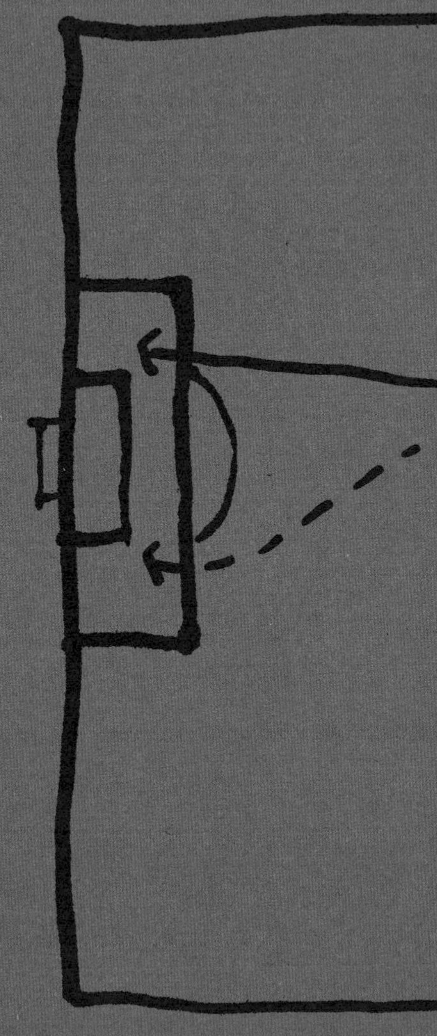

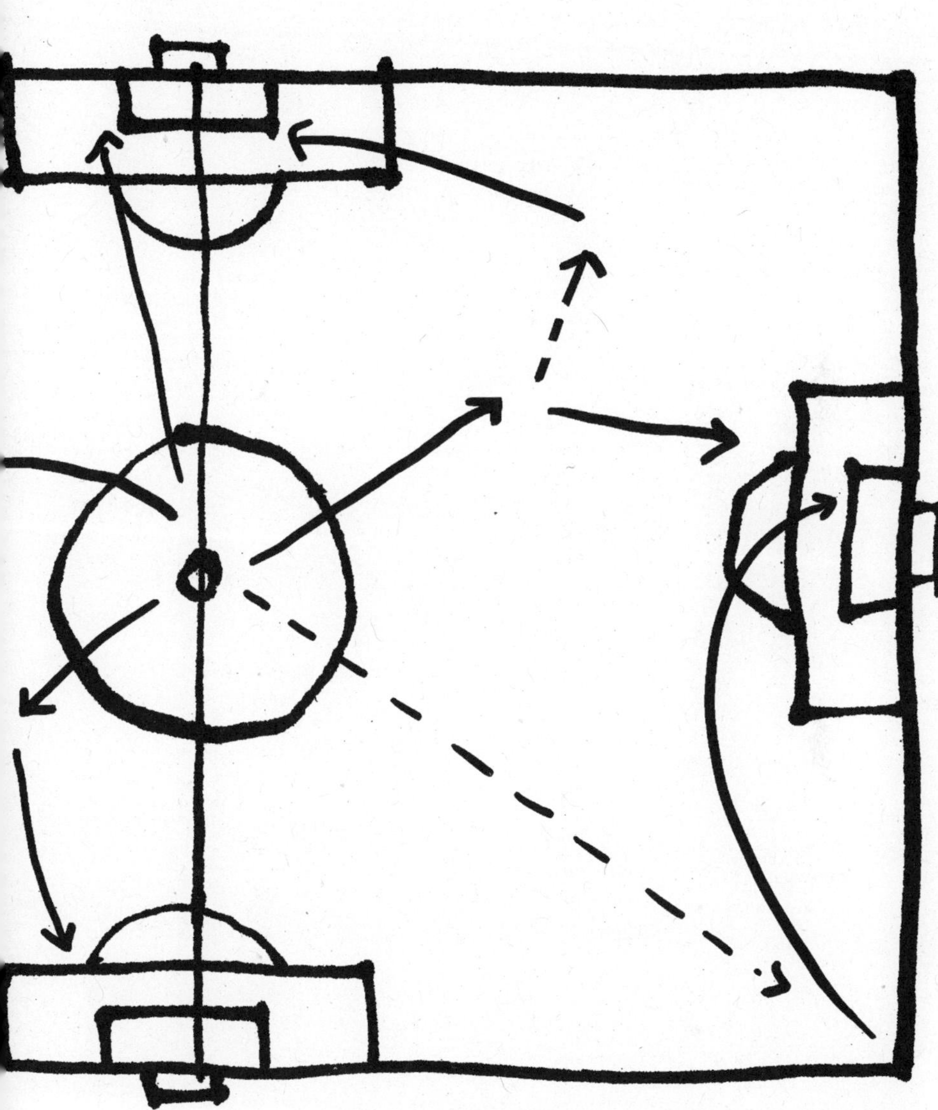

total *football* with many *goals*

Harvest drawings by Andrés Villalobos (left) and Daniella F Praptono (right)

Assalamualaikum

# ABOUT THE LUMBUNG PROCESSES AND HOW THE GUEST BECOMES THE HOST

ruangrupa is an art collective started in 2000 in Jakarta, Indonesia. Our experimentations with lumbung began critically. A vernacular agrarian term in Bahasa Indonesia, "lumbung" refers to a rice barn where a village community stores their harvests together, to be managed collectively, as a way to face an unpredictable future. Its initial use was as a metaphor, to explain the possibility of putting financial resources in a central account to be managed together.

This centralized financial account and our initial approach to resources as purely financial both proved to be false. Only after several trial-and-error attempts did we realize that even shareable resources can be held by different hands, put in different pockets, and communally governed whenever different needs arise over time. Since 2013, we—ruangrupa with other Jakarta-based collectives—have tried to build ekosistems based on an understanding that even a group of people, a collective, cannot stand alone, but must purposefully play a part in their larger context—just as in nature, where different species have their specific functions and roles to keep an ecosystem in balance.

The first of these ekosistems was dubbed the Gudang Sarinah Ekosistem, taking the name of the former-warehouse complex we occupied together in Jakarta and turned into the center of many of our activities. This way-too-large experiment gave way to Gudskul Ekosistem, an informal educational platform ruangrupa established with two other collectives, Serrum and Grafis Huru Hara, in 2018. With Gudskul, the notion of lumbung as the operational system for the ekosistem that believes and develops as a collective of collectives carries on indefinitely. Against this background, when we were invited to make a proposal for the fifteenth edition of documenta, instead of integrating ourselves into the long-established documenta system, we decided to stay on our path. We invited documenta back, asking it to be part of *our* journey. We refuse to be exploited by European, institutional agendas that are not ours to begin with. We believe that we must make this experience of imagining an edition of documenta contribute back to our own endeavors.

Gudskul can be understood as a miniature of what is to come with documenta's fifteenth edition. What ruangrupa has achieved together with Serrum and Grafis Huru Hara through Gudskul and the collective of collectives cannot be transposed literally to other contexts, not least because the investment of time and space, with its build-up of trust and friendships, cannot simply be copy-pasted. After realizing this, the timeline we first proposed was as follows:

> 2019
> warming up and research phase
> 2020
> institutional and artistic
> building phase
> 2021
> articulation and content
> finalization phase
> 2022
> souk or *istiqlal* phase
> 2023
> sustainability schemes
> implementation phase

Yet, in time, it became clear that many different forces prevented us from implementing the protocols laid out in the original timeline. Covid-19 was one big element, but other realities became evident, which meant we had to be ready to be tactical. Negotiation became the name of the game.

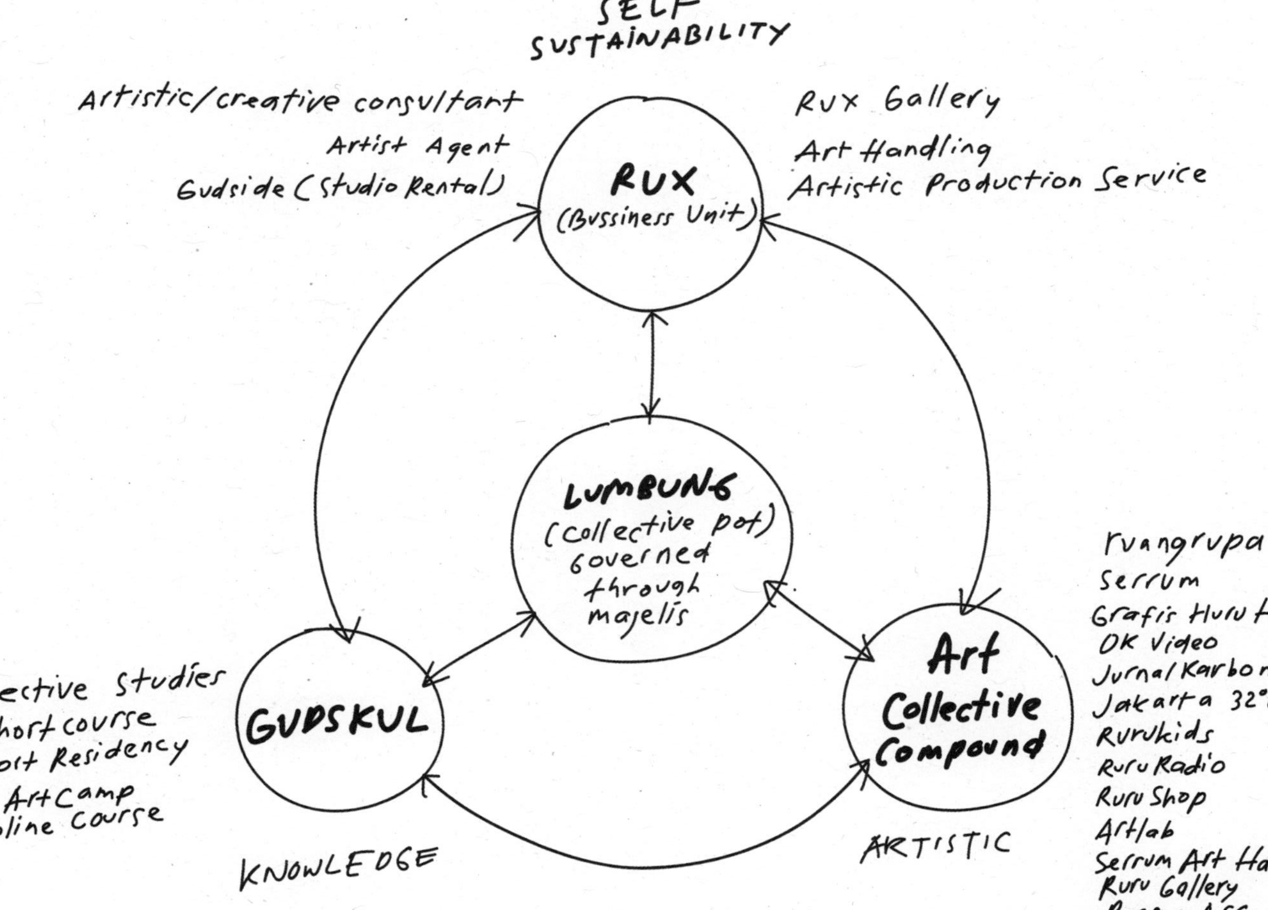



About the lumbung processes and how the guest becomes the host

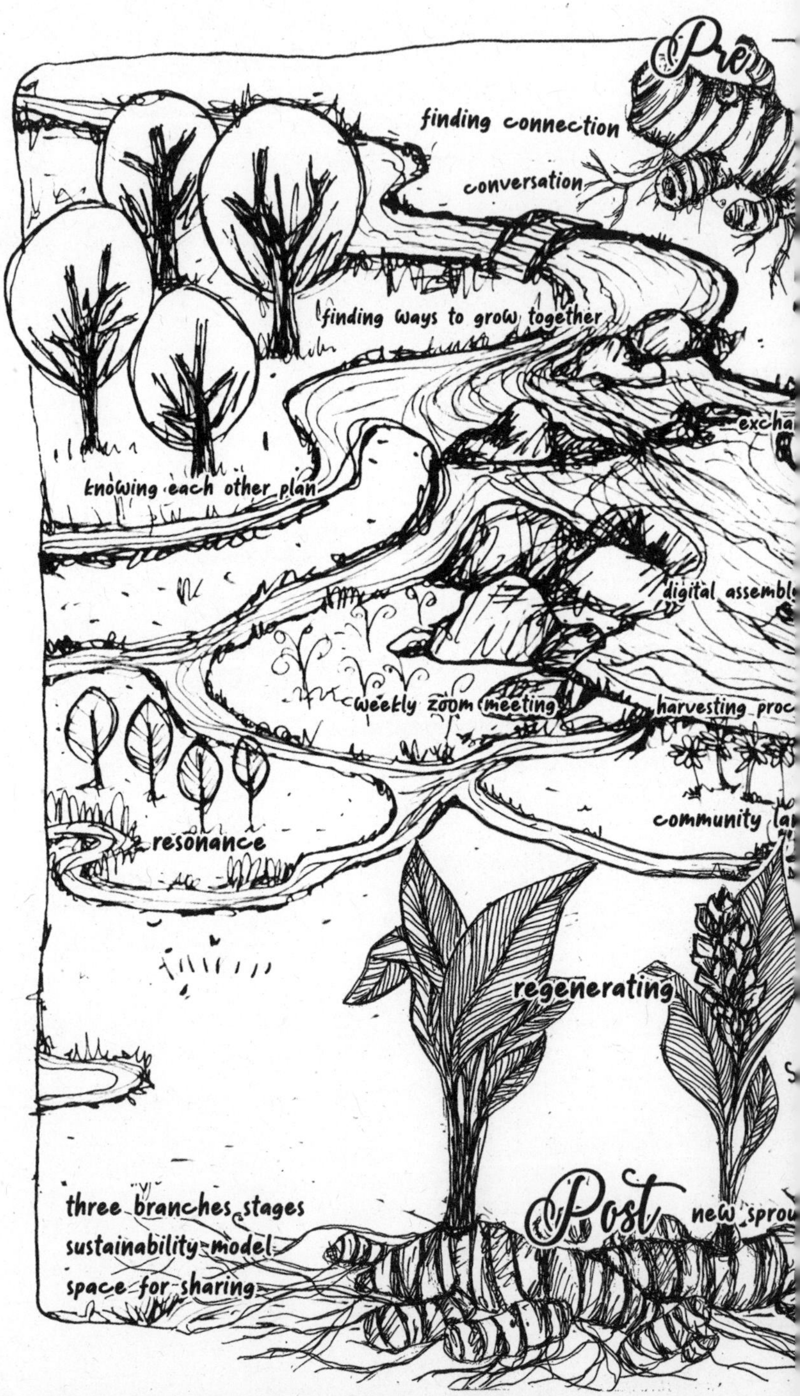
finding connection
conversation
Pre
finding ways to grow together
excha
knowing each other plan
digital assembl
weekly zoom meeting
harvesting proc
resonance
community la
regenerating
three branches stages
sustainability model
space for sharing
Post
new sprou

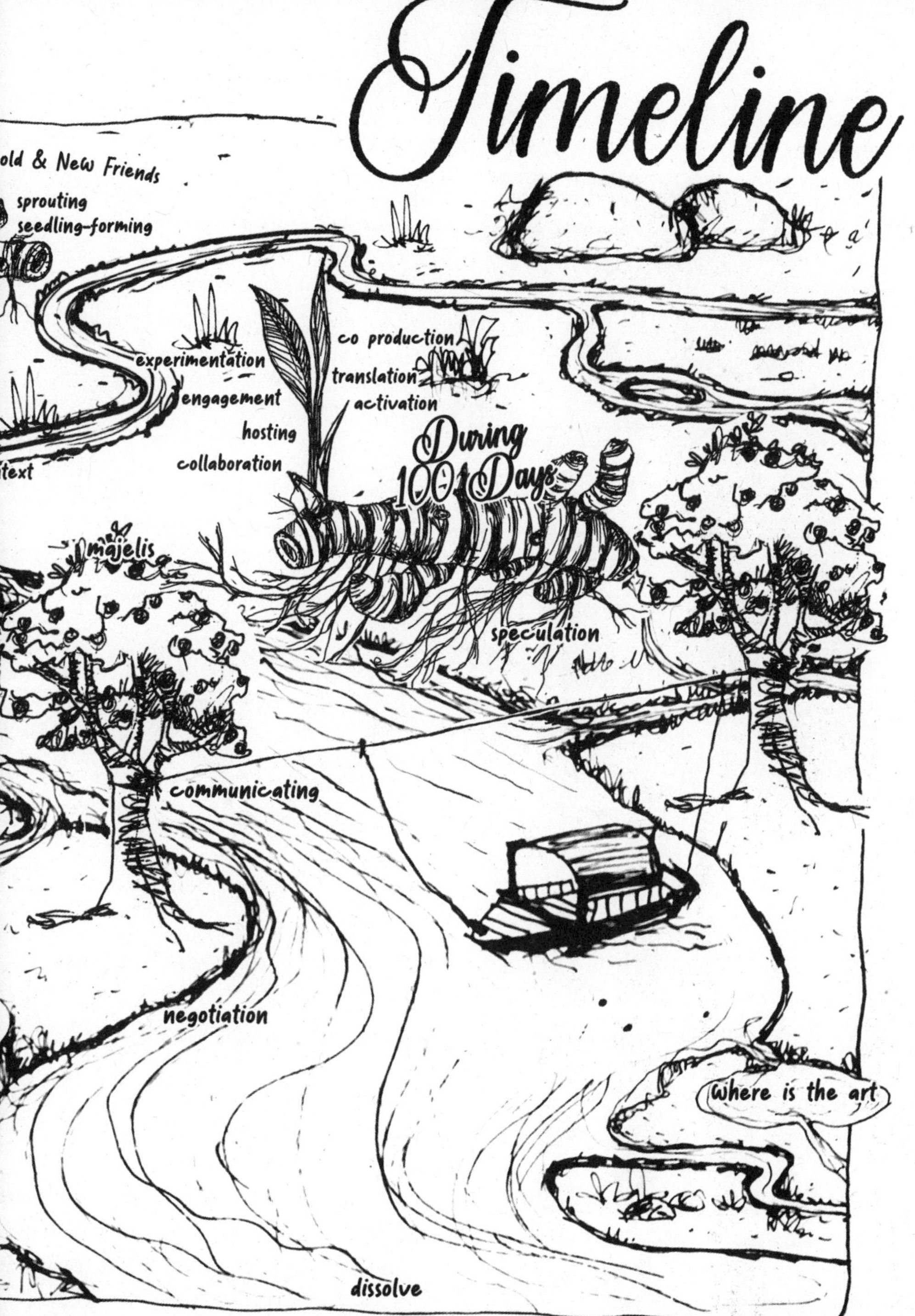

Timeline
old & New Friends
sprouting
seedling-forming
experimentation
engagement
hosting
collaboration
text
co production
translation
activation
During 1001 Days
majelis
speculation
communicating
negotiation
dissolve
where is the art
About the lumbung processes and how the guest becomes the host

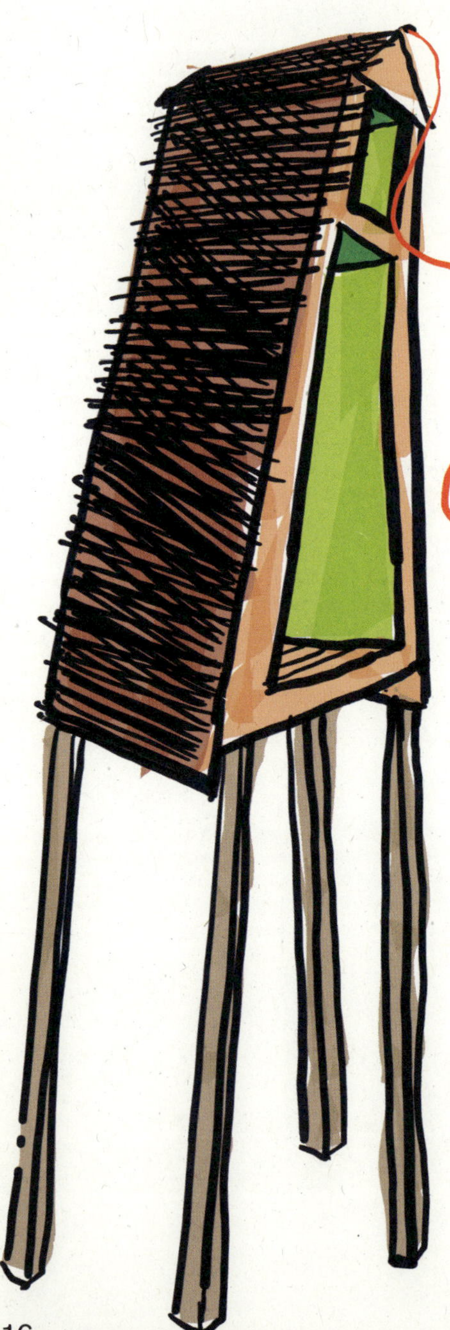

After documenta accepted our invitation to join our journey and to become part of our ekosistem, we decided—with their opportunities and support—to keep on extending invitations to different people. First, to five individuals in Kassel, Amsterdam, Jerusalem, and Møn, whom we believed could be an extension of ruangrupa. We thus formed the group that would become known as the Artistic Team. But there were also other initiatives in the world which we felt were already practicing lumbung and its values. We called on them to join us in imagining together what documenta fifteen could be. The first fourteen initiatives we invited committed to becoming part of lumbung-building processes before and beyond documenta fifteen. These initiatives became known as *lumbung inter-lokal* members. More than 50 other artistic practices, both individual and collective in nature, joined afterwards, forming what has become known as lumbung artists.

Besides these invitations, our own existence in our current localities had to be carved out more deeply in Indonesia, more broadly in our international circles, and newly in Kassel. Thus, together, *lumbung Indonesia*, *lumbung inter-lokal*, and *lumbung Kassel* were formed, with the aim of their members identifying what resources were in their power and deciding how to use them. This way, we were sure that documenta fifteen would not be solely ruangrupa's but would also belong to others.

This was a high-risk move, as, in the time of writing, we are still curious to see whether the 100 days of documenta fifteen will only result in pragmatic exercises—a temporary "time-off" for artists and initiatives to learn from—only to swing back to the old system of doing things, relapsing to state funding and/or free art-market systems, or even the biennial circuits. Based on our

Harvest drawings by Abdul Dyba (left) and Nino Bulling (right)

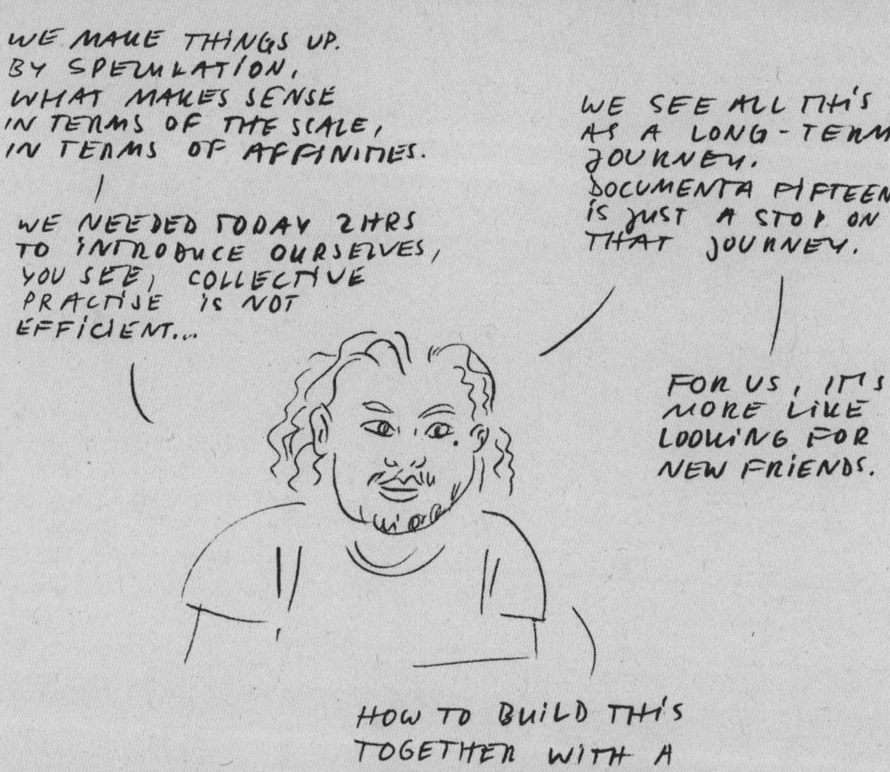


different past, collective experiences of operating within these existing systems, they have proven to be highly competitive, globally expansive, greedy, and capitalistic—in short, exploitative and extractive.

Will the much-needed dissolution of ownership and authorship happen in documenta fifteen? How will economy, credits, and aesthetics be practiced and therefore understood differently in the 100 days? These are things that we'd like to see happen.

There are different ways and practices of producing art (works). These practices are not (yet) visible, as they do not fit the existing model of the global art world(s). documenta fifteen is an attempt to clash these different realities against each other, showing that different ways are possible. Instead of fitting these various modes of production into what exists already, it should act as a series of exercises for reshaping and sow seeds for more changes in the future. Different ways of producing art will create different works, which, in turn, will ask for other ways of being read and understood: artworks that are functioning in real lives in their respective contexts, no longer pursuing mere individual expression, no longer needing to be exhibited as standalone objects or sold to individual collectors and hegemonic state-funded museums. Other ways are possible. In this way, we are resisting the domestication or taming of these different practices.

# "RURUHAUS" I

For many people
Kassel is an in-between,
before they move to
bigger cities.

A lot of people in
the cultural sphere
would like to change
that

Kassel has lots
of empty spaces,
even right here
in the center
of the city.

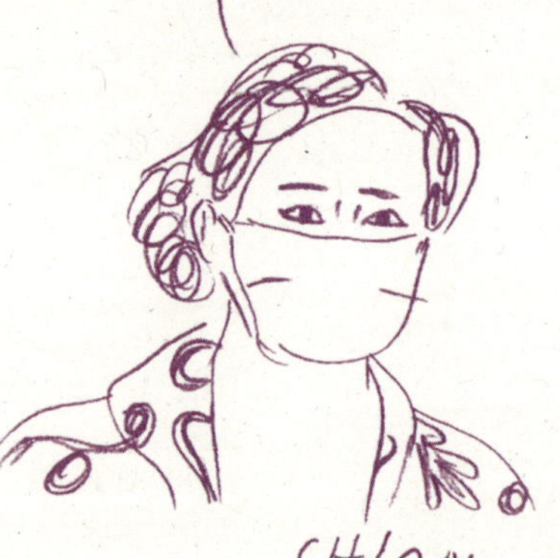



a lot of the
cultural spaces in the
city center are very
institutional spaces,
so the other things
happen off - center

(I missed the
beginning of
this presentation,
sorry)


Harvest drawings by
Nino Bulling (left)
and Abdul Dube (right)

# APPROACH TO KASSEL: RURUHAUS AND THE FACT THAT "WE COULD SLEEP IN THE LIVING ROOM"

From the off, we have experienced Kassel as an urban organism and ekosistem of local initiatives and collectives, rather than as exhibition context and history. To open a dialogue with surrounding ekosistems, we identified a number of interlinked "acupuncture points," using the analogy of the ancient Asian medical practice of healing the body with a slow but holistic method that looks at the workings of the body system and its millions of nerves and arteries. This logic of acupoints in a network of energy paths was used to approach the venues and spaces of documenta fifteen. Infiltrating the urban fabric of Kassel, decentralizing the center, and opening connections to the less culturally used areas in the East.

In Jakarta, out of necessity, ruangrupa would rent domestic houses and turn them into exhibition spaces, especially for art students to hang out, program, exhibit, and even live in. So, a bedroom and a living room could become exhibition spaces that would simultaneously be someone's living quarters. In keeping with this approach, we started ruruHaus in the center of Kassel as a shared living room in the city. While "ruru" is short for ruangrupa, the idea of ruruHaus is not for ruangrupa to occupy space in the city center, but to be part of a context where initiatives from Kassel (and visiting artists and members) can connect, and where they can extend themselves into the future as a collective of collectives.

In Europe, there tend to be very centrist ideas about knowledge, history, and art, ideas that we would like to decentralize or decompress within the ruruHaus. In the summer of 2020, amid the pandemic, two members of ruangrupa moved to Kassel when the first window since lockdown began made international travel possible again. Their focus became hosting the Kassel community along with all the visiting members and artists for whom ruruHaus would not be just a living room, but also a laboratory to test their planned translations from their own locales to Kassel's ekosistem.

Other than the 65-year tradition of documenta, we encountered many other local initiatives in the city, making it possible for lumbung to take on even more meanings in Kassel. We began looking at the initiatives to understand how (self) sufficient they were and if they had a surplus that they would like to share. This could be anything: from something educational to diverse experiences.

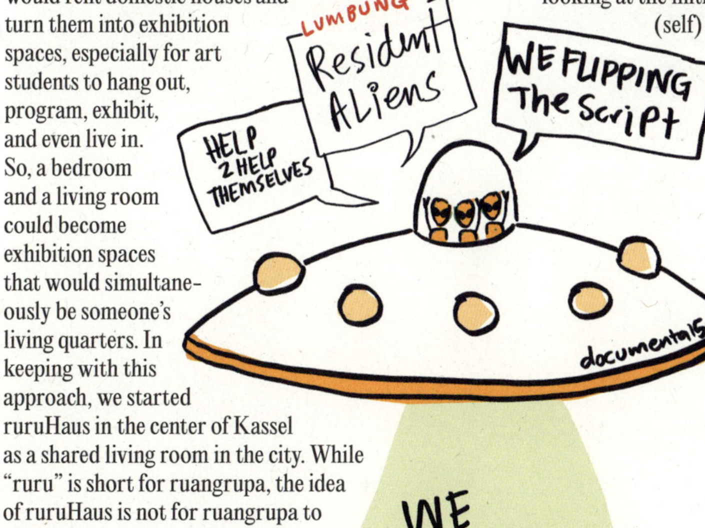

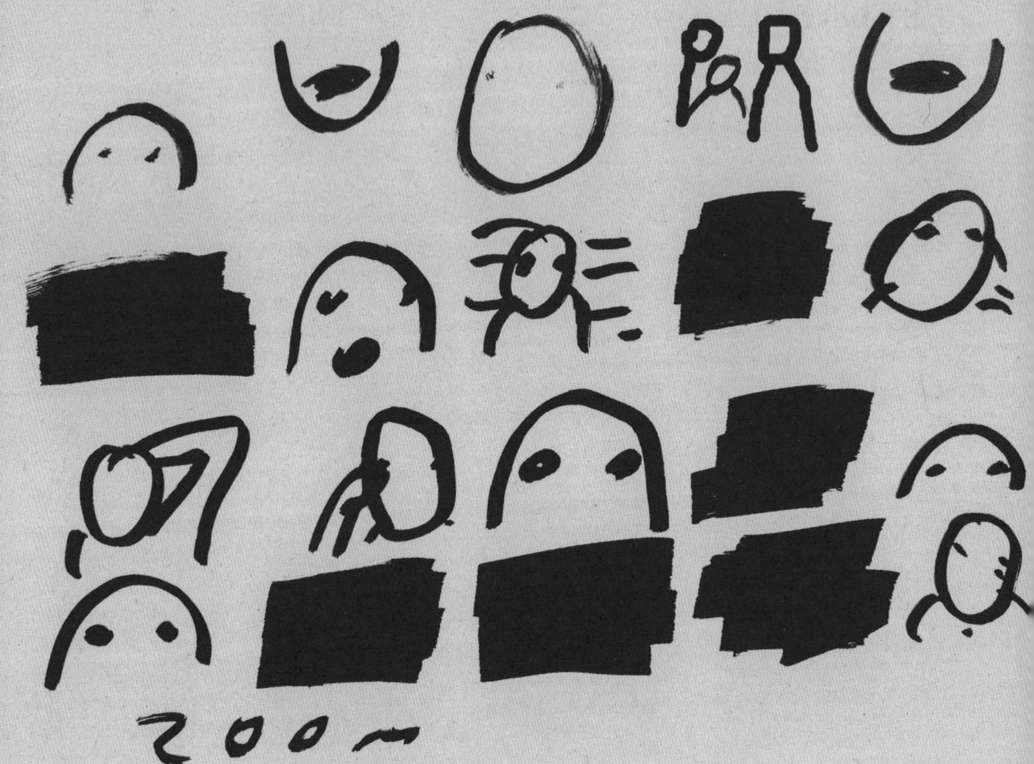




*    We later regretted this division of 20,000 Euro per artist, or communicating it this way to the artists. At times it created a sense of individual ownership of each 20,000 Euro in the common pot. If we had communicated the total sum, the conversations might have differed. In some mini-majelises, the conversations led to a consideration of the total sum of the budget, while in others the artists who were more present and active in the majelises felt like they could not govern the budgets of the absent artists, and so offered them back to the artists.

# "YOU ARE MUTE" (COVID-19 REALITY HITTING) AND GOING FROM FULL LUMBUNG TO GADO GADO

While our collective experiences under Covid-19 relegated us to the disembodied space of video conferencing, they allowed us to reflect again on the value of solidarity. We needed to go even further in fostering new networking models and more sustainable structures for small-to-medium arts initiatives. Consequently, we needed to rethink still further what artistic practices and events are, what they could and should be. All these issues relate to socio-political problems faced in the members' respective contexts, from Jakarta and Chocó in Colombia to Jerusalem; Nairobi, Kenya; Havana, Cuba; Dhaka, Bangladesh; and many other cities and villages where lumbung members practice.

Following ruangrupa's longstanding practice of dividing money and resources according to needs (a duo has different needs to a large collective, the needs of a person living alone and a parent with a big household are not the same), we considered our options, one of them being paying basic income to everyone for the entire time of working with documenta fifteen. Having looked into the figures, we faced the fact that, if we paid everyone a basic income, we wouldn't have sufficient budget for even a medium-sized exhibition. One solution, which we dubbed "full lumbung," was to stick to the 25 lumbung members that ruangrupa proposed in their original invitation to documenta and ask them to involve more of their ekosistem in their translation of their local practice to the exhibition in Kassel. The stakes were high, given that many commentators in Germany and beyond took ruangrupa's appointment and the lumbung concept to mean there being no exhibition at all, or an exhibition of non-art, in 2022. Furthermore, we were having Zoom visits with many artists who were



working in and out of collectivity in their locales, and whom we felt would enrich the lumbung process and the exhibition.

So, we had to come up with a model that would be fair, even if not ideal, that we called *gado-gado* (a dish with a bit of everything from the Indonesian kitchen).

In the end, we decided to stick to the fourteen members we had already invited for the long haul and invite about 50 artists, mostly collectives, to commit to the lumbung process and the 100 days in Kassel. The production budget for each lumbung inter-lokal member is 180,000 Euro, and 25,000 Euro seed money. Seed money is a budget paid upfront, which we see as an acknowledgment of the years of work in the artists' localities and as a seal of our agreement to find translations of that work to Kassel in 2022. This translation in its turn is made in such a way that it becomes (re) generative for the work beyond documenta fifteen. For many, the budget came at a crucial time, strengthening their sustainability during the pandemic. While the artists received the equal amounts of 60,000 Euro for production, with 10,000 Euro seed money for collectives, and 5,000 Euro for individuals. This came out of a long discussion among the Artistic Team members and the documenta gGmbH. The discussion started with the aim to distribute part of the available budget to all the involved artists as basic income, or for basic needs. However, as the discussion ensued the idea of a common pot occurred, with 20,000 EUR per participating group in collective management, in order to leave it to the artists themselves to decide how to use it in the exhibition.*

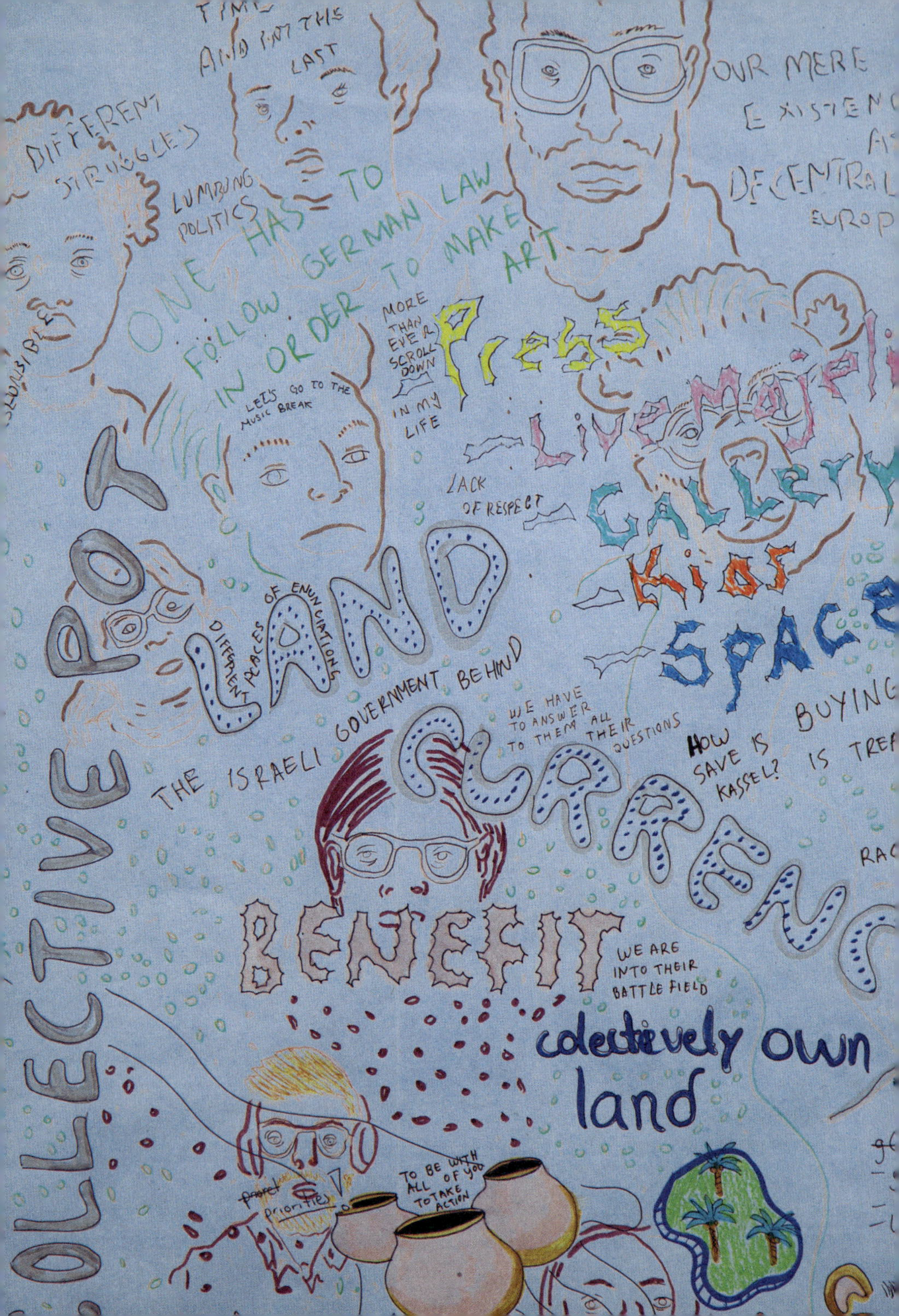

DIFFERENT STRUGGLES
TIME AND INFO THIS LAST
OUR MERE EXISTENCE AS DECENTRAL EUROP
LUMBUNG POLITICS
ONE HAS TO FOLLOW GERMAN LAW IN ORDER TO MAKE ART
MORE THAN EVER SCROLL DOWN
IN MY LIFE
Press
Live more
LET'S GO TO THE MUSIC BREAK
LACK OF RESPECT
GALLERY
KIDS
SPACE
COLLECTIVE POT
LAND
DIFFERENT PLACES OF ENUNCIATIONS
THE ISRAELI GOVERNMENT BEHIND
WE HAVE TO ANSWER TO THEM ALL THEIR QUESTIONS
HOW SAVE IS KASSEL? IS TREA
CURRENC
BENEFIT
WE ARE INTO THEIR BATTLE FIELD
collectively own land
project priorities
TO BE WITH ALL OF YOU TO TAKE ACTION

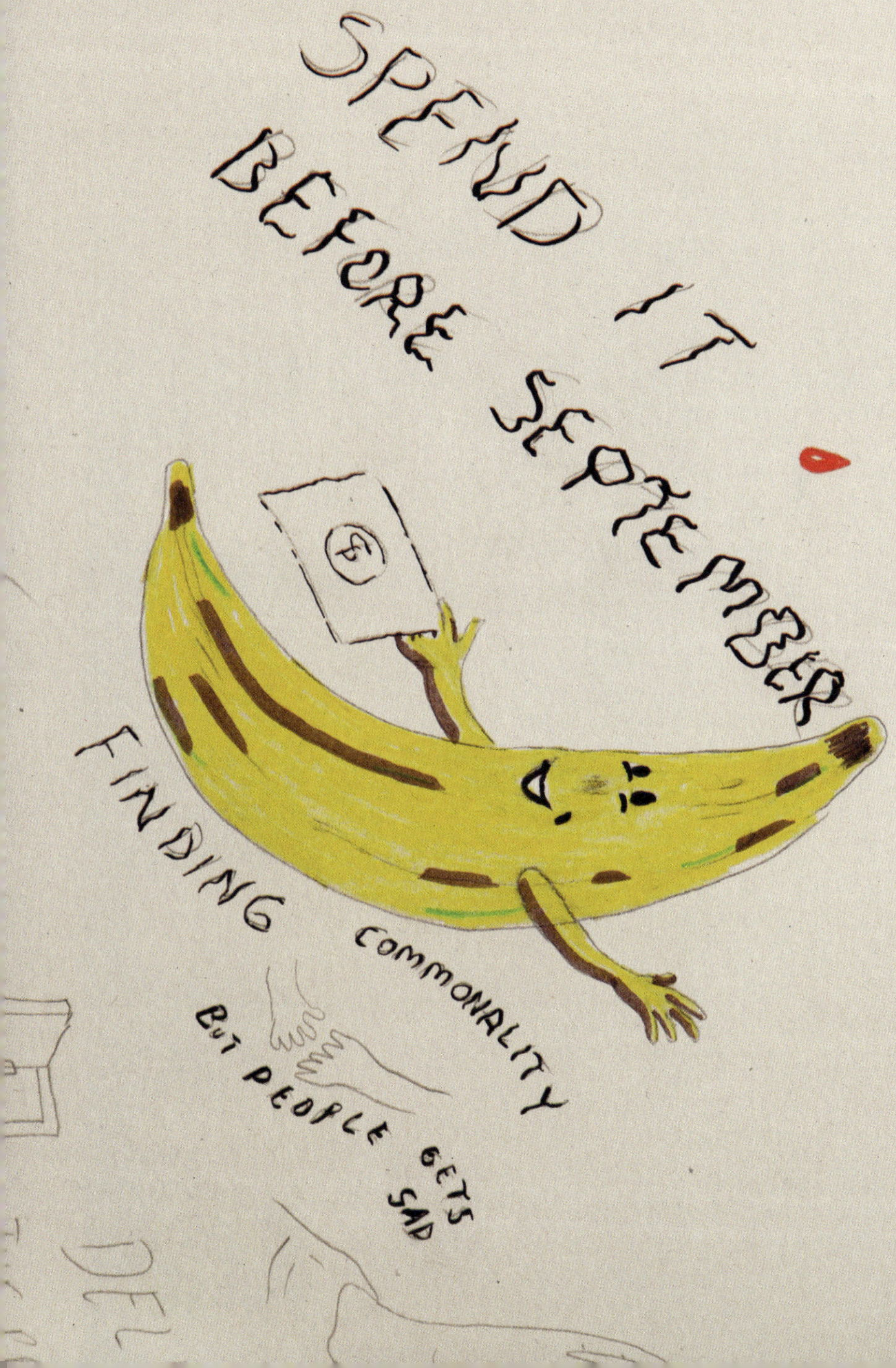

SPEND IT
BEFORE SEPTEMBER
FINDING COMMONALITY
BUT PEOPLE GETS SAD

# FROM MINI TO AKBAR: "WE ARE NOT IN DOCUMENTA FIFTEEN, WE ARE IN LUMBUNG ONE"

Through majelises, the lumbung artists and lumbung members could become part of the collective curatorial process and the wider documenta economy, or documenta lumbung. Before the pandemic, our idea was for majelises to occur every 100 days in order to decide collectively on the building of the exhibition, the principles of how to distribute resources, and other matters. The majelis is a learning space, where there is no competition. The majelises were to be held in a different city every time, and to be hosted by lumbung members. However, as a result of the pandemic, it was necessary to hold the majelises online.

The fourteen lumbung inter-lokal members have been discussing how to build both the exhibition and the longer term lumbung economy—beyond documenta fifteen—since June 2020, at first in bi-weekly majelises with the entire lumbung inter-lokal, and later in smaller groups. These discussions have produced several working groups that have taken on topics that are of common necessity. Most collectives in the lumbung inter-lokal come from contexts where the state had failed to support the development of infrastructure and a support system for art and culture.

Since the model of the stable institution had failed, they had seized the opportunity to rethink institutions. So, the questions of economic survival and autonomy were central in the lumbung inter-lokal. An economy working group grew out of discussions around what sustainability is and various experiments with currencies and circular economy, inviting economists to work sessions and putting forward ideas and mechanisms. Out of this working group, new ones formed: *lumbung Gallery*, *lumbung Kios*, and *lumbung Currency* working groups were set up to experiment practically with various ways to sustain and ask cultural questions through economic projects, as well as sustaining the lumbung pot after documenta fifteen. Another pressing issue in the lumbung inter-lokal mem-

bers' localities is land, since, whether endangered by corporate, political, or urban infringement, the sustainability of the members' ekosistems is at stake in the long run. The important discourse around the lumbung members' artistic practices led to another dynamic discussion and what we called the *"Where is the Art?"* working group. *lumbung.space* and a lumbung of Independent Publishers grew out of the need to amplify those discourses, where art and life are one.

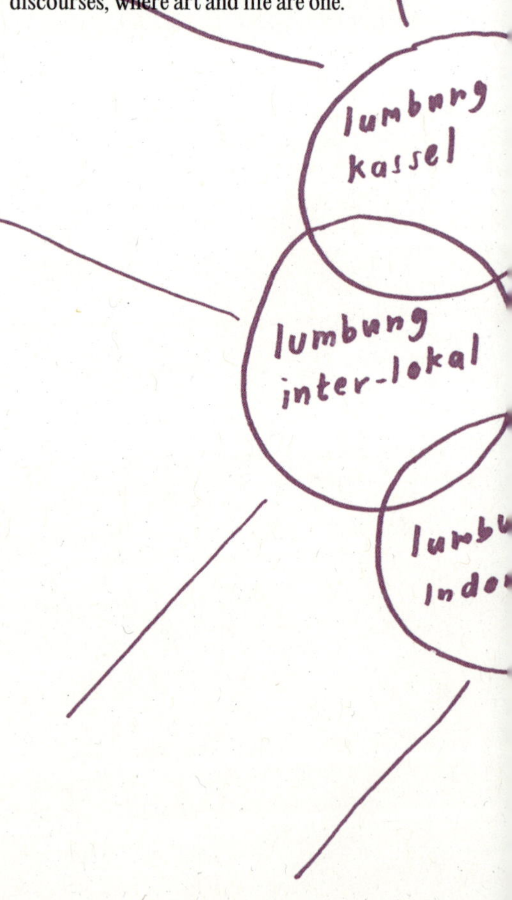

lumbung
artist

-IBAWIKRRR
REINAART VANHOE
RICHARD BELL
TARING PADI
WAKALIGA UGANDA

AGUSNURAMAL PM TOH
ARTS COLLABORATORY
BLACK QUANTUM FUTURISM
CHIMURENGA
JUMANA EMIL ABBOUD
NINO BULLING
SUBVERSIVE FILM

CINEMA CARAVAN + TAKASHI
KURIBAYASHI
KIRI DALENA
NGUYEN TRINH THI
SAFDAR AHMED

ATIS REZISTANS / GHETTO
BIENALLE
MARWA ARJANIOS
SOURABH PHADKE
YASMINE EID SABBAGH
+FOUNDATION CLASS

ALICE YARD
ERRCK BELTRAN
LE 18
MADE YOU LOOK
PARTY OFFICE
SERIGRAFISTAS QUEER

AMOL K PATIL
BOLOHO
CHEN JIANJUN & CAO MINGHO
CHONG EN-MAN
SA SA ART PROJECTS

HAMJA AHSAN
JIMMIE DURHAM
LA INTERMUNDIAL HOLOBIENTE
PINAR OGRENCI
SAODAT ISMAILOVA

ROHM NOORG COLABORANVE
ARTS & CULTURE
DAN PERJOVICHI
ASPARAS
NHA SAN
THE REST

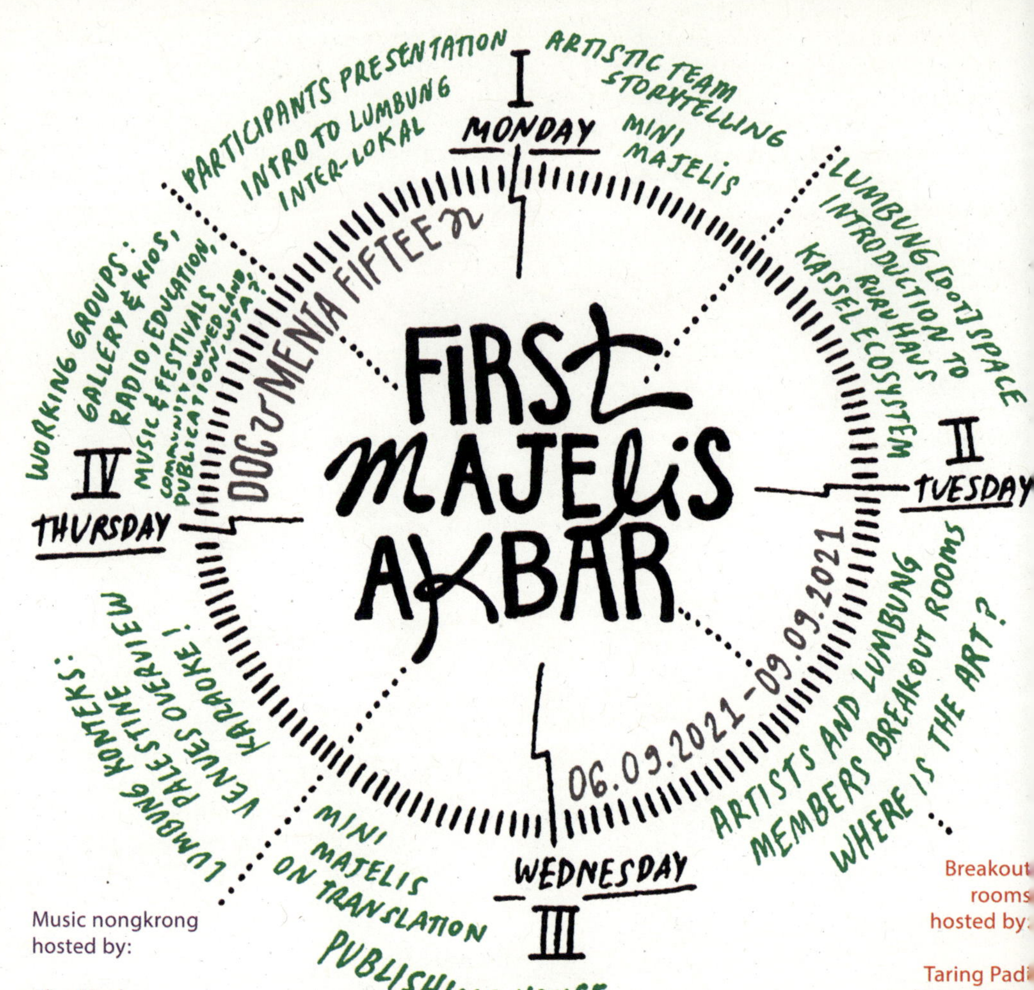


Music nongkrong
hosted by:

Alice Yard
Indra Ameng
Fondation Festival sur le Niger
Radio Rasclat
PMTOH

Breakout
rooms
hosted by:

Taring Padi
Party Office
Asia Art Archive
Amol K Patil
Cao Minghao & Chen Jianjun
Jumana Emil Abboud
La Intermundial Holobiente
Cinema Caravan
Britto Arts Trust
Jatiwangi art Factory

Harvest drawings by
Sari Dennise (left) and
Andrés Villalobos (right)

With all the different majelises established—ten in total—we needed a gathering space for the majelises to come together and to get an overview of all the discussions going on. Our answer was to host a mega assembly, known as *majelis akbar*, on a regular basis. These online meetings have been attended by 150 to 200 artists and members. In these meetings, members and artists talk about specific projects for artists and members to collaborate on, as well as on how to be in solidarity with each other, and how to share space, knowledge, program, and equipment together during the 100 days. Examples of this are: Cinema Caravan opening their cinema for others to use, the ZK/U turning their building's roof into a boat and bringing it to Kassel for other artists in the lumbung to activate, Party Office opening up the public program they host in their venue in WH22 for other artists to organize, and Richard Bell opening his *Tent Embassy* for artists to converse in during the hundred days and many more.



The majelis akbar was also a place for discussions about issues in the local context of lumbung members, for exchanging ideas about collaboration, and for forging solidarity. For example, we also talked about how we should respond to accusations of anti-Semitism that emerged from a Kassel blog in January 2022 and were picked up by German media. documenta fifteen, the artistic direction, team members, and individual artists were attacked in a way that we understood as racist. This was a shock to us and even led to concerns for our safety. During majelis akbar in January 2022, the artists discussed how both the lumbung and documenta could stand behind and, in the spirit of lumbung, support those affected. documenta also published several statements in which it rejected the accusations and made it clear that anti-Semitism and racism have no place at documenta fifteen. At the same time, it emphasized the right to freedom of expression in art, culture, and science. The majelises have been important tools to develop common understandings and

solidarity with everyone's local contexts, allowing us to learn from differing situations and conditions in each of the lumbung localities, especially where there has been political upheaval over the two years leading up to documenta fifteen, such as in Colombia, Palestine, Cuba, and Mali. This has also compelled us to develop a common discourse on our artistic practice.

The Where is the Art? working group grew out of this strong, shared necessity among lumbung members and artists to discuss how art is rooted in life and their social, activist, economic practices, and not limited to disciplines or definitions. Every inter-lokal member experiences a distortion in the way their practices are translated to the mainstream international art scene, and what it tends to define as "art." We established a working group that organizes workshops in local ekosistems and among artists and members, which formed the basis of building a collective language and knowledge base across practices and contexts.

The *lumbung land* working group, on the other hand, has been discussing developing a way of "investing" by using the collective pot in specific land projects run by members—projects that question ownership of land, that start from community needs and collective use and governance, and that combine agriculture, biodiversity, culture, and the spiritual. Combining experimentation on land with experimentation on currencies and decentralized autonomous organizations would be a start towards building a true, inter-locally connected and collectively governed economy.

While the conversations in the economy working group about how to sustain ourselves beyond documenta fifteen were ongoing, we learned from the permanent staff that has produced previous editions that most of the artworks exhibited are sold backstage by gallerists during the hundred days of the exhibition and shipped to the collectors afterwards. We decided to move this to the front stage to make questions about economy, ownership, labor, and exchange a matter of culture while at the same time attempting to secure resources for the lumbung members. As a visitor to the exhibition, you will come across the lumbung Kios; a network of decentralized and self-run kiosks trading goods made by the artists. In the lumbung Kios and Gallery, most of the returns will be stored into a collective pot, which is shared with all lumbung artists and members through a majelis mechanism.

Since the members and artists of the lumbung need to be constantly in touch with each other and the wider ekosistems, we needed digital platforms which are not conditioned by liberal market economy and institutional politics. lumbung.space, but also *lumbung Press* are mediums for lumbung artists and members to communicate with each other and the larger public. While lumbung. space is an experimental social and publishing platform for sharing harvests by all the members online, the lumbung Press is a physical space and tool to realize artistic printing projects. lumbung.space is non-extractive, co-governed by the users, and is built on open platforms. It functions as a lumbung with a members-only backend for artists to store, discuss, and organize content and a frontend where users can see and interact with the published content. Centrally stationed in documenta Halle and active from well before the opening and throughout the 100 days of documenta fifteen, lumbung Press is a proper offset printing workshop where artists can be closely involved in the printing process of their own publications, host events, and acquire skills needed to operate the printing press for the long haul, should the lumbung have the needs and means to keep it running after the exhibition.

SOCIALLY ENGAGED ART COMES FROM THE EXPERIENCE OF COMMUNITY AND THE NEEDS OF PEOPLE.

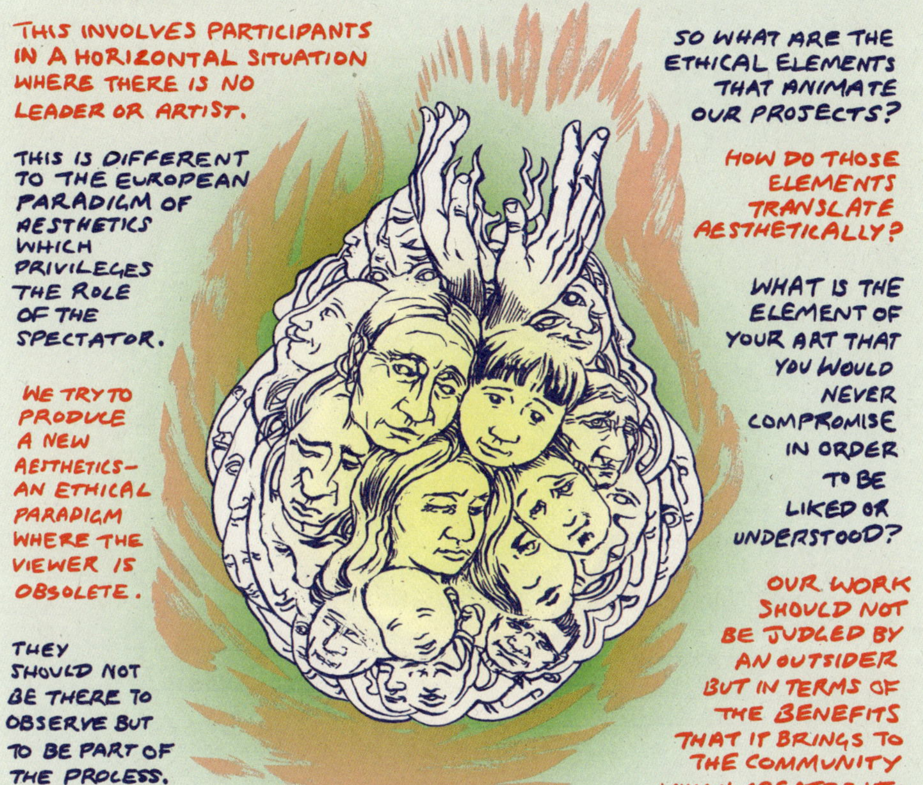



DRAWN BY SAFDAR AHMED ON THE UNCEDED LANDS OF THE GURINGAI PEOPLE IN SO-CALLED AUSTRALIA 2021

Harvest drawings by Andrés Villalobos (left) and Safdar Ahmed (right)

From Mini To Akbar

# "KEEP ON DOING
WHAT YOU'RE DOING ..."

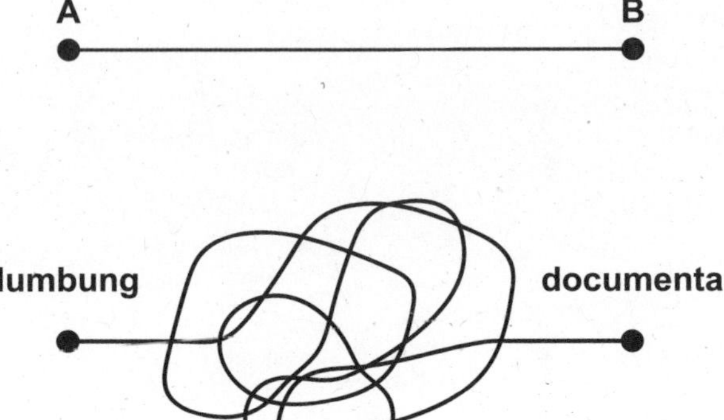



documenta fifteen is practice and not theme based. It is not about lumbung, or the commons, or any such notion. When we started, we realized that making a "showcase" of collective practices, done by many already in many art centers, would be a trap. Instead, this exhibition and journey are with collectives and artists who have longstanding experience with practicing and not preaching (much)—walking the talk—and who would like to learn new tricks, strategies, and approaches from one another to enrich their local communities. So, in a way it is a study of many models.

How do people create the material and immaterial infrastructures they need to nurture and sustain themselves and their ekosistem? Artists, collectives, and artist-led-institutions joined the lumbung based on how they practice. This was sometimes not immediately visible in their artistic work, but rather in the artists' and collectives' larger roles forming or participating in social and political movements. We are more interested in *how* the artists are working in their respective localities, and their practiced values.

Art is rooted in life. The ensuing objects and methods help in thinking through the issues at hand and in finding solutions that are useful to the community. In this way it is impossible to separate art and life, and it is meaningless to exhibit the objects in Kassel without finding translations of the processes that give rise to them. So, instead of following the logic of commissioning new or exhibiting existing work, we asked all lumbung members and artists to keep doing what they are doing while harvesting it and to think about how to translate their practices to Kassel. Making one's resources shareable within the lumbung is already a translation in itself. To make documenta fifteen the least extractive it can be, we continue to question how the artists' "contributions" to documenta fifteen can also cycle back to each of the artists' local context and ekosistems, and how meaningful it is.

# ... AND FIND A TRANSLATION TO KASSEL

Translation should not be understood too literally, but more as a poetic way of bringing something already existing in touch with more potential users. In contrast to commissioning, which would mean bringing more stuff into the world, translation thus became a way for the artists and collectives to continue practicing in their localities, without having to put their often longstanding work on hold in order to be part of a big art event such as documenta. Some have harvested assemblies in their localities and brought them to Kassel as models and challenges to learn from and in conversation with others. Many have moved their practice to Kassel as temporary occupations of the city. Others have extended their invitation and budgets to colleagues from their ekosistems to work alongside them in Kassel. Connecting their localities on the one hand and Kassel on the other, all artists have redistributed resources in a circular flow of money and cultural capital between the two sites.

When we started hanging out in conversation with the artists it was shortly after Covid-19 was declared a pandemic. We thought we had two years to build and fill the lumbung with resources for both the everyday and crises alike. With Covid, the collapse came much earlier and with such brute force that it pressured us to consider how we could speed up and start sharing resources straight away. At the same time, we insisted on going slow, meeting several times, and building up trust. We wanted to get to know everyone better and to let them experience us and our dynamics, beyond simply discussing their artworks.

Speaking to the artists about how they coped with Covid in their local communities helped us understand more about their survival strategies and to decouple from their actual artworks. In this manner, we have developed a way of working collectively where we present practices or projects and the people behind them to each other, and then discuss them in several steps that allow for time to revisit and reflect. Our different processes follow different paces and modes, but common to them all are trust, intuition, collectivity, and accepting that we might be wrong and make mistakes.

In the beginning, we spoke a lot about finding mechanisms for practicing lumbung values at an expanded scale. Mechanisms that can be shared without becoming mechanistic, or disciplines that one would need to follow to be lumbung. Just as lumbung is not a theme, neither is it a discipline. Intuitively, every time we invent a principle, we don't see it through completely; we happen to leave a part open and unruly, like when we decided to turn Fridericianum into a school but still needed the space for work that demands controlled museum conditions. Our approach is nonsystematic, not crystalline or exhaustive. It is dynamic, and changes according to conversations between people and their needs, rather than based on one static line of conceptual thinking.

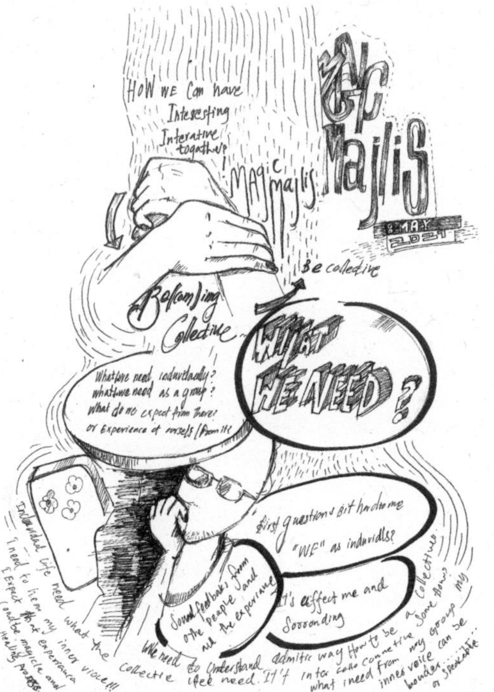

In thinking about translation to Kassel, we grouped the lumbung artists in what we termed *mini-majelis*, small assemblies of four to five artists (individuals and collectives), put together according to time zones, due to digital meetings, and to existing friendships predating Covid that could nurture trust-building online. The first mini-majelises started meeting in February 2021. Artistic Team met with the groups a few times, but then left it to the artists and a curatorial assistant to decide on the rhythm and way of meeting, and, crucially, on how to make decisions around their common resources, known as the common pot. As one of the artists pointed out, the common pot is like a totem pole, something highly symbolic that holds the community together. On one hand the artists have been generous with their time and knowledge with each other, and on the other it was a challenge for them to decide on the common pot together because they didn't know each other so well. It was also a challenge that the budget had to be spent by September 2022 and that all budgets pertaining to documenta are conditioned by traditional exhibition logics, with the bulk of spending being allocated to the narrow time frame of a limited exhibition period and not the extended spacetime of lumbung building.

The mini-majelises adopted different ways of running the majelis and making decisions. One group used *agraw*, an assembly from the North African Amazigh tradition, which takes the physical form of a circle where the moderator walks around the circle, while participants stop the moderator if they wish to speak. A Zoom version of this was adapted in the majelis. Another mini-majelis met over dinner on Zoom and spoke in depth about their recipes and food as well as their practices. Another group would always decide on two hosts each time, who would prepare the session together and ask questions of everyone, passing the mike around, as well as taking turns to present their art practices for each other.

These meetings happened over the course of almost a year and a half for some groups online. Some of the mini-majelises met in Kassel, as we tried to organize their trips to coincide with each other. In early 2022, we asked them for their final decisions on their common pot budgets. Some of the artists redirected the budgets back into their production budgets, mostly to be able to host more collaborators from their ekosistem in Kassel, or to support them in their localities after discussing with the rest of the members of their mini-majelises. Many of the artists decided to invite artists to present work in the exhibition, such as Nino Bulling, Jumana Emil Abboud, Safdar Ahmed, Alice Yard, Kiri Dalena, and Saodat Ismailova. Many worked on common projects, such as the mini-majelis that BOLOHO is part of, as they developed an online shop for which the whole mini-majelis is making artworks and developing artistic advertisements. Another majelis made a public program together called "chasing the sunset" to be held during the 100 days to allow lumbung members and artists to get together. Some members and artists have managed to use funds from the common pot to visit each other before the opening, such as Jatiwangi art Factory visiting Más Arte Más Acción in Colombia.

Many majelises are still trying to use the common pot for meeting and exchanging after the passing of the 100 days of documenta, and are trying to find ways to do so, despite the conditions of the funds. Fridskul is somewhat of a different mini-majelis, as the group also share the Fridericianum. Through their majelises they have come to see it as a neighborhood, where in addition to their project spaces, they share living spaces, a library, as well as a public program.

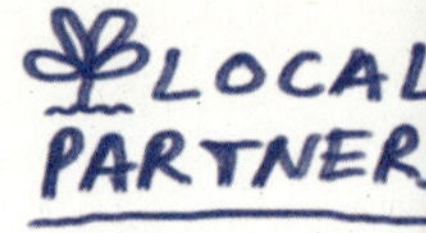


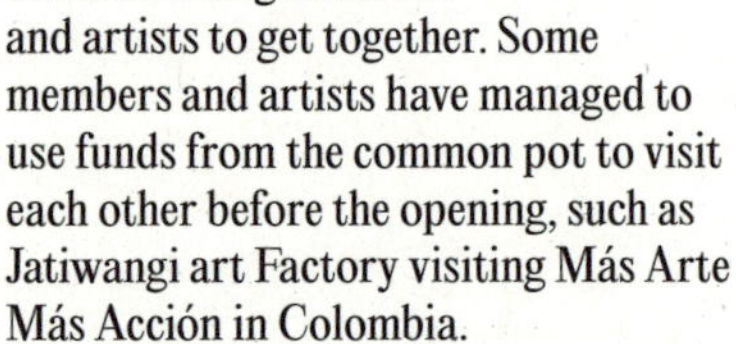

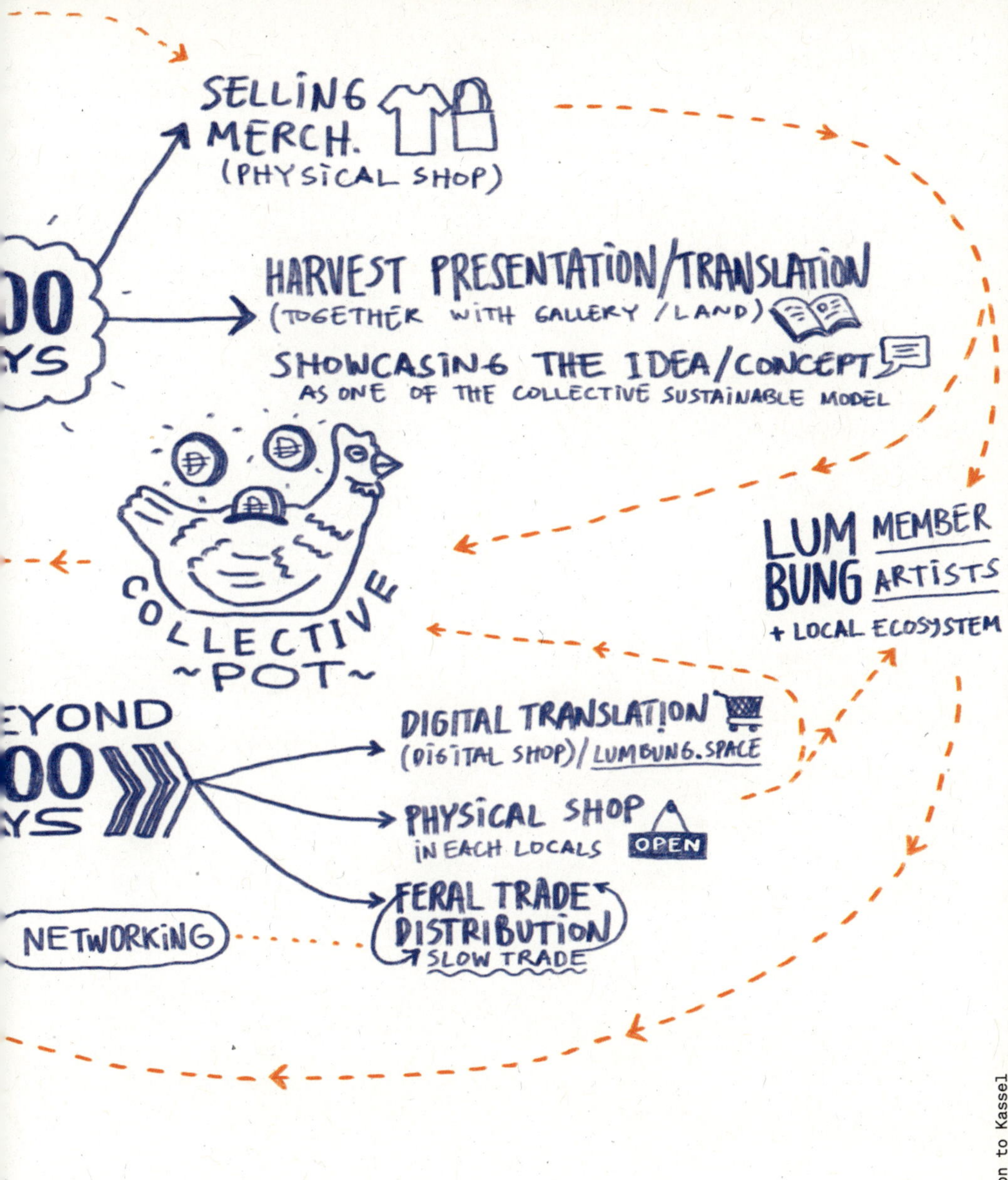

SELLING MERCH. (PHYSICAL SHOP)
HARVEST PRESENTATION/TRANSLATION
(TOGETHER WITH GALLERY /LAND)
SHOWCASING THE IDEA/CONCEPT
AS ONE OF THE COLLECTIVE SUSTAINABLE MODEL
00 YS
COLLECTIVE ~POT~
LUM BUNG MEMBER ARTISTS
+ LOCAL ECOSYSTEM
EYOND 00 YS
DIGITAL TRANSLATION
(DIGITAL SHOP)/ LUMBUNG.SPACE
PHYSICAL SHOP IN EACH LOCALS
OPEN
FERAL TRADE DISTRIBUTION
SLOW TRADE
NETWORKING
... and find a translation to Kassel

# NEIGHBORS FOR A HUNDRED DAYS?

Since artists were neither responding to a theme nor to venues in the city of Kassel—unless through collaboration with collectives and artists in our Kassel ekosistem or because they find it regenerative for their own locale and ekosistem—we had to approach the distribution of venues differently. Function became an important aspect in locating a venue for a project. The spaces were matched with artists according to the functional needs and use of the spaces. For example, one difficulty was finding affordable accommodation for the collectives who have to inhabit Kassel for longer periods. Parts of venues were converted into living space, apartments, and dormitories by the artists. This is also connected to many of the artists' practices in their localities that combine living and working space, private and public, art and life. Many artist collectives who were inhabiting the same venues also started to form majelises to discuss how to share the building together.

The process of the distribution of the venues was dynamic. Apart from using the functional distribution of artists to venues, another proactive approach was for artists to find venues which fit within their practices. In some cases, the needs and uses of different collectives overlapped in the same venues. Another way of organizing the artists in the venues grew organically; especially with lumbung inter-lokal members, who had more time to develop collaborations. Artists started to choose spaces that were spatially close to the artists or members with whom they felt for various reasons more affiliated. Even though the process was more time consuming, it is very important to see the "artists' space" as an entity within a larger venue ekosistem, where they nurture each other. They share common spaces such as kitchens, meeting spaces, classes, and even dor-mitories and libraries rather than form a collection of "showcases" or "window displays" of artworks.

The venues are also a resource in the lumbung common pot. Typically, the centrally located venues, such as Fridericianum and documenta Halle, are seen as the main venues and are accordingly the most and sometimes, even, the only ones visited. Although we have tried to distribute the venues in a more decentered way, where the route linking them dips south in an arch and brings visitors back to the west across the city, the main venues remain central because we cannot reformat visitors' memories. Since different venues have different symbolic capital which in turn partly endows the works exhibited within them, a fair distribution entailed giving more marginalized practices more priority at times. In our first—and due to Covid, as we write, so far only—Artistic Team assembly in Kassel, we hung a big map of an acupunctured Kassel next to a schematic drawing of the Gudskul Ekosistem diagram. Juxtaposing the two, we came up with the analogy and strategy to decenter the Fridericianum. We thought the center should be the lumbung building, where all the harvest is kept, the storage of all knowledge, stories and experiences, and that it should be dynamic and keep changing. Also breaking with the audience tradition of seeing Fridericianum as the central or main venue of documenta.

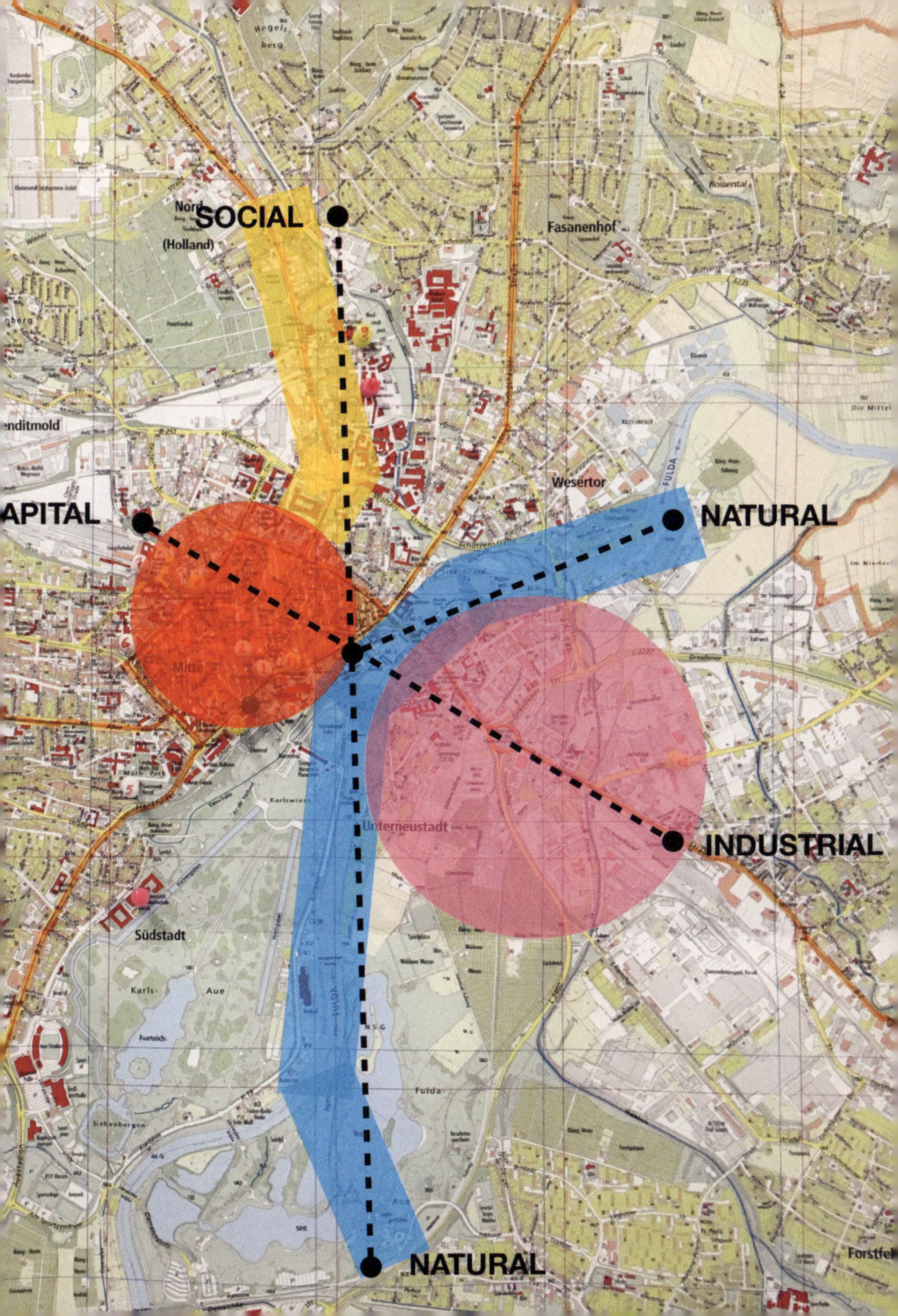

SOCIAL
(Holland)
CAPITAL
NATURAL
INDUSTRIAL
NATURAL
Südstadt
Unterneustadt
Wesertor
Fasanenhof
Bossental

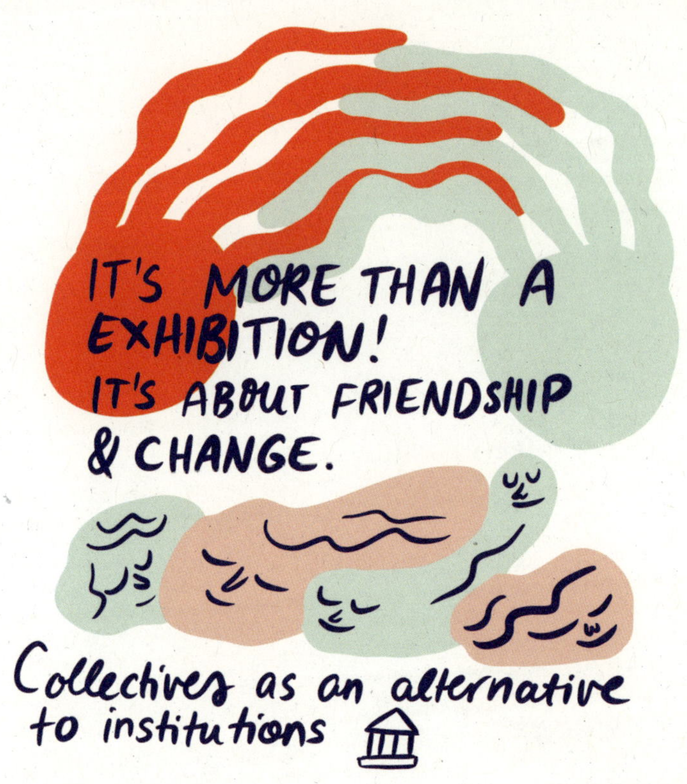


The *Fridskul* (Fridericianum as a school) hosts dynamic activities that are experienced rather than viewed as static objects. The contributions of the artists and guests develop into a program that will continuously update and change the place in 100 days. Looking at the architecture of the lumbung or rice barn, knowledge has a place everywhere, such as in the social, living, and storage spaces. The artists and participants of their respective projects live and sleep, and eat and drink together in this place and take care of the knowledge-generation processes to which everyone contributes.

Fridskul turns the Fridericianum from a museum into a living space where one is likely to get a whiff of home cooking and hear the sound of kids playing. Here you find RURUKIDS, a space where children and artists can connect 1:1. At RURUKIDS, knowledge and practice are closely entangled. In collaboration with lumbung artists, Kassel initiatives, and the sobat-sobat, RURUKIDS builds a safe and stimulating environment to learn and discover through play for babies, children, and adults alike.

# FRIDERICIA NUM AS AN ALTERNATIVE SCHOOL

"FRID-SHOOL"

→ kitchen

Library! → COMMUNICATE WITH PUBLIC

living space! → COLLECTIVES CAN COME TOGETHER

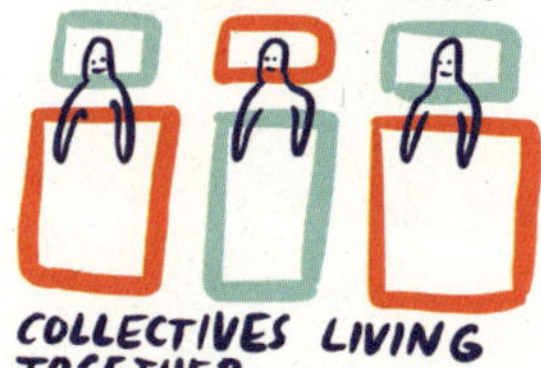


HOW? There are still many issues and questions.

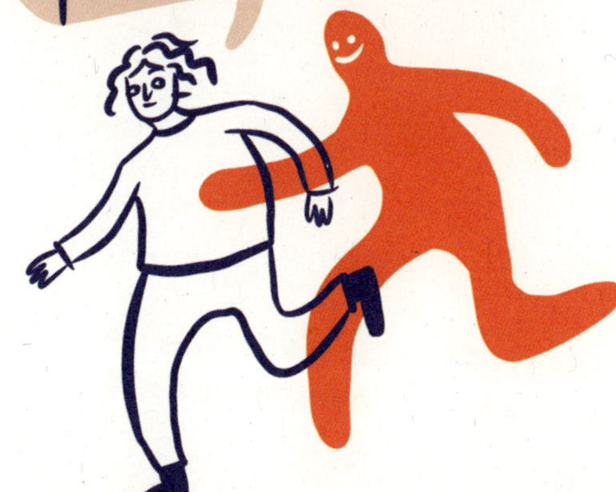

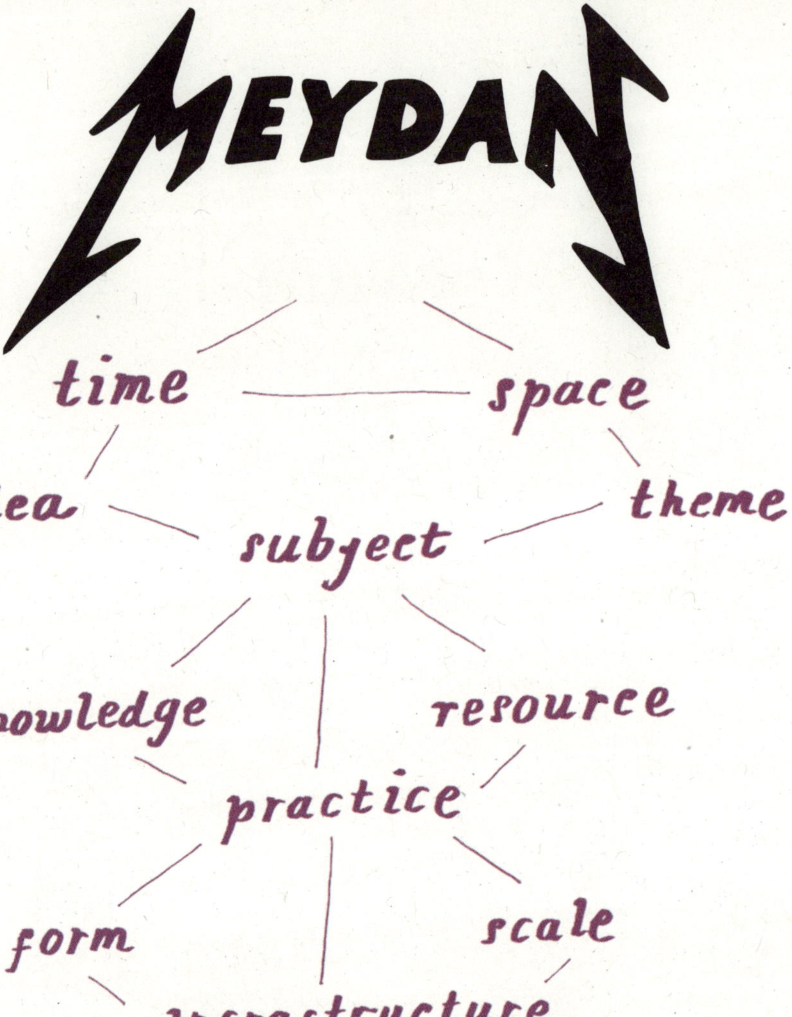

Harvest drawings by Indra Ameng (left) and Daniella F Prantono (right)

# MAKING SOBAT-SOBAT OR PLUG IN AND AMPLIFY IN THE MEYDAN

The sharing of knowledge between guests and artists is hosted by a team of what were formerly known as art mediators. For lumbung they are called the sobat-sobat (Indonesian for friends or companions). The sobat-sobat consists of more than 100 people from different backgrounds, most of them Kassel residents. They host guests and artists during the 100 days, based on their respective interests in artistic approach, research, and subject. Sobat-sobat are an active and, most importantly, creative part of lumbung. Through their hosting and harvesting processes, knowledge production and dissemination happen everywhere organically, inseparable from the art.

Because documenta fifteen will be brimming with lumbung members and artists activating their spaces and installations, it didn't make sense to us to make a classic public program to accompany the exhibition. We decided instead to plug in to existing public spaces in Kassel and the infrastructure they hold and what they could share. It's not about owning those spaces but about inspiring others to think about how we can use the public space together. It's a learning process more than a program, under the banner of Meydan.

Meydan is a word used in Urdu, Persian, and Arabic to refer to a public area used for coming together, a square or a public park. It's an accessible space for having assemblies to discuss, to dissent or to celebrate. The Meydan program of documenta fifteen is based on various forms of social gathering that takes place every second weekend of the month throughout the 100 days of the exhibition, in one of three different areas in Kassel that are each home to local initiatives in the Kassel ekosistem. The Meydan program will take place in cooperation with initiatives, organizations and communities in Kassel. The infrastructure used and created for Meydan will be shared with members, artists, and the Kassel ekosistem.

Meydan also occupies digital space through our different online platforms where we experiment with meeting, publicizing, and of course storing and redistributing surpluses.

On documenta fifteen's website, for instance, you find the seven-part conversation series *lumbung calling*. Each edition is dedicated to one of the lumbung values: Local Anchor, Humor, Generosity, Independence, Transparency, Sufficiency, and Regeneration, asking how these values can be translated into artistic practice and open up new spaces for conversation.

*lumbung konteks* is the sequel. This online conversation series addresses the importance of the localities of the lumbung inter-lokal members, the conditions for practices and learning from each other's models of education, ecology, and economy. Among the longer-lasting initiatives in our digital storage are *lumbung Radio* and *lumbung Film*, a server full of films from lumbung members and artists that are not on show in the exhibition but can be curated by the different ekosistems according to their local needs throughout the 100 days of documenta fifteen and 100 days beyond.

# HOW WE COULD HAVE DONE THINGS DIFFERENTLY

The sustained discussions, negotiations, and struggles with our ever-growing circles of collaborators, artists, neighbors, and our host, the documenta gGmbH, have blessed us with lessons that we will use for the future of lumbung after documenta fifteen.

From all these elements, a vital constituent in forming the lumbung process is the lumbung inter-lokal, for which we still utilized the logic of membership. Ideally, lumbung can be a model that can be owned, adapted, developed, and utilized by many, without rigid control. This way membership is not needed.

To further dissolve memberships, awareness of scale is paramount; how to keep it small-to-medium and agile, never too big. How cellular organisms or rhizomatic structures split themselves up in order to keep themselves small is a useful model to learn from. Large scale brings unsustainable consequences. Not enough systematic thought has been given to scale.

The hardest part of constituting lumbung is building trust and affinities. Our trust-building phase between actors of documenta fifteen has not been enough. One way to further foster this is through building collectives of collectives, in different localities with different manifestations and strategies.

Connections should happen directly, not mediated through entities that hold large resources. What we are making is a documenta version of lumbung, as our relations are still mediated (with a price) by documenta. One of the biggest challenges is how to sustain the relationships we have started, not by following the old logics of resources and therefore always mediated, domesticated, and tamed, always systemized and institutionalized.

Connections should happen not with the illusion or promise of capitals (be it financial, social, cultural, and so on). Would lumbung sustain using a non-transactional approach, where financial gain is not the starting point for relating to each other?

Regular harvest celebrations should happen with transparencies exercised from the outset. Resources should be shared, discussed, and co-governed both within and outside of a collective of collectivities, with stories made through financial spreadsheets, from planning up to the realization phase, for anyone to learn from.

In documenta fifteen, lumbung is still approaching the economy using old paradigms. If we are supporting different types of art production then the artworks and their forms, their positions and agencies, the way they are being made public and understood, the infrastructures built around them, and how ownerships are fostered, should also be made differently. Changes in both their production and the economical construction, need to be further rethought.

documenta fifteen is still using the language of—and can be understood as—a conventional artistic mega-event, despite the attempts to approach it in a more bottom-up, organic, and accessible way. It is our hope that you, as visitors, can feel the differences in your own experiences. Enjoy this public harvest celebration as much as you can. lumbung is not only ours now, it's also yours. Own it, while it lasts, and make it last. Make your own lumbung.

ruangrupa & Artistic Team
documenta fifteen

Harvest drawing by Nino Bulling

NOW WE ARE
LOOKING
BACK AND ASKING:

# WHAT IS HARVEST?

Harvest refers to artistic recordings of discussions and meetings. Harvesters listen, reflect, and depict this process from their own perspectives, forms, and artistic practices. Harvests can be humorous, poetic, or candid. They can take the shape of a sticky note, a written story, drawing, film, sound piece, or meme.

The process of the making of lumbung where members share resources together is an integral part of documenta fifteen. Harvesting can be seen as a way of collective writing that enables continuous collective learning, from different sensory experiences. Harvests are made to share what is being discussed with absent members and the general public and they are present throughout the handbook and the exhibition to illustrate and expand our thinking and methodologies. They are also published in books, zines, on social media, and on the lumbung's digital publishing platform lumbung.space.

Due to the nature of harvesting, it is difficult to come up with a complete list of all individuals who contributed to lumbung with their harvests. In this space we highlight practitioners whom we have invited especially to harvest our meetings. The list of harvesters includes many others, from lumbung members and artists who were harvesting their meetings, to the Artistic Team, sobat-sobat, and visitors who are invited to contribute to the rice barn with their harvests during the 100 days.

Abdul Dube and Putra Hidayatullah have been invited to accompany the artistic team, lumbung inter-lokal and majelises since the beginning. They harvested through graphic recordings and creative writing, respectively.

Having followed and been part of ruangrupa's practice since the early 2000s, Sebastián Diaz Morales and Simon Danang Anggoro collaborate to produce artistic work that can be seen as harvest. Nonkrong is used as a method for creating films. The films can be seen in several locations of the exhibition and will continue after documenta fifteen.

Victoria Lumasko has been invited to harvest the making of the exhibition with an illustrated book. The book harvests her witnessing the practice and ekosistem of lumbung members and artists while the exhibition is opening.

Cem A. is known for running the art meme account @freeze_magazine and he works as a curatorial assistant for documenta fifteen. He has been invited to harvest his experiences working for documenta fifteen through internet memes and situated memes.

There are several lumbung artists for whom harvesting is an integral part of their practice and thus have been very active in harvesting meetings. reinaart vanhoe has harvested and (self-)published his note-drawings. Arts Collaboratory has published several *documentamtam*, and keeps on doing so during the 100 days. *documentamtam* includes harvests from Arts Collaboratory members, as well as the work of other harvesters. *documentamtam* can be read at www.artscollaboratory.org. Other artists who have harvested include Safdar Ahmed, Nino Bulling, Keleketla! Library and Dan Perjovschi.

Radio Alhara, Tropical Tap Water and Community Immunity have accompanied us during several Majelis Akbar and working groups and made audio and visual harvesting out of it, as well as a glossary of terms.

Sheree Domingo, Tupac, and Melani Budianto have also contributed generously with their harvests, as well as many others who have contributed after this book went to print.

# Documenting vs harvesting

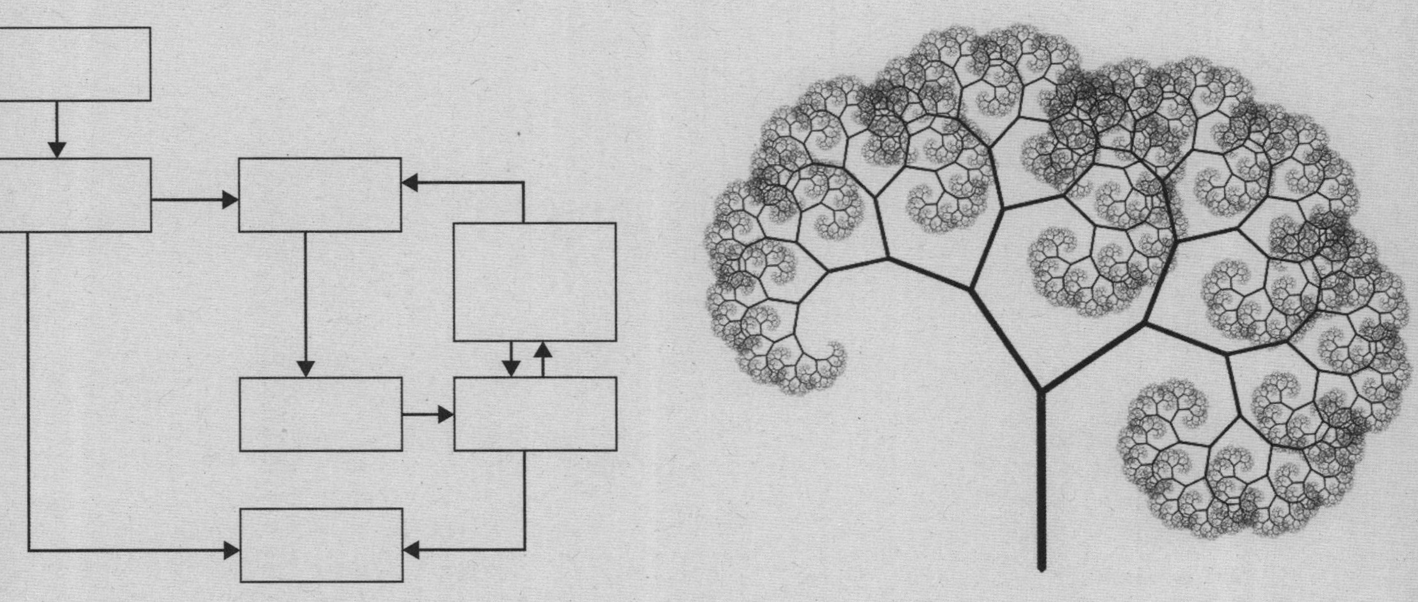

Harvest drawing by Cem A.

What is Harvest?

# a–z INDeX

14 lumbung members and 53 lumbung
artists participate in documenta
fifteen, as invited by ruangrupa
and the artistic team. In the
following pages, you will find
insights on the lumbung members'
and lumbung artists' contexts in
their home localities, as well as
details on their specific
interventions, projects, and
contributions for documenta
fifteen in Kassel and beyond.
A full list of invited guests
is printed in the appendix
at the back of this handbook.

## LUMBUNG MEMBERS AND LUMBUNG ARTISTS

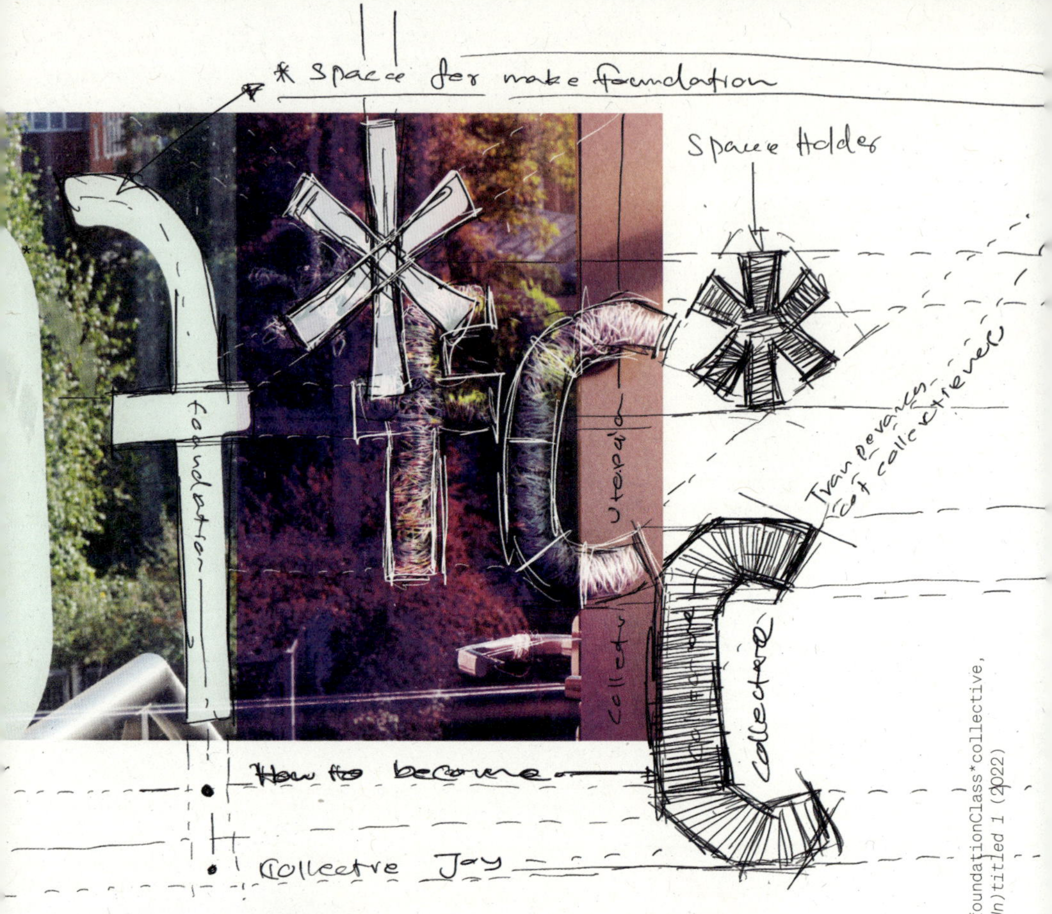

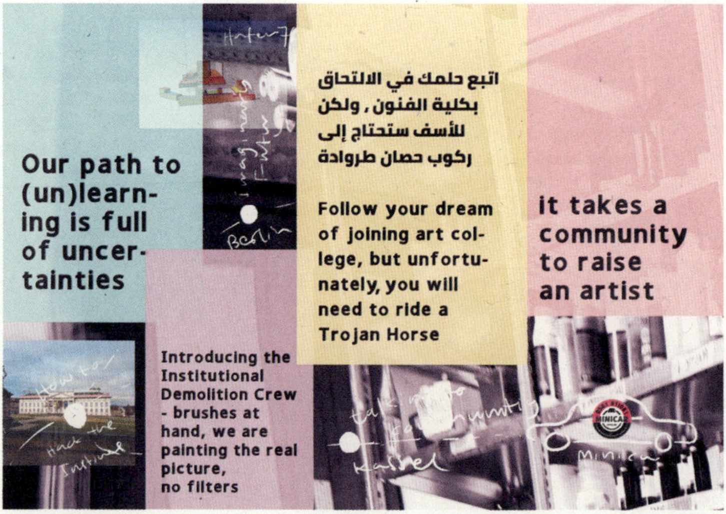

## Our path to (un)learning is full of uncertainties

اتبع حلمك في الالتحاق بكلية الفنون ، ولكن للأسف ستحتاج إلى ركوب حصان طروادة

**Follow your dream of joining art college, but unfortunately, you will need to ride a Trojan Horse**

## it takes a community to raise an artist

**Introducing the Institutional Demolition Crew - brushes at hand, we are painting the real picture, no filters**

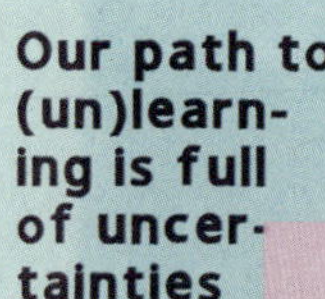

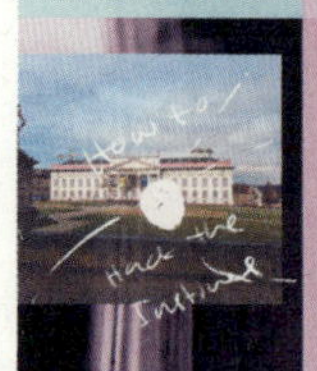

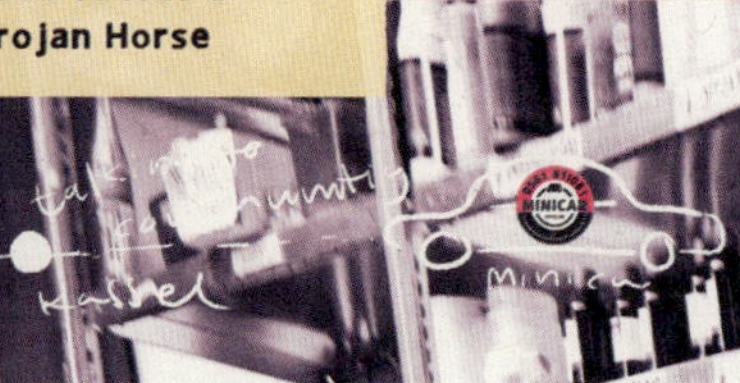

# *FOUNDATIONCLASS* COLLECTIVE

*foundationClass*collective's projects for documenta fifteen depart from Kassel's particular migrant and community ecologies.

Founded in 2016 at Weißensee Academy of Art Berlin (KHB), *foundationClass*collective proposes a dissident-minded art education platform and resistance toolkit to facilitate access to art academia for migrant communities who have been affected by structural discriminations in Germany. They operate from the crack as a breaking point, a sign of destruction, but also as an undefined space from which opportunities arise.

From this program, *foundationClass*collective was developed in 2021 and together imaginary models of learning, living and personal development analogous to the solidarity practice lumbung has been explored. *foundationClass*collective are among others: Fadi Aljabour, Ulf Aminde, Susan Azizi, Yemisi Babatola, Carolyn Amora Bosco, Mohamad Halbouni, Nadira Husain, Ali Kaaf, Katharina Kersten, Cam-Anh Luong, Abiye Okujagu, Krishan Rajapakshe, Miriam Schickler, Hatef Soltani, Vera Varlamova, Noureddin Yassin and Mc3BArts.

The collective's initiatives for documenta fifteen respond to Kassel's particular migrant landscape and community ecology. Their work uncovers methods of developing self-driven economies from migrant standpoints and reiterating their visions of art in education. Their footing in the city of Kassel is down-to-earth and examines how the city lives before and after the 100 days of documenta, bridging older conflicts with newer ways of learning and sharing. Together with Mini-Car, the migrant-driven cab network, they devised a mobile audio sculpture that circulates throughout the city in MiniCar cabs. A second project, *Hafenstraße 76*, is a spatial laboratory to imagine a possible project space in the future (in Berlin); a laboratory to enable the politics of self-representations, it includes hosting workshops, mutual learning, and setting up a space for artistic interventions and experiments. The third venue is the Fridskul at the Fridericianum, where the *foundationClass* collective contributes with an installation of banners. The banners, like book pages, vocalize *fC* practices on art education, sharing strategies with audiences about how to survive in an art school, with its inherent powerful mechanisms of inclusion and exclusion.

Övül Ö. Durmuşoğlu

VENUES
- Fridericianum
- Hafenstraße 76
- Mini Car Kassel

MINI-MAJELIS
- Atis Rezistans | Ghetto Biennale
- Marwa Arsanios
- Sourabh Phadke
- yasmine eid-sabbagh

"

# AGUS NUR AMAL PMTOH

Agus Nur Amal PMTOH facilitates a
series of storytelling sessions
based on the Sundanese life principle.

A

Public space contains a multitude of narratives,
all competing for how they can function as truths.
Within the context of an authoritarian state, alternative histories become a site to find answers and
explanations for difficult issues. Mainstream media
outlets and state-made historical textbooks do not
provide spaces for other voices. Oppression leaves a
lasting effect and intergenerational traumas in the
bodies of communities.

In Agus Nur Amal PMTOH's practices,
storytelling emerged as an informal method to
write and allow people to rewrite their histories. It
opens up difficult conversations and makes visible
hidden stories and repressed memories—military
violence, ecological destruction, human right
oppression, forgotten wisdom. Agus is a storyteller
who is able to transgress limits by changing roles as
a journalist, researcher, neighbor, or friend.

Agus bases his storytelling method on a
threatened Acehnese storytelling style combined
with music performances, known as *hikayat*. The
continuity of the *hikayat* tradition risks being
broken due to a lack of new generations of storytellers. A large part of the *hikayat* stories exist
only in oral forms and their existence depends on
the lifespan of the living storytellers. While Agus
preserves the *hikayat* tradition, he also revitalizes
it. He incorporates various domestic objects in his
repertoires. This adds a new material dimension
to his performances. Agus's realm provides the
condition to stretch the meaning of the objects.
They become arbitrary, makeshift, and subjective.

The playfulness liberates the audience to engage in
the performance and tell the tales of their lives.

For documenta fifteen, Agus creates a series
of storytelling sessions based on the Sundanese life
principle, *Tri Tangtu*. The storytelling workshop
sessions are conducted with schoolchildren from
the Friedrich Wöhler Schule and Reformschule
in Kassel. Three storytelling sessions performed
around the city are augmented by further
sessions occurring during documenta. *Tri Tangtu*
represents a vernacular thought system in which
the mystical, rational, and natural intersect with
each other and serve as the basis to guide the
relational position of humans with other inhabitants of Earth. Central to storytelling is the joy
of just being and interacting with many people:
remembering the past, thinking about the present
and speculating about futures.

Nuraini Juliastuti

VENUE
 Grimmwelt Kassel

MINI-MAJELIS
O Arts Collaboratory
O Black Quantum Futurism
O Chimurenga
O Jumana Emil Abboud
O Nino Bulling
O Subversive Film

Agus Nur Amal PMTOH,
Production stills from
*lumbung Stories* (2021)

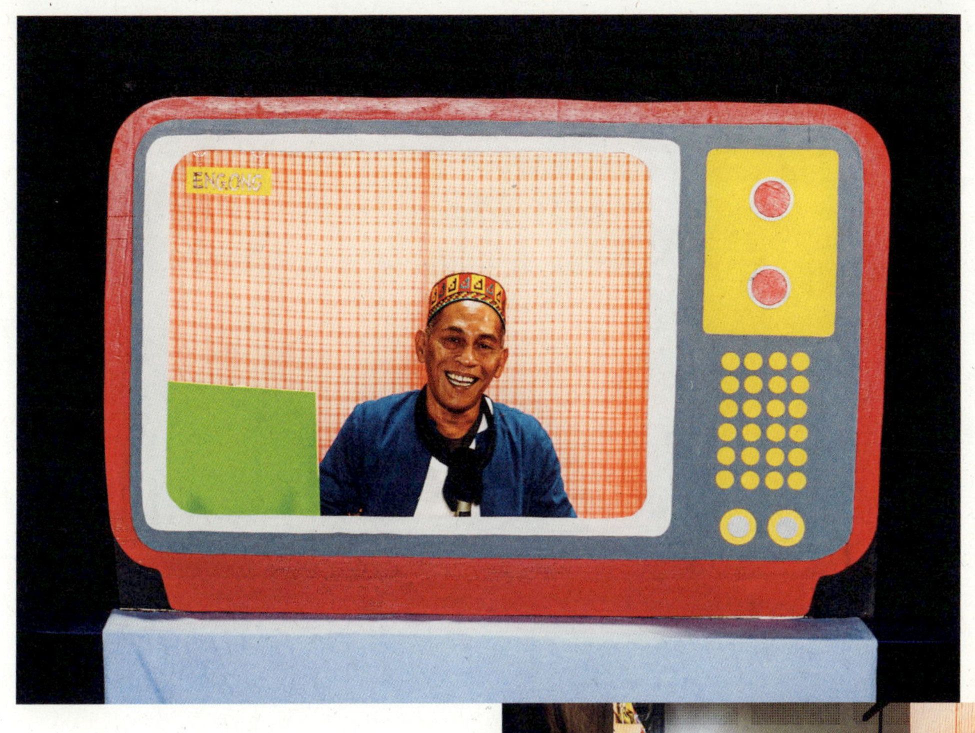




"*The* lumbung Stories *give us an understanding that lumbung can broadly reach the aspects of human life. Lumbung can be understood and adopted through many ways. Gudskul and Jatiwangi art Factory are the collectives that develop archetypes of contemporary lumbung.*" —*Agus Nur Amal PMTOH*

A

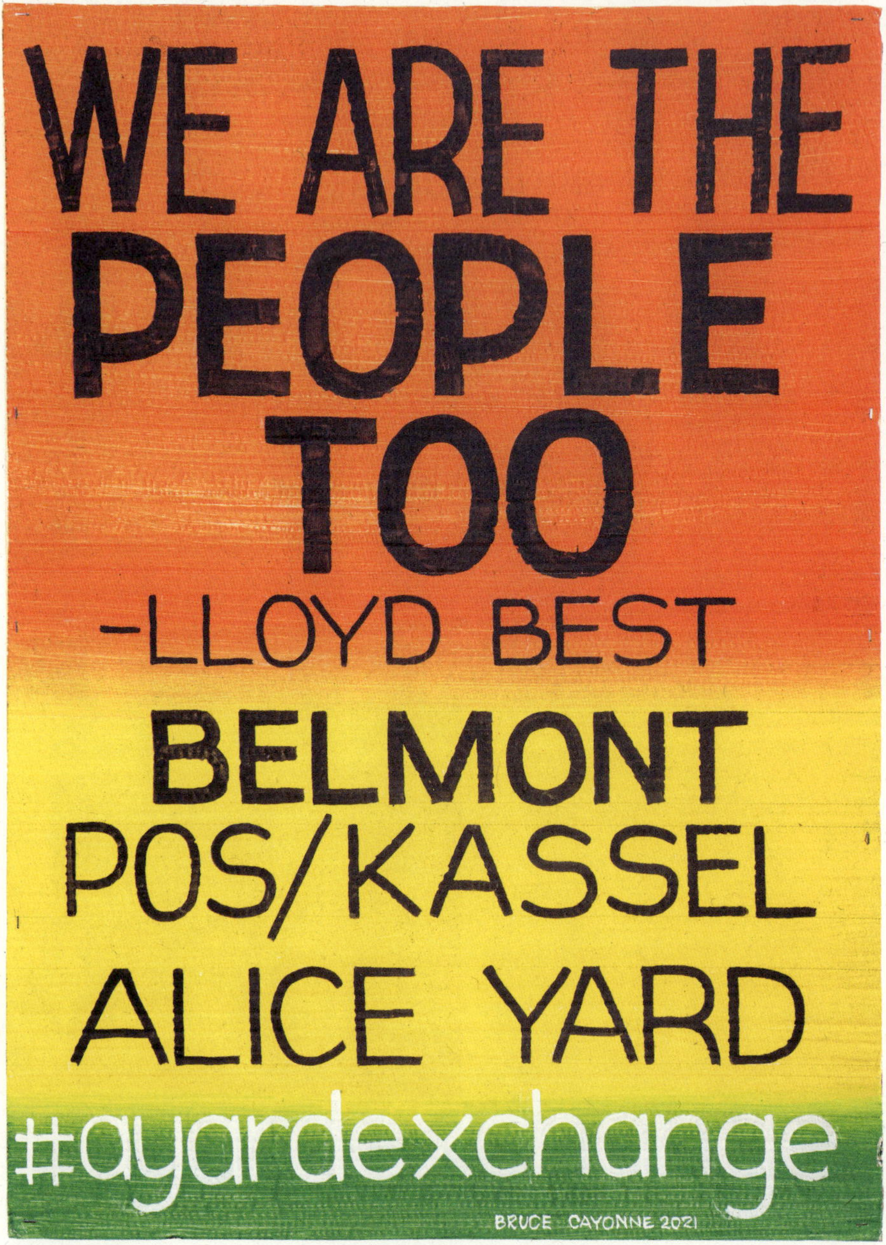

Hand-painted sign by Bruce Cayonne at ruruHaus, Kassel, 2021

**VENUES**
- Grimmwelt Kassel
- Trafohaus
- WH22

**MINI-MAJELIS**
- Erick Beltrán
- LE 18
- MADEYOULOOK
- Party Office b2b Fadescha
- Serigrafistas queer

Since its start in the early 2000s, Alice Yard has been a touchstone in Caribbean arts. Through interventions, residencies, installation, and printing, they link Port of Spain, Trinidad and Tobago, with Kassel.

Alice Yard was formed as a contemporary network and arts space in the neighborhood of Woodbrook, in Port of Spain, Trinidad and Tobago, in 2006. Architect Sean Leonard proposed and discussed its idea with curator and visual artist Christopher Cozier, and writer and editor Nicholas Laughlin, following conversations on the need for independent art initiatives that could provide a space to support the work and practice of artists in the Caribbean and internationally.

Over the years, Alice Yard has hosted artist residencies, exhibitions, and live music, talks, and workshops. Its original physical space was the backyard of the house of Alice Gittens, Sean Leonard's great-grandmother. That space is also where generations of children in the family grew up and played. In 2020, Alice Yard relocated permanently to Granderson Lab, a larger building located in the Port of Spain neighborhood of Belmont, and which from a few years prior had been working as an Alice Yard space. At this time, graphic designer Kriston Chen also joined the team.

Since its start in the early 2000s, Alice Yard has been a touchstone in Caribbean arts, illustrative of the great impact and possibilities of independent art spaces and networks in the region. It has followed the notion of play as an investigative practice of inquiry and reverie partly drawn from Caribbean Carnival. Over the years, collaborations with established and emerging artists, writers, curators, and scholars, as well as other art and cultural spaces in the region, have further strengthened the arts ekosistem in the Caribbean.

Collaboration, experimentation, and sharing—central to ruangrupa's artistic philosophy and the practice of lumbung—are true to the vision of Alice Yard. For their participation at documenta, the team decided both to continue and adapt their practice and philosophy through an outpost, offering a residency space and studio hosting visiting artists, events, and conversations attuned to the context and curatorial concept of lumbung.

During the 100 days of documenta fifteen, Alice Yard hosts nine artists in residence in Kassel: Shannon Alonzo, Bruce Cayonne, Blue Curry, Nicole Delgado, Michelle Eistrup, Versia Harris, Amanda Hernandez, Ada M. Patterson, and Luis Vasquez La Roche. They are physically based at WH22, which serves as a living and working space, while creating and presenting site- and time-specific works in diverse media at additional venues including Grimmwelt, Trafo Haus, and informal outdoor locations around the city. Each artist is invited to instigate further activations with their own past and present collaborators.

At Grimmwelt, Alice Yard will present *Telling After All…* (2022), a digital video and editorial project with works by five Caribbean artists who explore questions of folklore and mythology in the digital era—after the era of state construction, regulation, and assertion of national identity. Participating artists are Razia Barsatie, Versia Harris, Gwladys Gambie, Tessa Mars, and Oneika Russel. Alice Yard is also hosting a screening program co-curated with the Third Horizon Film Festival, presenting short film and video works by Caribbean and diaspora artists at WH22. In parallel, during the 100 days, Alice Yard is instigating a series of spontaneous activations in Kassel with artists to be later announced, as well as a series of events at their home base in Port of Spain, including artist Cass'Mosha Amoroso-Centeno, and others.

Marta Fernández Campa

*"This piece of improvised public furniture in Port of Spain — incorporating the wheeled legs of a discarded office chair into a traditional bench form Trinidadians call a* peera *—fascinates us not merely as an example of improvised Creole technology, but as an embodiment of a kind of freedom and a kind of refusal. It belongs to someone but also to no one and everyone. The bench is a place to pause, to daydream, to talk, or just to be silent."—Alice Yard*

A

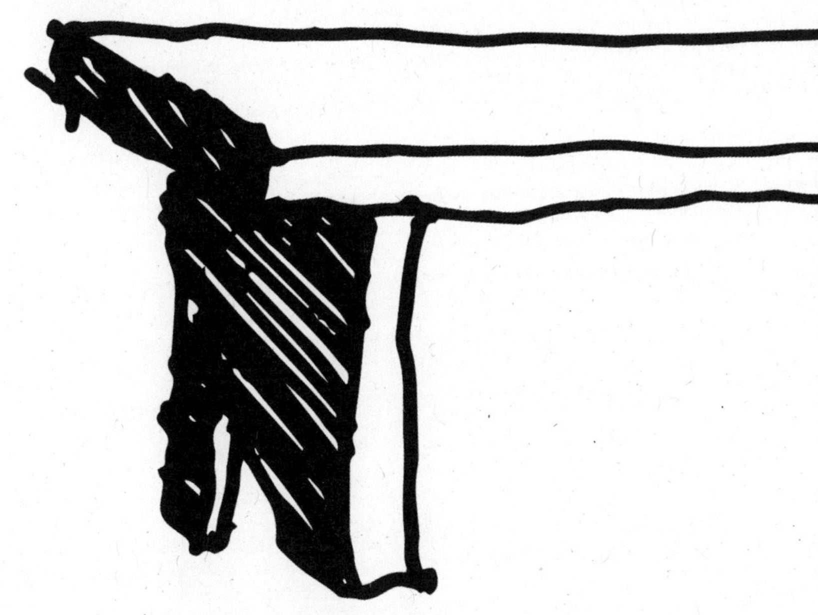

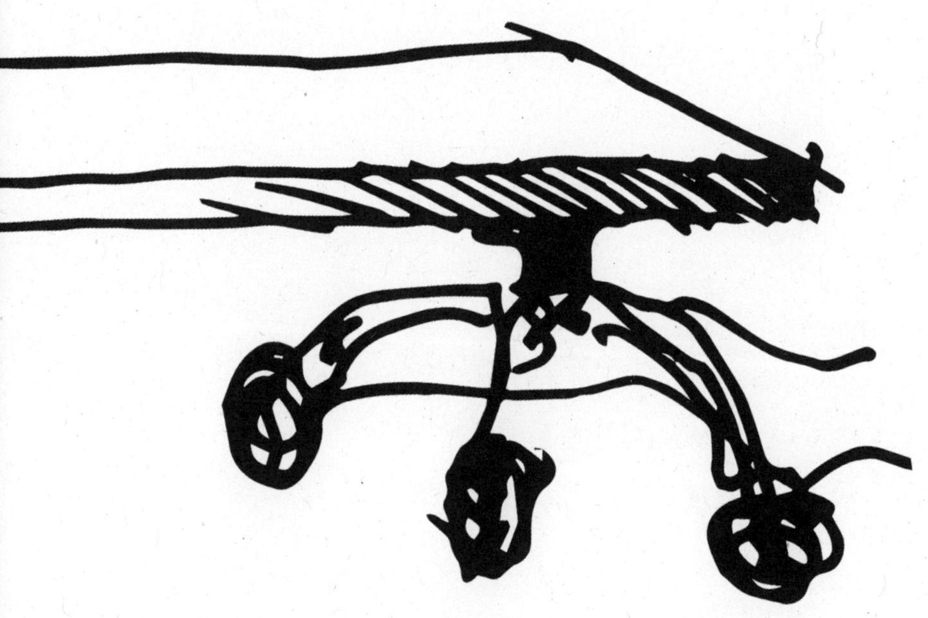



Sketch from the notebooks of
Christopher Cozier, 2021

**Alice Yard**

# AMOL K PATIL

Amol K Patil brings to Kassel
a tradition of anti-colonial,
working-class musical performance.

A  "I vibrate with a legacy," he says. There is an insurrectionary history that Amol K Patil comes from. In Kassel, he reawakens it. *Black Masks on Roller Skates* (2022) encompasses kinetic sculpture, holographic video, music, and performance. Map-lines of migration and transformation outline a stage, with performers, as if beneath the surface. "They are breathing, watching the land, living, moving. It's a wave movement, between places."

Patil builds on theater and performative traditions nested in working-class neighborhoods in Mumbai, India, as well as his own family history. His grandfather was an anti-colonial *Powada* performer who mixed his critique of empire with that of a violence embedded in the graded inequality of the caste system that hierarchically divides not just labor but laborers. His father—an avant-garde writer who wrote and produced protest theatre that critiqued severe labor conditions—intensified this experimental, emancipatory ethos. "In my father's scripts are comma sections, with gestures and moods. I access these clues, this other body language," he says.

*Powada*, a musical performance of traveling troupes, can be traced to the thirteenth century where, in kings' courts, poets composed songs praising gods. In Maharashtra, India, over the last century, the Dalit movement turned this devotional bias into a radical idiom to reimagine society with equality and new ideas of fraternity. A tumult of revolutionary lyrics provokes a reconstitution of publics and arenas. "Many, from different cultures, backgrounds, suddenly together, in *chawls*, made adjustable stages, performed, and rehearsed."

Patil invites collaboration across time. Young *Powada* writers and musicians, the Yalgaar Sanskrutik Manch, weave their lyrics with his grandfather's. "It's a way to think the now, combining what's harsh and polite, sweet and silent, pitching a criticism of land politics and social separation."

Patil draws us into journeys within the city from his childhood. His father's friend, Anil Tuebhekar, moved on skates, a broom in hand and a radio at his waist, sweeping the street, every day. "He cleaned the city, but knew he wasn't welcome into the bus or in the hotel for a drink of water. Shutting the world out with music was his individual protest."

In *Sweep Walkers* (2022), performers move through exhibition spaces on roller skates with cleaning brushes, radios playing the composed songs. In Hübner, with immersive sculptures of map-lines of the journeys of his grandfather and many others, from village to city, a radio plays, its waves permeating the underground.

The city's factories, mills, municipality, and public sector have contained millions as workers, helpers, craftsmen, caregivers, and cleaners. *Chawls*, an early modern form of neighborhood housing unique to Mumbai, were turned by migrant laborers into dynamic sites of protest, words, theater, and music. The battle with memory, time, and politics accelerates. "Construction is ongoing; there is a pit with water, it looks still, but small bubbles keep appearing, like someone's breathing inside, someone who created this land."

Skye Arundhati Thomas

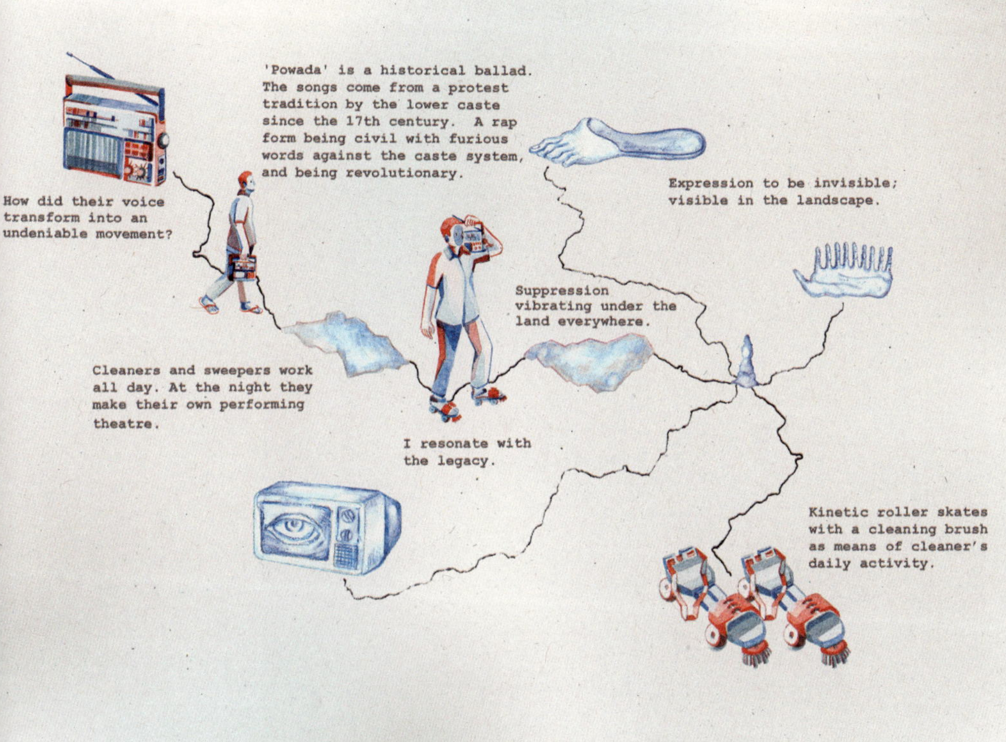


Amol K Patil, drawing illustrating a map referring to the journey of a Powada singer from Kokan to Bombay to Kassel. Also shown is a roller-skate performance on a theatrical stage installation, and sculptures.

**VENUE**
◉ Hübner areal

**MINI-MAJELIS**
○ BOLOHO
○ Cao Minghao & Chen Jianjun
○ Chang En-Man
○ Sa Sa Art Projects

Amol K Patil

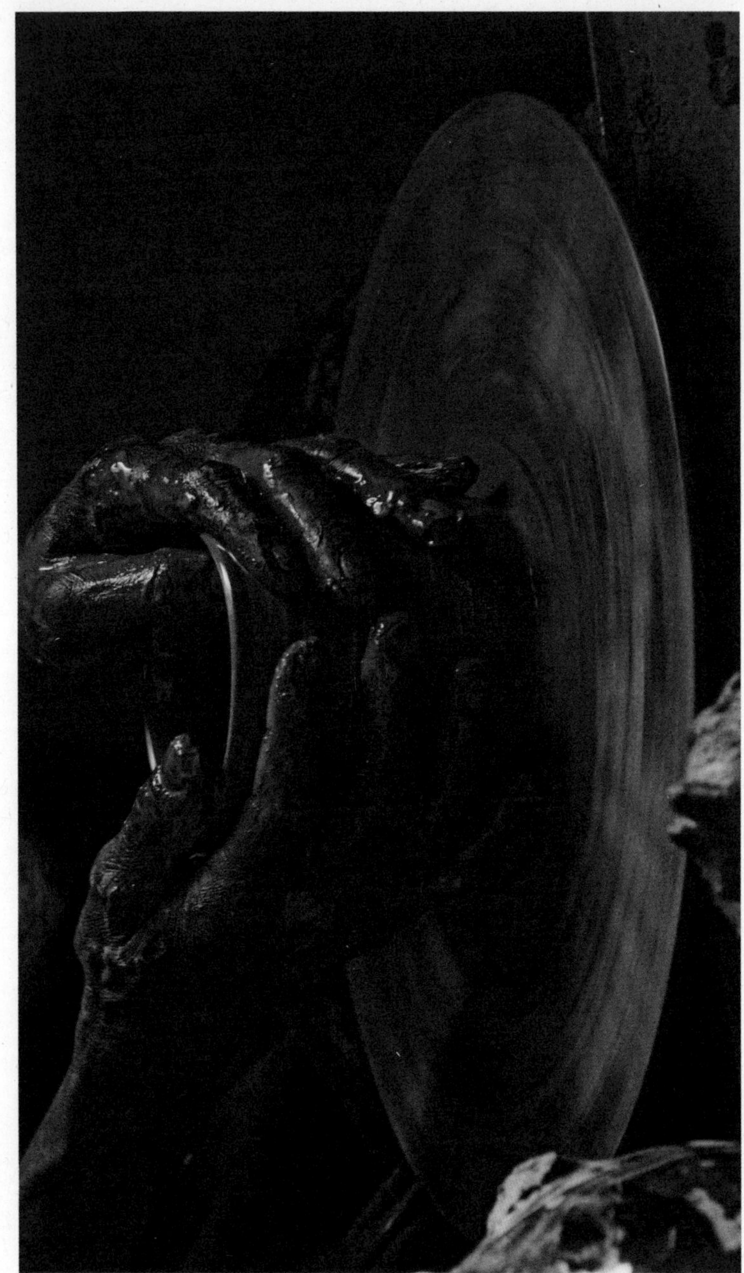

*"For ARAC, process is practice. Multiple practices harmonize across ARAC to produce materials relevant to its members' different locations."—ARAC*

# ANOTHER ROADMAP AFRICA CLUSTER (ARAC)

Founded in Uganda in 2015, ARAC
builds bridges in art education
across the African continent. In
Kassel, they open up their work
process to the public.

Another Roadmap School is a network of individuals working in museums, cultural institutions, and educational centers in 22 cities on four continents. Their mission is to rethink art education in order to focus on what's often left out of academic contexts: international connection, community building, and social engagement.

The network operates through specific working groups that are geographically defined. Another Roadmap Africa Cluster (ARAC), founded in Uganda in 2015 and focusing on the African continent, initiates conversations about art and education, particularly in relation to the theoretical and aesthetic legacies of colonialism. Participants develop a common knowledge base, together with structures of collaborative learning.

Over the years, ARAC has organized numerous colloquia, creating lively forums. There, its own methods have emerged, as well as a new vocabulary of art education—one divergent from the hitherto dominant Western or Eurocentric understandings of art and education. *The Schoolbook Project*, which takes center stage at documenta fifteen, draws from this wealth of experience. The results of ARAC's work to date are made accessible through three publications, called *Provocations*, *Exercise*, and *Glossary*.

In keeping with the practice of collaborative knowledge transfer and collection, ARAC is opening up the work process to the public. As part of documenta's public program, one-week editorial workshops are being held in which the diverse material is selected, organized, and jointly reflected upon. *Provocations* brings together central questions that have guided and challenged ARAC's research and action in recent years. *Exercise* provides concrete applications of knowledge to audiences, and *Glossary* compiles African words that describe concepts in art, aesthetics, and design.

Ann Mbuti

VENUE

 Fridericianum

MINI-MAJELIS

O Archives des luttes des
  femmes en Algérie
O Asia Art Archive
O Centre d'art Waza
O El Warcha
O Graziela Kunsch

O Keleketla! Library
O Komîna Fîlm a Rojava
O Sada [regroup]
O Siwa plateforme -
  L'Economat at Redeyef
O The Black Archives

# ARCHIVES DES LUTTES DES FEMMES EN ALGÉRIE

A In Kassel, Archives des luttes des femmes en Algérie builds a chronology of women's movements and mobilizations in Algeria, including interviews with female activists, focused on a pivotal date in Algerian history.

In 2019, Algeria experienced one of its largest popular uprisings, known as the *Hirak*. Millions took to the streets to protest against the government and led a movement that lasted more than a year. In this context of renewed collective political imagination, Archives des luttes des femmes en Algérie (Archives of Women's Struggles in Algeria) was founded by anthropologist and researcher Awel Haouati, later joined by researcher Saadia Gacem and photographer and archivist Lydia Saïdi and a large group of contributors.

The independent initiative's mission is to digitize and make accessible written, visual, print, and photographic materials produced by women activists and women-led associations both in Algeria and the diaspora since Algeria's independence in 1962.

Highlighting connections between present and past political struggles, Archives des luttes de femmes en Algérie builds a scenography with the material collected, proposing a fragmented chronology of women's movements and mobilizations in Algeria. The historical narrative places a particular importance on a pivotal date—March 8, 1990—when the largest women's rights movement protest took place. Prior to the new constitution of 1989, which abolished the single party, political parties and associations were not authorized, and movements were clandestine or informal. The March 8 protest culminated years of political action and mobilization led by women activists.

The project, installed at the Fridericianum, aims to reconstitute a history of these movements through the selection of archival documents where visitors are invited to read and go through over 60 reproductions of different materials from this period, such as political tracts, posters, photographs, and film rushes. The exhibition also includes recent interviews conducted with three women activists who participated in these emancipatory movements and who gave access to their personal archives.

In addition to rendering visible the traces that these women have left over the decades yet which remain unknown to a wider audience, the exhibition presented in Kassel is an opportunity to reflect on the genesis of the project. By documenting the individual practices of the initiative's members in the framework of this larger project, the exhibition also focuses on the gestural work that an archival project demands, raising important questions around the conditions of the archive itself: how bodies move around and handle such fragile documents and what emanates from unearthing these narratives.

Rayya Badran

VENUE
🖉 Fridericianum

MINI-MAJELIS
O Another Roadmap Africa
  Cluster (ARAC)
O Asia Art Archive
O Centre d'art Waza
O El Warcha
O Graziela Kunsch
O Keleketla! Library
O Komîna Fîlm a Rojava
O Sada [regroup]
O Siwa plateforme -
  L'Economat at Redeyef
O The Black Archives

"

Archives des luttes des femmes en Algérie

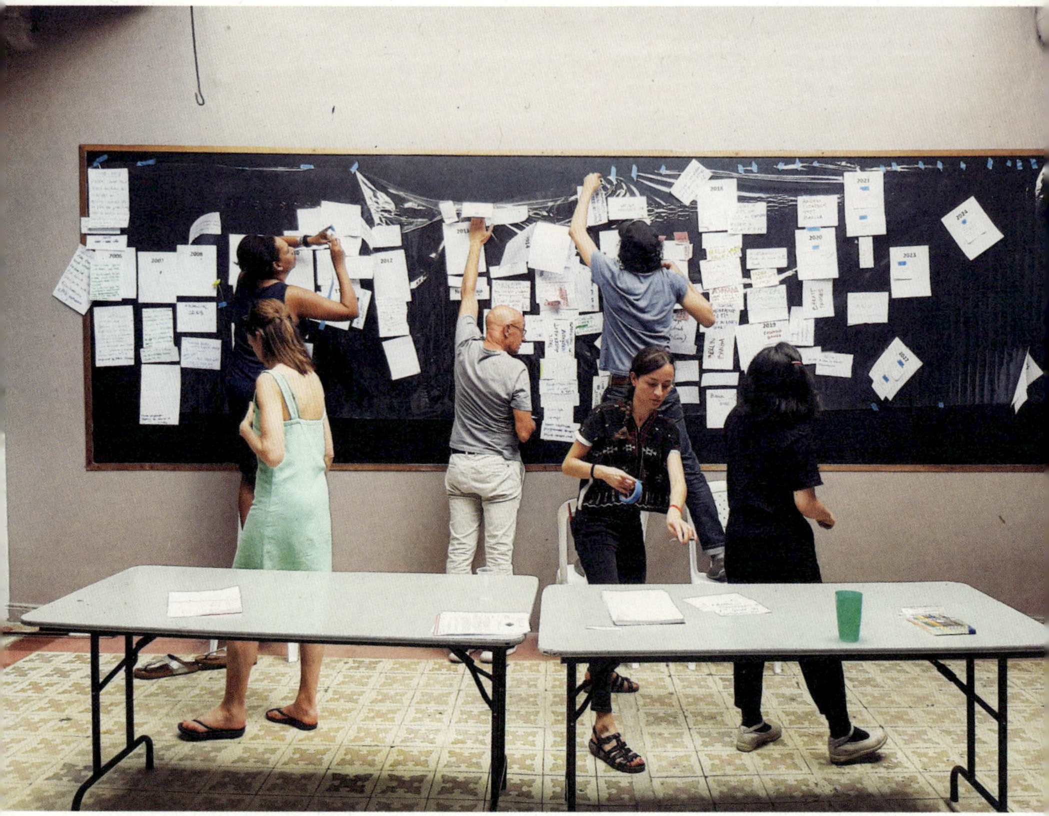

*"Arts Collaboratory School is sustained by the work of many people
that are part of the network and many people that are outside,
those who are active right now and also the ones that have been part
in the past. People from 25 organizations around the globe and
people from each of their own local ekosistems, Arts Collaboratory
has gathered all its knowledge and their imaginaries to become
what it is now. What is being shared in documenta fifteen is part
of this knowledge that comes from the time the network has existed
and beyond 2022. Arts Collaboratory School is an ongoing process
in which our togetherness will grow and degrow. Therefore, we
acknowledge the limit of this acknowledgement to contain what is
Arts Collaboratory School and what it can become in the future."*
— *Arts Collaboratory*

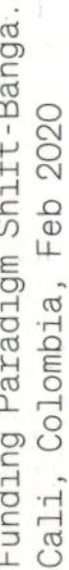

"Funding Paradigm Shift-Banga.
Cali, Colombia, Feb 2020

# ARTS COLLABORATORY



Arts Collaboratory (AC) emerges as a "collective of organizations" operating across the globe from Latin America, Africa, the Middle East, Europe, and Asia. Founded in 2007, and operating since 2015 as a self-organized ekosistem, it includes 25 entities that interact through collaborations, as well as face-to-face meetings known as *banga* (meaning "time and space" in the Ugandan language Luganda), and with a general assembly held almost annually in different countries including Costa Rica, Indonesia, Kyrgyzstan, Senegal, and Uganda. Their practices bridge visual arts and social activism, highlighting questions of solidarity, collective governance, sustainability, and shared political struggles. The network works on paradigm shifts in ways of living and being, organizational structures, funding, power relations, and collective governance.

In Kassel, the collectives materialize under the common umbrella of Arts Collaboratory School (AC School), sharing the acquired practice and knowledges of the network and its members, and expanding upon the physical and conceptual architecture developed by other participants in documenta fifteen.

AC School comprises an array of initiatives that unfold in ruruHaus, Trafohaus, and a range of spaces that otherwise spring to life for the purpose of different projects. Based on the idea of openness and exchange, and bringing together a diversity of "times and spaces," AC School has set up, among others, a radio station, a newsroom, a living room-library, as well as a presentation of printed materials across the city of Kassel and a series of meetings, including cooking sessions.

Arts Collaboratory's tool for communicating content, known as the TAM-TAM, a hybrid newsletter and magazine, has been transformed into *documentamtam*, available online on the collective's web page. Several issues have been published before the 100 days of the exhibition connecting the experiences of the network to that of the lumbung members and artists on collectivity, collective pots, assemblying, shared political struggles and artistic practice that is entangled with the social.

Krzysztof Kościuczuk

VENUES
Ⓡ ruruHaus
● Trafohaus

MINI-MAJELIS
○ Black Quantum Futurism
○ Chimurenga
○ Jumana Emil Abboud
○ Nino Bulling
○ Agus Nur Amal PMTOH
○ Subversive Film

AC School is a collaborative working group amongst Arts Collaboratory organizations and ekosistems.

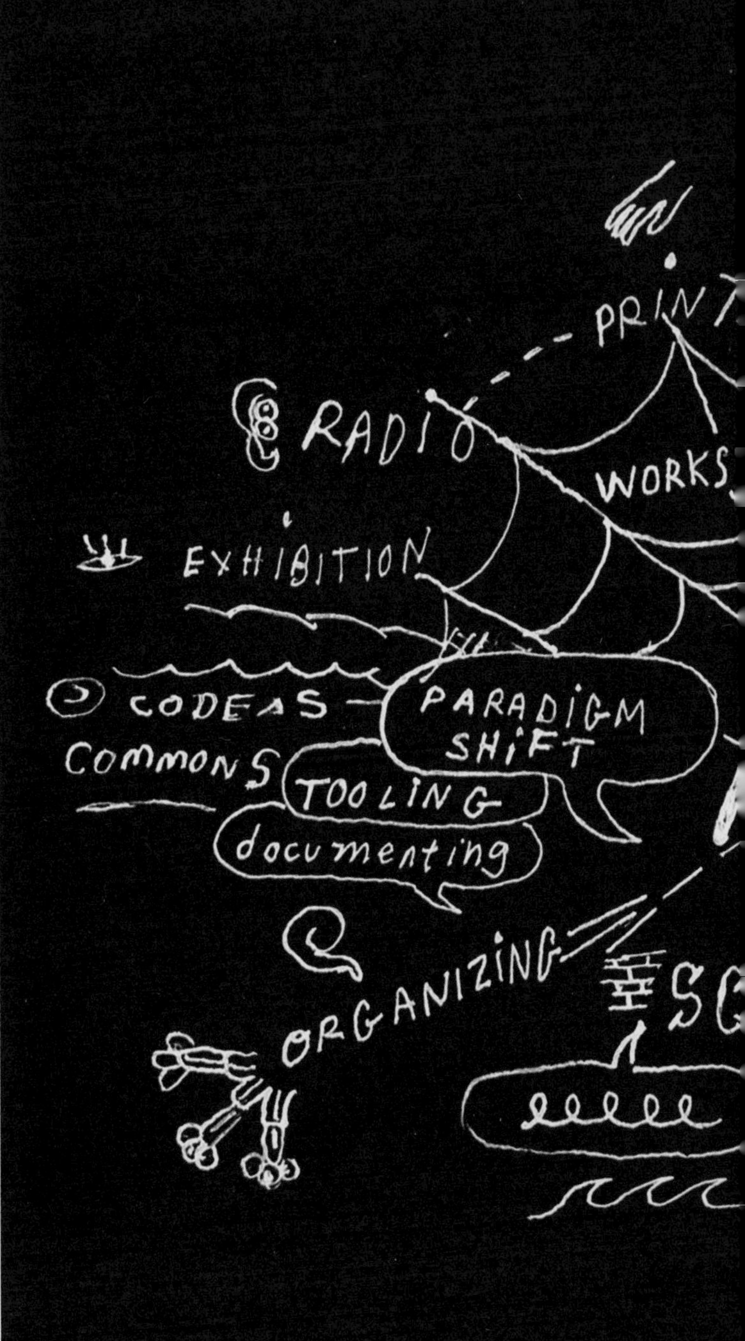

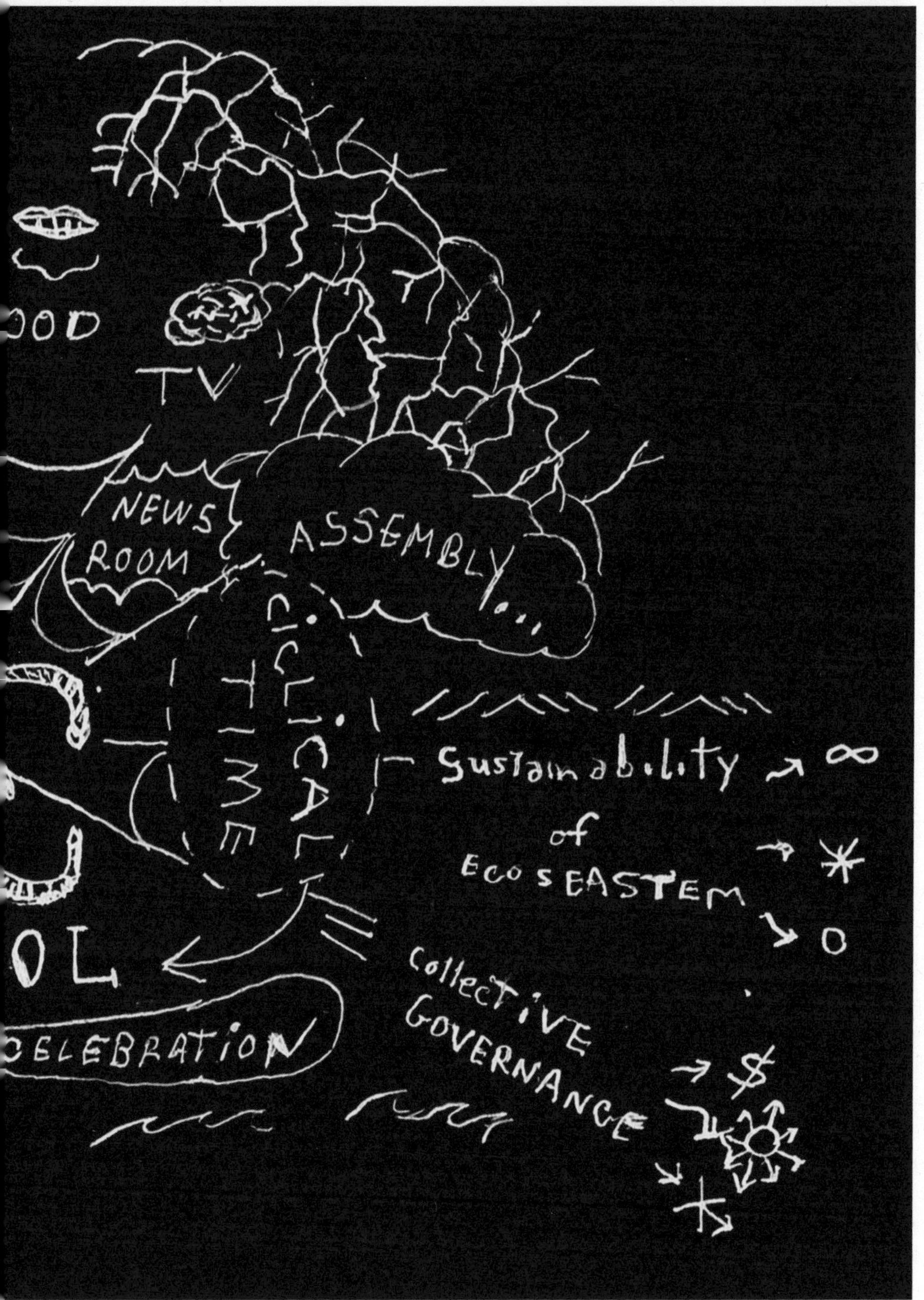
OOD
TV
NEWS
ROOM
ASSEMBLY...
CYCLICAL TIME
Sustainability → ∞
of
ECO S EASTEM
→ *
→ 0
OL
CELEBRATION
collective
GOVERNANCE
→ $

# ASIA ART ARCHIVE

AAA's presentation at documenta fifteen foregrounds the active role artists themselves have played in preserving and mediating knowledge about art.

A

Asia Art Archive (AAA) was founded in Hong Kong at the turn of the century to fill a void resulting from the lack of organizations documenting the rapid rise of contemporary art across Asia. Since then, motivated by the belief that art must be preserved not only as artifact but also—perhaps more importantly—as knowledge, AAA has set itself the task of collecting and sharing that knowledge as the crux of its endeavors. In the process, they have become one of the foremost custodians of primary and secondary materials about recent art from the region. Headquartered in Hong Kong and subsequently at two satellite offices in New York, USA, and New Delhi, India, the organization's vision is grounded in a keen awareness of the complex but less visible histories—from rich local traditions to the legacies of colonialism—that continue to shape Asia's heterogeneous cultures and artistic networks.

As part of a group of collectives and organizations who are dedicated to collaboration and knowledge sharing, AAA's presentation at documenta fifteen foregrounds the active role artists themselves have played in preserving and mediating knowledge about art. Weaving together archival material from the AAA Collections and artworks on loan, this presentation zooms in on three clusters of artist-collectives committed to documenting and reinterpreting practices rooted in everyday vernacular cultures across Asia: artists connected to the Faculty of Fine Arts, Vadodara, India, who participated in the Living Traditions movement in postcolonial India; Womanifesto, a feminist art collective and biennial program in Thailand, most active from 1997 to 2008; and the network of performance art festivals that blossomed across East and Southeast Asia starting in the 1990s.

The section on Vadodara traces the role of Jyoti Bhatt, Nilima Sheikh, K.G. Subramanyan, and others associated with the Faculty of Fine Arts, Vadodara, in preserving and integrating vernacular art forms such as rangolis (threshold paintings) and stencil-making into their artistic practice. In addition, this section demonstrates how the school made space for artistic experimentation with such traditions through activities such as the extracurricular Fine Arts Fairs. The Womanifesto section, meanwhile, highlights the work of the eponymous feminist biennial collective, in pushing beyond ostensible rural-urban divides by connecting its network of international women artists with the community around one particular farm in the Isaan region of Thailand, thereby allowing these artists to serve as bearers of knowledge of local craft traditions. Finally, the festivals and gatherings that were nodes in the performance art network that sprung around the same time as Womanifesto, though often thought of as hotbeds of experimentation, more often than not featured artists who adapted everyday gestures and settings into their work. Furthermore, many of these artists, including Ray Langenbach and Lee Wen, made it a point to chronicle their peers amid the rapid expansion of the performance scene in Asia. These interwoven recent histories, as retold by Asia Art Archive, are an active testament to the collective ethos at the root of contemporary art across the region, and its engagement with the everyday local.

Alvin Li

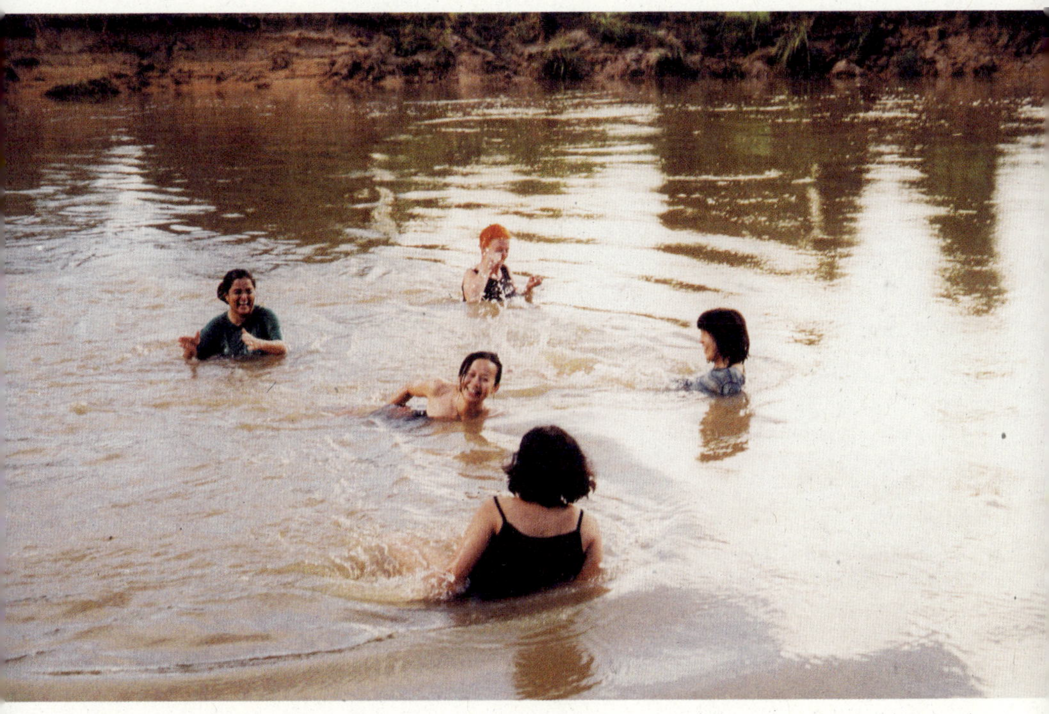

Enjoy (Womanifesto Workshop
River Bathing Photo) (2001)
The Womanifesto Archive, Asia
Art Archive Collections

VENUE
◖ Fridericianum

MINI-MAJELIS
○ Another Roadmap Africa
  Cluster (ARAC)
○ Archives des luttes des
  femmes en Algérie
○ Centre d'art Waza
○ El Warcha
○ Graziela Kunsch
○ Keleketla! Library
○ Komîna Fîlm a Rojava
○ Sada [regroup]
○ Siwa plateforme - L'Economat
  at Redeyef
○ The Black Archives

Atis Rezistans (Resistance Artists) is a fluid collective of artists working in the Grand Rue neighborhood of Port-au-Prince, Haiti. Grand Rue is a large avenue that runs from north to south of the city's downtown. The collective, which was founded by sculptors André Eugène and Jean Herald Celeur in the late 1990s, is composed of established artists working largely on sculpture, and younger, emerging artists working in sculpture, painting, and other art forms. As new artists have continued to join the collective, they have added further forms of artistic expression, incorporating performance, slam poetry, photography, and music.

The large sculptures of Atis Rezistans embody the artistic sensibility and spirit of the collective. Their style draws influences from Haitian popular culture, history, and vodou religion. Using a range of found and recycled materials, carved wood, as well as human remains, such as skulls, the artists in the collective create structures that have been described as assemblages and recuperations. This assemblage of elements reflects a meeting of art in conversation with the social and physical landscape of Port-au-Prince, Haiti and world history, especially the role of Haiti in the global history of Black revolution and liberation.

In 2009, André Eugène and British artist, curator, and critic Leah Gordon (a collaborator of the collective) first organized The Ghetto Biennale; the biennale has since gone on to play a major role in the collective's practice, furthering dialogue about Haitian and Caribbean art and fostering generative conversations with other artists and art critics regionally and internationally. The core members of Atis Rezistans include André Eugène, Jean Claude Saintilus aka Kaliko, Jean Robert Palanquet aka Ti Jean, Evel Romain, Wesner Bazile and Riko. A loose larger group of around twenty younger artists also form part of the collective, and have participated in editions of the Ghetto Biennale. Inspired by the writing of Gloria Anzaldua, and proposed by Gordon, curator of the biennale, the biennale is organized following the question "What happens when first world art rubs up against third world art? Does it bleed?" Another founding premise of the Ghetto Biennale was to confront the class inequalities of mobility, movement, and the art market.

Their participation in documenta fifteen is wide-ranging; it includes multimedia sculpture, various exhibition spaces and artist residencies, performances, screenings and discussions. It features a series of sculptures in St. Kunigundis Church, and a structure designed by British architect, and former Ghetto Biennale participant, Vivian Chan in collaboration with André Eugène and Leah Gordon. The shape of the ceiling floating structure mirrors the geometry and cacophony of the streets in the neighborhood behind Grand Rue in Port-au-Prince, and is inspired by the visual representation of place and space in the work of Haitian master painter Préfète Duffaut. A major sculpture of Papa Legba—a welcoming spirit—will stand in the garden of the church, where recordings made during the Ghetto Biennale, at Radyo Shak, will be broadcast. Haitian artists Michel Lafleur, Katelyne Alexis and Harold Pierre Louis will also be producing artwork during a residency at Kassel that will be exhibited at the entrance of the church. Other featured works include a memorial tent created by André Eugène and Michel Lafleur, honoring the memory of the artists lost during the 2012 earthquake in Haiti. A series of film screenings will feature the work of the Ghetto Biennale and work by collaborating artists. Similarly, a number of conferences will focus on the historical context of Atis Rezistans and the Ghetto Biennale exploring the role of the Kreyol concept *konbit* (traditional form of collective labour), global class politics in art, and the history of the Haitian revolution and vodou, challenging previous narratives and memorialization of the revolution and inviting new ones. Atis Rezistans | Ghetto Biennale's intervention at documenta showcases the collaborative experiences and work that has emerged from Atis Rezistans and the various editions of the Ghetto Biennale, revealing its connection to the lumbung spirit of collaboration.

Marta Fernández Campa

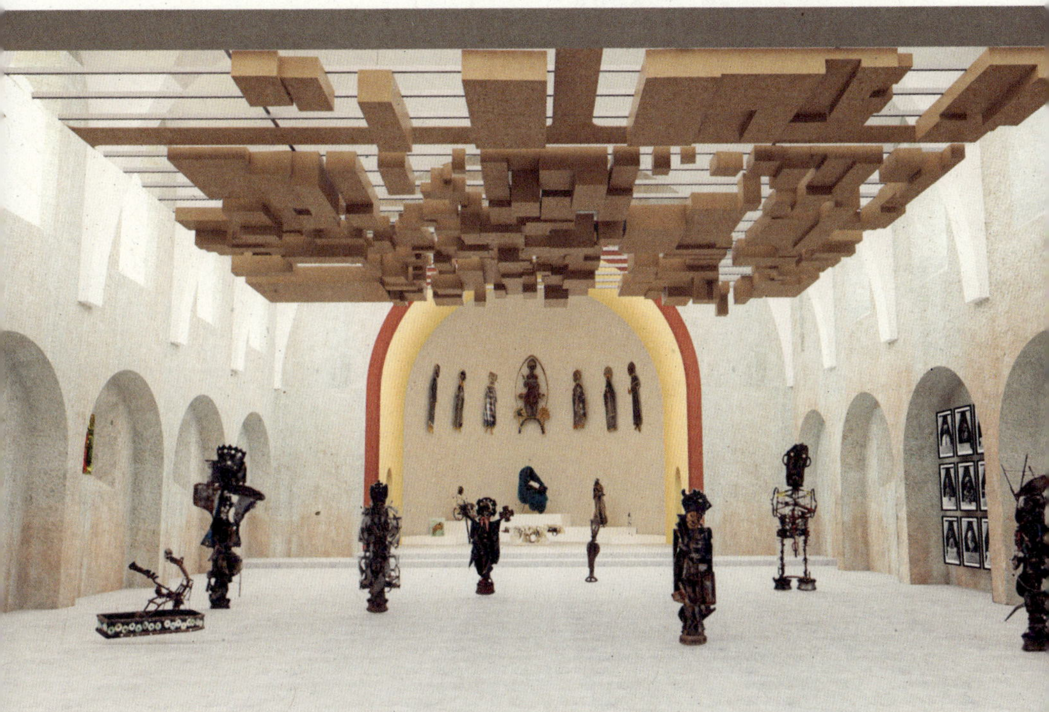

Plan for Atis Rezistans | Ghetto Biennale space
at St. Kunigundis Church, Kassel, Germany
Digital Rendering

**VENUE**
St. Kunigundis

**MINI-MAJELIS**
O Marwa Arsanios
O Sourabh Phadke
O yasmine eid-sabbagh
O *foundationClass*collective

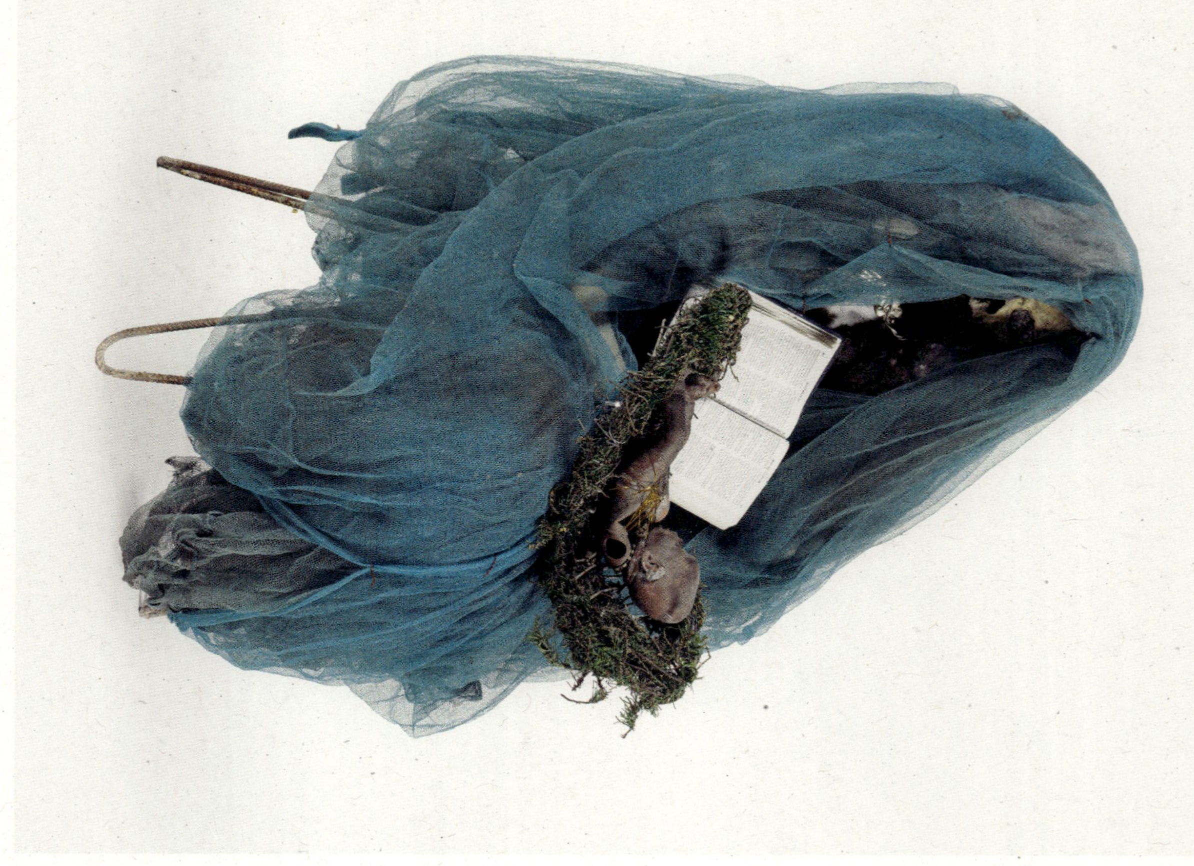

Jean Claude Saintilus, *Vyej Mari (Virgin Mary)*, 2015. Metal, skull, net cloth, glazed paper, bible, clock, doll, plastic chair, and balsam, 292.1 × 139.7 × 137.2 cm

# List of participating artists and contributors

**ATIS REZISTANS**
Katelyn Alexis
Wesner Bazile
Jerry Reginald Chery
 aka Twoket
Patrick Elie aka
 Kombatan
André Eugène
Londel Innocent
Louis Kervans aka
 Bakari
Michel Lafleur
Jean Muller Milord
 aka Soso
Jean Robert Palenquet
Herold Pierre-Louis
Mario Pierre-Louis
 aka Prela
Evel Romain
Jean-Claude Saintilus
Reginald Senatus
Wilerme Tegenis

**GHETTO BIENNALE**
Leah Gordon
Cat Barich
Vivian Chan
Henrike Naumann
Bastian Hagedorn
Tom Bogaert
L
Laura Heyman
Elizabeth Woodroffe
Roberto N Peyre
Camille Chedda
Emilie Boone
Simon Benjamin
Whit Forrester
Edouard Duval-Carrie
Demar Brackenridge
Sheldon Green

**PERFORMANCE**
Carima Neusser
Joe Winter
Richard Fleming –
 Radyo Shak
Pedro Lasch

**CONFERENCE**
Nanne Buurman
John Cussans
Marta Fernández Campa

A

Installation of the Caribbean *InTransitProject* at the 3rd Ghetto Biennale 2013, Port-au-Prince, Haiti

# BAAN NOORG COLLABORATIVE ARTS AND CULTURE

Between Kassel and Nongpho,
Thailand, Baan Noorg engage with
urban subcultures and mythic
rituals.

Founded in 2011 by artists jiandyin (Jiradej Meemalai and Pornpilai Meemalai), Baan Noorg Collaborative Arts and Culture is a nonprofit collective dedicated to community-oriented, socially engaged, and intercultural practices. Baan Noorg is the name of the village in Nongpho district, Ratchaburi province, Thailand, where jiandyin live and work.

Baan Noorg's collaborative and exchange-driven work brings different communities together, engaging with urban subculture and mythic ritual. In 2014, for the first Day Off Laboratory—a venture dedicated to lifelong, non-institutional learning—Baan Noorg invited intergenerational Thai and overseas participants to make and display artworks at community sites across Nongpho. For NongpoKiDdee (NPKD), initiated in 2011, they organized moving-image workshops and festivals for children in Nongpho. Baan Noorg facilitates social enterprise to promote community ecological and economic sustainability.

For documenta, Baan Noorg have focused on non-human animals and extended their operating methodologies through a three-part project comprising a dairy farm exchange program, *Nang Yai* (Thai shadow puppetry), and skateboard activities. Baan Noorg envisage these interventions as dynamic, dialogical platforms that facilitate knowledge exchange between Kassel and Nongpho.

In 1968, due to a global economic depreciation of rice, Nongpho villagers switched from rice cultivation to dairy farming. In order to enable farmers to develop more sustainable dairy farming practices, especially in light of global food shortages, Baan Noorg established an exchange program between a farm in Kassel and Nongpho. Footage shot in these locations is displayed in a four-channel video.

The agricultural shift also precipitated significant social changes, as traditionally interfamilial rice cultivation was replaced by relatively segregated husbandry activities. Baan Noorg, advised and trained by experts at the Khanon Temple, a regional-based cultural heritage center, is organizing daily workshops and performances of *Nang Yai*, which utilizes the hides of dead or pregnant cows as surfaces to depict gods and characters from the Ramayana epics—and here, by the Brothers Grimm, too.

Finally, inspired by a Ramayanan myth in which gods and demons conspired to churn the ocean of milk for a nectar of immortality, Baan Noorg has built a functional skateboarding ramp in documenta Halle. With the Kassel-based group Mr. Wilson Skatehalle, they have organized workshops and social activities related to skateboarding culture, including a skateboard donation and exchange program between Kassel and Nongpho.

Wong Binghao

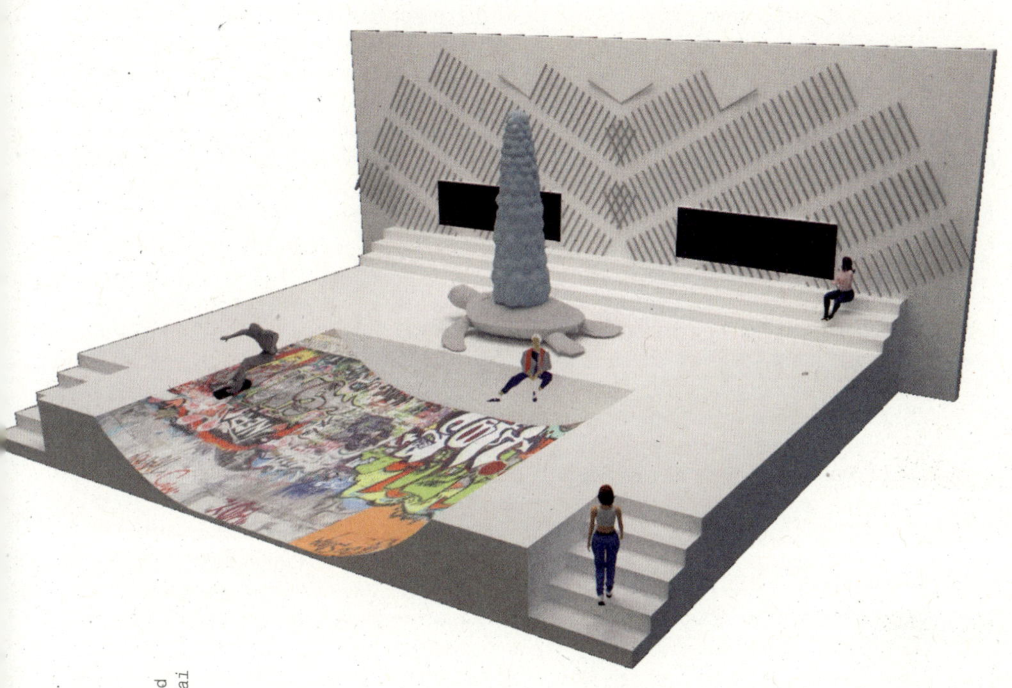



Plan for *Churning Milk: the Rituals of Things* (2022).
Multimedia installation 14.00 × 12.00 × 1.20 m.
Include: 85" LCD monitors, VDO 4 channel full HD B/W
and color-sound, speakers, horn-speaker, subwoofer,
mixer, fluorescent light tubes, prepared motor,
steel, inflatable air object, spray paint, skateboard
mini-ramp, Nang Yai, live piece performances, Nang Yai
carving workshop

**VENUE**
*documenta* Halle

**MINI-MAJELIS**
O Dan Perjovschi
O Fehras Publishing Practices
O Nhà Sàn Collective
O The Nest Collective

Baan Noorg Collaborative Arts and Culture

# BLACK QUANTUM FUTURISM

Based in Philadelphia, USA,
Black Quantum Futurism draws on
Afro-diasporan temporalities and
speculative fiction. In Kassel,
the collective has built a stage
that's a hub for memories, stories,
and concerts.

Based in Philadelphia, USA, Black Quantum Futurism (BQF) is the collective practice of Camae Ayewa and Rasheedah Phillips. Their work sets forth new connections of time and space, thereby becoming liberated from the constraints of linear time. Their writing, films, and performances draw on sources such as alternative futurities, Afro-diasporan temporalities, quantum physics, housing futures, and speculative fiction as frameworks through which to reconnect to the past and create new futures.

> *Return of the echo*
> *Reversal is memory*
> *The spin that influences itself*
> *The Time Reversal of Water Waves*
> *Future information technologies*

At documenta fifteen, BQF are represented by three projects. *The Clepsydra Stage* (2022) is an interactive installation on the banks of the river Fulda. An abstracted water clock, consisting of three entangled circles, serves as a hub for memories, visions, and stories. Two of the circular elements that make up the stage construction are set in motion by the water. Different experiences of space and time as well as identities meet; the personal always intersects with the universal.

But, more concretely, through the work, new spaces are opened for local marginalized communities for expression and exchange. Conceived as an interactive space, in the course of documenta fifteen *The Clepsydra Stage* is also activated as a floating stage by other participants. Responding to each visitor's movements, it gives voice to varying temporalities, spatialities, and identities. BQF uses it for its own concerts, as well as one by Camae Ayewa's jazz ensemble, Irreversible Entanglements.

The other two works also collect and make accessible the memories and experiences of audiences. *Black Grandmother Clock (Oral Futures Booth)* (2021) is installed in the underpass and collects ideas of the future and audio testimonies of Kassel visitors. A questionnaire encourages audiences to develop their own visions; stories from the past that have long since disappeared from public memory can thereby be documented. Suggestions for additional contributions such as speeches, songs, or sounds from the city can be submitted to BQF. All of these collected audio elements are incorporated into an evolving soundscape, merging archival sounds, song snippets, and voices of the neighborhood that plays from sound sculptures called the *Sonic Shades* (2021). In these novel forms, BQF brings local memories together with nascent visions of the future, creating a unique archive.

Ann Mbuti

VENUES
- Frankfurter Straße / Fünffensterstraße (Underpass)
- Rondell

MINI-MAJELIS
- Arts Collaboratory
- Chimurenga
- Jumana Emil Abboud
- Nino Bulling
- Agus Nur Amal PMTOH
- Subversive Film

Black Quantum Futurism, *Reclamation: Space-Times* (2021)
Installation view, Philadelphia, USA

Black Quantum Futurism, *Nonlinear Histories & Quantum Futures* (2020)
Installation view, Marseille, France

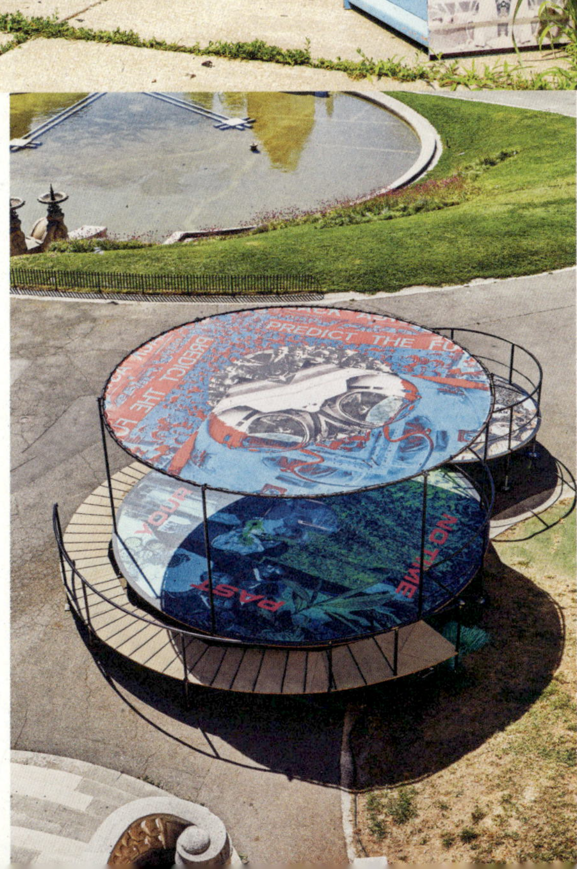

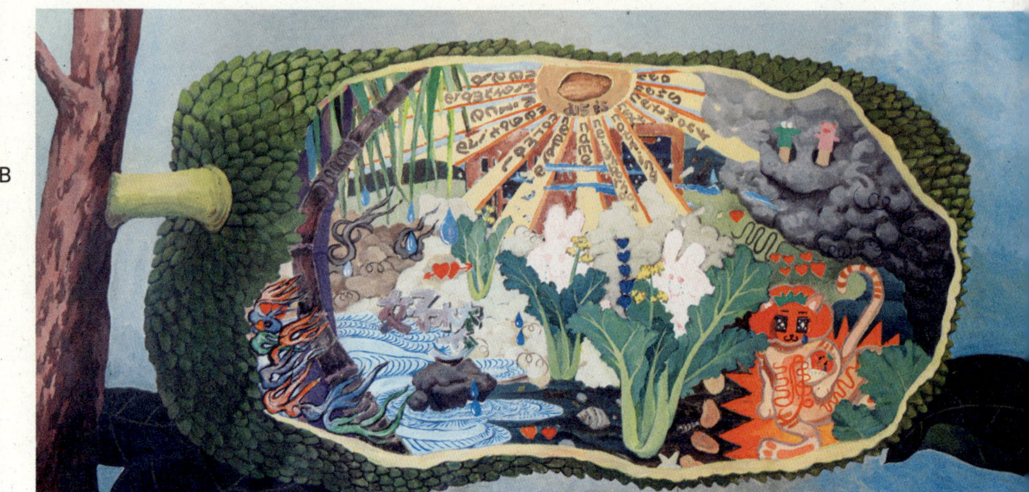

B

THE DREAM OF BOLOHOPE (2022)
Acrylic on canvas
198 × 96 cm

Formed in Guangzhou, China, in 2019, BOLOHO is a collective centered on social practice and embodied knowledge, from food to co-working. In Kassel, BOLOHO has turned a factory cafeteria into a Cantonese-style café, together with a collaboratively-designed menu, and a self-produced sitcom.

Just as a fruit's meat grows around its pit, BOLOHO—a romanization of the Chinese word for "jackfruit pit"—coalesced around a nexus. In early 2019, Bubu and Cat started searching for an office for their new design company. They invited friends to join them in an apartment in an old residential neighborhood of Haizhu District in Guangzhou, China, which gradually grew into a hybrid spatial practice.

Part co-working space and part collective centered on social practice, BOLOHO houses the BOLOHO Company, whose services range from advertisement and exhibition production to graphics and event organization; the company office; and the Reading Room, a publication project initiated by Xiaotian Li, Di Liu, and Siyan Xie. BOHOLO continues the lineage of Pearl River Delta art collectives, sharing the belief in collectivity and experimentalism, while practicing novel forms of decentralization and mutual aid, further knitting their practice into the fabric of life. At BOLOHO you will find its five core members working while guests peruse publications in the reading room. In the evenings, members and guests share home-cooked meals and food plays a crucial role in BOLOHO's practice, as a social experience and a form of embodied knowledge.

For documenta fifteen, the collective has turned a factory cafeteria into a Cantonese-style café. The space is divided into four rooms, each featuring an episode of the self-produced sitcom *BOLOHOPE*. The members, part of a generation raised on maudlin sitcoms with sentimental narratives bound by traditional family values, chose to shoot *BOLOHOPE* as a contemporary adaptation of this ideology-laden genre. On the screens separating the rooms, drawings and paintings by the group earnestly and humorously express their aspirations and anxieties. *The Dream of Bolohope* (2022), for instance, depicts a microcosm operating inside a jackfruit. Radiating from the pit, here labeled "d15," are streaks of light bearing words such as "nice" and "negative," which describe a certain collective euphoria mingled with ambivalence towards participation in a canonical exhibition. But surely any problem can be solved with a good meal. Working with other participating collectives, BOLOHO has designed a menu including recipes from places as far away as Cambodia, India, and Chengdu in China.

Alvin Li

B

VENUE
● Hübner areal

MINI-MAJELIS
○ Amol K Patil
○ Cao Minghao & Chen Jianjun
○ Chang En-Man
○ Sa Sa Art Projects

# BRITTO ARTS TRUST

In Kassel, the Bangladesh-based Britto Arts Trust creates a bazaar, a family kitchen, and a large-scale mural, all exploring geopolitics, land rights, and food.

B

Founded in 2002, Britto Arts Trust is an artist-run, non-profit contemporary art hub in Dhaka, Bangladesh, providing support and infrastructure for cultural practitioners across Bangladesh. At documenta fifteen, Britto (meaning "circle" in Bangla) creates a vivid interconnected landscape devoted to food politics, displacement, and culture.

The first is an organic *palan*—a Bengali kitchen garden—which feeds the *pak ghor*, the family kitchen-cum-living room, where meals are prepared and stories swapped. In Kassel, Britto's *pak gor* serves food and gathers people from its immigrant population, who prepare meals, share their histories, memories, and host events, presenting the food cultures of 100 nationalities in 100 days.

In the large-scale installation *rasad* (2022), Britto has recreated a small-town bazaar stocked with food items in crochet, ceramic, metal, or embroidery, produced collaboratively through workshops in Dhaka in 2021. Each handmade object makes the ubiquitous supermarket item precious. They underscore how foodstuffs are divorced from their natural origins, surviving only through chemical conditioning and false environments.

A team of artists have spent a year combing through old Bengali movies for scenes of food, famine, and war, renditions of which form a large on-site mural *Chayachhobi* (2022), painted by the artists and Bangladeshi cinema banner and rickshaw painters. Alongside, there are screenings of videos and photographs, both freshly captured and long conceived.

Britto has organized *Re-Visit* (2021–2022), which travels across remote Bangladeshi villages revisiting communities they have worked with in the past, and documented for display in Kassel. Here, Britto scrutinizes the geopolitical issues facing rural and border locations in Bangladesh and their loss of land rights, environment, and culture. Since 2009, Britto has invited artists to work with local communities on a project entitled *Prantiker Prakritajan*, where performances, cultural, and ritual events were held alongside artistic projects, and then celebrated with the villagers with feasts of traditional food and drinks. Revisiting the communities, Britto has collected recipes as well as oral histories. Through their ambitious project, Britto exercises agency over food and community; an important advance against the mass corporatization of food. Not product-oriented, but the opening up and explication of a process, food here is a manner by which to record what is disappearing as the direct result of displacement and the dispossession of land and resources.

Skye Arundhati Thomas

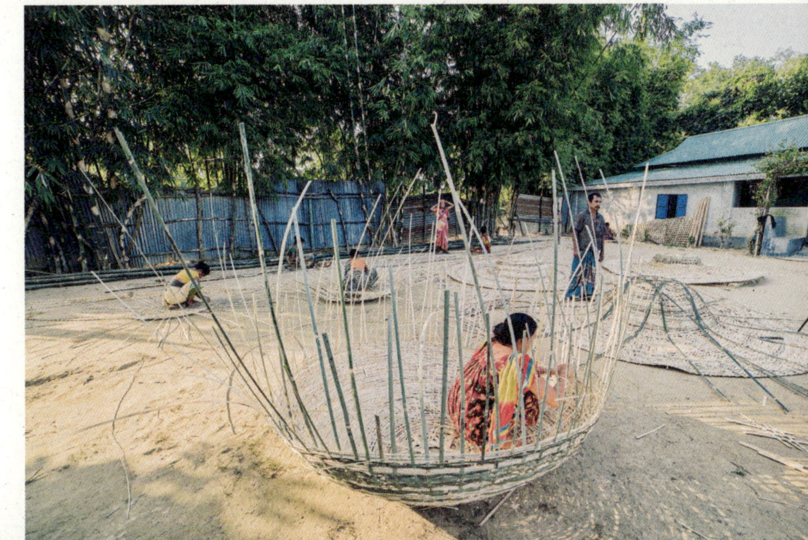

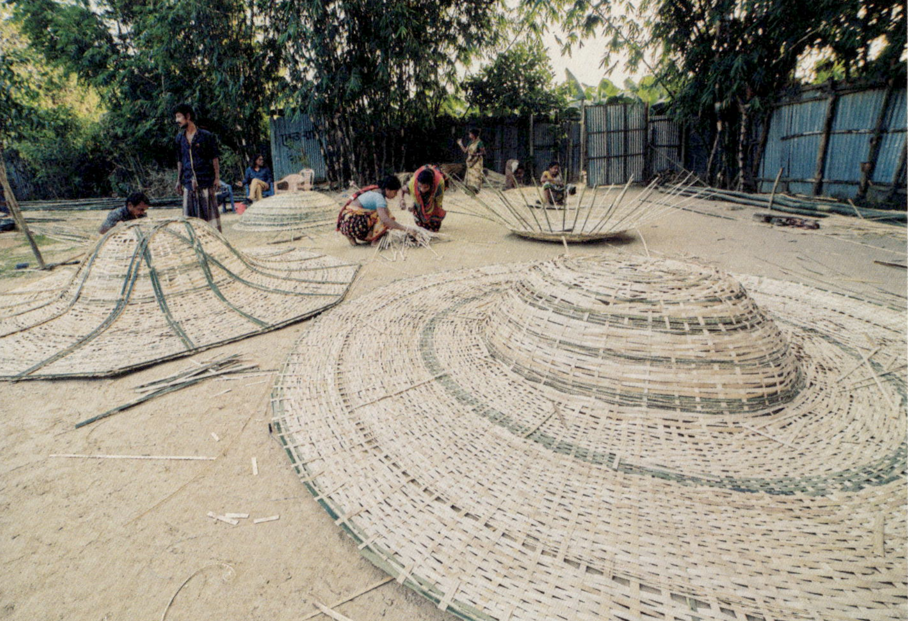





**VENUE**
🟡 documenta Halle

**LUMBUNG INTER-LOKAL**
- ⭘ FAFSWAG
- ⭘ Fondation Festival sur le Niger
- ⭘ Gudskul
- ⭘ INLAND
- ⭘ Instituto de Artivismo Hannah Arendt (INSTAR)
- ⭘ Jatiwangi art Factory
- ⭘ Más Arte Más Acción (MAMA)
- ⭘ OFF-Biennale Budapest
- ⭘ Project Art Works
- ⭘ The Question of Funding
- ⭘ Trampoline House
- ⭘ Wajukuu Art Project
- ⭘ ZK/U – Center for Art and Urbanistics

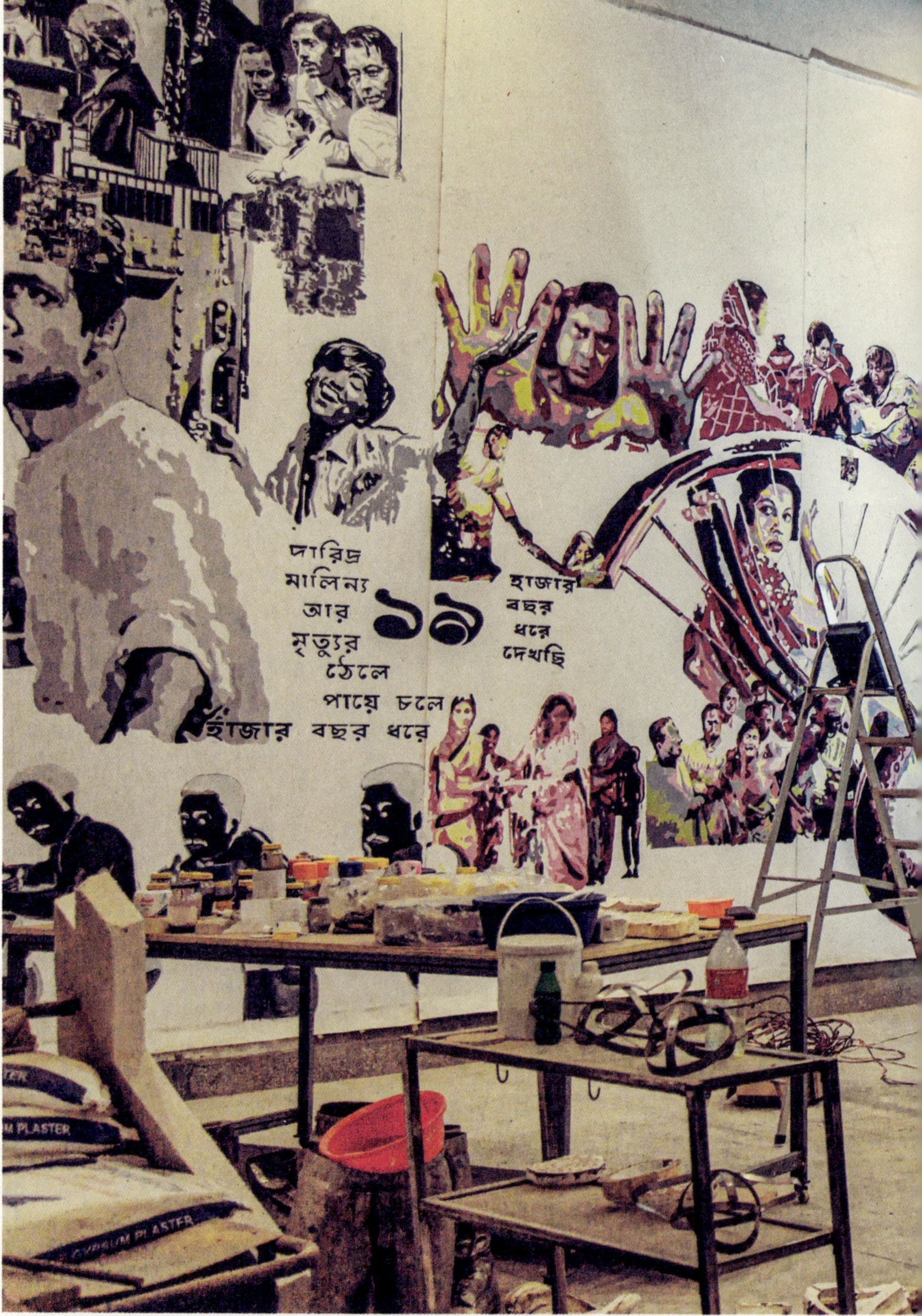


B

Artists in action making Britto Art Trust's ছায়াছবি (Chayachobi) / Mural for documenta fifteen.

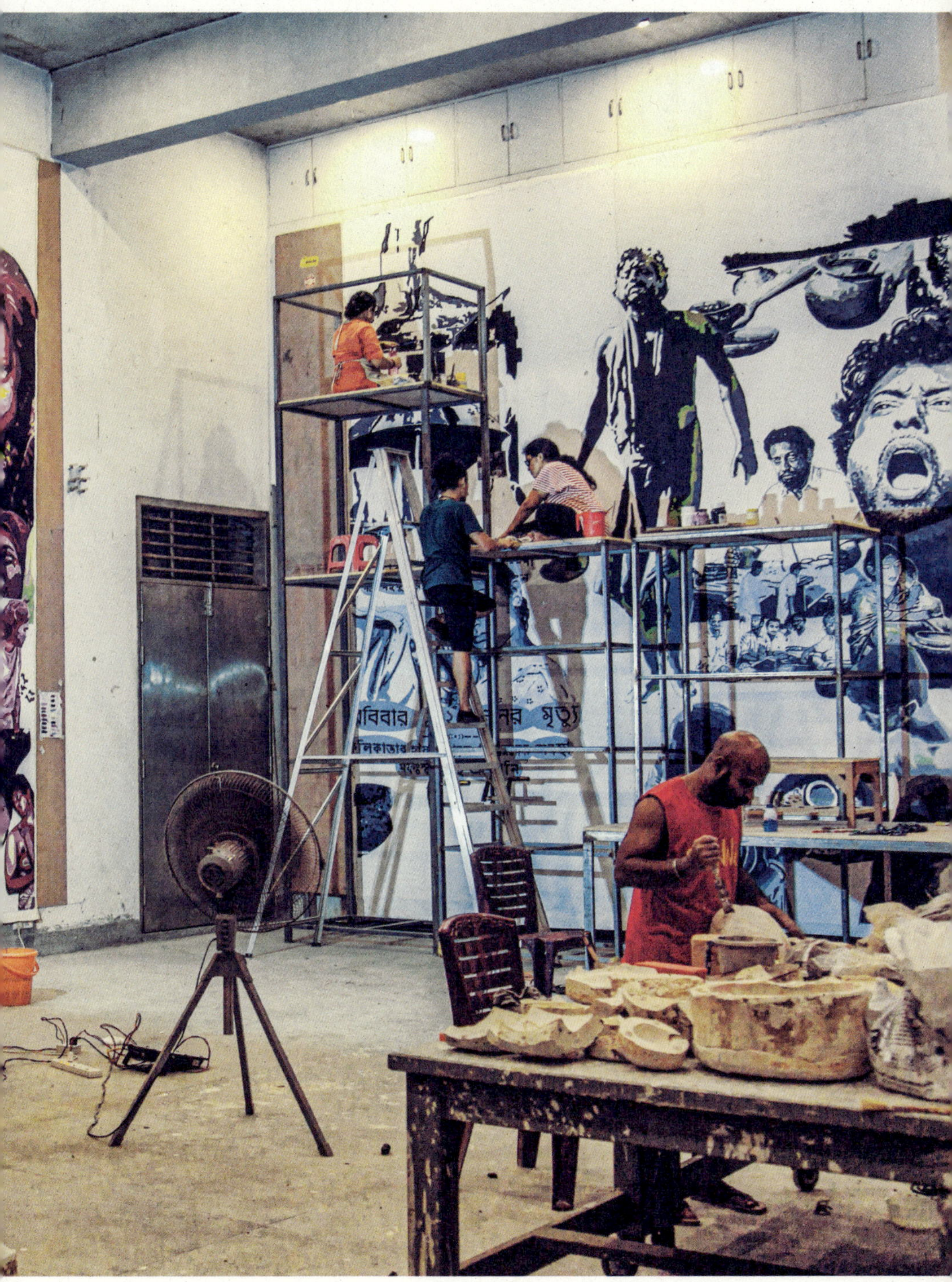

# CAO MINGHAO & CHEN JIANJUN

A tent, installed outside the
Orangerie, by Cao Minghao and Chen
Jianjun brings together herders,
pastoralists, artists, and
C  visitors.

The Chengdu, China-based artists Cao Minghao and Chen Jianjun reconceptualize how we can take refuge within the environment without alienating ecological wisdom. Their research-based practice attempts to overcome anthropocentrism, summoning ways to relate to the environment amidst climate challenges faced by all—be it lands, waters, skyways, animals, or their long-standing human caretakers.

*Water System Refuge #3* is the latest in their long-term research series, set in Sichuan province and focused on water systems in multiple locations: source areas in the upper reaches of the Minjiang River; the Zoigê alpine wetlands on the eastern Tibetan Plateau; and Kassel's environment, with its 250 years of industrial consumption and transformation.

Their project brings together many people—herders and pastoralists, Kassel's diverse communities, scientists, geologists, anthropologists, documenta artists, and visitors. The site for interactions is a black tent—woven in animal hair and mixed fabric—installed in a park outside the Orangerie. The tent takes the form of nomadic housing used by herder groups in a region stretching from the shores of the Atlantic Ocean to the eastern Tibetan Plateau. These groups use the tent not only for refuge, but as sites for governance and ritual. The specific tent in Kassel is partly made of yak hair, by herders and craftspeople from the Zoigê Wetlands,

a dense peatland area of rich biodiversity that supplies water to the Upper Yellow River.

Within this tent, viewers can see other components to the project: research from workshops, presentations, a new publication titled *The Ecology of Sands and "Black Beach"*, and the video *Grass, Sand and Global Environmental Apparatus*. The video draws from the 28 tangkas collected in the book *Thangka Paintings of the World and Beings of Kurti Kachukha* by the environmentalist Trachung Palzang. Tangkas are paintings relating traditionally to gods and mythology; here they act to transmute knowledge about ecological methods in grasslands.

While the tent will be partly biodegradable by the end of the exhibition, its yak hair does not live and die at documenta. Minghao and Jianjun have worked with the Grassland Ecological Planting Farmers' Cooperative to facilitate production of yak hair slippers. This experimental initiative hopes to help reduce the region's reliance on imported industrial products, while also facilitating an economy of subsistence for sedentary herders whose lives are affected by changing ekosistems.

Carol Que


Ⓚ Karlswiese (Karlsaue)
Ⓗ Hafenstraße 76

MINI-MAJELIS
O Amol K Patil
O BOLOHO
O Chang En-Man
O Sa Sa Art Projects

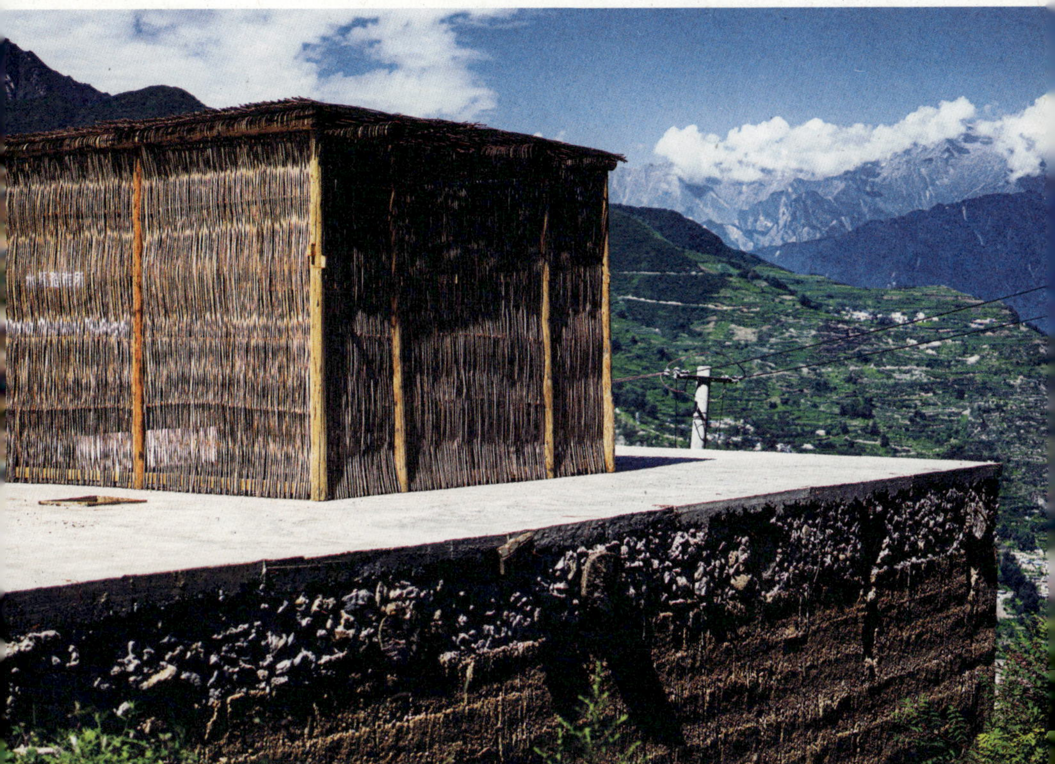

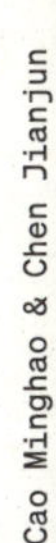

Cao Minghao & Chen Jianjun

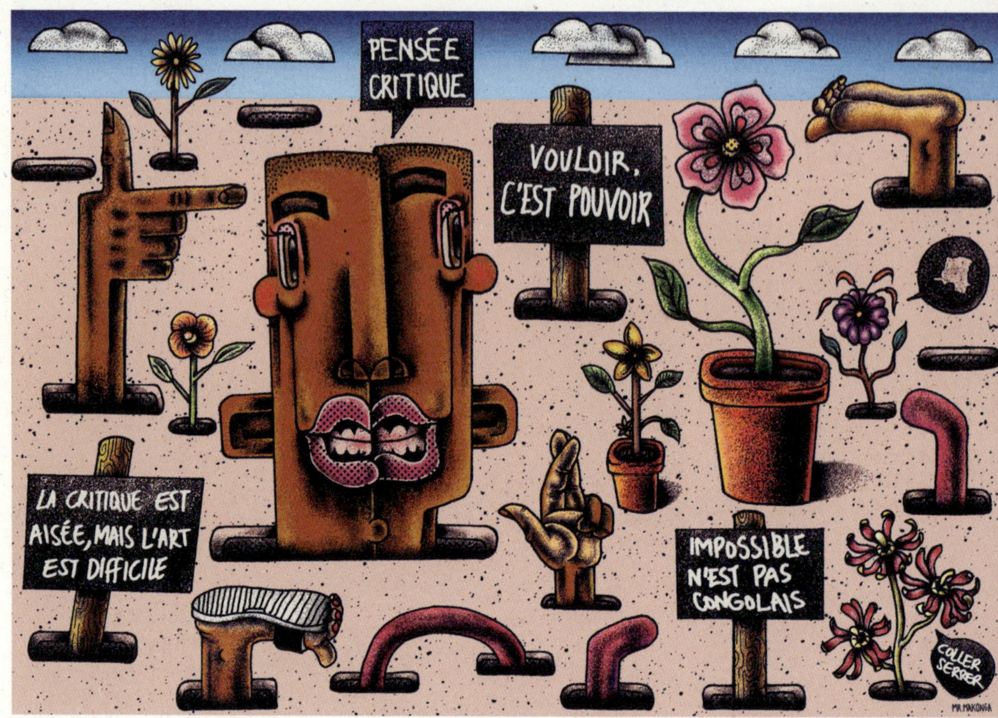


c

Embodied harvesting of the Kirata process in Lubumbashi, February 2022. A visual harvesting of the dialogues with the Waza team, the Kirata participants and the community of Lubumbashi. Drawing by Prodige Makonga

# CENTRE D'ART WAZA

For documenta fifteen, Waza presents a platform of curatorial experiences informed by their work in D. R. Congo.

Waza, which means "imagine" in Swahili, is an art center founded in 2010 by a group of artists and curators based in Lubumbashi, D.R. Congo. Waza develops exhibitions, publications, and other cultural productions for the emergence of grassroots experimental artistic practices and the promotion of alternative ways of knowledge sharing and consciousness raising. In its physical space, Waza hosts art collectives, social entrepreneurs, and individual artists from a wide range of disciplines (visual art, comics, music, writing, dance, among others). It also has a library, sound studio, a web radio, and a zine lab. Its recent projects explore various themes such as the restitution of African cultural heritage (such the project *Disolo, Convers(at)ion avec les collections du musée* in collaboration with Witwatersrand University), the commons (such as *Power to the Commons* in collaboration with Ker Thiossane, Platohedro and SALTS), art education, emancipation from paternalistic organization of labor (such as *Revolution Room*), and alternative uses of cyberspace in the global south (such as *AfricaTube*, in collaboration with AfricaMuseum). Waza's program alternates sequences of research as an experimental laboratory (*Kazi 2.0*) and with presentation or mediations towards communities (*Mitaani Moments*).

At documenta fifteen, Waza presents its platform of curatorial experiences inspired by the practices of commons studied in South Eastern Congo. More than twenty cultural workers take the title of Kirata, an accented form of "curator", to both claim their legitimacy to construct their own discourse on art practices and to distance themselves from the extractive methods of hegemonic international exchanges. During the 100 days in Kassel, Waza presents a collaboration with the traditional smelters of Walemba in the Congolese copper belt; discussions with the community of Kalera, caught between a natural reserve and a hydroelectric dam project; and the archives of the Verbeek-Mwewa collection, which gives an account of the artistic sensitivities of the working classes of Lubumbashi during the last five decades. The triple installation is an embodied harvesting of the process of Kirata, used as triggers for the *baraza*, the public program encouraging cultural empowerment through artistic production.

As a contribution to the Fridericianum library, Waza presents research on archiving contemporary art practices in Africa developed since 2014 in collaboration with Visual Art Network South Africa for PAN!C, the Pan-Afican Network of Independent Contemporaneity. Waza will also join the programs of Arts Collaboratory and Another Roadmap, of which it is a member.

Dagara Dakin

VENUE
Fridericianum

MINI-MAJELIS
O Another Roadmap Africa Cluster (ARAC)
O Archives des luttes des femmes en Algérie
O Asia Art Archive
O El Warcha
O Graziela Kunsch
O Keleketla! Library
O Komîna Film a Rojava
O Sada [regroup]
O Siwa plateforme - L'Economat at Redeyef
O The Black Archives

# CHANG EN-MAN

Departing from the trajectory of invasive snail species, Chang En-Man's projects look to colonialism and the Indigenous Paiwan people of Taiwan. In Kassel, she geotags parts of Kassel along the routes of giant African snails, publishes snail recipes, and makes a boathouse that sets sail on the Fulda, together with an archival waiting room.

In Taiwan, a common snack with beer is wok-fried giant African snails *(Achatina fulica)*. Originating in East Africa, the snails came to Taiwan in 1933 as a food source on the order of Shimojō Kumaichi, a public health administrator in Taiwan during the Japanese Occupation (1895–1945). One of the world's worst invasive species, they wreaked havoc on local agriculture, invading the Malay Peninsula, North Borneo, Indonesia, and the Hawaiian Islands. The Paiwan people, from whom Chang En-Man is descended matrilineally, use the meat for *cinavu*, eaten at celebrations. The slime (that the snails emit even after death) is removed with paper mulberry leaves gathered from trees that symbolize the Indigenous. They trace the voyages of Austronesian peoples beginning 4000 years ago as they were transplanted across archipelagos. Following this logic, Chang confirmed anthropological assumptions that Austronesian peoples emigrated from Taiwan.

Chang has been following this slime trail since 2009, with exhibitions and presentations in Taipei, Yilan, Kaohsiung, and Pingtung, Taiwan, Singapore, Hong Kong, Kathmandu, Nepal, Kelowna, Canada—and now Kassel—of recipes, embroidery, maps, moving image, performance, and collaborations. They derive from Chang's interest in Paiwan culture and its entanglements with colonialism in the Age of Exploration and the later colonial period in East and Southeast Asia. The documenta fifteen project contains three parts.

First, the boathouse and waiting room, fashioned out of painted glass in the shape of paper mulberry leaves, will set sail on the Fulda River as an homage to sea voyages—the boathouse simulates a journey made of legends, inspired by oral tradition; the waiting room contains an archival display examining the collection of snails.

Secondly, the *Project Invasion* investigates themes including colonial history, industry and economics and food cultures. Working with research collaborators Tsou Ting and Wang Han Fang, Chang has distributed QR codes throughout documenta fifteen sites as a sort of invasion in itself: leading visitors to a digital space of glossary networking and remapping Kassel onto that of the giant African snails' own routes.

Hera Chan

VENUE
🌑 Bootsverleih Ahoi

MINI-MAJELIS
O Amol K Patil
O BOLOHO
O Cao Minghao & Chen Jianjun
O Sa Sa Art Projects

*Floating system for snails* (2022)
Boats, glass inlays, videos, cross-stitch, botanical specimens, invasive project.
Variable dimensions

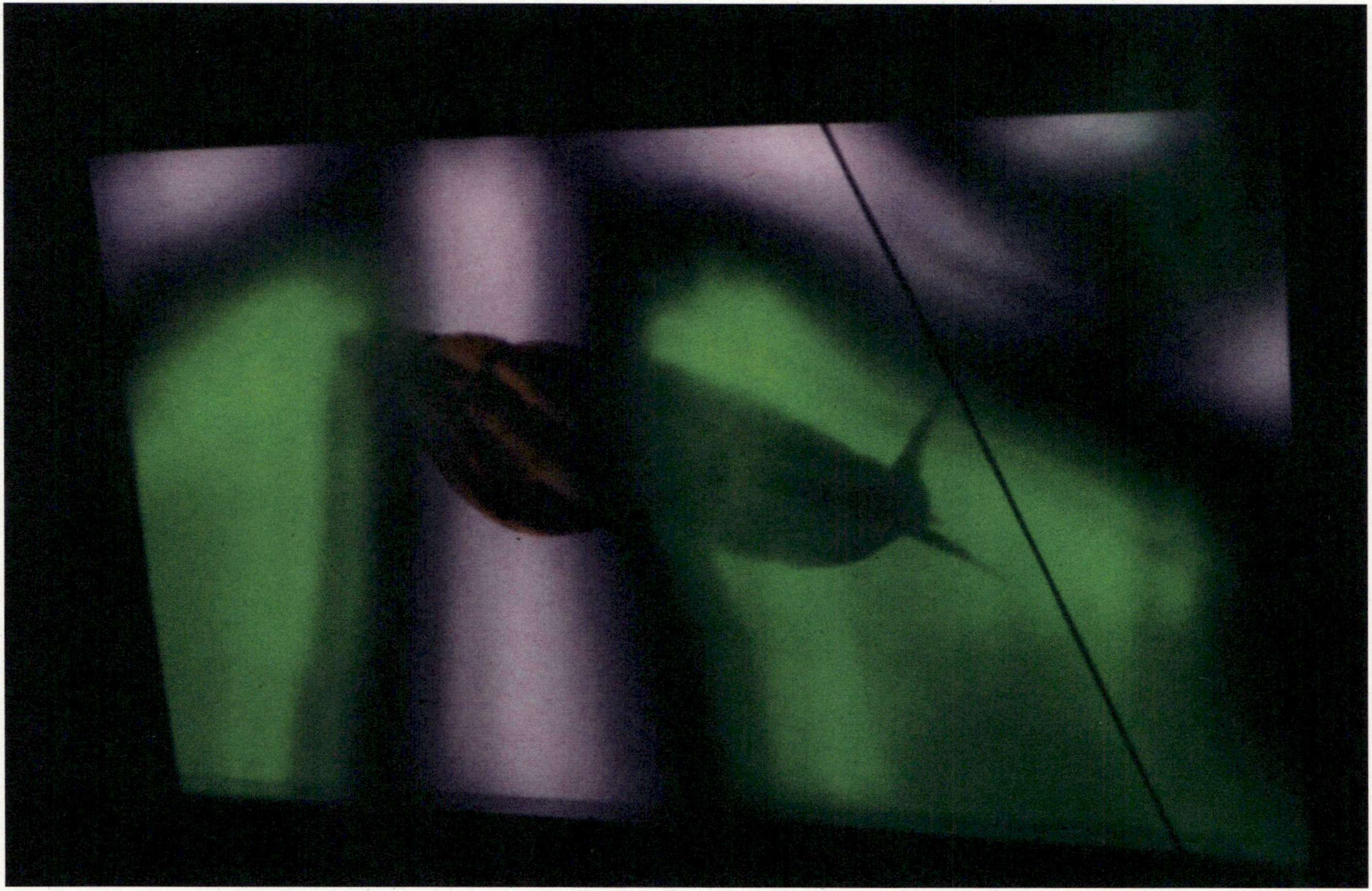

Chang En-Man

# CHIMURENGA

Through pop-up radio stations and publications, Chimurenga reactivates liberation movements across Africa.

C A core notion for Chimurenga is that of 'rethinking'. Since 2002, the collective has been in a constant act of reconfiguration and reorganization in an era of global upheavals.

Founded by Ntone Edjabe in Cape Town, South Africa, Chimurenga has continually redefined its media through regular publications like *The Chronic*, *Chimurenga Magazine*, and the *African Cities Reader*, which gather voices from across Africa and its diaspora. Chimurenga concerns itself with an African rewriting of the history of the continent, to further enable alternative imaginaries of Africa's future.

Broadcasting has been a preferred medium for the group since 2008, when the independent radio station Pan African Space Station (PASS) was founded. It acts as a regular pop-up radio studio, as well as a performance and exhibition space.

For documenta fifteen, Chimurenga has developed a new season of its radio program, *Radio Freedom*, which the collective will stream for five days from Dar es Salaam, Tanzania. The program is part of Chimurenga's ongoing enquiry on knowledge production via African sound worlds, and long-term research on broadcasting and cultural initiatives by liberation movements across the continent. The research focuses on the city-studios of Cairo, Accra, Conakry, Algiers, Lusaka, and Dar es Salaam: revolutionary capitals which hosted and disseminated anti-colonial radio broadcasts through their own national infrastructure. The chapter of *Radio Freedom*, which follows Cairo in 2018, focuses on the anti-apartheid struggle in Southern Africa, and features artists and collectives from across the region. Contributors would reactivate the broadcasting liberation archive of their country, and collaboratively reimagine the programing of stations such as ANC's Radio Freedom, MPLA's Angola Combatante, SWAPO's Voice of Namibia, FRELIMO's A Voz da FRELIMO, and many more. Just like the Radio Tanzania of old, which hosted broadcasting by liberation movements from across Southern Africa during the 1960s and 1970s, *Radio Freedom* presents transnational and multi-lingual programming that challenges territorial and cultural borders.

Chimurenga intervenes in the soundscape of Kassel through the broadcasting of *Radio Freedom* via Freies Radio Kassel (Free Radio Kassel) and other local non-commercial stations, as well as through sound systems at undisclosed venues around the Am Stern public square—the shops and public-private spaces which constitute the center of Kassel's migrant communities.

Ann Mbuti

Excerpts from Planning notes for
*The Pan African Space Station* (2008)

VENUES
Freies Radio Kassel,
August 10-14, 2022,
105,8 MHz

MINI-MAJELIS
O Arts Collaboratory
O Black Quantum Futurism
O Jumana Emil Abboud
O Nino Bulling
O Agus Nur Amal PMTOH
O Subversive Film

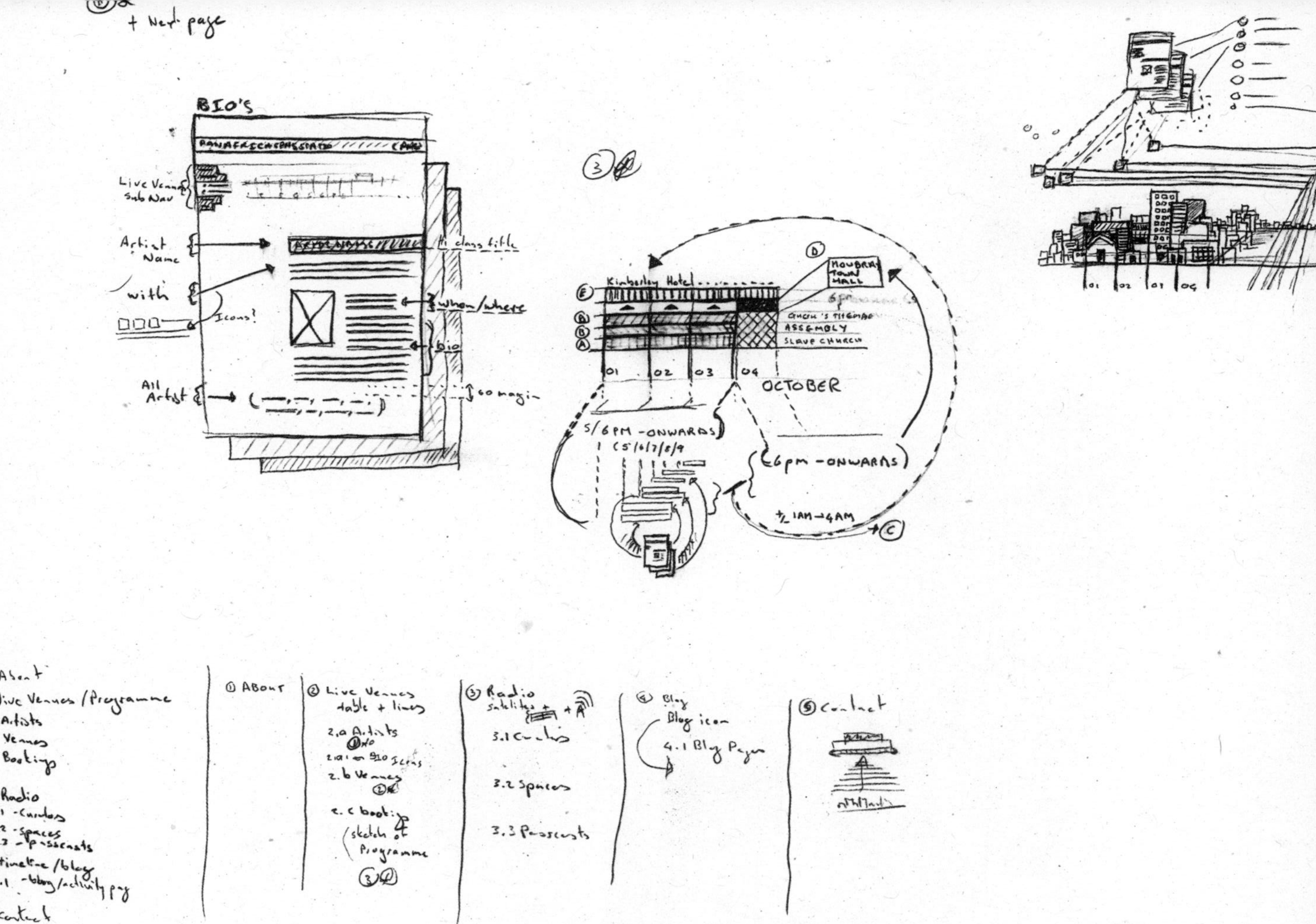
+ Next page
BIO'S
PANAFRICANSPACESTATIO ( PASS )
Live Venue Sub Nav
Artist Name
with
Icons?
All Artist
Hi class title
when/where
bio
no magi-
OCTOBER
Kimberley Hotel
MOWBRAY TOWN HALL
CHURCH'S THEATRE
ASSEMBLY
SLAVE CHURCH
01 02 03 04
5/6PM - ONWARDS
( 5/6/7/8/9
(6PM - ONWARDS)
1/2 1AM→4AM
01 02 01 04
1 About
2 live Venues / Programme
2.a Artists
2.b Venues
2.c Booking
3 Radio
3.1 - Curados
3.2 - Spaces
3.3 - P-ssecasts
4 timeline / blog
4.1 - blog / activity pg
5 contact
1 ABOUT
2 Live Venues table + lines
2.a Artists
2.a1 or Bio Icons
2.b Venues
2.c booking (sketch of Programme
3 Radio satelites + + A
3.1 Curados
3.2 Spaces
3.3 Passcasts
4 Blog Blog icon
4.1 Blog Pages
5 Contact

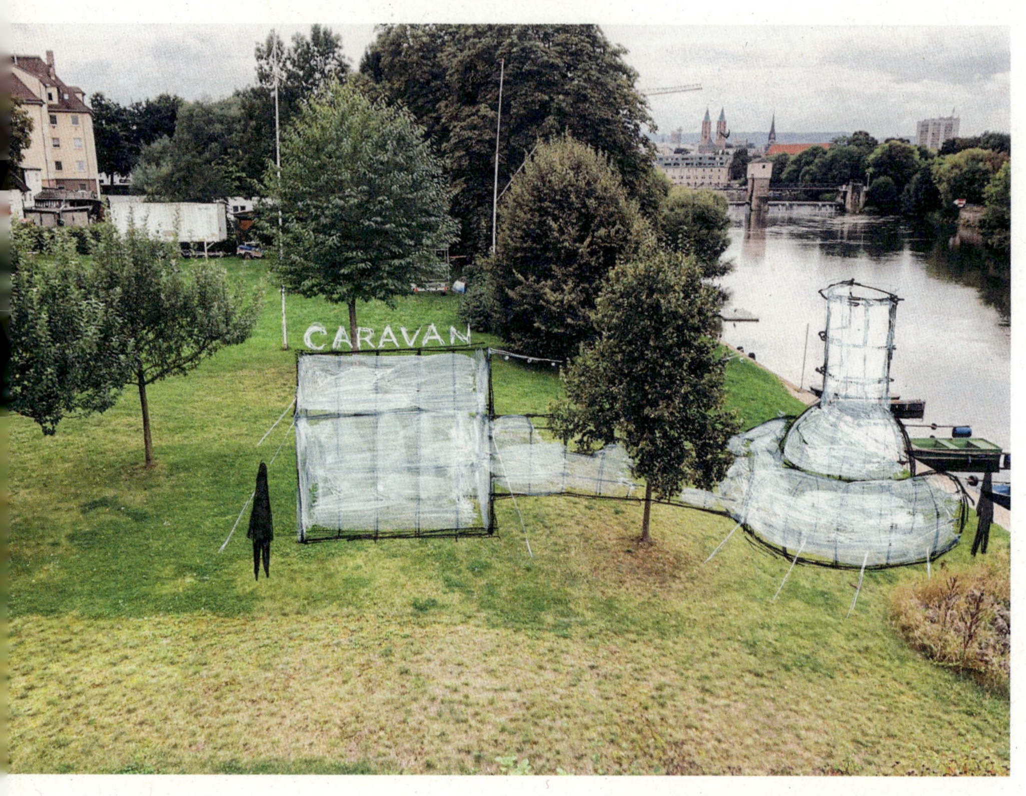


Cinema Caravan and Takashi Kuribayashi
Concept sketch for Outside of Mosquito
Net, 2022

# CINEMA CARAVAN AND TAKASHI KURIBAYASHI

A fluid, roving community of like-minded artists, carpenters, designers, and musicians, Cinema Caravan and Takashi Kuribayashi ask viewers to reconsider their perceptions of nature and their place in it. In Kassel, they are presenting a large, mobile space made out of mosquito nets, drawing audiences into an evolving net as it drifts around the city.

Conviviality is a form of consciousness raising for Cinema Caravan and artist Takashi Kuribayashi. A fluid, roving community of like-minded artists, carpenters, designers, and musicians, as well as cooks and surfers, the collective has produced open-air cinemas for venues ranging from natural sites, to festivals and art events. Since graduating from Kunstakademie Düsseldorf in 2002, Kuribayashi, who is now based between Japan and Yogyakarta, Indonesia, has made a career of producing large-scale installations that invert the relations of visible and invisible, using wonder as a mechanism for viewers to reconsider their perceptions of the world and their place in it.

Both Cinema Caravan and Kuribayashi are united in their long-standing concern for ecology and energy issues—a concern that was only heightened after the Tohoku earthquake and tsunami and concomitant Fukushima nuclear disaster of March 11, 2011. Their work encourages visitors to immerse themselves into problems that can often feel remote or hard to visualize, such as the effects of radioactive contamination on the environment, while also taking time to recharge themselves spiritually.

In Kassel, the artists are driven by the motto "make friends not art." Building on previous works, such as Kuribayashi's *Genki-Ro* installation (2021), a functioning herbal sauna modeled on the Fukushima reactors, and his ongoing *Yatai Trip Project* (2009–), which uses the mobile food stall as a device for creating spontaneous communal sites, they are presenting a large, mobile space made out of mosquito nets. The choice of material is inspired by the Japanese idiom *kaya no soto*, or "outside of the mosquito net," which corresponds in usage to the English "out of the loop." Instead of practicing exclusion, the project invites unforeseen audiences into the mosquito net and evolves in dialogue with local contributors as it drifts around Kassel.

Exemplifying the *lumbung* spirit informing documenta fifteen, Cinema Caravan and Takaashi Kuribayashi's projects cumulatively point to the caravan as a model of community where individuals retain their autonomy while each contributing in their own way to an unfolding experience of togetherness.

Andrew Maerkle



VENUE
🅚 Karlswiese (Karlsaue)

MINI-MAJELIS
O Kiri Dalena
O Nguyen Trinh Thi
O Safdar Ahmed

# DAN PERJOVSCHI

Through his *Horizontal Newspaper*, Dan Perjovschi connects Kassel with his hometown of Sibiu, Romania by hand-drawing its massive pages outside on the pavement.

"The 1989 Revolution, when the dictatorship fell in Romania, was fundamental for me. Each of my drawings celebrates this exceptional event where, as a citizen and an artist, I gained the freedom of expression."

Perjovschi has embraced drawing as his primary mode of expression, and after the collapse of Communism, began publishing in the Romanian press, especially the magazine *Revista 22*. He developed a visual idiom allowing drawings to function equally on a page or installed on gallery walls.

Perjovschi's drawings often use an altered and polyglossic English, mixed with other tongues, and so cannot be claimed by any single group. Traversing scale and contexts, the works comment on current events. "I do not call my drawings cartoons, comics, or graffiti, but press drawings," says Perjovschi.

Perjovschi "publishes" the *Horizontal Newspaper* that addresses current events through observations, conversations, and hearsay, hand-drawn over a 30-meter stretch of wall in the artist's native city of Sibiu, Romania. He updates from one edition to the next. Unlike today's media outlets, pushing news items directly to their consumers, Perjovschi examines the act of "updating"—which in his practice is analogue and obsolete—questioning the very character of the news, the way it is delivered and digested.

For Kassel, Perjovschi is publishing a special edition of the *Horizontal Newspaper*, with reports on culture, politics, society, and sports, to be updated over the course of documenta fifteen. It can be perused on the pavement in the square in front of the KulturBahnhof, a station serving local lines. It's a newspaper that can't be picked up, on a central station that does not connect beyond the city's immediate surroundings, speaking about events condensed into drawings and filtered through the experience and sensitivity of a single artist.

On the occasion of documenta, Perjovschi's presence in Sibiu connects the two newspapers, while forging a local network of social and cultural institutions called the Visual Art Platform. Meanwhile, the columns on the Fridericianum's façade have been transformed into "columns" of a yet different magazine, devoted to the values that underlie ruangrupa's lumbung concept: Generosity, Independence, and Regeneration, with Humor as the overarching value. Inside the Fridericianum, Perjovschi shares his inquiries into branding, identity-formation, and sponsorship—trajectories that connect with lumbung. Or, in his words: "My practice is individual, but for the collective good."

Krzysztof Kościuczuk

VENUES
- Fridericianum
- Rainer-Dierichs-Platz

MINI-MAJELIS
- Baan Noorg Collaborative Arts and Culture
- Fehras Publishing Practices
- Nhà Sàn Collective
- The Nest Collective

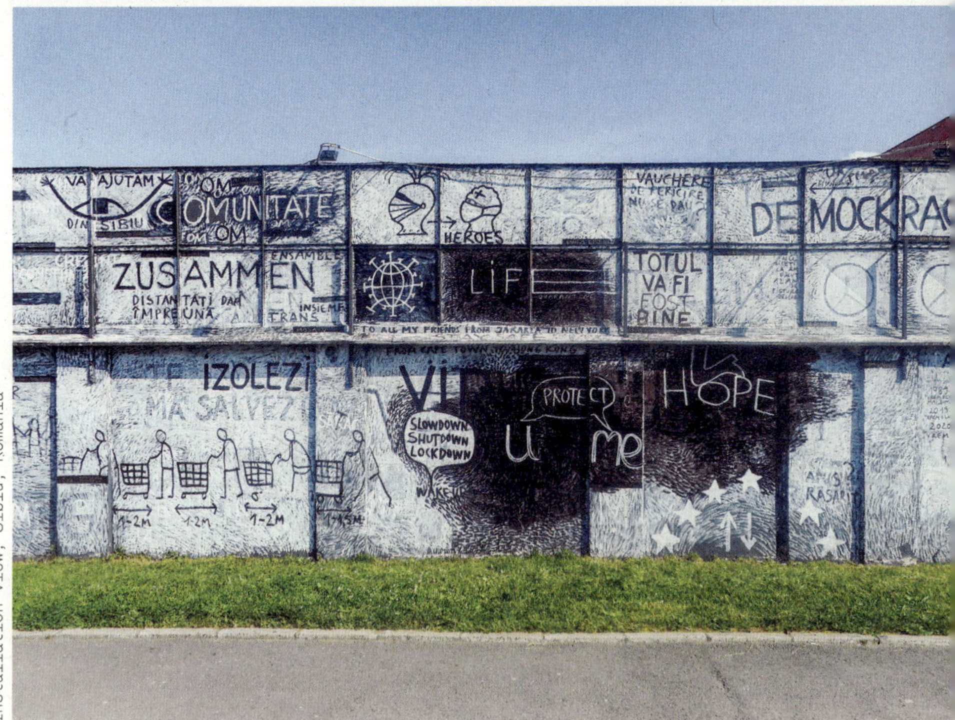




Dan Perjovschi, The Horizontal Newspaper Sibiu (2010–ongoing).
The Pandemic Edition 2020–2021, work-in-progress
Installation view, Sibiu, Romania


SOL
SOLID
ID
SOLIDARITY


Dan Perjovschi,
Harvest Drawing, 2022


Dan Perjovschi

*"El Warcha means 'workshop' in Arabic, a space where we come together and play. We tend to accumulate things, bits and bobs from past projects, furniture that needs repairing, and found materials. Once in a while we take what we can out on the street, trying to make some sense of what we really need and we start all over again."*
*El Warcha, Hafsia, Tunis, Tunisia, 2021*

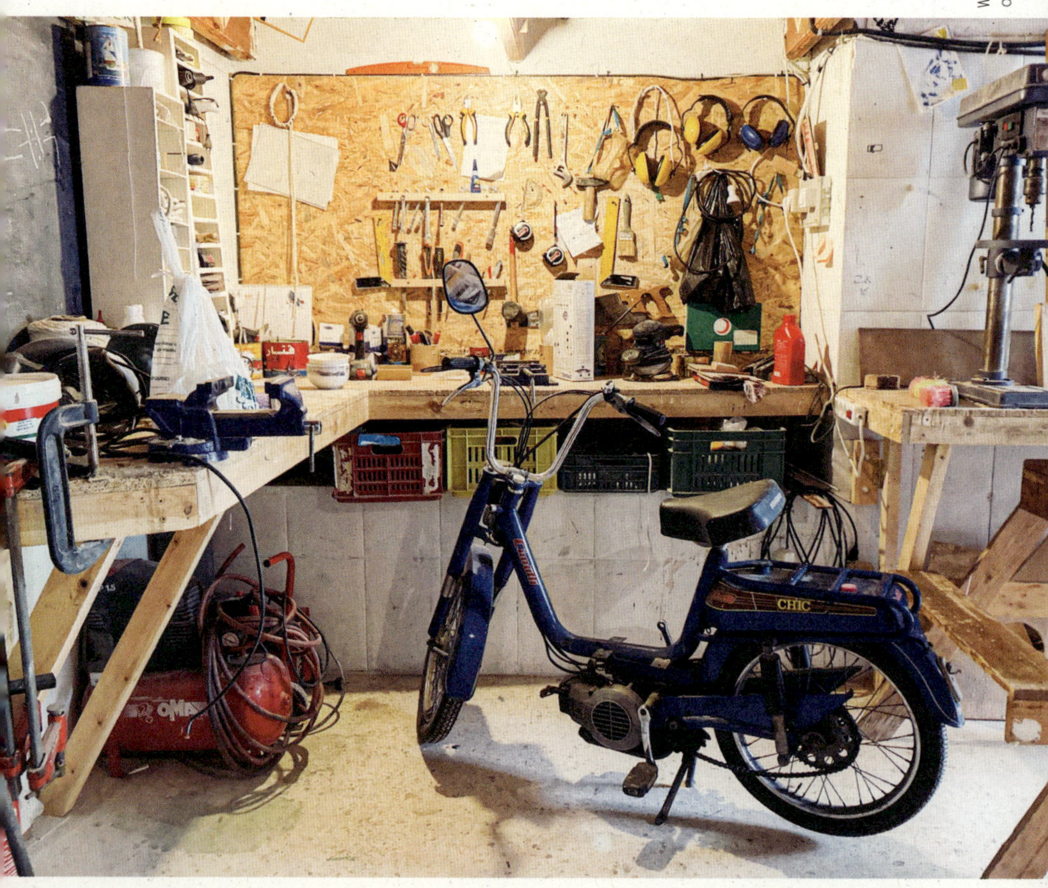

Workshop in Hafsia, Medina of Tunis, Tunisia, 2021

# EL WARCHA



Based in Tunisia, in El Warcha's work, collaborative design meets performance and narrative. In Kassel, El Warcha has built a rowdy workshop for DIY prototyping.

Rooted in the heart of the Medina of Tunis, Tunisia, El Warcha is a collaborative design studio with trans-local tentacles, spreading over three continents. Whether working in cities such as Lisbon, Nefta, London, Davis (California), or now in Kassel, their designs unfold in relation to their immediate surroundings, with the rhythm of daily life in different neighborhoods.

Initiated in 2016 by a mixed group of designers and residents, their practice has taken shape through various participatory forms. Using simple materials, El Warcha devises intuitive interdisciplinary assemblage techniques to make urban furniture and art installations. In their work, the process of collaborative design has developed as a sustainable practice with performative and narrative elements.

For documenta fifteen, El Warcha has experimented with new ways of occupying and inhabiting the space of the Fridericianum and its surrounding neighborhood. They have constructed an open and welcoming space that enables collective playful practices where everyone can contribute to live projects by prototyping their ideas through three-dimensional sketches. By drafting a friendly and festive space, El Warcha works in the hyphen between Kassel and Tunisia, improving existing prototypes inspired by themes emerging through facilitated collaborative processes.

In this space, a wooden boxing ring constructed earlier in Hafsia square for a televised quiz might be transformed into a stage where artists can challenge each other. A floating cinema built for a theatrical procession in the coastal town of El Kram can be adapted to drift on one of Kassel's rivers. In this self-made prototyping factory, the insights gained around the dining table might circle back to Nefta and improve its water shortages. Rather than showing pre-existing artworks, the museum space has been transformed into a noisy workshop, allowing for a collective work-in-progress full of possibilities to emerge. The pile of wooden sketched furniture and prototyped installations, constructed with various found materials, have been rearranged in a library. The library constitutes the perfect image for El Warcha's collaborative design practice, where knowledge formation does not happen through books, but through the very practice of making as a form of language and a tool for mediation.

Joachim Ben Yakoub



---

VENUE
 Fridericianum

MINI-MAJELIS
○ Another Roadmap Africa
  Cluster (ARAC)
○ Archives des luttes des
  femmes en Algérie
○ Asia Art Archive
○ Centre d'art Waza
○ Graziela Kunsch

○ Keleketla! Library
○ Komîna Fîlm a Rojava
○ Sada [regroup]
○ Siwa plateforme -
  L'Economat at Redeyef
○ The Black Archives

# ERICK BELTRÁN

Working with publications, installations, diagrammatic displays,
and lectures, Erick Beltrán ana-
lyzes and reflects upon social
values and systems. For documenta
fifteen, he has asked viewers to
reflect on their image of "power."

E "It is well-known that the individual is an idea that emerged only recently, about 300 years ago," says the Mexican artist Erick Beltrán, who lives in Barcelona. "My work tries to introduce a clash between Western thought structures and other ways of understanding the appearance of things in the world."

Beltrán's work for documenta fifteen, *Manifold* (2022), is a study of the relationship between unity and multiplicity, and of the forms and images we create in the contemporary psyche to represent that relationship.

We tend to perceive things as unities: me, you, another person. Multiplicity is the totality, interrelated and interconnected, of those things. Their relationship is the tension that opens in reality as it is perceived. But how does the universe present itself to us? Are there ways to approach reality from multiplicity?

Here Beltrán carries out his research. "The search for a form or a body is an effort to define a boundary between the totality and its parts," he says, "between the will of the individual and the invisible and omniscient order of the totality. How do we decide on what we see? Who tells the story? Who has the power?"

*Manifold* attempts to investigate how, from this relationship, something appears and is embodied in the world. Inspired by the theories of Furio Jesi, Aby Warburg, and Horst Bredekamp, among others, Beltrán and researchers from the School of Fine Arts at the University of Kassel conducted interviews with Kassel residents, who were asked about the image that emerges when thinking about the image of power. The goal was to generate a projection between the interviewee (the unity) and their imaginative and iconographic relationship with forms of power, as mediated by social filters (the multiplicity).

The resulting sequence, on display at the Museum of Sepulchral Culture in Kassel, displays the products of this research: a complete set of images that emerged from the interviews as well as the theories and diagrams that explain its relations. Together, they now appear as a difficult-to-describe body, which can only be completely understood through fragments of time—at once single and multiple and moving, and sharing the same spaces and time. *Manifold* shows conflict, but also resolution: unity and multiplicity as entities that inhabit the other simultaneously.

Camilo Jiménez Santofimio

VENUE
 Museum for Sepulchral
 Culture

MINI-MAJELIS
O Alice Yard
O LE 18
O MADEYOULOOK
O Party Office b2b Fadescha
O Serigrafistas queer

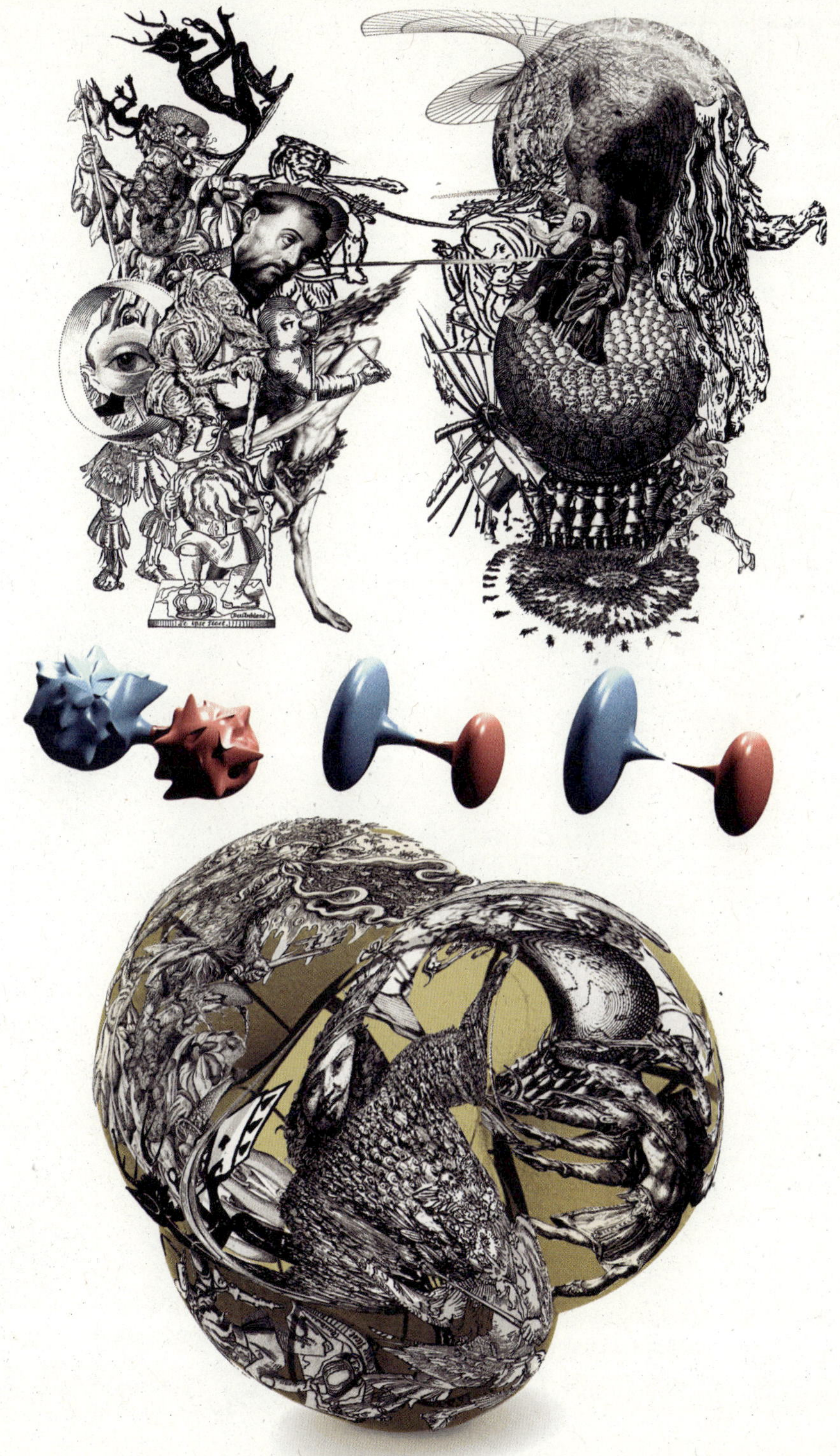



Iconological surface and Ricci flow (2022)
Digital models

Erick Beltrán

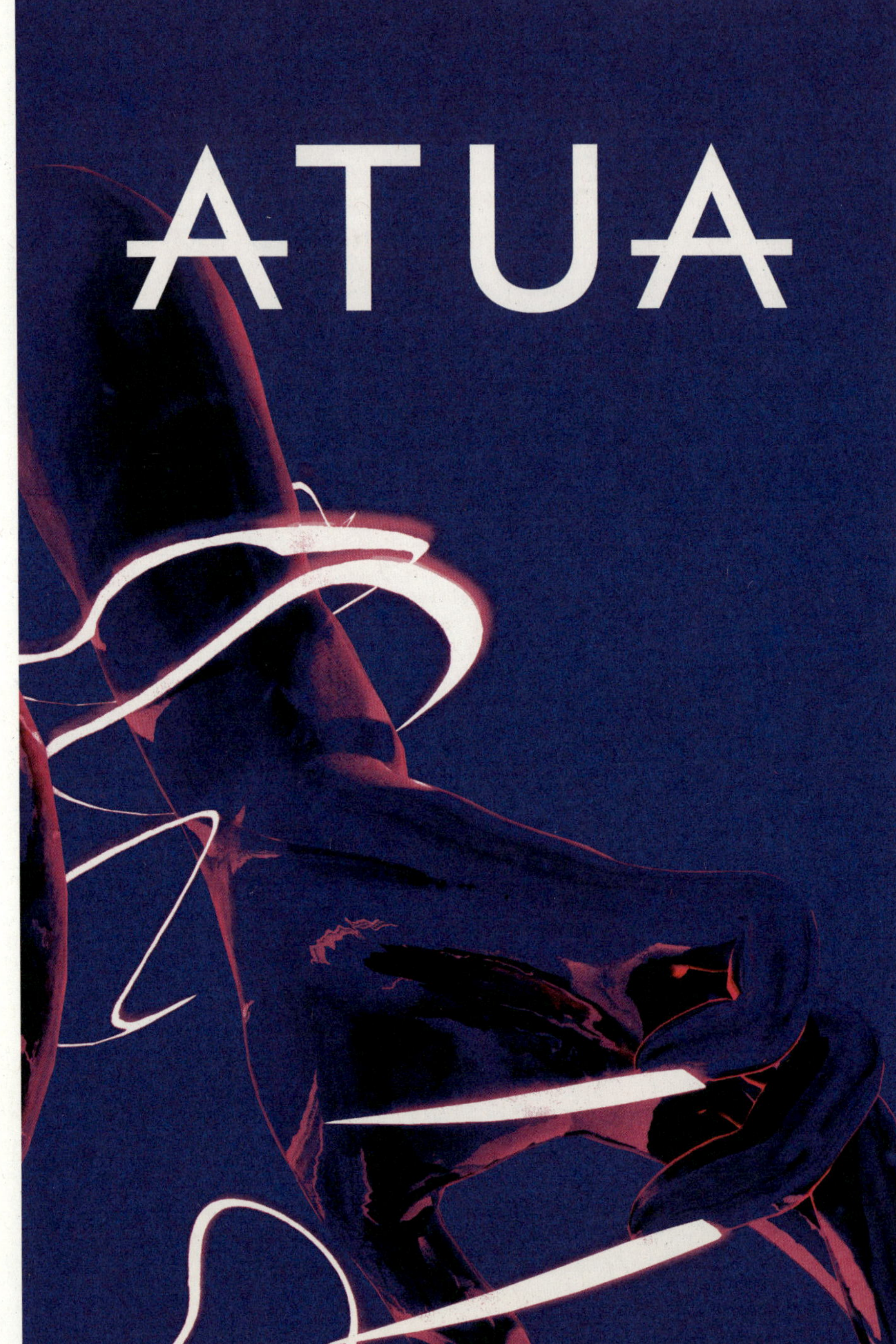


F

Tanu Gago & Mahia Jermaine Dean
ATUA (2022)

Through active collaborations with Aotearoa's Indigenous, LGBTIQ+ scenes, FAFSWAG creates intimate and inclusive spaces where queer, brown bodies are rejuvenated and celebrated. In Kassel, FAFSWAG presents installations, an augmented reality sculpture, and a mixed-media archive.

FAFSWAG is a Indigenous queer artists collective based in Aotearoa/ New Zealand that works across the Pacific Islands connecting the region's diverse cultural and social contexts. Through active collaborations with local LGBTIQ+ scenes, creating intimate and inclusive spaces where queer brown bodies are rejuvenated and celebrated through the art of voguing, FAFSWAG flourishes.

"Cultural restoration" best describes what FAFSWAG does. This is reflected by its body of works that address the ongoing erasure of gender diverse people and identities in contemporary Pacific cultures due to the legacy of colonization and traditional conservatism. The name blends the words *fa'afafine*—a non-binary role in Samoan cultures—and *swag*, a stylish confidence. Since its inception in 2013, FAFSWAG has had various changes in personnel, and currently numbers twelve members. The different artists-activists involved share a common practice of working in an interdisciplinary way. Their artistic practices operate through multiple forms of public and digital engagement that tell self-determined narratives of joy and pleasure in being a part of LGBTIQ+ community in Oceania.

For documenta fifteen, FAFSWAG presents three site-specific works that draw from their own spiritual connections to ancestral practices of storytelling and Indigenous cosmology. The first is a moving image installation, a collaborative work resulting from a 2019 workshop process. Through this installation, FAFSWAG wishes to publicly share their aspiration for a deepening narrative-based digital practice to navigate the increasingly uncertain world that we live in. It is a means for making meaningful connections to the Moana diaspora and other migrants who are culturally displaced.

FAFSWAG'S second contribution is an augmented reality (AR) sculpture called *Atua*, derived from deity figures that occupy the underworld in pan-Pacific cosmological belief systems. Here, Tanu Gago and Jermaine Dean seek to recuperate the connection—ruptured by violent colonization and suppressed throughout modernity—between ancestral divine beings and queer Indigenous folk.

The third contribution in documenta fifteen takes shape as an archival exhibition, which bears witness to FAFSWAG's artistic embeddedness in Pacific heritage as they journey across translocal contemporary art scenes. Comprising large mixed-media works, and items of traditional material culture, this collection is a platform for engaging with collective organizing and resource-sharing, issues that are encapsulated by the current documenta curatorial framing of lumbung.

Ferdiansyah Thajib

VENUES
- Hübner areal
- Hessisches Landesmuseum
- Stadtmuseum Kassel

LUMBUNG INTER-LOKAL
- Britto Arts Trust
- Fondation Festival sur le Niger
- Gudskul
- INLAND
- Instituto de Artivismo Hannah Arendt (INSTAR)
- Jatiwangi art Factory
- Más Arte Más Acción (MAMA)
- OFF-Biennale Budapest
- Project Art Works
- The Question of Funding
- Trampoline House
- Wajukuu Art Project
- ZK/U – Center for Art and Urbanistics

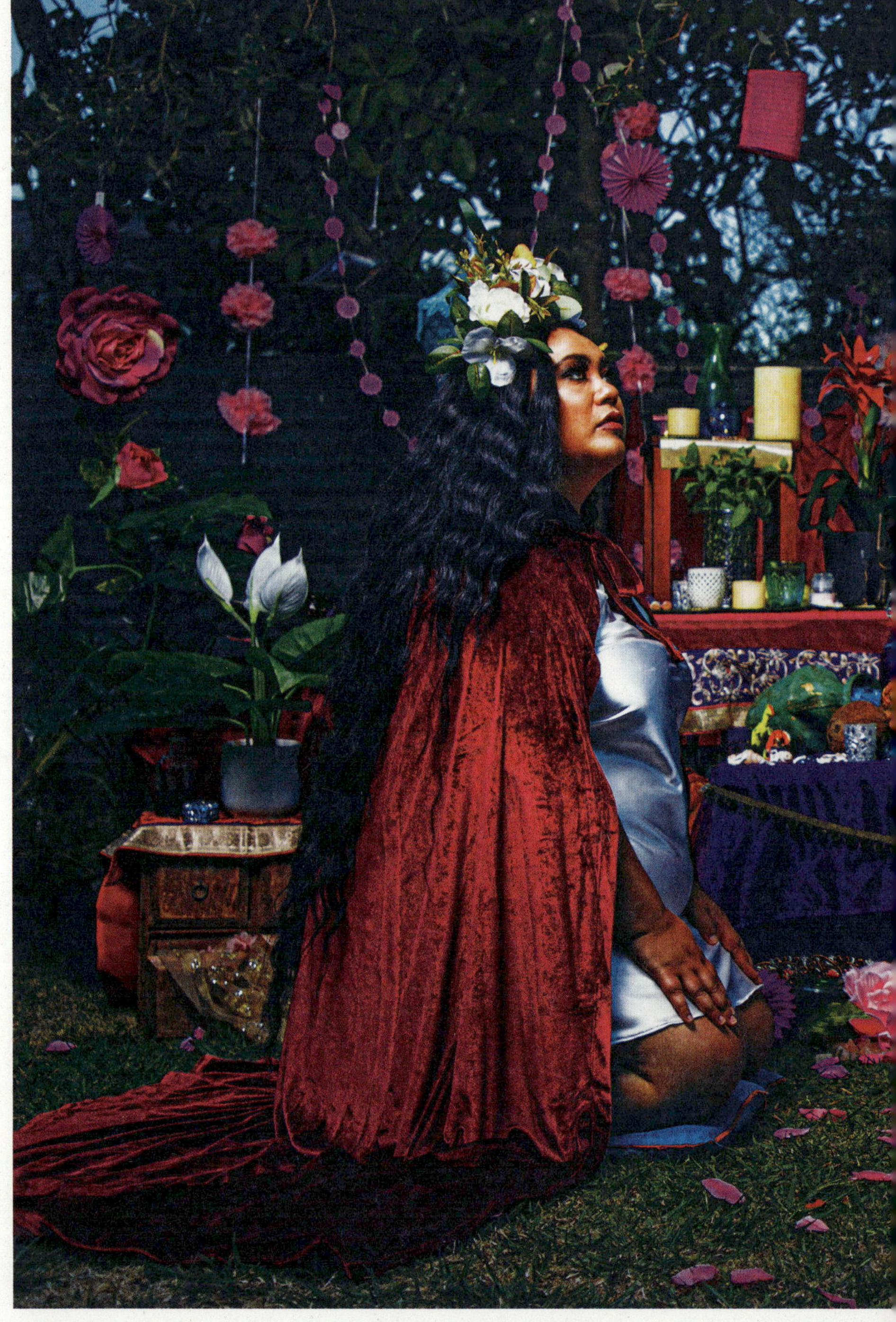



Elyssia Wilson Heti & Ria Hiroki
*Only I Can Name Me* (2021)

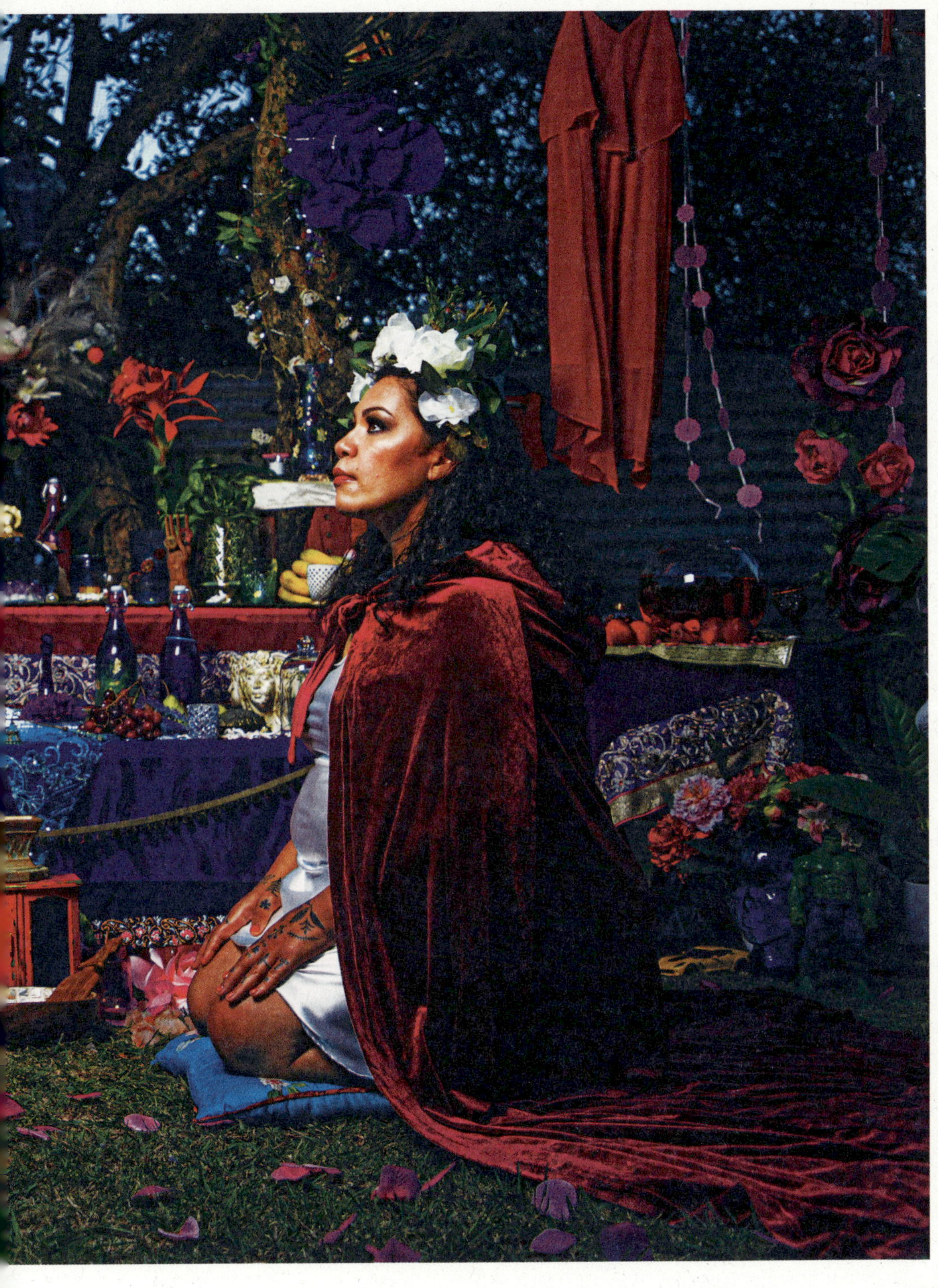

# FEHRAS PUBLISHING PRACTICES

F Formed in Berlin, Germany, in 2015, Fehras Publishing Practices investigates the curious histories of Arab-language publishing across the Mediterranean, North Africa, and the Arabic diaspora. In Kassel, they are presenting the latest of their photo-novel *Borrowed Faces*, focusing on the feminist women behind the Afro-Asian Solidarity Movement.

Archive is a fever of modernity—yet is archiving enough by itself to own the stories that make up who we are today? How can we own these stories? Fehras Publishing Practices was founded in 2015 in Berlin, Germany, by Sami Rustom, Omar Nicolas, and Kenan Darwich. Together they delve into the curious histories of Arab-language publishing in the Eastern Mediterranean, North Africa, and the Arabic diaspora. The collective initiates installations, films, publications and lectures aiming to extend the notion of publishing, such as *Borrowed Faces* (2019–ongoing), which addresses cultural practices during the Cold War.

This was the era that set in place the conditions of globalization, a period considered among the most fertile and critical in the history of Arab publishing, when the entanglements between politics and cultural production reached new levels, and which saw the emergence of the tutelage wars the region has violently experienced over the last decades. After intensive research in different cities and networks, Fehras Publishing Practices created fictional stories, which enable them to raise their questions about the historical narratives they had heard. They chose the photo-novel—a classic format of this period—to publish them.

Queering the usual ways these archival narratives are shared, *Borrowed Faces* tells the story of three fictional characters—Afaf Samra, Hala Haddad, and Huda Al-Wadi—who become friends. The first *Borrowed Faces*, published in 2019, problematized the American Franklin Book Programs and the Soviet book market. The second edition, commissioned by documenta fifteen, focuses on the Afro-Asian Solidarity Movement and their publishing practices. It also observes the counter-project, the American CIA-funded Congress for Cultural Freedom, and its intervention in cultural production. The narrative woven among Beirut, Cairo, Bandung, Rome, Paris, New York, and Moscow is guided by a feminist discussion around the role of intellectual women during the 1960s. These photo-novels also function as playful guides to trigger publics in a study room where archives are researched and digitized by the collective. As Fehras attempts to own the stories that made them, they propose ways to get out of the maze of history towards a new kind of non-binary citizenship.

Övül Ö. Durmuşoğlu

VENUE
H Hafenstraße 76

MINI-MAJELIS
O Baan Noorg Collaborative Arts and Culture
O Dan Perjovschi
O Nhà Sàn Collective
O The Nest Collective

Fehras Publishing Practices
*Borrowed Faces: Future Recall*, no 4. Huda,
Hala, Afaf on a magic carpet, somewhere over
the Atlantic to Kassel (2021)
Color photograph, ChromaLuxe print
84 × 150 cm

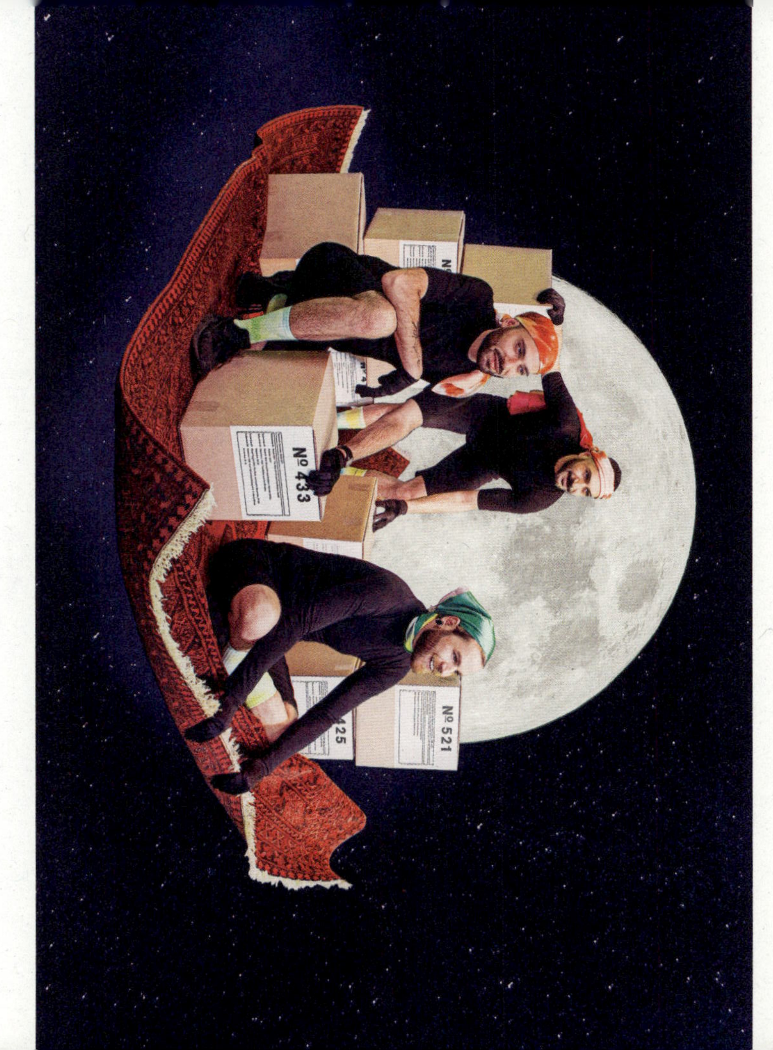

# FONDATION FESTIVAL SUR LE NIGER

F

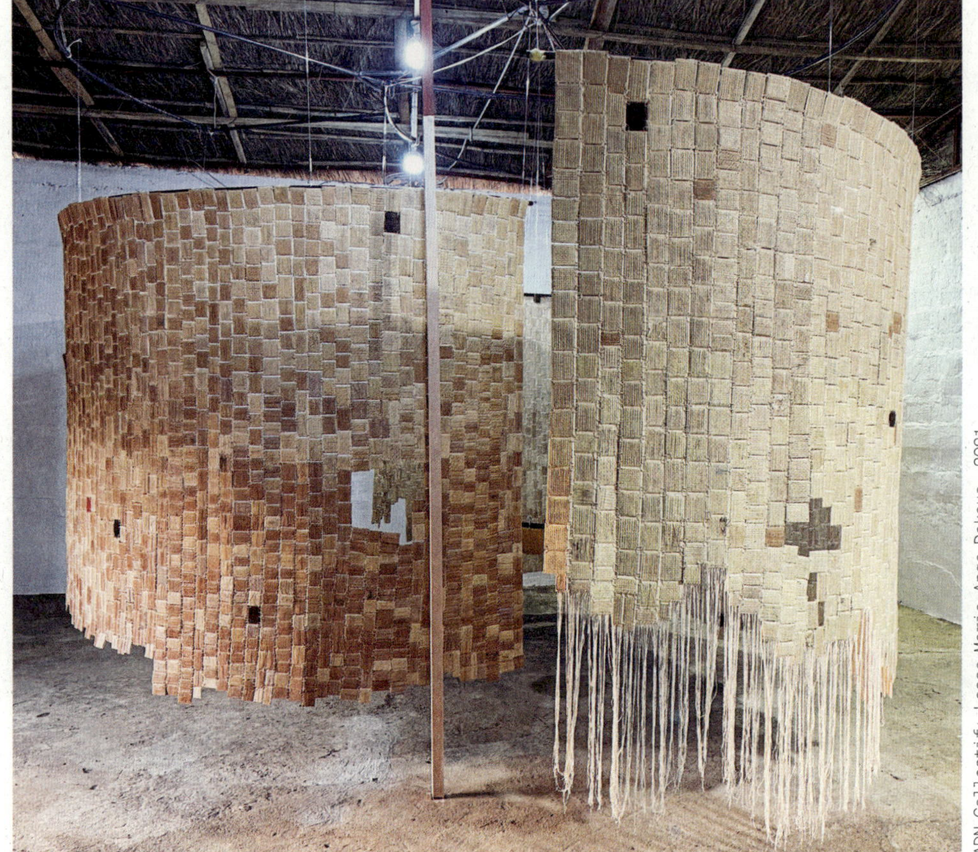

ADN Collectif: Losso Marie-Ange Dakouo, 2021
Cardboard, newspapers, cotton threads, acrylic paint

---

**VENUES**
⊕ Hübner areal

**LUMBUNG INTER-LOKAL**
○ Britto Arts Trust
○ FAFSWAG
○ Gudskul
○ INLAND
○ Instituto de Artivismo
  Hannah Arendt (INSTAR)
○ Jatiwangi art Factory
○ Más Arte Más Acción (MAMA)

○ OFF-Biennale Budapest
○ Project Art Works
○ The Question of Funding
○ Trampoline House
○ Wajukuu Art Project
○ ZK/U – Center for Art and
  Urbanistics

Fondation Festival sur le Niger presents a series of artistic actions that resonate with the social practices that produce change in Malian society.

The Foundation Festival sur le Niger (FFSN) was created in August 2009 by Mamou Daffé—a multi-talented Malian creative entrepreneur—and his team. The birth of this cultural institution was prompted by the success of the Festival sur le Niger, an international music and contemporary art event held annually in February in Segou, Mali.

The work of the Foundation Festival sur le Niger is grounded in the traditional Maaya philosophy, bringing it to contemporary society in Mali and Africa at large. Maaya is an integral concept with which to discuss the relationship between the individual and the community. It is grounded in values such as generosity, *jatigiya* (hospitality), *dambe* (knowing oneself and self-limitation), *sinakunya* (humorous cousinhood) and humor.

These values are the base of the artistic, educational, and economic activities organized by the three legs of the Foundation: the yearly festival and Ségou Art, the Centre Culturel *Kôrè*, and IKAM, the educational center. Through training young artists and cultural entrepreneurs, deep mentoring and support, producing artistic work, and developing distribution circuits, the whole spectrum of culture and arts in Mali, and across Africa, is strengthened.

Working from Maaya values—and combining it with principles of entrepreneurship and constant negotiation of the needs of the involved artists and communities—has helped the Foundation to build many artistic and solidarity networks in Mali and beyond. It has also aided them in finding answers to the multiple crises hitting the country since 2012, and to overcome the competitive culture created by the problems of our times.

For documenta fifteen, the Foundation Festival sur le Niger, as a member of the international collective called lumbung, presents a series of artistic actions that resonate with the social practices that influence change in Malian society. These artistic proposals are presented in *Le Maaya Bulon / Vestibule Maaya*, a name given to a specific room in Malian architecture where decisions are made. The "Bulon" designates a room in the house, which, because of its multifunctional character, is generally larger than the other rooms. It is in this space that hospitality is practiced (welcoming, chatting, exchanging with the host), a central notion in Malian culture.

The device is also a way of translating into action the principles of the Maaya. Numerous artistic events of a multidisciplinary nature take place there throughout the duration of the exhibition. In this ekosistem elaborated by the members of the FFSN team, the performing arts (music and theater) rub shoulders with the visual arts (paintings and photographs). Some key figures from the Malian art scene bear witness to the humanist values of sharing and mutual aid of the Maaya, including Abdoulaye Konaté, Losso Marie Ange Dakouo, Yaya Coulibaly, Mama Koné, Lamine Diarra, Lassina Koné, Seydou Camara, Fatoumata Coulibaly, Yacouba Magassouba, N'fana Diakité, Cheick Tidiane Seck, NDji Yacouba Traoré, Samba Touré, Adama Keita, Salomé Dembélé, Salif Berthé, Amaïchata Salamata and Tieble Traoré, among others.

Dagara Dakin

F

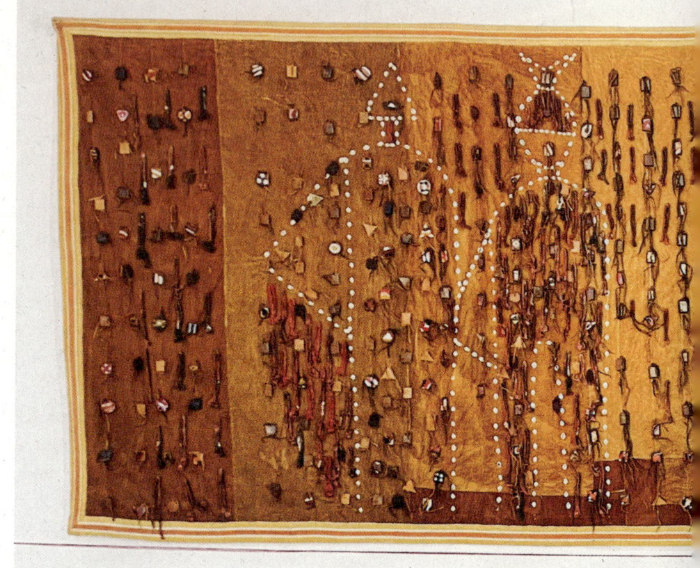

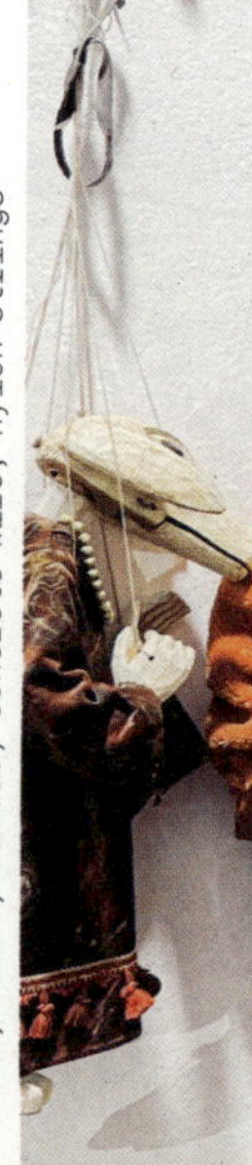

Yaya Coulibaly: *Wall of puppets* (2022)
Wood, masks, bamboo, concrete wire, nylon strings

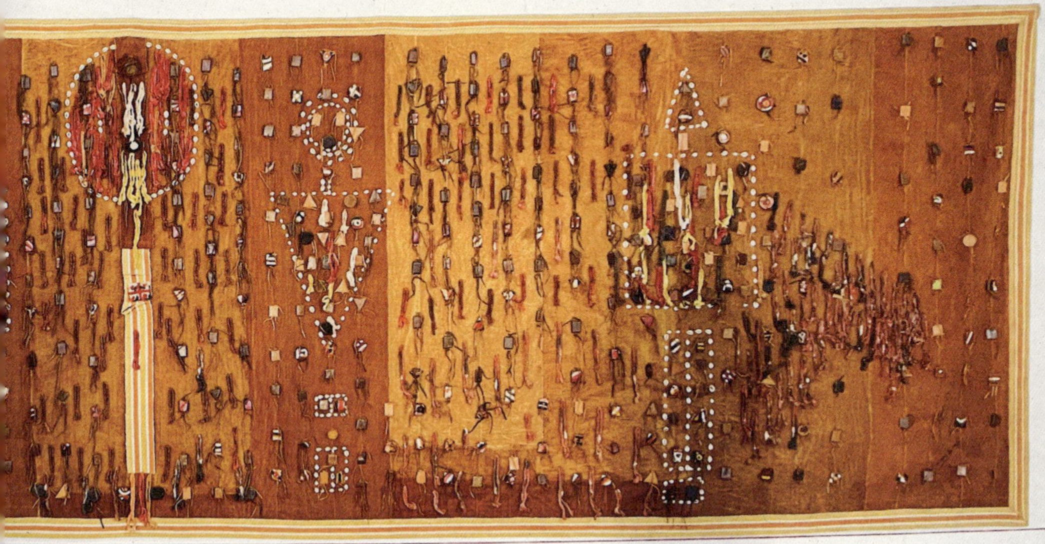

Abdoulaye Konaté:
*Tribute to the Mandé
Hunters* (1996)
Mixed-media

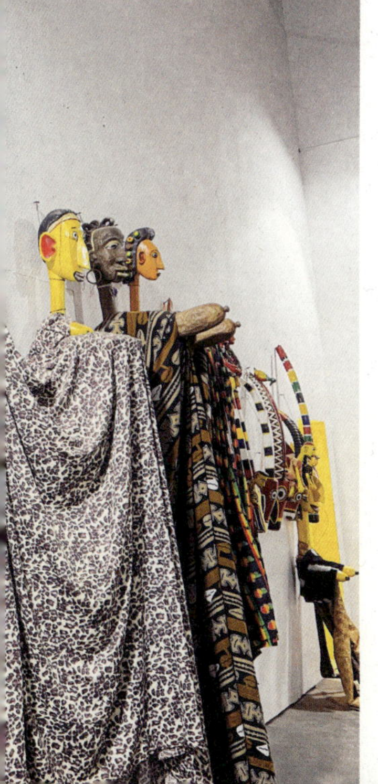

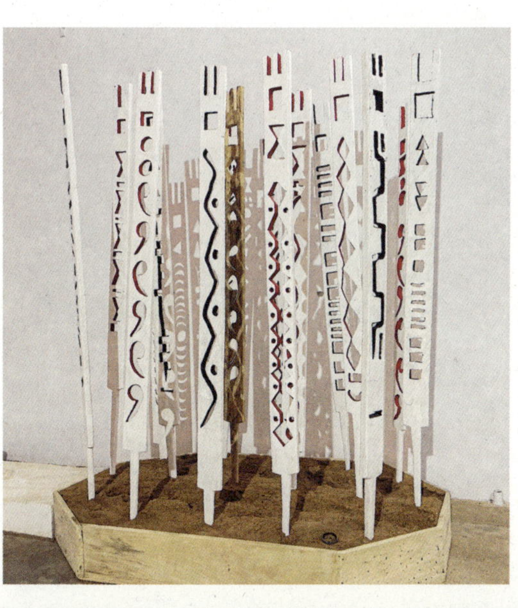

*Karaw* (2021) (made by local craftsman)
Carved wood

**Fondation Festival sur le Niger**

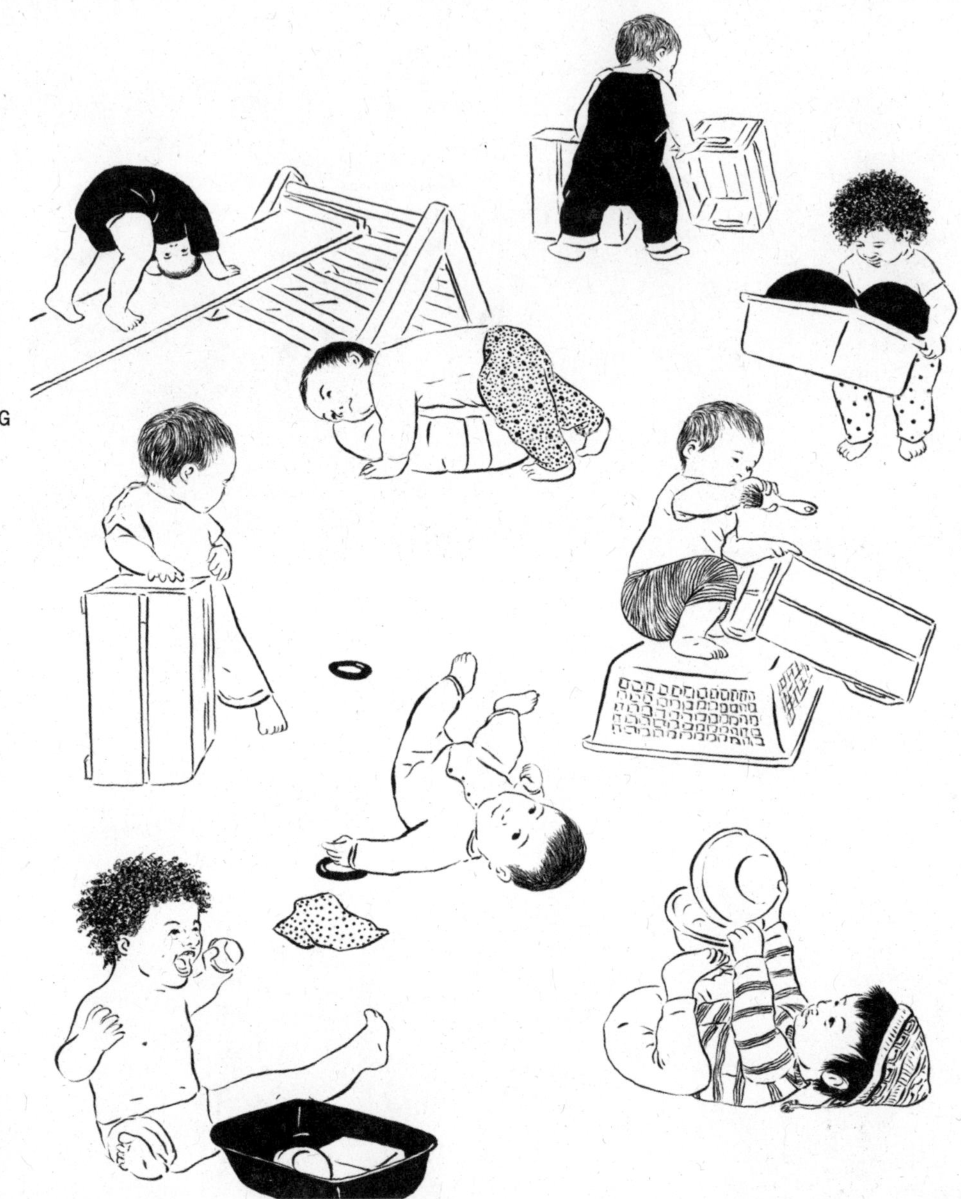

Drawing by Deborah Salles in dialogue with Graziela Kunsch

G

VENUE
 Fridericianum

MINI-MAJELIS
- Another Roadmap Africa Cluster (ARAC)
- Archives des luttes des femmes en Algérie
- Asia Art Archive
- Centre d'art Waza
- El Warcha
- Keleketla! Library
- Komîna Fîlm a Rojava
- Sada [regroup]
- Siwa plateforme - L'Economat at Redeyef
- The Black Archives

# GRAZIELA KUNSCH

Graziela Kunsch has set up a
daycare in the Fridericianum,
creating a space where babies and
parents can learn together.

In one of the rooms of the Fridericianum, there are parents and small children who accessed the museum through its back door. Mothers and fathers carry their babies into the eating, sleeping, and changing spaces, looking after their babies. In other, larger spaces, the babies move around freely and look after themselves. Their parents are there, but they do not direct the play. This is the proposal of *Public Daycare*, inspired by the pedagogical approach of twentieth-century Hungarian pediatrician Emmi Pikler.

The daycare is open from 10 am to 5 pm, and is free of charge for babies aged 0 to 3 years and those responsible for them. According to Graziela Kunsch, "it is a space where we, adults, more than teaching our babies, can learn with them, and also among us. For example, it is common for adults to anticipate babies' motor positions—sitting the baby, making the baby stand, helping the baby walk—hoping that, as soon as possible, babies will become part of the 'adult world.' What if we inverted this relationship, getting down to the floor, allowing babies to fully live their first years of life, or the 'baby world?' Babies are capable of developing motor positions on their own, given time and a safe environment. Here, carers will have the opportunity to combine respectful care moments along with the respect for the baby's need to move and unfold at her or his own pace."

Visitors without babies have access to reading and video rooms. On the walls, they can see photographs by Marian Reismann, who for decades documented babies playing, and the relationship between babies and carers, at the Pikler-Lóczy residential nursery, in Budapest, Hungary. In the library, in addition to books on early education, there is a *Library of Playful Objects*. Videos show recordings the artist made of her daughter's free motor development. After 6 pm, any visitor can circulate throughout the whole area and see furniture designed for babies' growing autonomy and environments set up for play, with open-ended materials and no predefined use.

The transformation of the monumental museum building into an everyday living space is a collaboration between Kunsch and Elke Avenarius. Avenarius worked as a civil engineer before becoming a mother and co-founding Kleine Entdecker (Little Discoverers) in Kassel, a nursery that recognizes the child as the protagonist of their own development. Kunsch and Avenarius met during a visit to Kassel by the São Paulo, Brazil-based artist, whose work often engages people outside the art context. Her creative strategy consists of making an initial proposition that she opens up to co-creation and transformation.

Camilo Jiménez Santofimio

CO-OPERATORS
Elke Avenarius
Deborah Salles
Carmen Orofino
Nina Kanitz
Michaela
  Brüning-Lilienfeldt
Patrícia Lima Zahn
Ute Strub
Laura Lazzarin
Barbara Lackner
Suzana Macedo Soares
María Rozas
Sylvia Nabinger
Daniel Guimarães
Manuela Guimarães
  Kunsch
Kleine Entdecker
  Kinderkrippe
Strandgut Spielraum
Plackner Werkstatt für
  Spiel + Pädagogik
Kokomoo Spielsachen
Magyarországi Pikler-
  Lóczy Társaság
Associação Pikler
  Brasil
Ateliê Carambola
  Escola
Ateliê Arte Educação e
  Movimento
Cooperativa
  Emprendedoras Sin
  Fronteras
Casa do Povo

# GUDSKUL



Rooted in Jakarta, Indonesia, Gudskul sustains the role of alternative art spaces as sites of visionary, collective gathering.

Gudskul is a shared space designed to consolidate intellectual and creative resources. Three Jakarta, Indonesia-based collectives—ruangrupa, Serrum, and Grafis Huru Hara—formed the space in 2018. The existence of Gudskul can be contextualized within critiques made of conventional art education institutions. It sustains the role of alternative spaces as visionary spaces to provide contextual responses to inhabit post-authoritarian Indonesian cultural landscapes. It also reflects the recent development of various independent initiatives and artist collectives that develop various educational or learning activities as the basis of their works.

In operating the organization, collectives and collectivism serve as the main models and principles to develop an experimental pedagogical platform. Gudskul proposes a set of learning methods which are based on informality. Knowledge is dispersed and embodied in personal experiences. In an earlier phase, Gudskul was a space where friends would *nongkrong* (hang out together), where long-term comrades and collaborators shared their capacities to design and teach short courses. Gudskul emerged as a collective site of knowledge to provide a learning space for younger generations of artists and art collectives. It functions as a niche in the public education infrastructure and a sustainable support system within the local art ekosistem.

For documenta fifteen, Gudskul replicates the collective learning model and creates *Sekolah Temujalar* (Temujalar School). Temujalar derives from two Indonesian words — *temu* (meet) and *jalar* (spread). Temujalar School is envisaged to be a gathering space and a starting point to make connections with others. Using nongkrong as a method for learning, the school develops a "Nongkrong Curricula." Conviviality and friendship characterize the organization of Temujalar. The Nongkrong Curricula will be conducted through three main activity clusters: Friend-Making, Learning from Friends, and Self-Organizing. All the components in the clusters perform as moments to gather abundant tacit knowledge through nongkrong and living together. Temujalar stemmed from the Gudskul's ongoing collective study program. It functions as an artistic and sustainability model where the participants use the opportunities to experience being in a collective, collaborating, expanding networks, harvesting knowledge, and creating self-organized modules for managing resources. The duration of Temujalar is initially 50 days, but it is expected that participants can further the collective spirit beyond this planned duration.

Nuraini Juliastuti

VENUE
 Fridericianum

LUMBUNG INTER-LOKAL
O Britto Arts Trust
O FAFSWAG
O Fondation Festival sur le Niger
O INLAND
O Instituto de Artivismo Hannah Arendt (INSTAR)
O Jatiwangi art Factory
O Más Arte Más Acción (MAMA)
O OFF-Biennale Budapest
O Project Art Works
O The Question of Funding
O Trampoline House
O Wajukuu Art Project
O ZK/U – Center for Art and Urbanistics

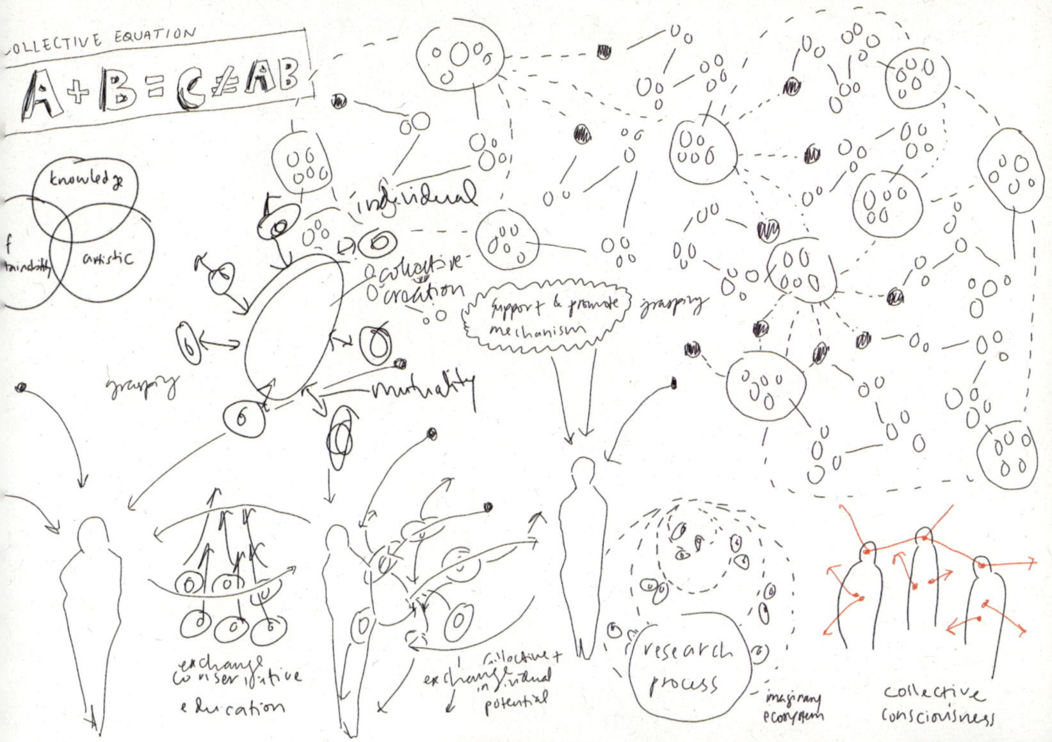

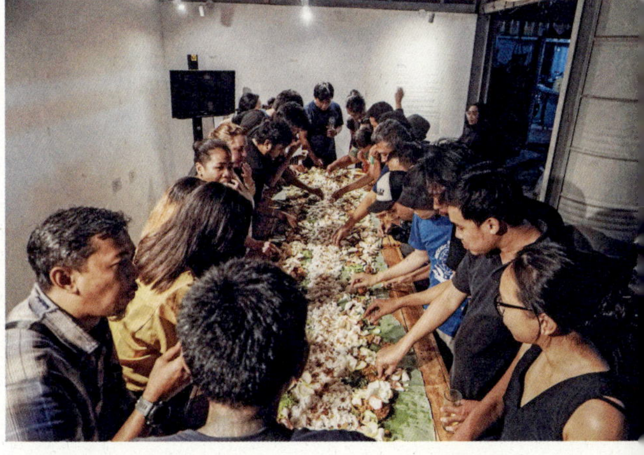

*Gudskul temujalar doodle mechanism (2022), Gudskul, Jakarta, Indonesia*

*Gudskul Ngeliwet (2019), Gudskul, Jakarta, Indonesia*

**CO-OPERATORS**
Infazio
UnconditionalDesign
Essbare Stadt
Tokonoma
Feinmechanik
Game Department
  Kunsthochschule Kassel
Office of Community Art
Städelschule
blaxTARLINES KUMASI
Ba Bau Air
Omni Space
Yayasan Tonjo Foundation
Load Na Dito
Scutoid Coop
Pangrok Sulap
Salikhain
Bishkek School of Contemporary
  Art
PAYON
Nordland kunst- og
  filmhøgskule
Gud RnD
Stuffo Labs
Ekstrak Kolektif
PSS Duren
Sudut Kalisat
Lifepatch
Hysteria
TIGA (Tindakan Gerak Asuh)
Arab Theatre Studio
Floating Project
Asia Art Archive
Rifandi Septiawan Nugroho
Cemara Weda Chrisalit
Rifandi Septiawan Nugroho
Cemara Weda Chrisalit

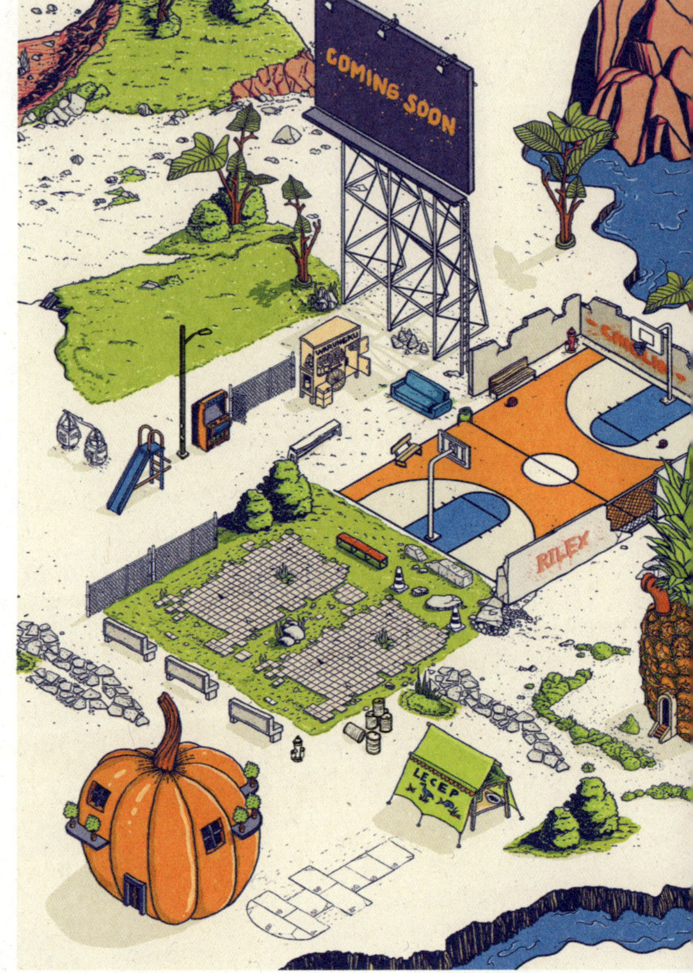

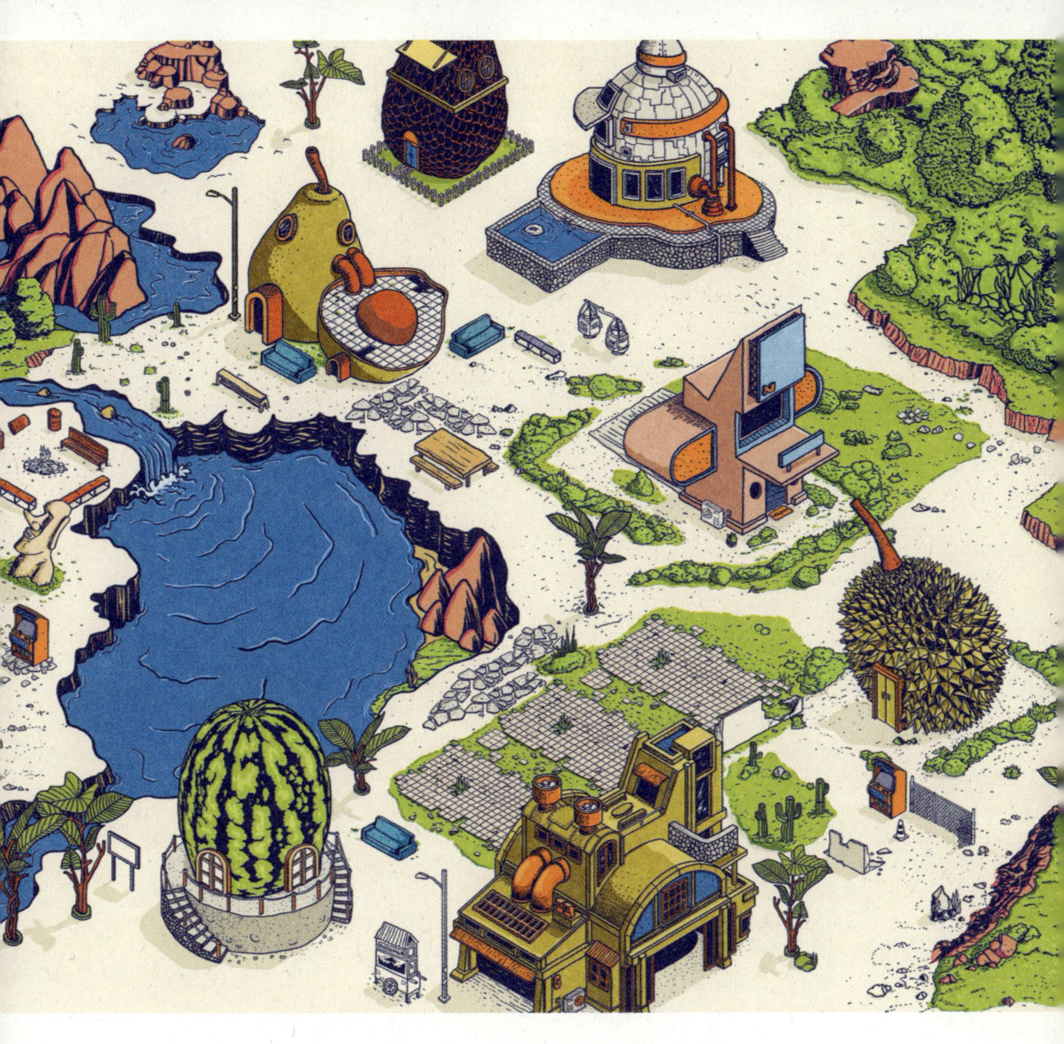

Gudskul's temujalar art sitemap, an online art collective ekosistem platform to build connectivity and sustainability in different localities

# HAMJA AHSAN

Hamja Ahsan's halal fried chicken franchises are taking over Kassel. His work exposes the fractures of social exclusion—in this case, with regard to Islamophobia and xenophobia.

From offices to boardrooms, in museums or social settings, to command visibility is to win. Yet, social imperatives to be seen are, in themselves, exclusive. Who is left out? What about those who won't, or can't, speak, show, or stand up?

Working in publishing, conceptual art, satire, and activism, Hamja Ahsan addresses the exclusionary mechanisms that proliferate in contemporary life. Ahsan's 2017 satire *Shy Radicals: The Anti-Systemic Politics of the Militant Introvert*, for example, founds a fictional country for the introverted, and is a call-to-arms to end "extrovert supremacism." Ahsan articulates the aspirations of the (by definition) under-acknowledged: the shy, the introverted, the neurodivergent, the differently-abled, or those stigmatized due to religious or ethnic affiliations.

His project for documenta fifteen likewise employs vernacular iconography and humor in order to expose the fractures of social exclusion— in this case, with regard to Islamophobia and xenophobia.

His contribution is to found a universe of competing halal fried chicken franchises, complete with LED signage, displayed across documenta venues. A new, ongoing series of *khutbah* (Islamic sermons) videos on fried chicken, theology, and politics—titled *Theological Positions around Fried Chicken*—is being streamed on documenta's social media platforms. Panel discussions form part of documenta's Meydan public program.

Touching on questions of assimilation, classism, religious discrimination and racism, Ahsan's work is a form of serious satire. Some background: fried chicken and halal chicken shops have proliferated throughout majority-Muslim nations—and, in recent years, within Western European cities, too. Along the way, there were some who came to conflate the growth of Islam in the west with food habits they may have found hard to understand, sub-cultural or impenetrable. For instance, in the 1990s in London—during the time of genocidal atrocities against Bosnian Muslims (1992–1995) in Serbia—a jihadist network in the UK was said to have been recruited through South London's chicken shops. Islamophobia rose after the US's so-called "War on Terror," when long-established forms of Islamic activism were shoehorned as terrorism. As Muslims grew in number, the right-wing UK media spoke of a "Londonistan" in South London, noting the proliferation of Middle Eastern chicken restaurants there. As recently as its 2019 anti-knife crime campaign, the British Home Office distributed its slogan (#knifefree) through fried chicken boxes. While Ahsan's work remains satirical, it is grounded in a reality that may itself appear farcical. Below the surface, Ahsan's work is a scathing rebuke of racist assessments against the many millions of Muslims who struggle for rights and recognition today.

Pablo Larios

حلال

# KALIPHATE
# FRIED CHICKEN
## FEEDING THE UMMAH SINCE 1924

Hamja Ahsan, Logo for
*Kaliphate Fried Chicken* (2022)

**VENUES**
- documenta Halle
- Fridericianum
- Grimmwelt Kassel
- Hübner areal
- Hafenstraße 76
- Museum for Sepulchral
  Culture
- ruruHaus
- WH22

**MINI-MAJELIS**
- Jimmie Durham
- La Intermundial Holobiente
- Pınar Öğrenci
- Saodat Ismailova

Hamnja Ahsan

113

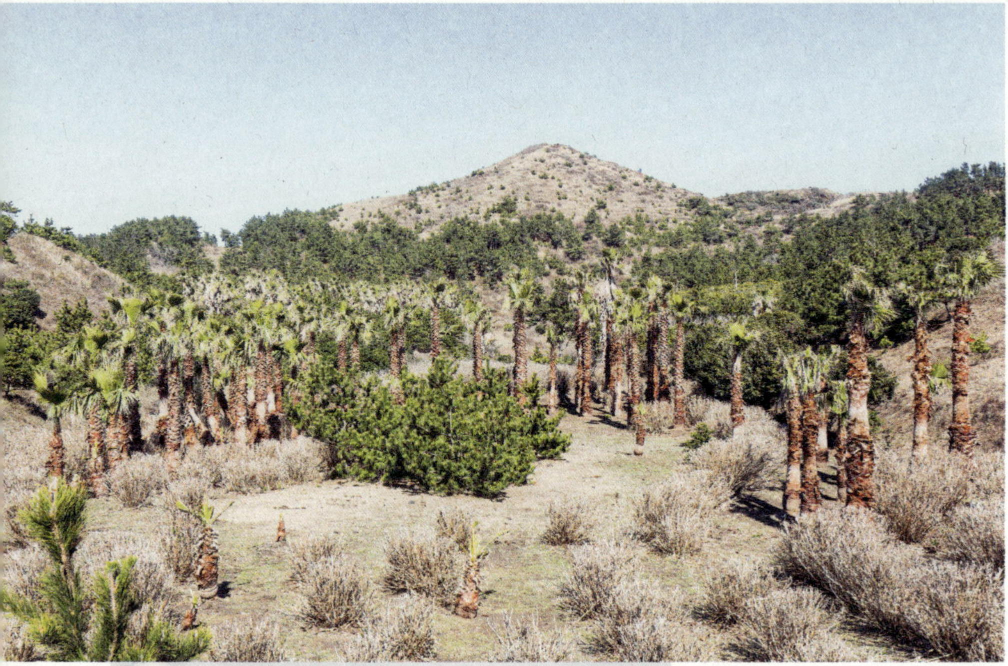

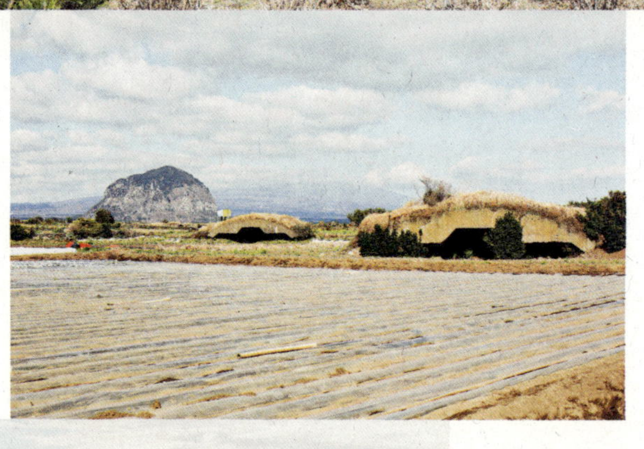

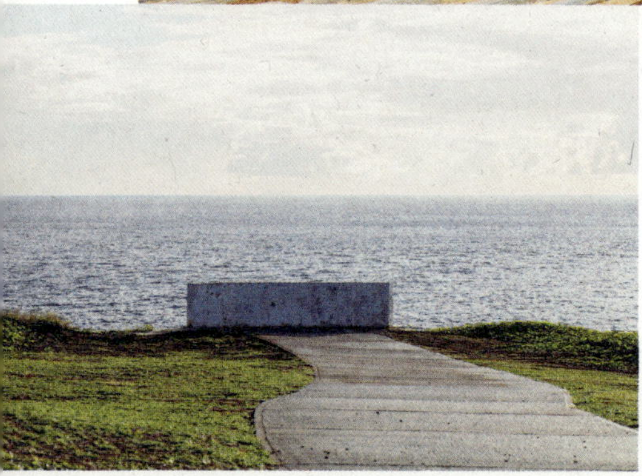

Research photos for *Tropics Story* (2022).
Top to bottom:
Songak Mountain, 2021;
Alddreu Airfield in Jeju Island, South Korea, 2019;
Suicide cliff on Tinian Island, the Mariana Islands, 2019

# IKKIBAWIKRRR

With a new video focusing on Korea's "sea women" divers, ikkibawiKrrr show how nature can unleash the power of destruction.

The visual research band ikkibawiKrrr was formed in 2021 in Seoul, South Korea, by KO Gyeol, KIM Jungwon, and CHO Jieun—members of an earlier collective, mixrice. Combining the words for "moss" (ikki) and "rock" (bawi) with an onomatopoeia (borrowed from Korean comics) for crumbling or rolling sounds (krrr), the name reflects both the artists' playful sensibility and their interest in exploring the shifting dynamics between plant life and human, nature and civilization, ecology and colonialism.

ikkibawiKrrr's projects for documenta fifteen traverse diverse topics connected to war, industry, the environment, and Korea's transnational twentieth-century history. *Tropics Story* (2022) finds the artists visiting war remnants at locations that were formerly occupied by the Japanese empire, ranging from Jeju, a large, South Korean island in the Korea Strait, to the Palauan island of Peleliu, site of some of the fiercest fighting of World War II. Accompanied by a display of photographs, the two-channel video's images of overgrown airstrips, abandoned cave fortifications, and burial grounds hint at how war is metabolized by nature.

Returning to Jeju, the single-channel video *Seaweed Story* (2022) focuses on the *haenyeo*, or "sea women" divers who harvest marine products—including the edible seaweed Ecklonia cava, another source of explosive components, along with herbal remedies—from the surrounding waters. Part of a centuries-long tradition, the *haenyeo* were once so successful that they were the primary earners in their families, upending Confucian gender norms. But access to education and less physically demanding work introduced by economic development in recent decades has led to a steep decline in their numbers. Interspersing footage of local war remnants with scenes of a *haenyeo* choir singing songs that reflect their lives and the Jeju sea, the video speaks to the complexities of balancing individual resilience and communal survival, while maquettes on view in the gallery represent the facilities where the *haenyeo* gather before and after their dives.

Incorporating reportage and performance with an element of what the cultural historian Saidiya Hartman calls "critical fabulation," *Tropics Story* and *Seaweed Story* reveal underlying histories of precarity and exploitation that, perhaps, are on the verge of being forgotten amid South Korea's twenty-first century ascendancy to global soft power status. And if they wryly acknowledge the joke nature plays on humanity, whereby something as innocuous as bird droppings or a floating frond of seaweed can unleash the power of destruction, they also suggest that we too have untapped potential for alternate ways of being.

Andrew Maerkle

VENUE
Ⓝ Museum of Natural History Ottoneum

MINI-MAJELIS
○ ook_
○ Richard Bell
○ Taring Padi
○ Wakaliga Uganda

# INLAND

In Kassel, INLAND and collaborators show the potential of agrarian economies.

INLAND *(campo adentro)* is a collaborative platform working on art, territories, and social change. As a para-institution, since its creation in 2009, INLAND has provided a platform for diverse actors engaged in agroecological and cultural production to explore and manifest possible ruralities.

During its first stage (2010–2013), and taking urban-rural frictions in Spain as a case study, INLAND, as initiated by Fernando García-Dory, was engaged with artistic production in 22 villages across the country. They made exhibitions and presentations, and hosted an international conference to examine the rural question today.

This was followed by a period of reflection and evaluation between 2013 and 2015, during which they launched study groups on art, ecology, and de-growth, and produced a series of publications. Today, INLAND functions as a collective focusing on land-based collaborations and economies, and communities-of-practice as a substrate for post-contemporary art. Through their involvement in global rural movements, INLAND promotes gatherings with Indigenous, nomadic, and pastoralist peoples, articulating a joint voice at UN forums, advocating for grassroots community rights and for trans-local mutual support. The collective is also coordinating the Confederacy of Villages network, connecting diverse, full-scale art projects across rural Europe.

For documenta fifteen, an installation presents INLAND's current areas of interest and development: in-habitation and expanded landscapes, economy and collaboration, and composed knowledges and learning. The social and artistic intervention and dissemination of the collective's work is varied, and carries a commitment to explore other ways of living together with the land and other beings within, through spaces of sharing—aspects which guide documenta fifteen's curatorial principle of lumbung.

Their contribution builds on Kassel's Museum of Natural History Ottoneum as a space of mutations—from a theater and cultural social space to an extended cabinet of curiosities and lifeforms from the Paleozoic to the Ice Age, back to the staging of displays and dioramas.

A cave, conceived as a geobiological vault, is built to contain primeval and algorithmic forms of representation, extinct animal spirits, and storage for INLAND's cheese production and mother lactic cultures. The ripening chamber and its microbiota of molds and fungi act as a counter server farm, minting INLAND's currency, the *cheesecoin*. Both artwork and money form, *cheesecoins* (in limited numbers) are placed in circulation through networks of exchange with local producers and via the dairy-pavilion at the Ottoneum's garden.

The currency is also used as part of the design and launch of INLAND's Eco-Social & Art Impact Bond (ESAIB), a financial instrument that experiments in metric designs that can account for both environmental restoration and a community's long term socio-economic wellbeing, for example by cultivating activities such as artistic expression. Developed with theorist Mi You and economist Vienne Chan, the bond articulates how an investment in art, beyond traditional art collection, could be a sound investment in society and the ekosistem, while reformulating art's economics.

How an economy can be informed by values associated with peasant cultures—such as giving away, and reproduction of the community instead of accumulation and productivism—is also examined in the In-habitation Room or unmuseum, containing INLAND source materials, references functioning as story vessels, documents of heterodox sociologies, and objects that manifest power relations.

Marta Fernández Campa and INLAND

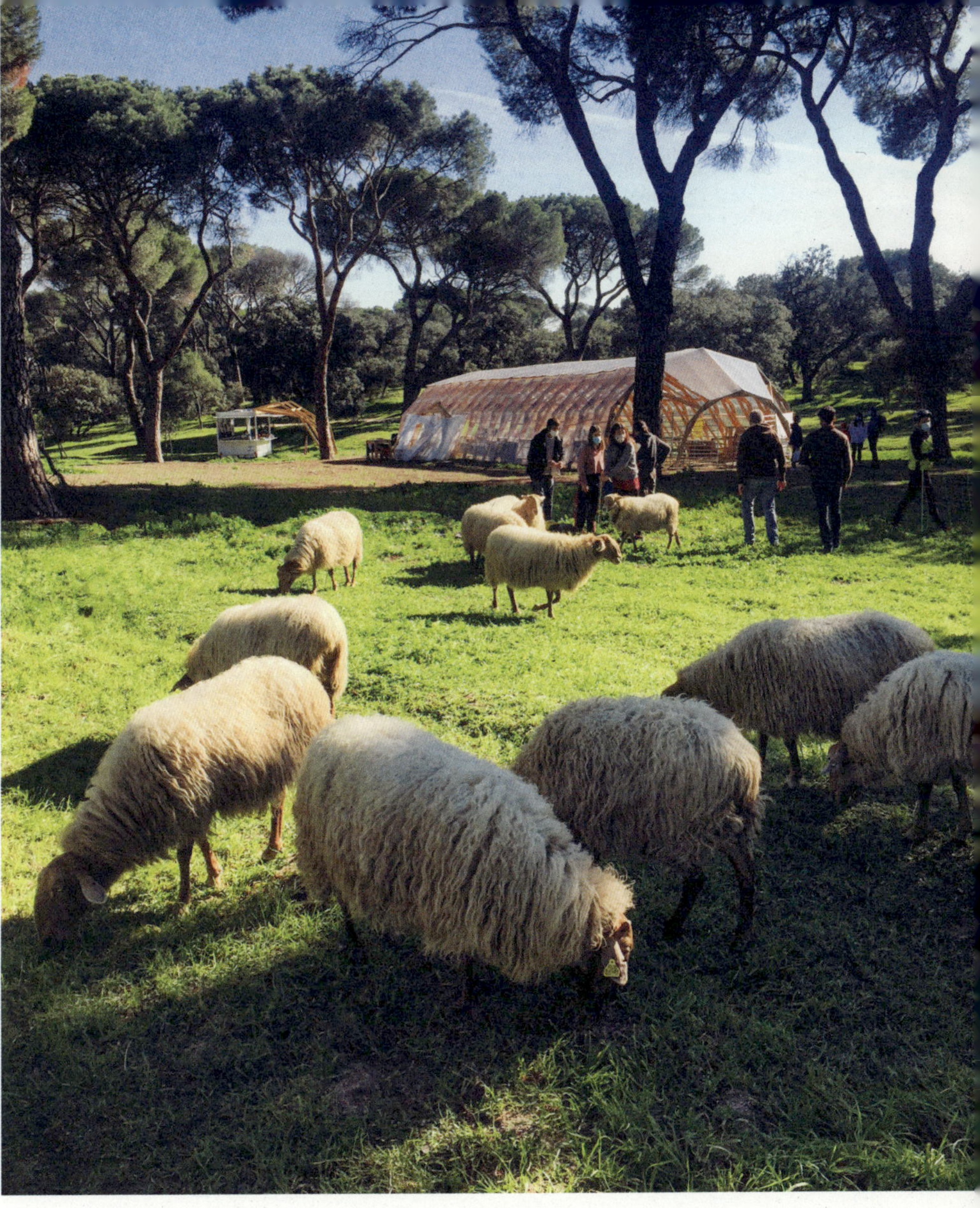



**VENUE**

Museum of Natural History
Ottoneum

**LUMBUNG INTER-LOKAL**

○ Britto Arts Trust
○ FAFSWAG
○ Fondation Festival sur le Niger
○ Gudskul
○ Instituto de Artivismo Hannah Arendt (INSTAR)
○ Jatiwangi art Factory
○ Más Arte Más Acción (MAMA)
○ OFF-Biennale Budapest
○ Project Art Works
○ The Question of Funding
○ Trampoline House
○ Wajukuu Art Project
○ ZK/U – Center for Art and Urbanistics

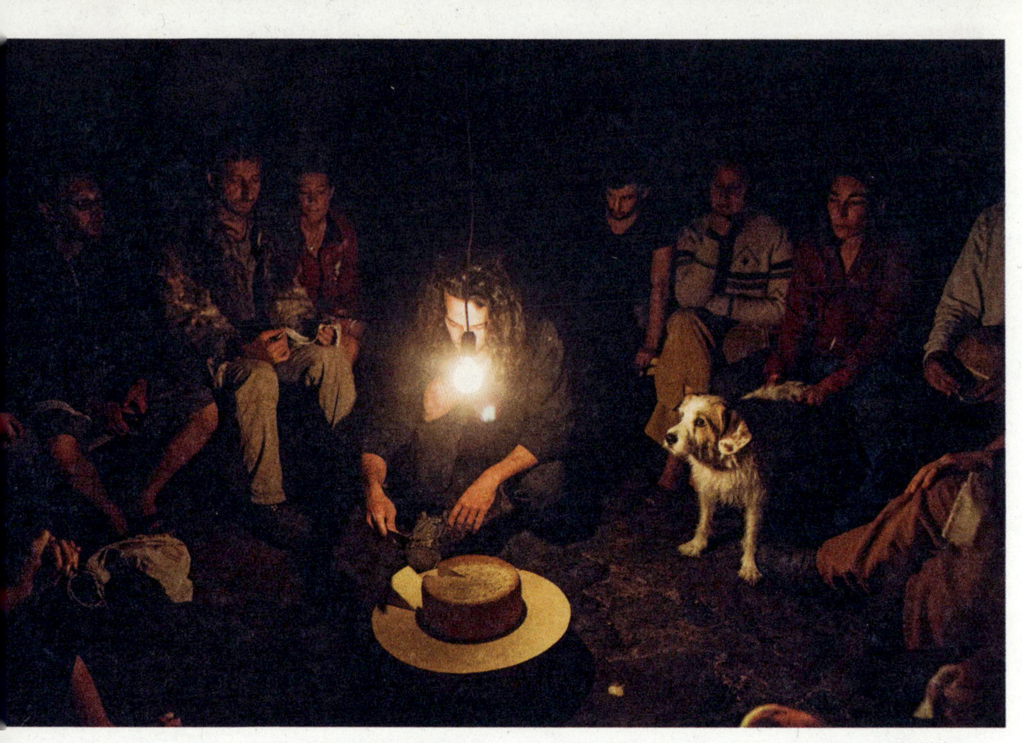

Left: Group dynamic embodying landscape characters during first
seasonal cheese tasting at *New Curriculum*, 2018.
Right: INLAND functioning organizational diagram, 2020.

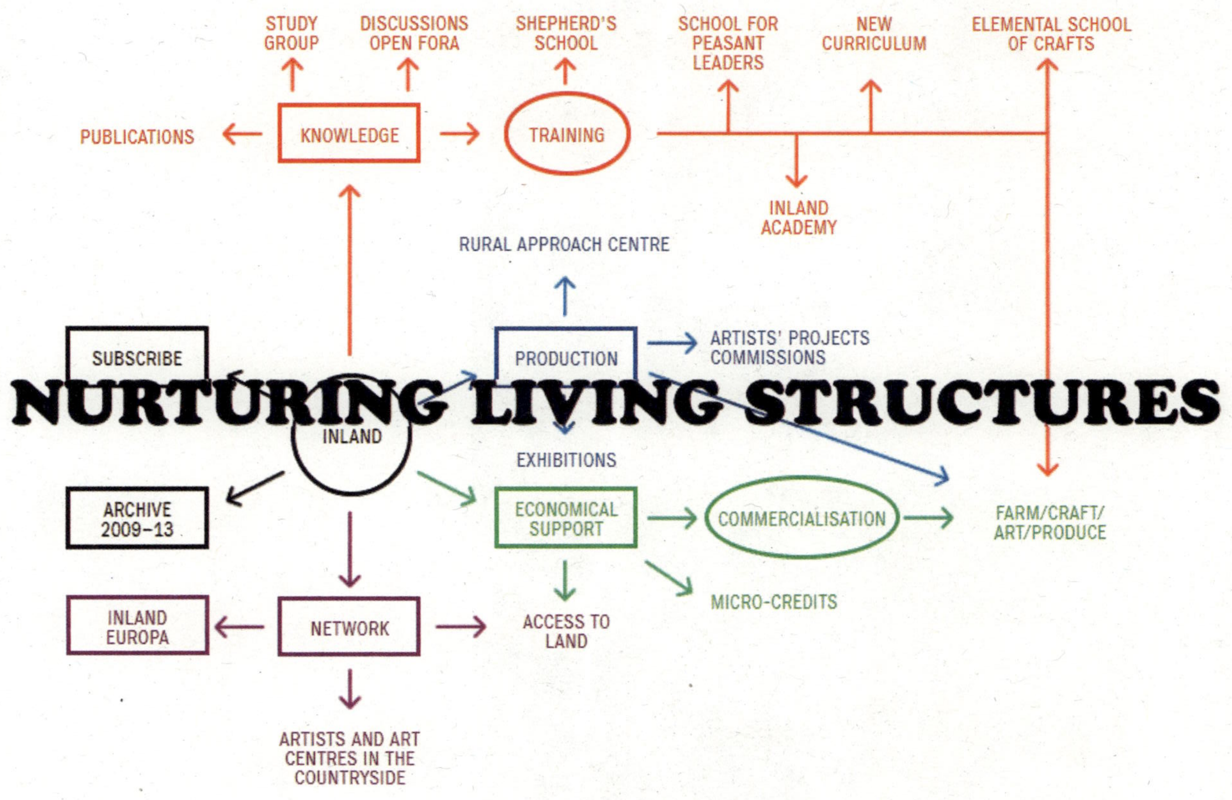

NURTURING LIVING STRUCTURES
INLAND
PUBLICATIONS
KNOWLEDGE
TRAINING
STUDY GROUP
DISCUSSIONS OPEN FORA
SHEPHERD'S SCHOOL
SCHOOL FOR PEASANT LEADERS
NEW CURRICULUM
ELEMENTAL SCHOOL OF CRAFTS
INLAND ACADEMY
RURAL APPROACH CENTRE
PRODUCTION
ARTISTS' PROJECTS COMMISSIONS
EXHIBITIONS
ECONOMICAL SUPPORT
COMMERCIALISATION
FARM/CRAFT/ ART/PRODUCE
MICRO-CREDITS
ACCESS TO LAND
SUBSCRIBE
ARCHIVE 2009–13
INLAND EUROPA
NETWORK
ARTISTS AND ART CENTRES IN THE COUNTRYSIDE

# INSTITUTO DE ARTIVISMO HANNAH ARENDT (INSTAR)

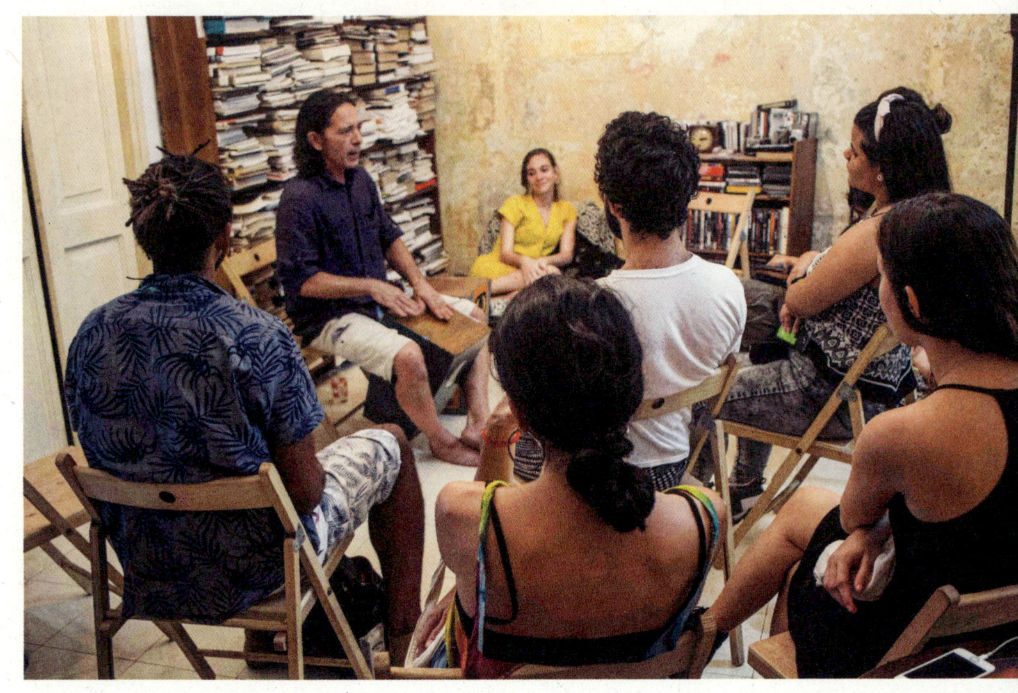

Poetry space *Lecturas en Tiempo (Readings in Time)*. Recital and exhibition by Omar Pérez, Havana, 2020

**VENUES**
🔹 documenta Halle

**LUMBUNG INTER-LOKAL**
○ Britto Arts Trust
○ FAFSWAG
○ Fondation Festival sur le Niger
○ Gudskul
○ INLAND
○ Jatiwangi art Factory

○ Más Arte Más Acción (MAMA)
○ OFF-Biennale Budapest
○ Project Art Works
○ The Question of Funding
○ Trampoline House
○ Wajukuu Art Project
○ ZK/U – Center for Art and Urbanistics

INSTAR is presenting a counter-
narrative of Cuban cultural
history, installed between Havana
and Kassel.

The Instituto de Artivismo Hannah Arendt (INSTAR) was born out of an artistic action in Havana, Cuba, when, in May 2015, the artist and activist Tania Bruguera held a collective reading of Arendt's *The Origins of Totalitarianism* (1951) in what are now INSTAR's headquarters. For 100 hours, people recited and discussed Arendt's classic study of totalitarian regimes, which is highly relevant to Cuba today. This action was the culmination of the #YoTambiénExijo campaign, which Bruguera initiated with a group of Cuban citizens in 2014–2015. They demanded transparency from the Cuban regime about conversations that established bilateral relations between Cuba and the United States during the terms of Raul Castro and Barack Obama, respectively. In an unprecedented event, within a few days, more than 20,000 people gathered on a public platform, activating a genuine civic campaign using social media. From that moment, the cultural sector became an agent of socio-political change in Cuba.

INSTAR—an acronym, and also a verb meaning "to encourage," "to instigate," or "to incite"—works at the fault lines between artistic practice and activism. The institute's main objectives are the promotion of civic literacy and social justice in Cuba. Operating collectively and by consensus, it creates a model of institutionality guided by freedom of expression, the observance of human rights, and the fulfillment of labor rights such as fair working hours and wages, zero tolerance to discrimination, and favorable working environments for single-parent families. INSTAR is a space that generates content through programming, developed through social networks and at its Havana headquarters: it institutes and promotes awards and scholarships for the financial support of independent practice on the island; and it aims for the restitution of historical memory through public programs and the archive created for this purpose.

INSTAR's project for documenta fifteen takes as a point of departure the Russian constructivist poet, journalist, and playwright Sergei Tretyakov. Tretyakov believed that artists should not only reflect reality but shape its economic and labor conditions. For two years, Tretyakov lived on a *kolkhoz*, or collective farm, in the rural northern Caucasus. Interested in forms of social reorganization, he engaged in administrative duties, edited a newspaper, and worked with farmers on inventory, literacy, and accounting. In the *kolkhoz* he devised an information tool: a mural newspaper that helped the community coordinate and visualize their many activities. He called this information tool an "operational factography."

INSTAR's *Operational Factography* (2022) creates the conditions for the crossover and coexistence of projects and ideas that lead to the restitution of historical memory and its dynamization in the present. Integrating art, economics, literacy, and political engagement, INSTAR's project takes place in two locations: at documenta Halle in Kassel, and in INSTAR's Cuban headquarters. Viewers can access an operant archive of INSTAR's activities an aims through ten exhibitions that INSTAR is putting on every ten days. Each show displays a specific project or or practice in Cuba, aiming to give justice to artists and intellectuals censored by the Cuban government. Together with a reading room, public program, and archive space documenting this process, INSTAR's presentation is guided by a counter-narrative of artistic and cultural history in Cuba.

Pablo Larios

INSTAR @ DOCUMENTA
  TEAM
Clara Astiasarán
Ernesto Oroza
Tania Bruguera

CORDINATORS DOCUMENTA
  FIFTEEN FOR INSTAR
Chiara Ianeselli
Thomas Engelbert

INSTAR SQUARE
**Public Events**
Tania Bruguera
**Assistant Public Events**
Marilyn Volkman
Solveig Font
**Guest**
Juan Francisco Elso[†]
**Objects Design**
Ernesto Oroza
**Textile**
Tomás Sánchez

**Graphic Design**
Claudia Patricia
Pérez Olivera

**General Timeline**
Ernesto Calvo
**INSTAR Timeline**
Camila Lobón

**Mural**
Carlos R. Cárdenas
Hamlet Lavastida

NEW RULES OF THE GAME -
  INDEPENDENT PRACTICES
  AND DISCURSIVE
  AUTONOMY IN CUBAN
  CULTURE
**Editor**
Tania Bruguera
Henry Eric Hernández
**Copy Editor**
Gilberto Padilla
**Authors**
Anaeli Ibarra Cáceres
Claudia González
  Marrero
Danae C. Diéguez
Dean Luis Reyes
Elvis Fuentes
Ernesto Menéndez-Conde
Ernesto Oroza
Grethel Domenech Henry
  Eric Hernández
Hilda Landrove
Jorge Enrique Rodríguez
  Lizabel Mónica
Marlene Azor Hernández
Rafael Rojas
Suset Sánchez Sánchez

**Artists in the Posters
  Series**
Ángel Delgado
Antonia Eiriz[†]
AR-DE (Arte y Derechos)
Ezequiel Suárez
Joel Rojas
Tomás Esson
Tomás Sánchez
Santiago Armada (Chago)[†]
Umberto Peña
#YoTambiénExijo

1. FACTOGRAFIA OPERATIVA
  (OPERATIONAL
  FACTOGRAPHY)
**Operatives**
INSTAR @ Documenta Team
**Catalog authors**
Documenta Team
**Guests**
El Toque
Proyecto Inventario
Raychel Carrión
Timeline INSTAR

2. CURADORES GO HOME
  (CURATORS, GO HOME)
**Operatives**
INSTAR @ Documenta Team
**Catalog authors**
Gerardo Mosquera
Sandra Ceballos
**Guests**
Ezequiel Suárez
Sandra Ceballos
Artists in *Curadores Go
  Home* (2008)

3. TIERRA SIN IMAGENES
  (LAND WITHOUT IMAGES)
**Guest Operative /
  Catalog Author**
José Luis Aparicio
**Guests**
Adriana F. Castellanos
Alán González González
Alejandro Alonso
Alejandro Brugués
Ana Alpízar
Arturo Infante
Carla Valdés
Carlos González Arenal
Carlos Lechuga
Carlos Melián
Carlos Quintela
Celia - Yunior
Damián Saínz
Daniela Muñoz
Eliecer Jiménez Almeida
Emmanuel Martín
Ermitis Blanco
Esteban Insausti
Fabián Suárez
Fausto Canel
Fernando Fraguela
Fernando Villaverde
Gabriel Alemán
Gustavo Pérez
Heidi Hassan
Henry Eric Hernández
Humberto Padrón
Ian Padrón
Irene Gutiérrez
Javier Labrador
Jorge Dalton
Jorge Molina
José Luis Aparicio

Josué García Gómez
Juan Carlos Alom
Juan Carlos Calahorra
Juan Carlos Cremata
Juan Pablo Daranas
Katherine Gavilán
Lisandra López Fabé
Lorenzo Regalado
Magdiel Aspillaga
Manuel Marzel
Manuel Zayas
Marcel Beltrán
Marcos Díaz
Maryulis Alfonso
Michelle Memran
Miguel Coyula
Miñuca Villaverde
Néstor Almendros[†]
Nicolás Guillén Landrián
Oneyda González
Orlando Jiménez Leal
Patricia Pérez
Pável Giroud
Rafael Ramírez
Raydel Araoz
Ricardo Acosta
Ricardo Figueredo
Ricardo Vega
Rolando Díaz
Sergio Fernández Borrás
Tomás
Piard[†]
Víctor Alfonso Cedeño
Yimit Ramírez

4. PEÑA DEL JUCARO MARTIANO
  (GATHERING AT MARTI'S
  JUCARO TREE)
**Operatives**
INSTAR @ Documenta
  Team
**Guest Operative /
  Catalog Author**
Joaquín Badajoz
**Guests**
Pedro Pablo Oliva
Rafael Almanza
**Árbol Invertido**
Francis Sánchez
Ileana Álvarez
**AlasTensas**
Ileana Álvarez
**Almenara / Bokeh**
Waldo Pérez Cino
**Casa Vacía**
Pablo de Cuba Soria
**Centro de Estudios
  Convivencia**
Dagoberto Valdés
**Ediciones Deslinde**
Francis Sánchez
Ileana Álvarez
**Hypermedia Magazine**
Gilberto Padilla
Ladislao Aguado

**La Maleza**
Léster Álvarez
**Mujercitos**
Claudia Patricia Pérez
  Olivera
Víctor Eduardo
  Iglesias Fernández
**No Country Magazine**
Carlos A. Aguilera
Carlos Aníbal Alonso
  (Rialta)
Carlos Manuel Álvarez
  Rodríguez (El
  Estornudo)
**Revista de la Vagancia
  en Cuba**
Julio Llópiz-Casal
**Revista Vitral**
Santiago Díaz
  Dagoberto Valdés

## 5. A TARRO PARTIDO (TO THE BITTER END)

**Guest Operatives /
  Catalog Authors**
Gean Moreno
Isbel Díaz Torres
Natalia Zuluaga
**Guests**
Ernesto Leal
Otari Oliva Buadze
**Guest Projects**
Guardabosques
Locación Cristo
  Salvador
Nuestra América
Observatorio Crítico
Voltus 5

## 6. OMNI

**Operatives**
INSTAR @ Documenta
  Team
**Catalog author**
Verónica Vega
**Guests**
Amaury Pacheco
Ángel Escobar[†]
Calvert Casey[†]
Carlos Augusto Alfonso
David D'Omni
Juan Carlos Flores[†]
Omar Pérez
Raúl Hernández Novás[†]

## 7. ACADEMIA DEL BEJUCO (CLIMBING VINE ACADEMY)

**Operatives**
INSTAR @ Documenta
  Team

**Guest Operatives**
Derbis Campos
  Hernández

Samuel Riera Méndez
**Catalog authors**
Orlando Hernández
Yenisel Osuna
**Guests**
Alberto Casado
Antonio de la Guardia[†]
Samuel Feijóo[†]
**Art Brut Project Cuba**
Bernado Sarría
Boris Adolfo Martín
  Carlos Javier García
  César Andrés León
  Rodríguez
Damián Valdés Dilla
Robaina Alonso
Dianelis Massip López
Duniesky Ávila Bordás
Esperanza Conde
  Rodríguez
Felipe
Gloria Caridad García
  Hernández
Guillermo Rigoberto
  Casola Marcos
Héctor González
  Herrero
Irving Antonio
  Beladiola Miranda
Isabel Alemán
  Corrales[†]
Jesús Espinosa
  Carrillo
Joan Ramírez Florez
Jorge Francisco García
  Lastayo
Josvedy Jove Junco
Julián Espinosa
  Rebodillo (a.k.a
  Wayacón)
Lázaro Antonio
  Martínez Durán
Luciano
Luis Jesús Sotorrio
  Fábregas
Marcos Antonio
  Guerrero Herrera
Miguel Ramón Morales
  Díaz
Roberto O'Farril
  Multan
Rubén Gerardo Guerrero
  Garrido
Taimy Linares Rabago
Víctor Miguel Moreno
  Piñeiro[†]
Yainara García
  Rousseaux

## 8. FESTIVAL ROTILLA (ROTILLA FESTIVAL)

**Guest Operative**
Michel Matos (sotam)
**Catalog Author**
Daniel Salas

**Staff**
Adrián Monzón (VjCuba)
Aminta D'Cárdenas
Hellman Avelle Soberón
Michel Matos (sotam)
**Guests**
Bárbaro Vargas (MC
  Urbano Vargas)
El Enano MC / Tattoo
Enrique Maresma (Dj
  Kike Wolf)
Jack Yglesias (Jack
  Attack)
Jasek Manzano
Joyvan Guevara (DJoy
  de Cuba)
Roger Rizzo
Yoel Antonio Diéguez
  (Dj Wichy de Helado)
**Contributors**
Carlos Michel
  Hernández
Gabriela Sánchez

## 9. A PIE DE OBRA (SURVEYING THE SITE)

**Guest Operative /
  Catalog Author**
Nara Mansur Cao
**Guests**
*Impulso Teatro*
Alexis Díaz de
  Villegas
*(Martica Minipunto)*
Martha Luisa Hernández
  Cadenas
*Teatro El Ciervo
  Encantado*
Mariela Brito
Nelda Castillo
*Teatro La Fortaleza*
Atilio Caballero
Agnieska Hernández
Karina Pino
Mercy Ruiz
Nara Mansur Cao
Noel Bonilla
Norge Espinosa
Rogelio Orizondo
Yohayna Hernández
Yvonne López Arenal
**INSTAR Guests**
*Perséfone Teatro*
Adonis Milán
Daniel Triana
*Teatro Kairós de LCAP*
Gorki Águila
Lynn Cruz
*Teatro Obstáculo*
Alcibíades Zaldívar
Bárbara María
  Barrientos
Víctor Varela
Daymé del Toro
Marianela Boán

**Magazine Design**
Ernesto Ferrán

## 10. INSTAR

**Operatives**
INSTAR @ Documenta
  Team
**Team INSTAR**
Aminta D'Cárdenas
Camila Lobón
Claudia Patricia Pérez
  Olivera
Marta María Ramírez
Tania Bruguera
Ulises Padrón Suárez
**Contributors**
Adonis Milán
Anaeli Ibarra Cáceres
Jorge Enrique
  Rodríguez
José Luis Aparicio
  Ferrera
Juliana Rabelo García
Leonardo Fernández
  Otaño
Maria Matienzo
**Catalog authors**
Team INSTAR



Instituto de Artivismo Hannah Arendt (INSTAR)

# JATIWANGI ART FACTORY

For documenta fifteen, the Jatiwangi art Factory has developed the New Rural Agenda—a transnational summit among rural community networks.

In Indonesia, the Suharto-led New Order regime established the principle of progress development *(pembangunan)* based on economic growth. Villages became contested zones of how to govern the hegemony of progress, the imagination, and the sense of communal security. There was an effort to instill villages with a sense of stability. An industrial, top-down farming policy was implemented to increase agricultural production. Villages ceased to become resourceful sites and were transformed into sites of global consumption. Many villagers were forced to seek work in cities, dreaming of becoming modern Indonesian citizens.

When Reformasi 1998 took place, many villages were already in decline. In this context, the Jatiwangi art Factory aims to restore the dignity and resilient power of village structures through emphasizing the community's cultural ownership of the land. Positioning themselves as part of the village community, Jatiwangi attempts to remake village identity through exploring local creative potentialities. Soil provides the material basis to develop collective strategies and ideas for dealing with pressing contemporary problems.

For documenta fifteen, the Jatiwangi art Factory has developed the New Rural Agenda——a transnational summit among rural community networks. The summit is preceded by the New Rural School, a series of knowledge and narrative exchanges in the form of conferences, amateur radio talks, and the *Bulletin Rural School*. The New Rural Agenda appropriated the high-level conference model, where elites perform the main diplomacy roles for the people. The logic of the summit is transformed into a space to discuss futures from rural-based perspectives. The development of the people's agenda is underway, through taking into account grass-root-level actors, who have been working to design futures in their communities. It emphasizes diverse perspectives from below and peripheries. It challenges the uniform ideas of progress and sustainability. The stakeholders include: youth, women, village heads, Indigenous leaders, policy makers, ambassadors, world institutions, and the non-human. According to Jatiwangi, rural-based perspectives need to be created and nurtured. Village knowledge should be utilized as a tool for thinking about future sustenance, resilience and collective safety. New Rural Agenda's summit will be held in Kassel where the stakeholders will convene and produce *Piagam Martabat Penghuni Bumi*——the Earth Inhabitants' Treaty of Dignities.

Nuraini Juliastuti

VENUES
- Hübner areal

LUMBUNG INTER-LOKAL
- Britto Arts Trust
- FAFSWAG
- Fondation Festival sur le Niger
- Gudskul
- INLAND
- Instituto de Artivismo Hannah Arendt (INSTAR)
- Más Arte Más Acción (MAMA)
- OFF-Biennale Budapest
- Project Art Works
- The Question of Funding
- Trampoline House
- Wajukuu Art Project
- ZK/U – Center for Art and Urbanistics

Project sketch for New Rural Agenda,
planetary summit to be held in Kassel, 2022

Jatiwangi art Factory

125

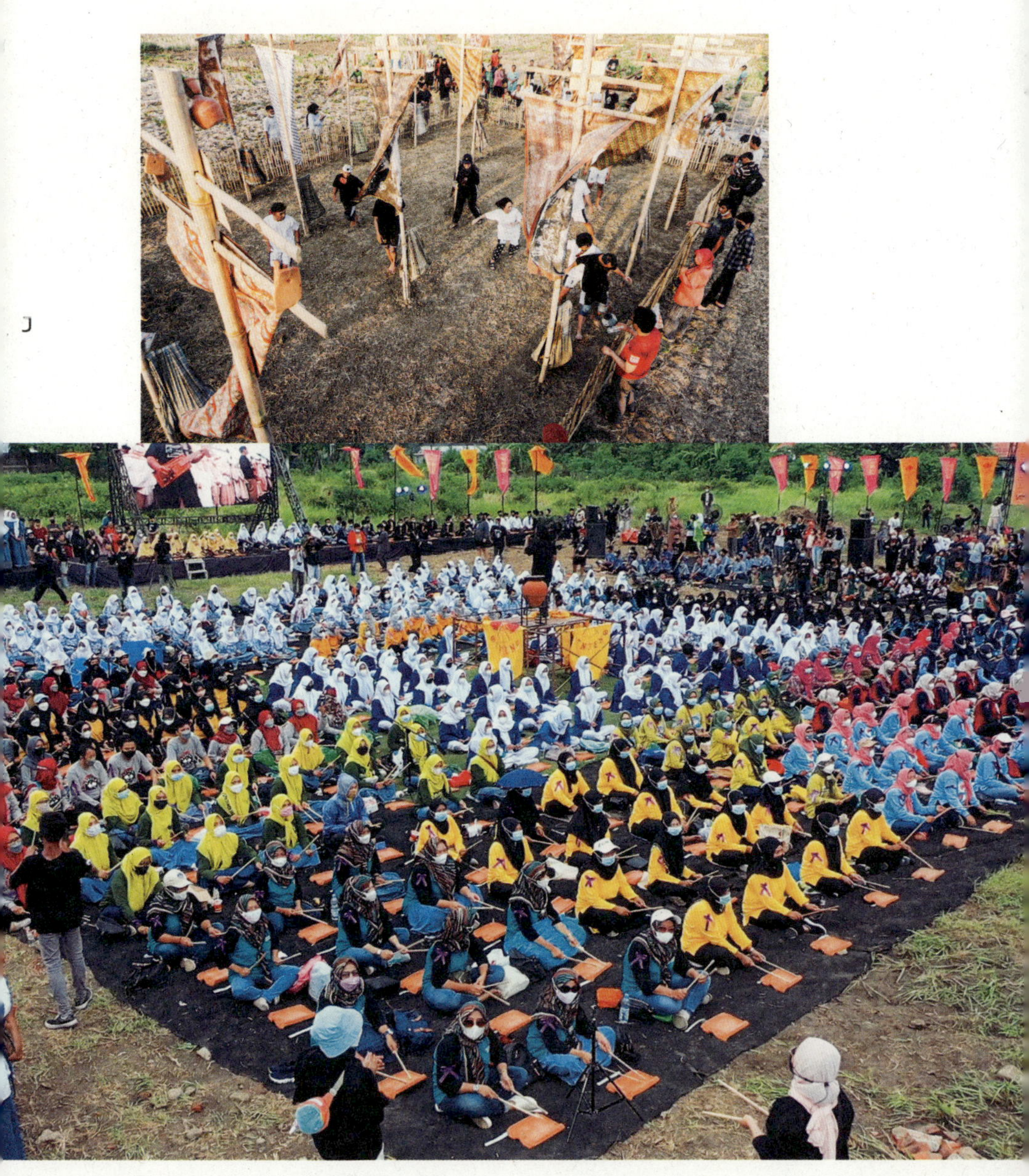

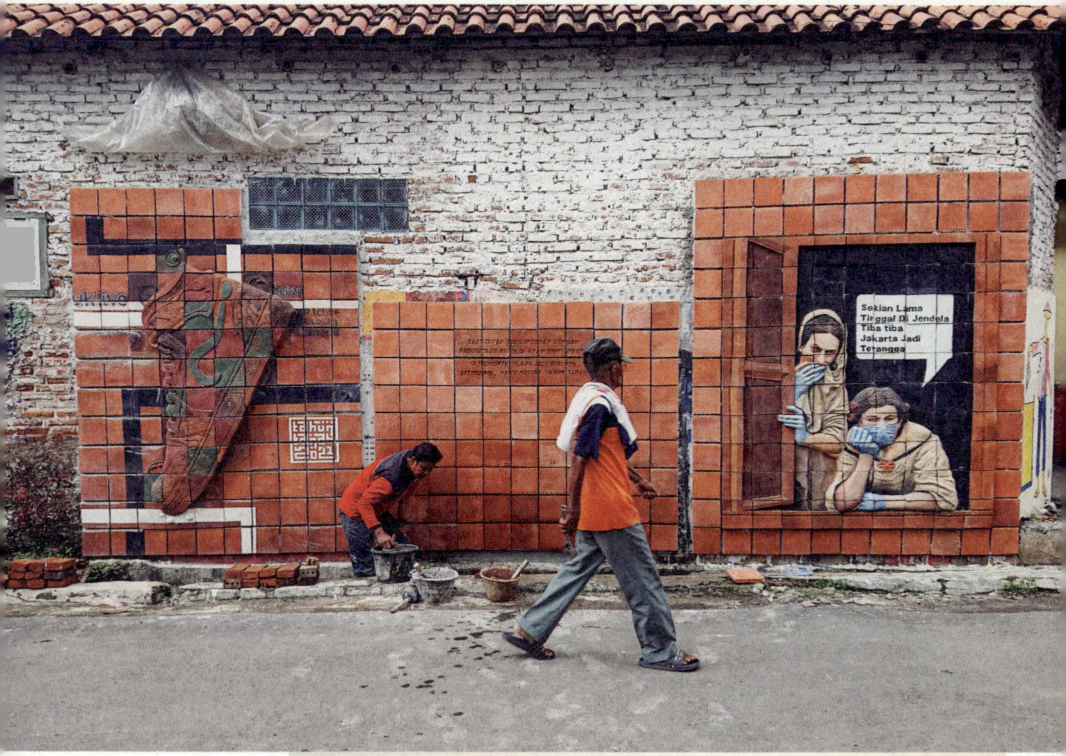

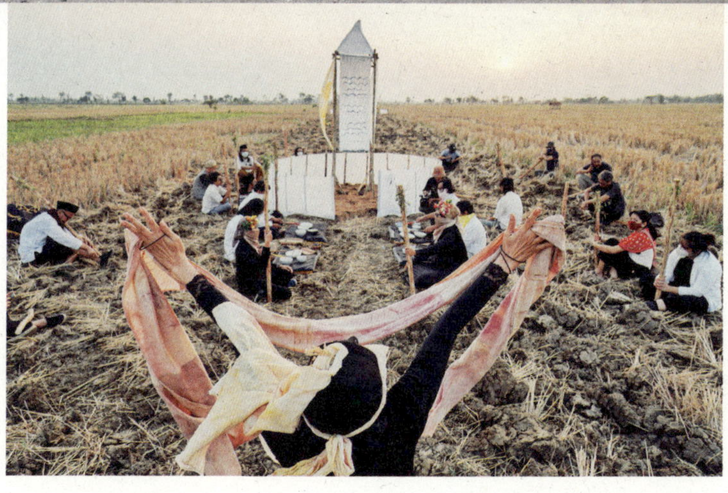



Offsite projects for documenta fifteen (clockwise):
*The Soil Bank, Terracotta Bombing, and Rampak Genteng*
(2021–2022), Jatiwangi, West Java, Indonesia

Jatiwangi art Factory

127

# JIMMIE DURHAM & A STICK IN THE FOREST BY THE SIDE OF THE ROAD


Jimmie Durham
Bev Koski
Elisa Strinna
Hamza Badran
Iain Chambers

Joen Vedel
Jone Kvie
Maria Thereza Alves
Wilma Lukatsch


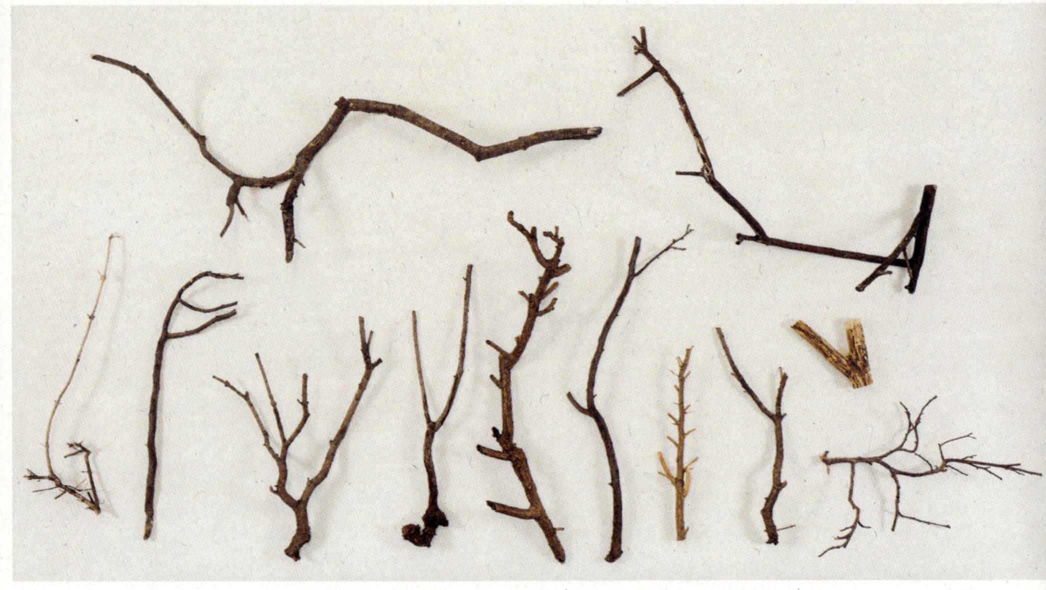



**VENUE**
Ⓚ KAZimKuBa

**MINI-MAJELIS**
⃝ Hamja Ahsan
⃝ La Intermundial Holobiente
⃝ Pınar Öğrenci
⃝ Saodat Ismailova

A new collective, formed after
Jimmie Durham's death in 2021,
departs from the late artist's
unfinished work.

A Stick in the Forest by the Side of the Road was born out of an idea of Jimmie Durham's. The artist, who died in November 2021, had the idea to bring together a group of eight people, mostly strangers, to share knowledge, empathy, and humor. On his last night, Durham said, "What a world we live in, a stick in the forest." After his death, the collective decided to make his absence part of the working process.

Durham, whose work moved between conceptual art, writing, and political activism, had a turtle skull on his worktable, in whose honor he had begun a sculpture. This, as well as artifacts he collected relating to physical theories about the expansion of the universe, are on display in documenta fifteen, together with works by nine individuals who use different ideas of knowledge to relate to different life forms.

Bev Koski's art explores memory, protection, and resilience within her beadwork practice. Elisa Strinna shows interventions from an ongoing research project entitled *People will miss the Earth* looking at plans to colonize space, how greenhouses replicate Earth's ekosistem, and the relationship of specific healing plants to the human body. Hamza Badran engages with historical apartheid in Cape Town, South Africa, tracing its continuation and relating it to a romanticization of peace and reconciliation. The text by Iain Chambers, *'…looking for connections that cannot, may be, should not, be made' (Jimmie Durham),* part of the workshop "The Colonial Clock and Critical Repair", engages with the violent mechanisms of the universalization of Western art to propose paths towards radical reconfiguration. Joen Vedel's sound and video works question processes of (un)learning, using live editing and montage to combine different forms of voices, temporalities, geographies, and levels of representation. Jone Kvie's installation, consisting of volcanic tuff rocks borrowed from the historic quarries around Kassel, offers space for pause and reflection. In addition, he deals with the topics of recycling and improvement of objects, and offers workshops on this subject. Maria Thereza Alves contributes two works, both in carpets and text. One looks at the political implications of the exotic flora of Naples, Italy, that arrived from former colonies. The other questions the lethal implications of a sixteenth-century text by a resident of Kassel, and explores its relationship to the continued contemporary colonization in Brazil. The contribution *How to Eat,* by Wilma Lukatsch, looks to food and recollections as social recipes in Kassel and Hessen. Through the richness of ingredients and their many embedded stories readers are invited to think about other ways to enjoy eating and to give a complex taste to our entangled history.

Ann Mbuti

J

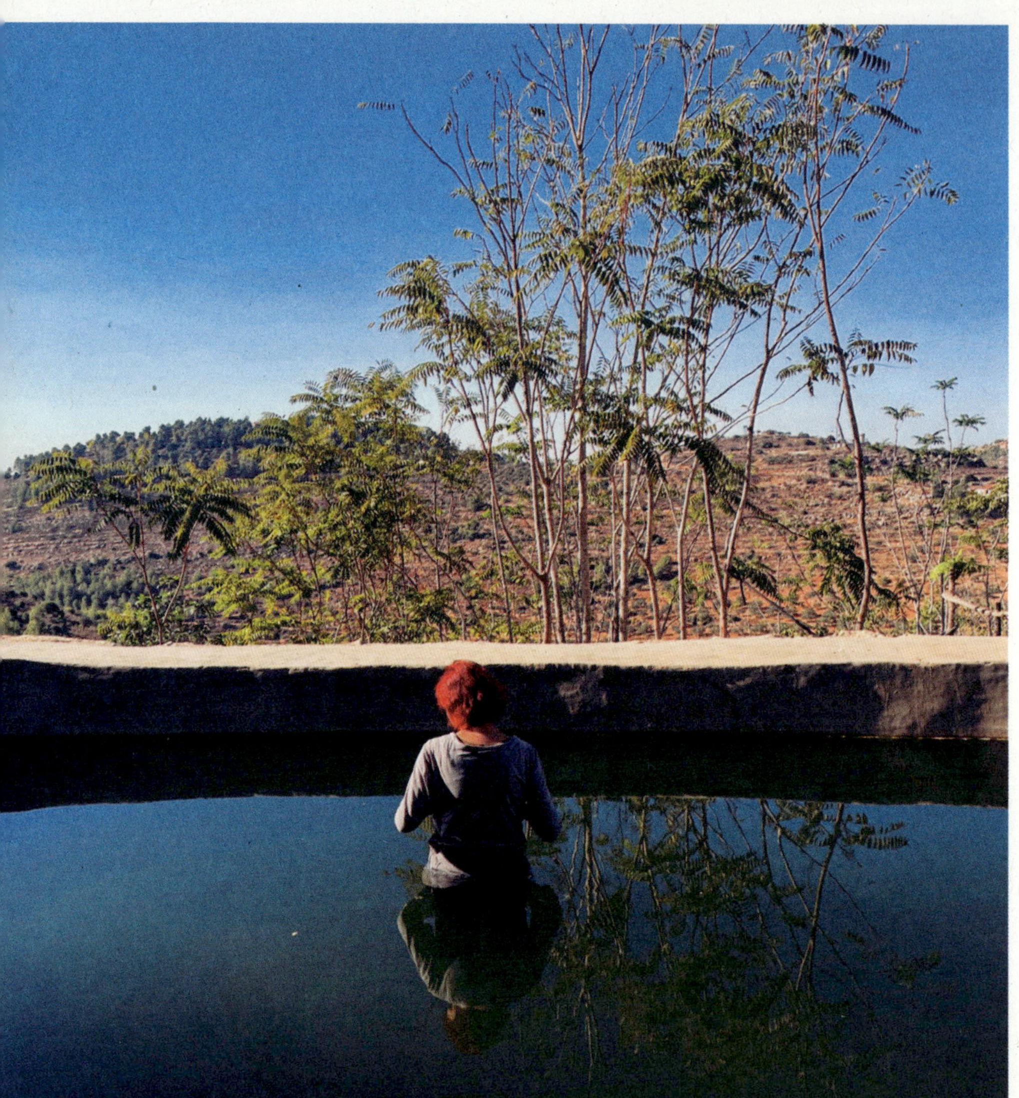





**VENUES**

- Fridericianum
- Grimmwelt Kassel
- Nordstadtpark
- Hafenstraße 76

**MINI-MAJELIS**

- ○ Arts Collaboratory
- ○ Black Quantum Futurism
- ○ Chimurenga
- ○ Nino Bulling
- ○ Agus Nur Amal PMTOH
- ○ Subversive Film

# JUMANA EMIL ABBOUD

Jumana Emil Abboud revisits
folktales collaboratively, showing
us how oral knowledge can remediate
endangered cultures.

Jumana Emil Abboud's works explore our intimate relationship with nature and landscapes, as collectively inhabited by humans and non-humans. Her practice in video, performance, drawings, and paintings assesses questions of longing, belonging, and separation—not through nostalgic iconography, but through a rediscovery and reimagining of the landscape. Her practice focuses on an exploration of places and sites in the topography of Palestine through folktales, popular stories, and oral traditions.

As an extension of her ongoing practice, Abboud's most recent work for documenta fifteen further delves into water sites as spirited places, now focusing specifically on seven endangered natural water sources in the Abu al-Adham hillside in 'Ein Qiniya, outside of Ramallah, Palestine. Through Water Diviner workshops that took place in 'Ein Qiniya, the group symbolically restituted their rights to water. Loss of water rights is seen as an integral part of dispossession, as water is taken and redirected from Palestinian sources to nearby settlements by the Israeli state. Water has also vacated our imagination due to the lack of our interaction with the landscape and with story-making; hence, here, the restitution of water is both physical and imaginary. Working from the understanding that stories are co-created, Abboud activates a re-visitation of water sources, through workshops and collective story-writing experimentation. Inspired by the natural water springs in Palestine, the stories continue to be co-authored as part of an ongoing collaborative process; a process that culminates in a storytelling performance for documenta fifteen—with new collaborations from Issa Freij, Anna Sherbany, Yasmine Haj, Mounya El Bakay, Lydia Antoniou, and Sourabh Phadke.

Additionally, Abboud has invited Issa Freij, Anna Sherbany, Yasmine Haj, Mounya El Bakay, and Lydia Antoniou to present their individual creative projects as part of the documenta exhibition, and separate from the performance collaboration with her. The aim of the collaborative processes, interventions and collaborations is like the interweaving of territory, time, language and culture with the past, present, the real and the mythical.

Also for documenta fifteen, Abboud presents drawings, video work and wax talismanic objects inspired by two Palestinian folk tales: the story of Half-a-Halfling (Nos Nsais), and the tale of The Orphans' Cow (similar to the Grimm Brothers' *Brother and Sister*). Abboud's revisiting of folktales through collaborative processes probes how oral knowledge can inform our contemporary reality and estrangement from the natural world. A publication published by Kayfa ta is also part of an evolving process. Stemming from her residency at Al Sakiya—Art/Science/Agriculture, she invites readers to participate and collaborate, to be with the earth in a gentle caring exchange, and to reunite with water with wonderment and imagination.

Tina Sherwell

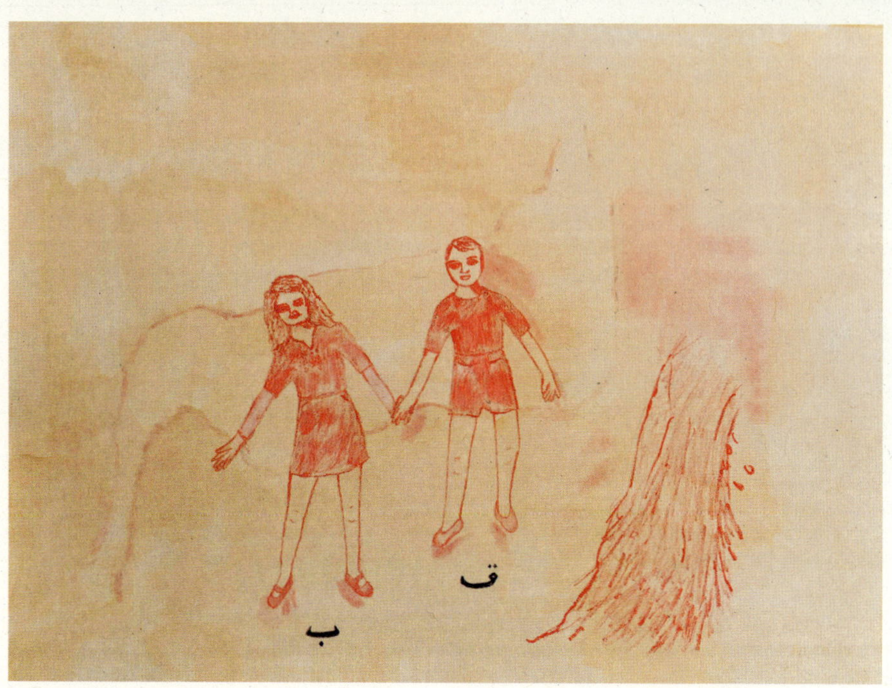

J



Jumana Emil Abboud, *Bdour and Qdour (II)* (2020)
Aquarelle pencil, lac dye on paper
57 × 76 cm

Jumana Emil Abboud, *RR-hood facing Tiger (I)* (detail, 2020)
Pigment gouache, pastel, acrylic, pencil, ink, charcoal on paper
57 × 76 cm

**THE WATER DIVINERS ARE:**
Raghad Saqfalhait
Lama Khatib
Haifa Zalatimo
Layla Taher
Amal Hajjaj
Zeina Nedal
Thurayya Shneina (Um Jum'a)
Ali Shneina (Abu Jum'a)
Suha 'Atta 'Alqam
Rahaf and Tabaraq 'Alqem
Sahar Qawasmi
Nida Sinnokrot
Issa Freij
Yusef Yacoub (Abu Omar)
Ayoub Yacoub
Danna Masad
Tareq Abboushi
Yazan Salem
Salma Kharouba
Sa'ad Dagher
Canaan Mazar'a (Abu Ibrahim)
Ishraq Awashra
Amany Kattom

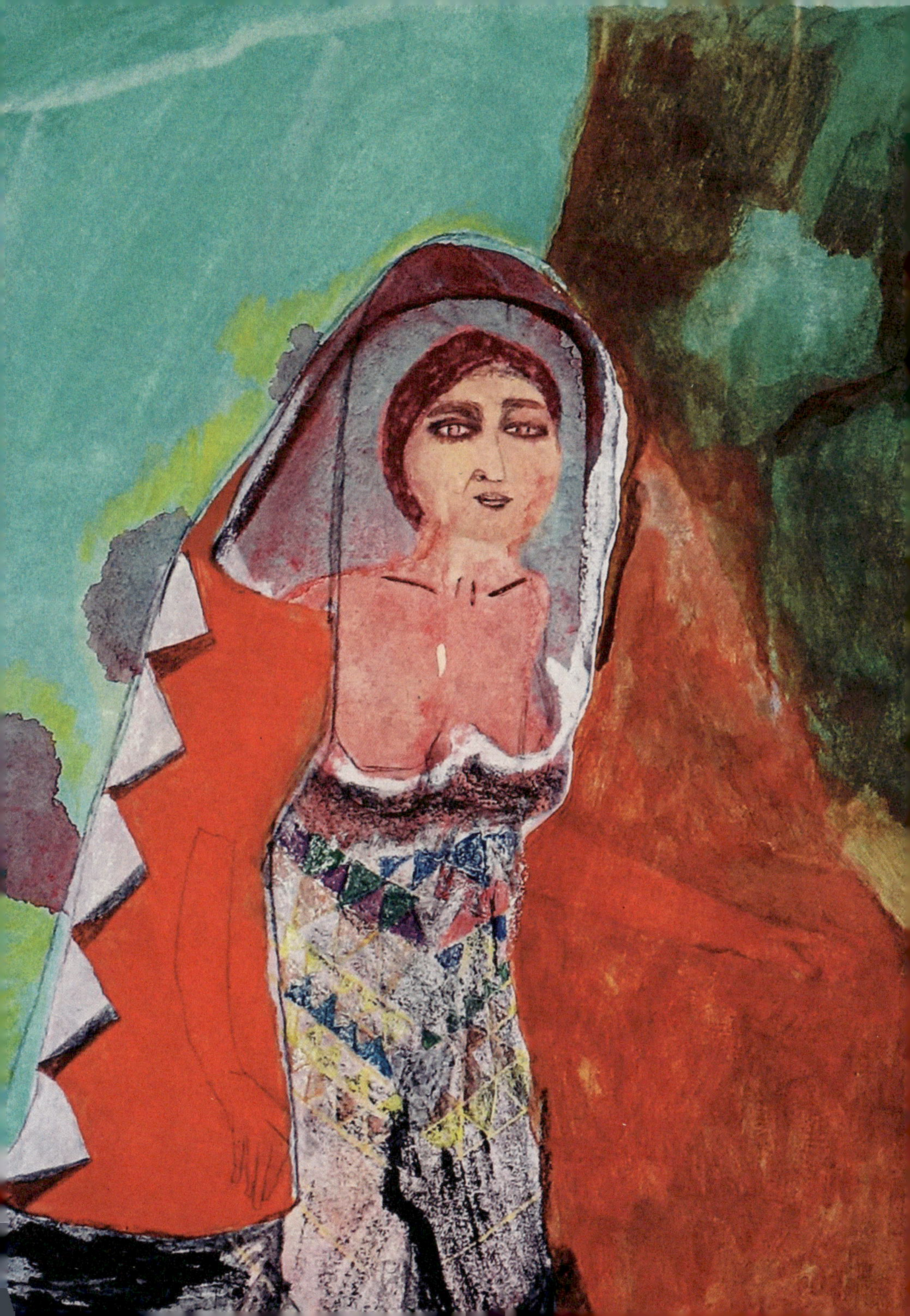

# KELEKETLA! LIBRARY

For documenta fifteen, Keleketla! Library reprises their social advocacy program, *Skaftien*.

Keleketla! Library positions itself as "a story-telling and narrative portal, an [arts] archive, cultural production and educational workshop and performance space" in Johannesburg, South Africa and worldwide through emergent platforms, media and collaborations. Their goal is to support and nurture autonomous and interdependent cultural production while, as they declare, "holding our governments accountable for just provisions of infrastructural support." Since its establishment in 2008, Keleketla! Library represents a rich legacy of multifaceted cultural presentations: literary, film, music, performance, installation, visual art, and more.

For Keleketla! Library, space is "a place where multiple narratives can exist parallel with each other in order to challenge dominant narratives." This is why the Drill Hall—a city block infrastructure mandated to advance community development, social welfare and arts, culture and heritage in Johannesburg—becomes a critical touch point. Drill Hall is a major cultural infrastructural stakeholder and beneficiary that forms the nerve center of Keleketla! Library discourse. Keleketla! Library recognizes that the Drill Hall represents a broader systemic neglect of cultural infrastructure, and as such is a rich case study for progressive, joint, participatory, and multi-stakeholder solution-making.

For documenta fifteen, Keleketla! Library reprises its project *Skaftien* (2011–ongoing). In this edition, to "skaftien" means to ask more out of a multi-stakeholder community. Instead of a shared meal in which the proceeds fund "compet-ing" communal-based initiatives, the evolution highlights the problematics of depoliticization of cultural work by demanding the accountability for neglect of infrastructure. In this reprise, *Skaftien* becomes a socio-cultural advocacy program that brings together stakeholders in cultural work and governance to diagnose and pinpoint mutual solutions to civil problems within the following paradigms: Public Space & Public Cultures; Architecture & Immovable Heritage; Public Transport, Spatial (In)Justice & Migrations; People are the Resources; Housing & Right of Law; Infrastructure & Governance.

The *Skaftien* model echoes the *Stokvel*, a trust or mutual community bank, traditionally run by women, for the upkeep and perpetuation of familial and communal ceremonies and developments. *Stokvel*, like *Skaftien* as articulated by Keleketla! Library, is a "a bridge between bureaucracy and cultural production." By making this link central to their documenta initiative, Keleketla! Library gets to the core of multi-stake-holder accountability (and solidarities), and the criticality of community to ensure survival by asking: "What do we bring to this *Skaftien*?" This understanding is not peculiarly South African or Sub-Saharan African—it is global, and also globally the epicenter of crisis.

Ashraf Jamal

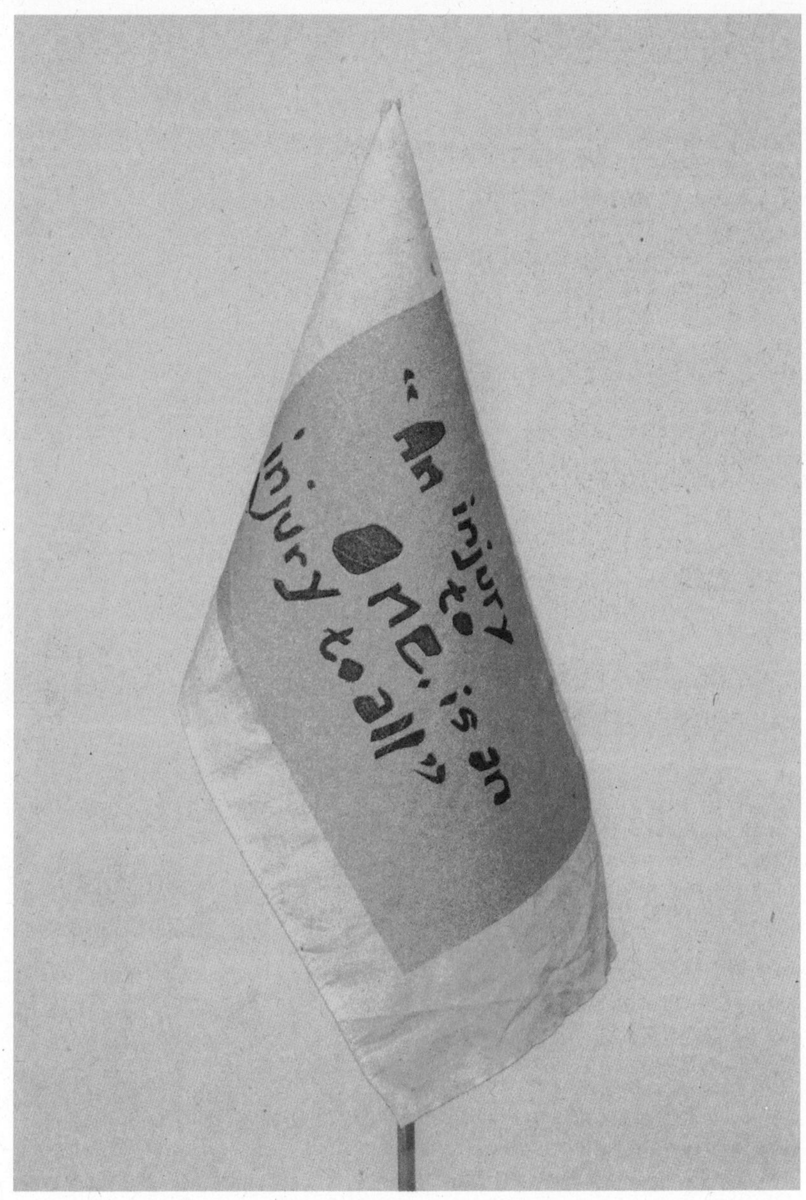


Keleketla! Library, *The Allure of Gold and Other Solidarity Stories* (2018)
Exhibition view (detail), Berlin, Germany


**VENUE**

🖊 Fridericianum

**MINI-MAJELIS**

- Another Roadmap Africa Cluster (ARAC)
- Archives des luttes des femmes en Algérie
- Asia Art Archive
- Centre d'art Waza
- El Warcha
- Graziela Kunsch
- Komîna Fîlm a Rojava
- Sada [regroup]
- Siwa plateforme - L'Economat at Redeyef
- The Black Archives

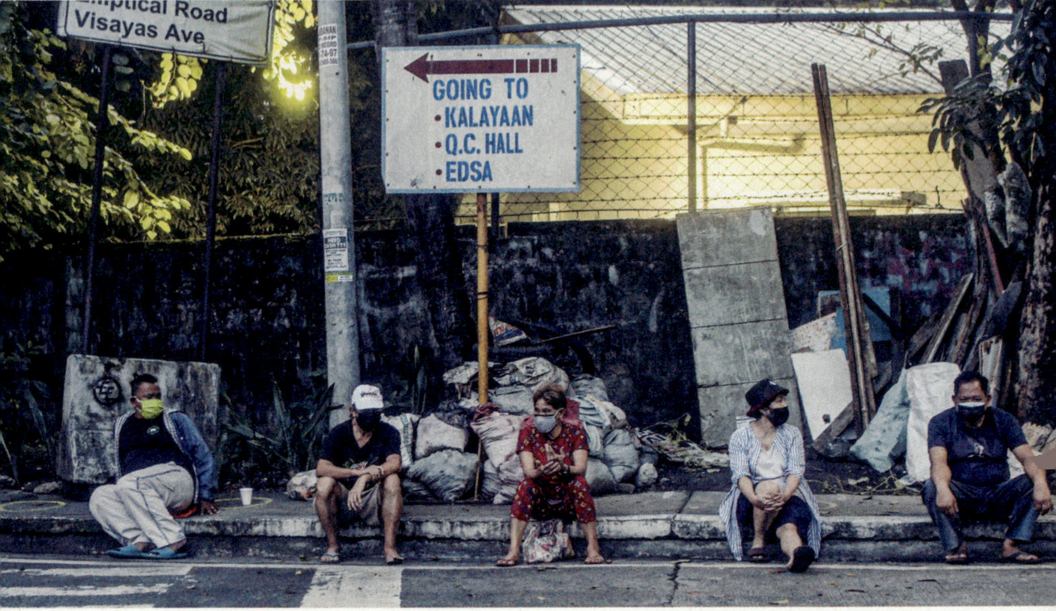




*Pila (Lines)* (2022)
Production still

Informed by the history of revolutionary struggle, Kiri Dalena's
art bridges activism and video.
In Kassel, Dalena shows new works
that depict a day in the lives of
activists under martial law, and
everyday politics in pandemic-era
Philippines.

Kiri Dalena's work begins with activism. In her early 20s, she left the Philippine capital to work as an organizer and artist-activist in various provinces in the Southern Tagalog region. Her haunting images offer us life under authoritarianism, the economics of food, and political promises. For documenta fifteen, a well-traveled protest banner unfurls across the facade of Kassel's Fridericianum. "STOP THE KILLINGS" is an address by RESBAK (Respond and Break the Silence Against the Killings)—an artists' collective of which Dalena is a co-founder—to organize against former president Rodrigo Duterte's War on Drugs in the Philippines. Up to 30,000 have died by police assassination and extrajudicial action since 2016. The words of the banner, which made its way through protests, are pixelated by mourning pins, traditional black acrylic markers worn by the bereaved.

The interminable waiting for the future is shown in *Pila (Lines)* (2022), a newly commissioned five-channel video and sound installation made during the pandemic. As the 18-month lockdown continued in the Philippines, food scarcity spread. Community pantries sprung up around the country with the imperative: "*Magbigay ayon sa kakayanan, kumuha batay sa pangangailangan*" (Give what you're able to give, and take only what you need). Dalena worked with community members to collect food donations for the table they've set up close to her house. The sky turns from night to day as people sit, sleep, talk, and wait for as little as 500 grams of rice. Dalena recorded (with their permission) conversations with those in line, asking them to speak freely of what they normally talk about while waiting—or, to continue resting quietly, if they prefer.

In a previous work, *The Guerilla is a Poet* (2013), Dalena told of an activist's journey under the martial law of the Marcos regime. Now, Dalena revisits a thread from the same story in *Nang Kumislap ang Mundo (When the World Sparkled)* (2022). In 1968, Jose Maria Sison reestablished the Communist Party of the Philippines. Under the Marcos regime, Sison, his partner and comrade Julie Delima, and other members were imprisoned for nine years. Before finding asylum in the Netherlands, their base was in the forest, away from the seat of power and in line with Maoist teachings toward re-education through immersion in the countryside. Through a lesser known story about their struggle to thrive and coexist with nature, Dalena reimagines a day in their life when the world throbs, glistens, and allows them to take an unexpected journey.

Hera Chan

VENUE
⊕ Hübner areal

MINI-MAJELIS
○ Cinema Caravan and
  Takashi Kuribayashi
○ Nguyen Trinh Thi
○ Safdar Ahmed

# KOMÎNA FÎLM A ROJAVA

The collective is curating a program of archival and recent films, as well as those from Kurdish cinema history.

Based in the autonomous region of Rojava in the Federation of Northern and Eastern Syria, *Komîna Fîlm a Rojava* (The Rojava Film Commune) is a collective of filmmakers founded in 2015. It works across the region to develop and build infrastructures for filmmaking, screening, and education, fostering new audiences and an awareness of filmmaking as a medium for empowerment and societal reimagination, and informed by their belief that the medium can be used by everyone for liberation and community-building.

Film has a tragic history in Rojava. In 1960, a fire in the region's only cinema, in the city of Amude, resulted in the death of 298 children. Cinema became associated with trauma and was stigmatized. However, the importance of film is nonetheless evident today: after the commune's first year, its more than 45 members screened over 300 films for children and the elderly across Rojava. Their intention was to bring the community back to cinema and filmmaking. They undertook a range of activities, including the Rojava Film Academy: a one-year educational program providing theoretical and practical classes, the production of films and documentaries, and infrastructure-building, all focused on giving voice to women and ethnic and religious communities. The academy is self-organized with students and commune members organizing its program taught by local and international film professionals. It "creates the possibility to imagine the *not yet present*, the permanent becoming that is the revolution itself." In 2016, the students produced the commune's first feature film *Stories of Destroyed Cities*, focusing on the aftermath of war on the local population, reappropriating their own language and culture using Kurdish as a working language and to research past history and myths. The commune are not film directors but rather use an ethos of "people to people" to create films. With the influx of foreign filmmakers and journalists to the region, the commune's work reclaims the space of representation, particularly in relation to dominant stereotypical images. In a place still entrenched in war, film can be a tool for reimaging society. They also archive local Rojava culture and the oral traditions.

For documenta fifteen, the collective curates a program of the commune's archival and recent films, as well as those from Kurdish cinema history. The program includes discussion panels with filmmakers and members of the commune and, in the Fridericianum, a video installation outlining the Rojava Film Academy as a model for alternative education.

Tina Sherwell

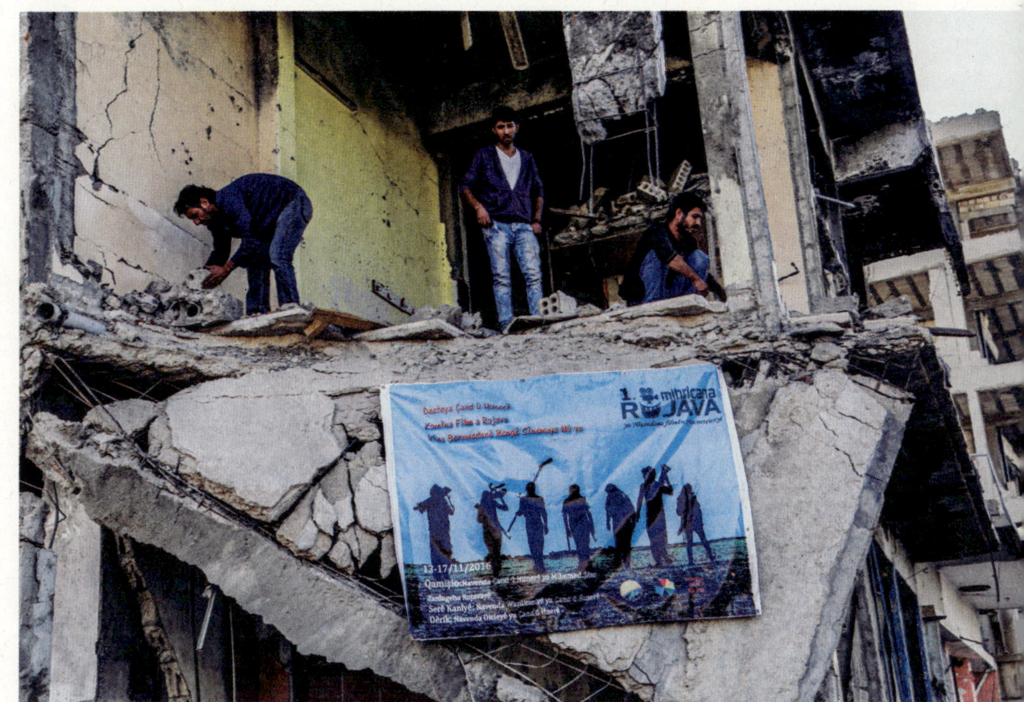




## VENUES

- Fridericianum
- Gloria-Kino
- Hübner areal

## MINI-MAJELIS

- Another Roadmap Africa Cluster (ARAC)
- Archives des luttes des femmes en Algérie
- Asia Art Archive
- Centre d'art Waza
- El Warcha
- Graziela Kunsch
- Keleketla! Library
- Sada [regroup]
- Siwa plateforme - L'Economat at Redeyef
- The Black Archives

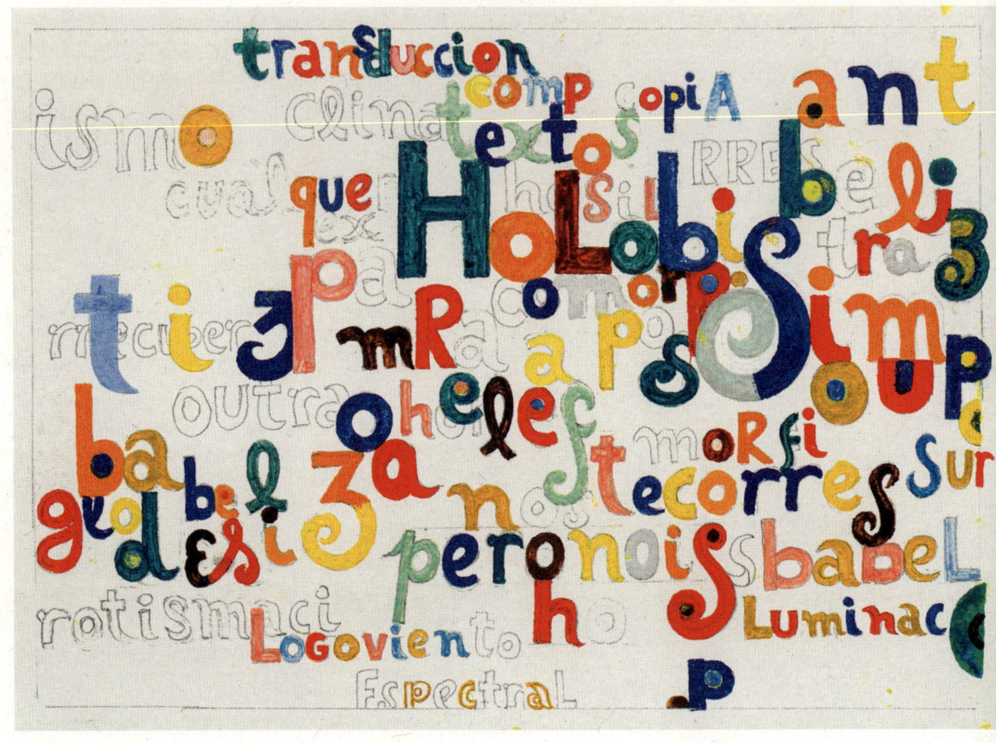



Drawing by Tulio de Sagastizábal in response to
the collective creative process proposed by La
Intermundial Holobiente for documenta fifteen

# LA INTERMUNDIAL HOLOBIENTE

La Intermundial Holobiente is a quartet dedicated to the invention of more-than-human imaginative practices. In Kassel, they have taken a feral area of the Karlsaue park and built a habitat to house a book written by a non-human being, designing a space for reading, writing, discussion and contemplation surrounded by living matter.

For two years, visual artist Claudia Fontes, philosopher Paula Fleisner, and writer and translator Pablo Martín Ruiz—all three from Argentina—met weekly to think about how to respond, through a methodology of collective creation, to the political problem of representation, authorship, and interpretation of the non-human. They decided to adopt a radically inclusive, non-extractivist, and non-hierarchical approach. They considered the capacity of all things on the planet to respond as well as to formulate their own questions. To this end they coined the word "holobient," by which they mean collective and more-than-human entities, and real and imaginary, non-binary consortiums of alliances that are not only human. Their conversation of three would become unrestrictedly inclusive: it would remain open to a fourth, a fifth, a potentially infinite number, and this potential member would be "the only irreplaceable one." Thus, *La Intermundial Holobiente* arose. They exhibit for the first time at documenta fifteen.

*La Intermundial Holobiente* plays an intermediary role in Kassel—and also in the preparations for the exhibition. Fleisner, Fontes, and Ruiz have chosen to work in a feral area of the Karlsaue State Park that has escaped human design. There, they have built a habitat to house *The Book of The Ten Thousand Things*, a book written and edited in a polyphonic way among fourteen artists and writers from Argentina: Erica Bohm, Virginia Buitrón, Gabriela Cabezón Cámara, Tulio de Sagastizábal, Lucas Di Pascuale, Carla Grunauer, Reynaldo Jiménez, Guadalupe Lucero, Anahí Rayén Mariluán, Leticia Obeid, Sergio Raimondi, Luis Sagasti, Ral Veroni, Susana Villalba, and the *intermundiales* themselves, all gathered under the idea of summoning non-human authors.

*La Intermundial Holobiente* has designed a space for reading, writing, discussion, and contemplation based on their own interpretation of lumbung. Here, the book expands and unfolds into images and actions surrounded by piles of local soil-mountains of living matter, and the groundwater rising from the ekosistem obliterated by the park. An English version of the book is available to explore and interact with as an open, unruly archive. Artist Graciela Carnevale collaborated with the archive and artist Chino Soria contributed to the design of the space. The Spanish edition of the book will find its definitive place in the documenta archive. The exhibition is accompanied by its own public program, "What's the Matter?"

Camilo Jiménez Santofimio





VENUE
Compost heap (Karlsaue)

MINI-MAJELIS
O Hamja Ahsan
O Jimmie Durham
O Pınar Öğrenci
O Saodat Ismailova

# LE 18

Based in Marrakesh, Morocco,
LE 18 is a multidisciplinary and
community-based cultural space.
In Kassel, LE 18 tells its story
through contributions of its
associated artists, together
with a public program of talks,
workshops, and screenings.

Since its creation in 2013, LE 18 has operated as an experimental cultural and artistic space hosting multidisciplinary art and research practices in Marrakesh, Morocco. The center focuses on gathering people together through exhibitions, public programs, and artists' residencies. Over the years, as different artists and cultural workers joined the team, a broader community of contributors and collaborators has led to diverse conversations, creating a common space in which different visions and practices could take place. LE 18 is invested in several research axes: photography and image production, the politics and poetics of water, and orality and storytelling. These became the focus of cycles of exhibitions, public programs, symposia, and workshops.

As a community-driven space, LE 18 connects with similarly invested initiatives and spaces in and out of Morocco, building different communities of shared interest. In this respect, LE 18 functions in concentric ways, working with regional collaborators and with young artists, cultural thinkers, and other local groups. The cultural space has always prioritized sharing the process of projects with their audiences: it develops visual arts practices with the artists that it hosts and accompanies them in Marrakesh to expand their projects in the ekosistem of the city and the rural regions around it. The experimental nature of LE 18 allows it to be a fluid and flexible place where conversations and their transmission are paramount.

At documenta, LE 18's history is told through artists who populated its space in Marrakesh throughout the years. It is an archival exhibition that aims to shed light on the different stages* and relevant themes of the space itself. An audio-guide, voiced by the artists, connects their individual projects to the broader history of LE 18. In addition, LE 18 has prepared a public program of talks, workshops, and screenings that brings together its closest collaborators, who will share and focus on the three main research axes. True to its mission of fostering spontaneous conversations and gatherings, LE 18 has erected a shared common space with a library where visitors can relax and look through published materials and other productions.

Rayya Badran

* At documenta, LE 18 transforms its former exhibition space at WH22 into a place for conversations and exchanges around the processes, challenges, and failures that emerged during our preparation for and participation at documenta. It therefore opens itself to addressing a sense of exhaustion and (self)-exploitation triggered by major art events. In this sense, it lends itself to the exploration of the structures cultural workers operate in and offers to collectively and openly deconstruct them.

This shift should not be understood as a withdrawing from, but rather as a putting in common with. Indeed, as the title of the proposal—*A Door to the Sky*—or a *Plea for Rain* already suggested, the site is reinforced as a space-time to rest. As such, it will be open to all invited artists at documenta as well as to the general public in order to find and share modes of regenerating and relearning after crisis. —LE 18

VENUE
(w) WH22

MINI-MAJELIS
O Alice Yard
O Erick Beltrán
O MADEYOULOOK
O Party Office b2b Fadescha
O Serigrafistas queer

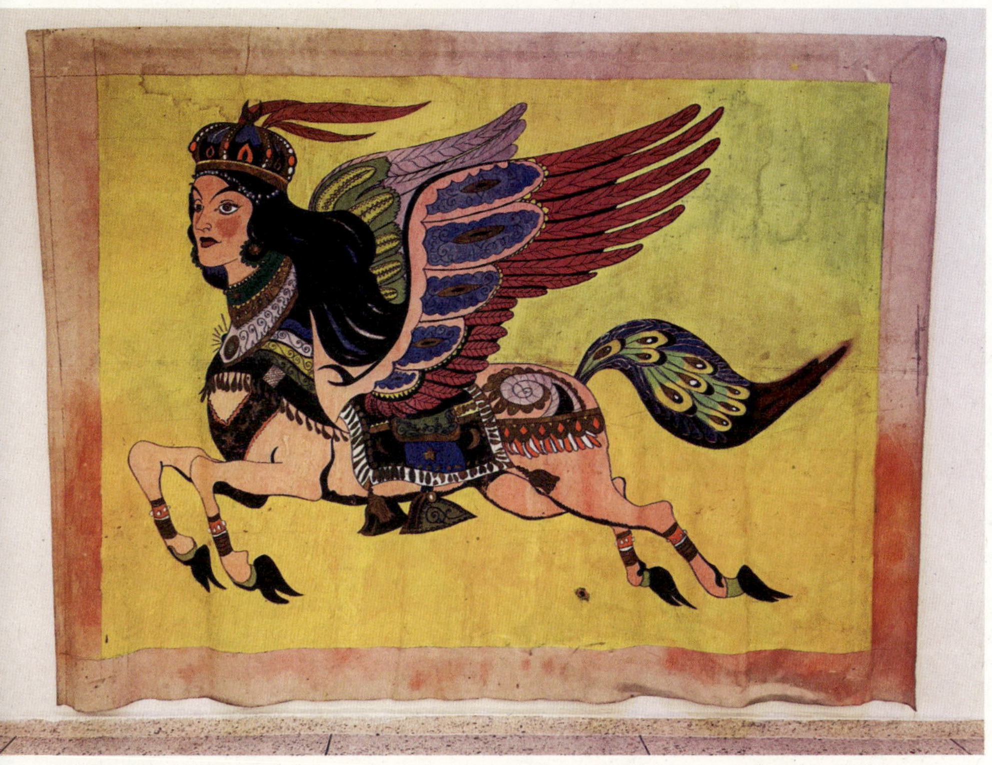

Al Bouraq illustrated by Mohamed Reggab
and painted by Naima Saoudi, 1979

L

LE 18

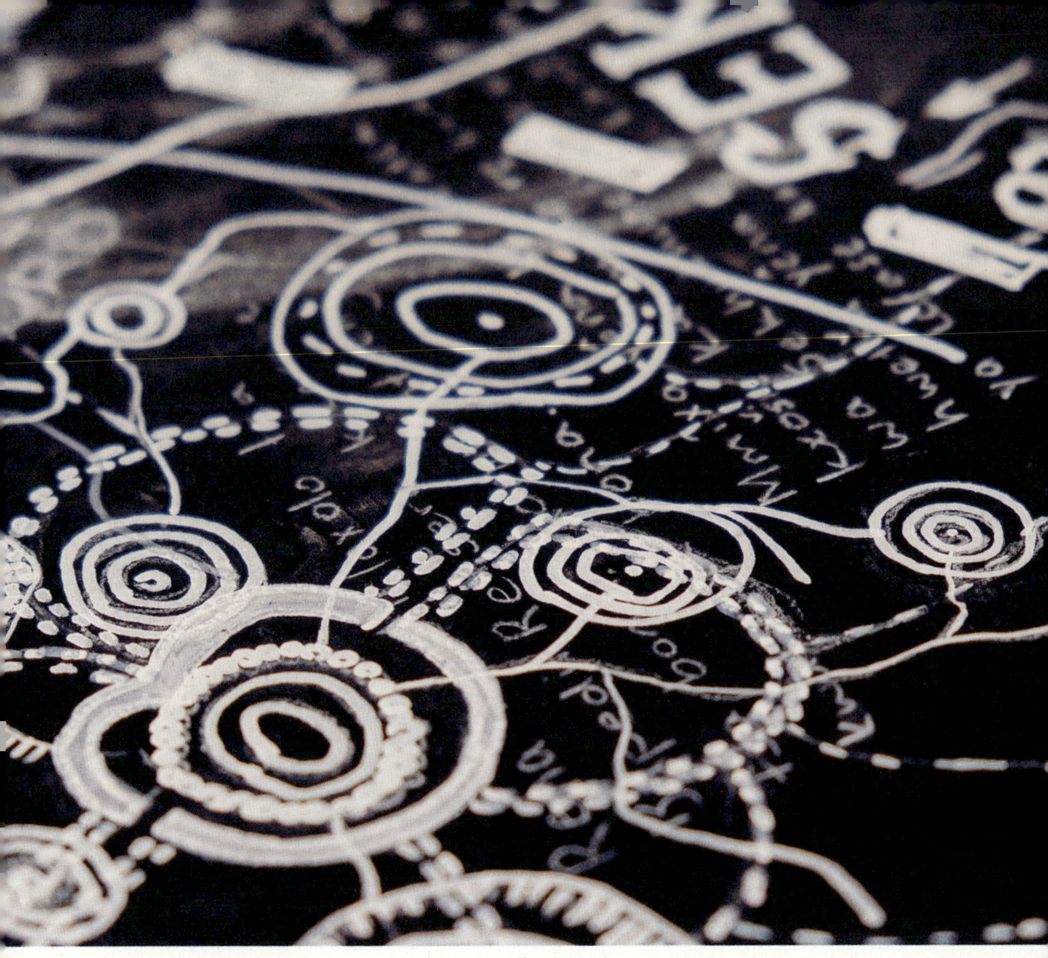

MADEYOULOOK, *Study for Bokoni floor map (detail)*, (2022) Graphite and pen on paper.

MADEYOULOOK has devised an undulating floor, an imprint of the inextricable nature of emotion, knowledge, and power, and of the psychic fallout of disconnection to the land.

Distracted by distraction, we barely have the capacity to look at the worlds within and around us with genuine interest and feeling. Aware of this dissociative relationship to others, the Johannesburg, South Africa-based pair behind the collective MADEYOULOOK, Molemo Moiloa and Nare Mokgotho, strive to reopen worlds that are historically overlooked or deemed inconsequential.

Their specific focus is Black life and Black love, which remain eccentric to the main event; Black suffering and Black oppression, which persist as the dominant register. MADEYOULOOK's counterintuition is to reexamine the cultural practice of everyday Black life, and, thereby, strategize projects which emphasize learning, repairing, and caring. Their projects are intuitive, immersive, compassionate. Moiloa and Mokgotho's emphasis on normative yet overlooked "Everyday Black Practices" is vital: they write, "In reworking and interrupting how we view ordinary Black lived experiences and the everyday, we are 'made to relook' and question societal relations."

For documenta fifteen, MADEYOULOOK emphasizes spatiality: how we manage space, how space manages us. Their project is a terraforming, a modification of a surface, to rethink and reexperience how we inhabit the world. MADEYOULOOK produce an undulating floor made of variable shifting heights, an anti-ergonomic exercise that refuses efficiency and comfort, that activates discomfort or unease as a trigger to re-evaluate the body's complacency.

The project's focal range is immense, yet interconnected, for what Moiloa and Mokgotho imprint upon their audience is the inextricable and spliced nature of emotion and space, knowledge, and power, and the psychic fallout of disenfranchisement, a disconnection to the land—the undulating floor. The defining moment of the catastrophe of Black South African experience is the Natives Land Act of 1913, which transferred 90 percent of the land to a white minority. The extent of the damage done to Black life is incomprehensible without recognizing the deliberate expropriation of the land that informed and defined them.

Moiloa and Mokgotho seek to "interrupt" a perverse economy, which was designed to render Black life aberrant. Given seismic disruptions in Europe right now, no one anywhere can ignore the precarity of the home-place-land. Nothing is certain, unrest is everywhere. MADEYOULOOK's documenta project, in which an undulating floor is an earthquake, is universal.

Ashraf Jamal

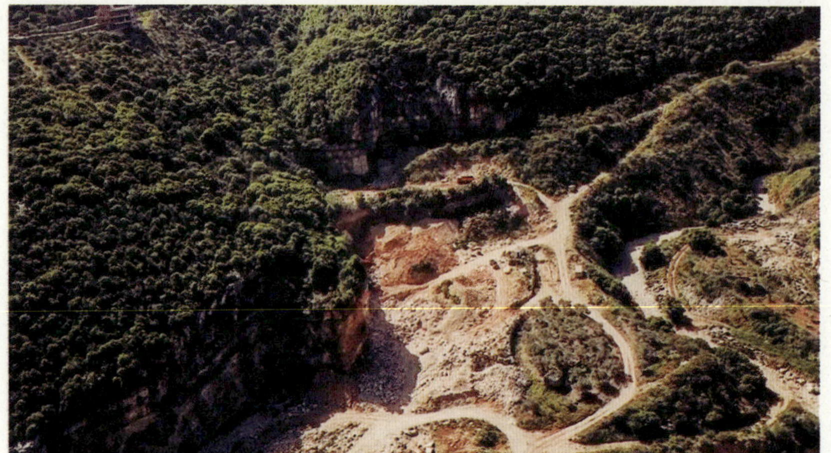

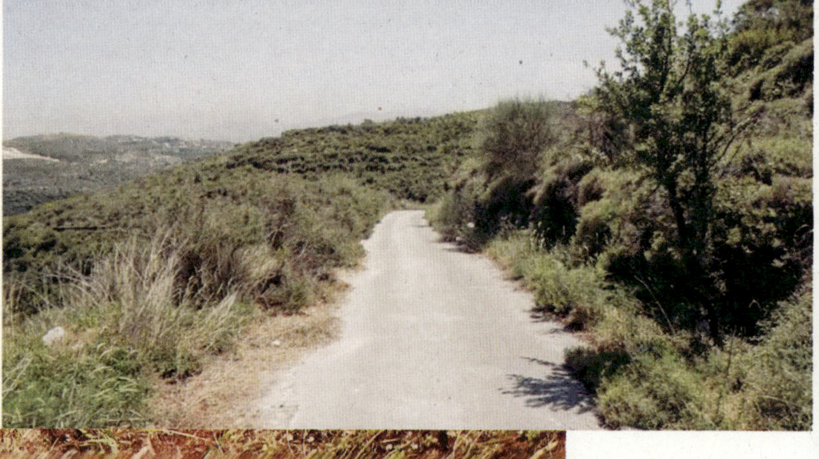

M

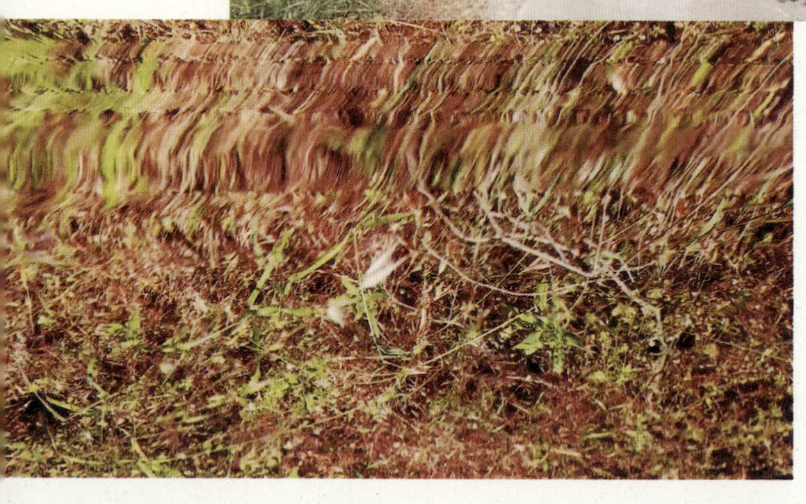

Video stills from *Who is Afraid of Ideology? part 4 "The reverse shot"*, 2022

Focusing on the resistance of women in places such as Syria and Colombia, Marwa Arsanios's work brings together anti-colonial and Indigenous struggle, seed protection, and land rights. For documenta fifteen, she shows the latest of her ongoing film series, set in a quarry in the mountains of northern Lebanon.

Self-defense, eco-feminism, ownership, healing, state control, autonomy, collectivity, Indigenous struggle, seed protection, and land rights—such acts of realignment with life are at the core of the anti-colonial struggle for wider social and political change today. Marwa Arsanios's film series *Who is Afraid of Ideology?* (2017–ongoing) weaves an intersectional path through the resistance of women on the frontline in places such as Northern Syria and Colombia to claim the unmediated right to land and water. Arsanios probes not only the ways in which ideology and theory coincide with living practices, but also asks whether those of us outside these circles of struggle can embody the answers.

In the fourth in the series, the artist takes the research, knowledge, and project's network to the north of Lebanon. The film we see is the beginning of a much longer effort that aims to set the groundwork for a different future. Arsanios's main goals in this endeavor are to communalize a section of private quarry in the mountains with the help of an agricultural cooperative, to work on the solutions for bettering the soil quality, and to make the local community part of the process.

In order to understand how to turn this particular land into a commons, the artist has initiated legal–historical research on other land ownership regimes in the region, dating from the Ottoman era (before the Industrial Revolution), during which farmers paid their taxes through working the land and keeping it fertile. The film bridges current acts of autonomy, seed protection, and land rights with older forms of land ownership. The idea of "taking matter into our own hands" takes on a new meaning in the context of Lebanon, which has experienced its crisis of dysfunction for some years now. Arsanios looks to the future, bringing together old and new knowledge, beyond ownership, to experiment with what is feasible in order to live and survive together before all codes, patterns, and habits of our world collapse completely.

Övül Ö. Durmuşoğlu

M

PROJECT IN
  COLLABORATION WITH
Maya Dghaidi (lawyer)
Wissam Saade
  (historian)
Amani Dagher and
  Wael Yammine from
  Soils Permaculture
  Association Lebanon
Further collaboration
  with the families
  of Mamlouk and
  Mohamad residing in
  the Batroun region,
  north of Lebanon

VENUE
⏺ Hafenstraße 76

MINI-MAJELIS
○ Atis Rezistans | Ghetto
  Biennale
○ Sourabh Phadke
○ yasmine eid-sabbagh
○ *foundationClass*collective

Marwa Arsanios

# MÁS ARTE MÁS ACCIÓN (MAMA)

MAMA reflects on climate change and deforestation by connecting the rainforests and their peoples in Colombia with the forests of Germany. In collaboration with Atelier Van Lieshout, who designed MAMA's residency space in Chocó, they have created the MAMA Doc Space next to the Orangerie, activated by members of their ekosistem of the Colombian Pacific and beyond.

In the Colombian Pacific there is the mangrove tree and the mangrove universe. The mangrove tree lives in the brackish water joining ocean to forest; the mangrove universe is the forest, the interconnected mangroves, with their complexity and rhythm, their fauna and water. There, tangled and tied by countless fibers, harmonious and pulsating, its meaning emerges—a symbol of life, of the world as a tangle.

Más Arte Más Acción (MAMA) has worked for ten years in a wooden house called the Chocó Base near Nuquí, a municipality in the tropical rainforest. It is embedded in the complexity of the beaches, rivers, and sea, and the Afro-Colombian and Indigenous communities that inhabit the region. Since its creation in 2011, MAMA has existed under the logic of mangrove entanglement, weaving a web to create ekosistems.

At its base, communities work with each other, and with artists, curators, museums, and funders from around the world. In this way, the foundation has succeeded, with more intensity than any other organization there, in creating ambitious interdisciplinary projects with the people of the region, and in unleashing individual and social processes of defense of the ekosistem and the vindication of cultural traditions, which are still in force today. Its value is decisive in a part of Colombia hit by armed conflict and drug trafficking, exclusion and poverty, extractivism and exploitation, and by the great threat of ekosistem destruction.

In Kassel, as a lumbung member of documenta fifteen, the foundation seeks to bring together artistic practices, political conceptions, ethnic and gender diversities, and to produce an "entanglement of cultural and artistic processes," as they call it. It has come, then, to build a network and an ekosistem here as well: to weave together artists, collectives, leaders, and academics; to unite conversations about climate justice, racial violence, about extractivism and the problems of progress—and to create its own forest.

In different parts of the city, the group has installed wooden stools cut from the trunks of the beetle-infested trees, small spaces for thinking, evoking the main function of Chocó Base. The work is a forest of soundscapes and wood from local beetle-infested forests that underscores the need for a common conversation about climate justice and biodiversity.

Camilo Jiménez Santofimio

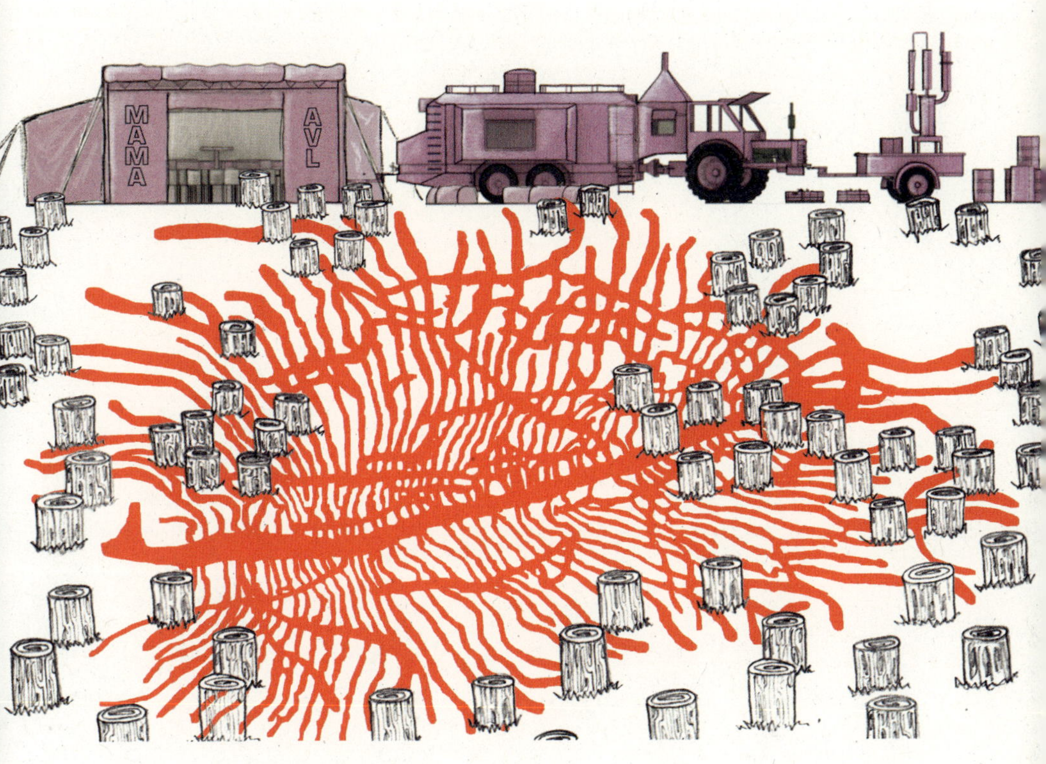

**VENUE**
- Ⓖ Greenhouse (Karlsaue)
- Ⓚ Karlswiese (Karlsaue)

**LUMBUNG INTER-LOKAL**
- ○ Britto Arts Trust
- ○ FAFSWAG
- ○ Fondation Festival sur le Niger
- ○ Gudskul
- ○ INLAND
- ○ Instituto de Artivismo Hannah Arendt (INSTAR)
- ○ Jatiwangi art Factory
- ○ OFF-Biennale Budapest
- ○ Project Art Works
- ○ The Question of Funding
- ○ Trampoline House
- ○ Wajukuu Art Project
- ○ ZK/U – Centre for Arts and Urbanistics

Más Arte Más Acción (MAMA)

*"For documenta fifteen, Más Arte Más Acción (MAMA) reflects on climate change and deforestation by connecting tropical rainforests and their peoples with the monoculture forests of Germany that are being destroyed by bark beetle infestations. Tree trunks from forests around Kassel that have been killed by beetles are installed in a glasshouse in the Aue Park, together with soundscapes. Stalls made from the trees are positioned around the park as spaces to reflect for visitors. Following their collaboration on the Chocó Base in 2012, MAMA has invited* Atelier Van Lieshout *to design the MAMA Doc Space that will be positioned between the Orangerie and Fulda River and host a documentation center and events during documenta fifteen.*

M

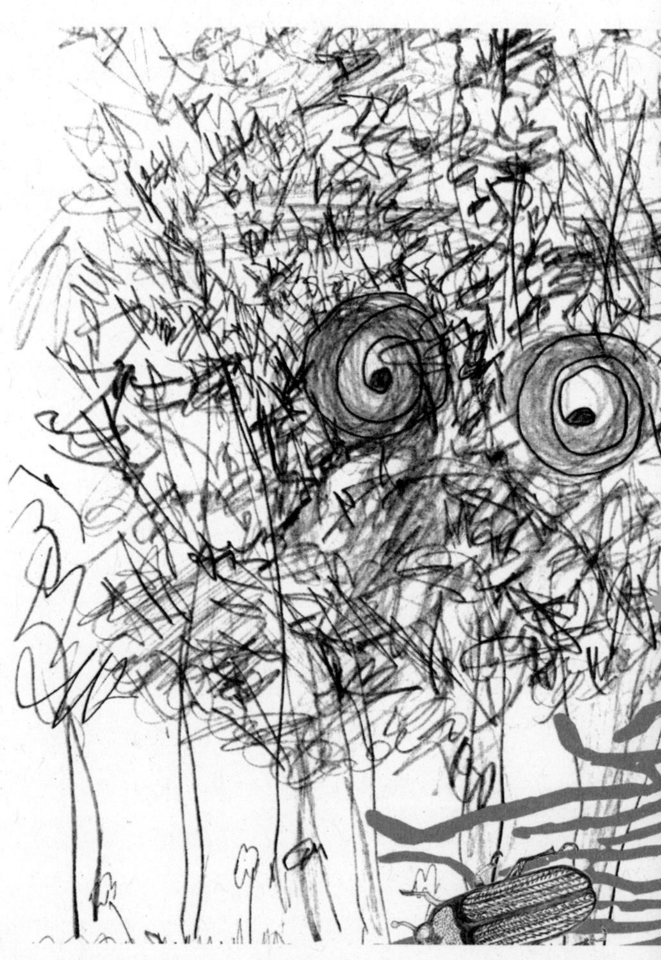

Collaborative Drawing by Fernando Arias
and El Honorable cartel, 2022

*Traces left by the beetles evoke MAMA's entanglement with its local ekosistem in Colombia. In this ekosistem, different ways of life, artistic practices, and relationships with the territory coexist. In MAMA's practice, Indigenous, Afro, and other groups that challenge the prevailing paradigm come together embracing differences, pursuing coexistence and expanding the limits of what is possible. Questions that have been raised in the past years of collaborations are shared in our MAMA Doc Space in Aue Park in the form of archives, film screenings, soundscapes, performances, dialogues, among others. The program comes to life with the participation of members of its ekosistem who are present throughout many of the 100 days of lumbung-building in Kassel."* — Más Arte Más Acción

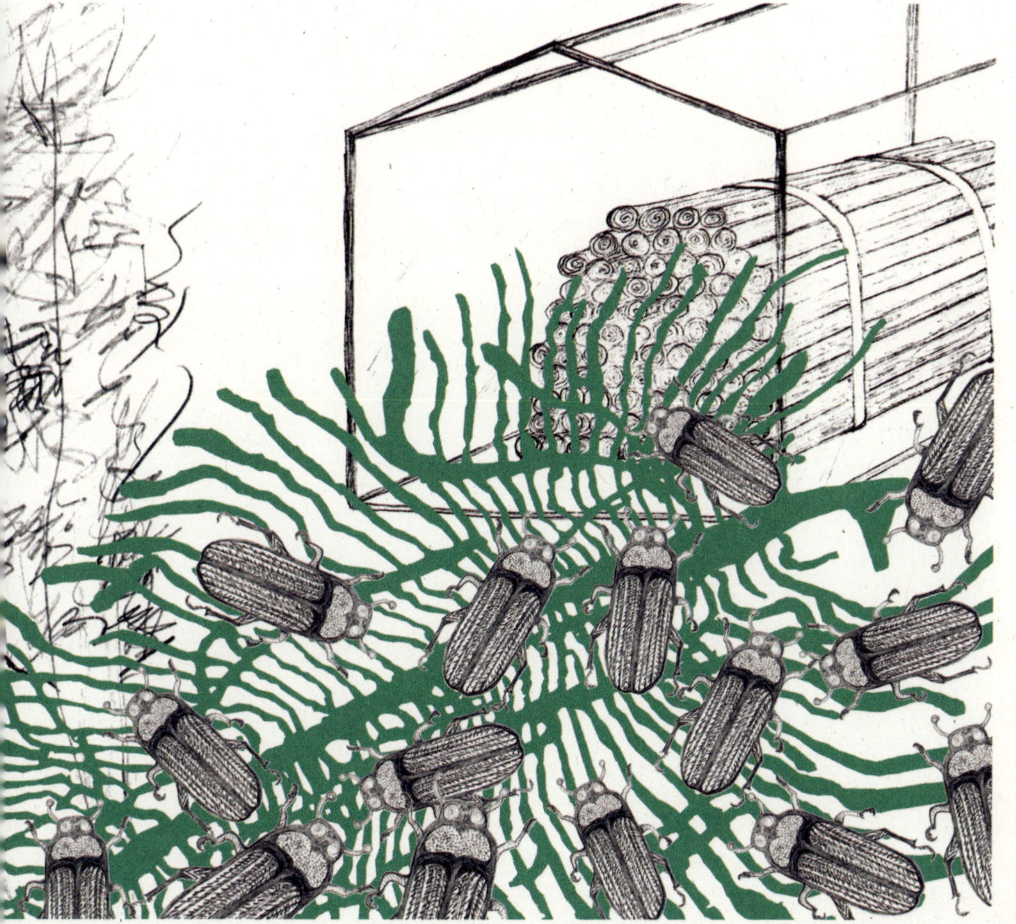

M

Más Arte Más Acción (MAMA)

# NGUYEN TRINH THI

Inspired by a vivid scene in a banned Vietnamese novel from 2000, Nguyen Trinh Thi stages an organic, hybrid media installation that is activated between Vietnam and Kassel, evoking ideas of political captivity and freedom.

Born in Hanoi, Vietnam, in 1973, Nguyễn Trinh Thi brings together her training in journalism, photography and ethnographic film to develop her artistic practice that uses archival footage and documentary, intermedial installations, and performances. Nguyễn creates interrogative essay film assemblages that use montage and episodic gestures. Her works engage with topics such as post-*đổi mới* Vietnam's fast-rising economy, expanding markets, political constraints, and the globalized circulation of images. Deeply concerned with themes of history, memory, land, indigeneity, ecology, and experimental aesthetic possibilities, Nguyen extends her practice through the curatorial and pedagogical activities of Hanoi DocLab (which she founded in 2009). These include screenings and filmmaking workshops that widen an appreciation and activation of audio-visual formats as an artistic methodology to represent contemporary Vietnamese life and its legacies.

At documenta fifteen, Nguyễn presents a new installation developed through working with organic materials and non-human forces, along with the experimental use of sound and image. The project is inspired by the auto-biographical novel *Tale Told in the Year 2000* by Bùi Ngọc Tấn, which was published in 2000, and immediately banned and destroyed. The novel depicts life in detention camps in northern Vietnam from the 1960s through 70s. The writer details the forests' flora and fauna: ecosystems that became sites where he and other prisoners were forced to perform hard labor. Tan also offers multiple reflections on freedom, including defining freedom as the taste of chili (which suggests a sense of home). Particularly evocative for Nguyễn is one fevered night scene where the prisoners stumble into a chili forest and become crazed and ravenous for its taste. The disruption results in the brutal shooting of an Indigenous ethnic minority prisoner.

At the Rondell in Kassel—with its historical torture chambers—Nguyễn resituates this *mise en scène* by presenting a sculptural installation of chili plant clusters. These are lit to project an immersive shadowy forest on its surrounding walls. A wind and wi-fi system set up in Vietnam's Vinh Quang-Tam Da area triggers the Kassel installation of fans, audiovisual effects, sound, and the haunting playing of the *sáo ôi* flute, an Indigenous musical instrument used by groups in the Northern mountainous areas including the Mường, Tày, and Nùng ethnic minorities. The installation maps the use of media technologies in artistic practice against the persistent anxieties of political oppression and surveillance, even within the context of the art-liberatory aspirations of global art events.

Annie Kael Kwan

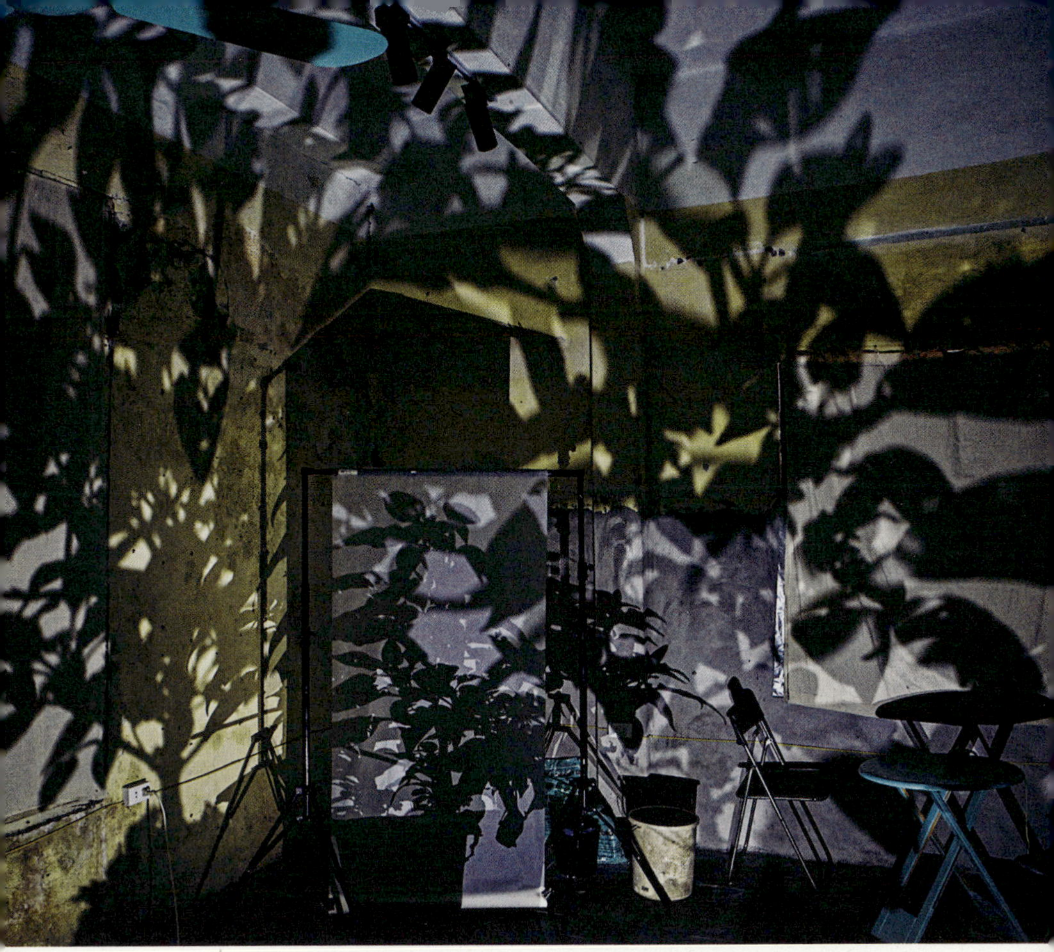

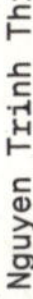



Landscape series #5: And They Die
a Natural Death, 2022
Light, shadows, chili plants, live
transmitted wind, automated flutes

*"The shadow of a chili forest is one of the two main performers in this trans-media work. The other performer is a set of žutes to be played automatically according to the wind that is live transmitted from a forest in northern Vietnam."* —*Nguyen Trinh Thi*

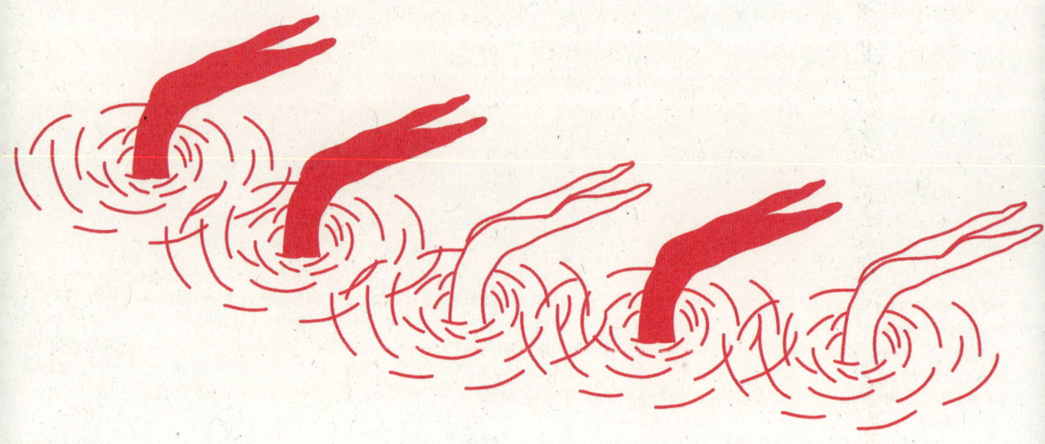

N



Drawing by Tuấn Mami

# NHÀ SÀN COLLECTIVE

For documenta fifteen, Nhà Sàn
Collective traces a metaphorical
connection from the Vietnamese *bến*
(wharf) to the Fulda River, transporting architectural materials
and community knowledge, performances, and joyful companionship.

Based in Hanoi, Vietnam, the formation of Nhà
Sàn Collective in 2013 can be traced back to Nhà
Sàn Studio, founded in 1998 by artists Nguyễn
Mạnh Đức and Trần Lương. Run from inside a
traditional house on stilts, it provided a hub for
the early development of contemporary art in
the city, drawing in younger artists and creatives.
Nhà Sàn (hut) provided a conceptual shelter for
artists seeking their critical and collective practices
amidst a landscape of precarity precipitated by
Vietnam's *đổi mới* policy of 1986 that unleashed a
set of fast-changing economic and cultural conditions. When Nhà Sàn was shut down in 2011 by
the authorities, Nhà Sàn Collective began working
with diverse disciplines and themes at different
temporary sites, presenting large-scale exhibitions,
screenings, workshops as well as a Queer Festival.

Rebuilding Nhà Sàn at *Ngọc Thụy* by the
Sông Hồng (Red River) is thus a hopeful collective
enterprise for a haven that will recuperate the materials from the old house, and reform them along
the shoreline between the city and nature, urban
dwellers and those on the periphery, its fishing
communities, artisanal heritage, and new horizons. The river that flows from Southwest China,
through Hanoi towards the Biển Đông / East Sea,
is the lifeline of movements of people, goods, and
ideas through Hanoi.

For documenta fifteen, Nhà Sàn Collective
traces a metaphorical connection from the Vietnamese bến (wharf) to the Fulda River, transporting the disassembled architectural materials, along
with its community and their lived experiences
and knowledge. The prefabricated architectural
intervention *Bến Kassel* recreates Nguyễn's space
and his beloved collection of wooden objects and
sculptures, utilising wood from his warehouse. By
the river in Kassel, two performance installations
stage their arrival. Nhà Sàn Collective and friends
invite visitors to join them in cultivating a garden
of migratory plants and narratives, joyful companionship inside a Queer House with a sauna, with
the celebratory imbibement of rice-based street
food and homemade wine, along with screenings,
discussions, and workshops.

Annie Jael Kwan

N



Nhà Sàn Collective

# NINO BULLING

Working in graphic arts, Nino Bulling's latest publication approaches the realities of climate change from a gender-fluid perspective.

Nino Bulling makes comics, illustrations, and books. Their practice is nonbinary: blurring the distinctions between fact and fiction and circulating freely between comic and contemporary art realms. Originally a student of ceramics and sculpture, Bulling turned to the comic form because of its accessibility and immediacy. They have worked flexibly within self-organized education spaces, the commercial illustration industry, and contemporary art institutions.

Bulling's previous works, published in both English and German, have communicated critical issues in contemporary culture. Their short story, *Water Level* (2020), speculates on environmentalism and the effects of climate change in the Brandenburg region of Germany. *Bruchlinien* (2019), or "fault lines" in English, is a graphic novel that explores the gendered undertones of right-wing terrorism and racism in Germany in relation to the infamous NSU trial.

While maintaining the political tenor of their previous works, Bulling's forthcoming and largest publication to date, titled *abfackeln* (firebugs), co-published by Colorama and Edition Moderne with the support of documenta fifteen, is decidedly more personal in nature. Equal parts hedonistic and poignant, and set against a backdrop of insidious climate change, *abfackeln* follows a couple who navigate the intermediary and ambiguous experiences of gender, intimacy, bodies, and kinship. The story embraces the realities of unresolved feelings and fluid self-presentations.

Underscoring Bulling's process-oriented and open-ended artistic methodology, *abfackeln* invites readers to stay with the unknown and interrogate the societal demand for fixed definitions, forms, and outcomes. For Bulling, the personal and processual intensities of, say, love, friendship, politics, and gender transition, cannot be compressed into any singular entity or art object.

At Hafenstrasse 76 Bulling will present selected drawings from *abfackeln*, as well as smaller hand-painted drawings on silk that expand on motifs and scenes from the book. Together with the Lebanon-based collective Samandal Comics, they are conducting a workshop with queer, trans and gender-nonconforming artists that will culminate in a collaboratively-created series of books, *Samandal*, to be published with Steidl and in conjunction with Kunsthaus Göttingen. Bulling is also part of a German comic artists' union: a nationwide network, currently in formation, that consists of about 15 comic artists. The union will officially inaugurate in September 2022. For documenta fifteen, the union is publishing a 60-page newspaper comprising comics, interviews, and a collective manifesto.

Wong Binghao

VENUE
⊕ Hafenstraße 76

MINI-MAJELIS
○ Arts Collaboratory
○ Black Quantum Futurism
○ Chimurenga
○ Jumana Emil Abboud
○ Agus Nur Amal PMTOH
○ Subversive Film

Ink and marker
21 × 29.7 cm

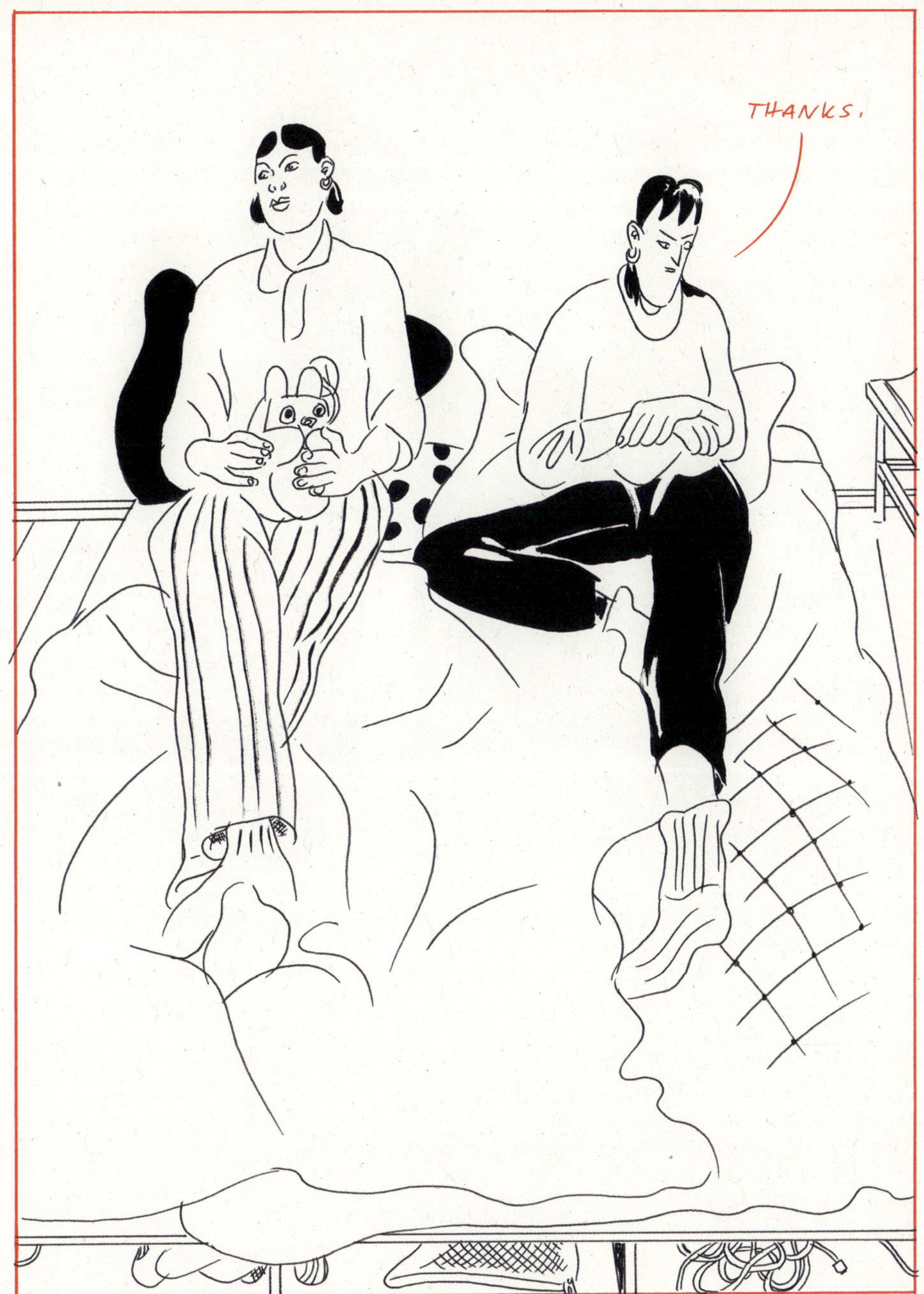


Nino Bulling

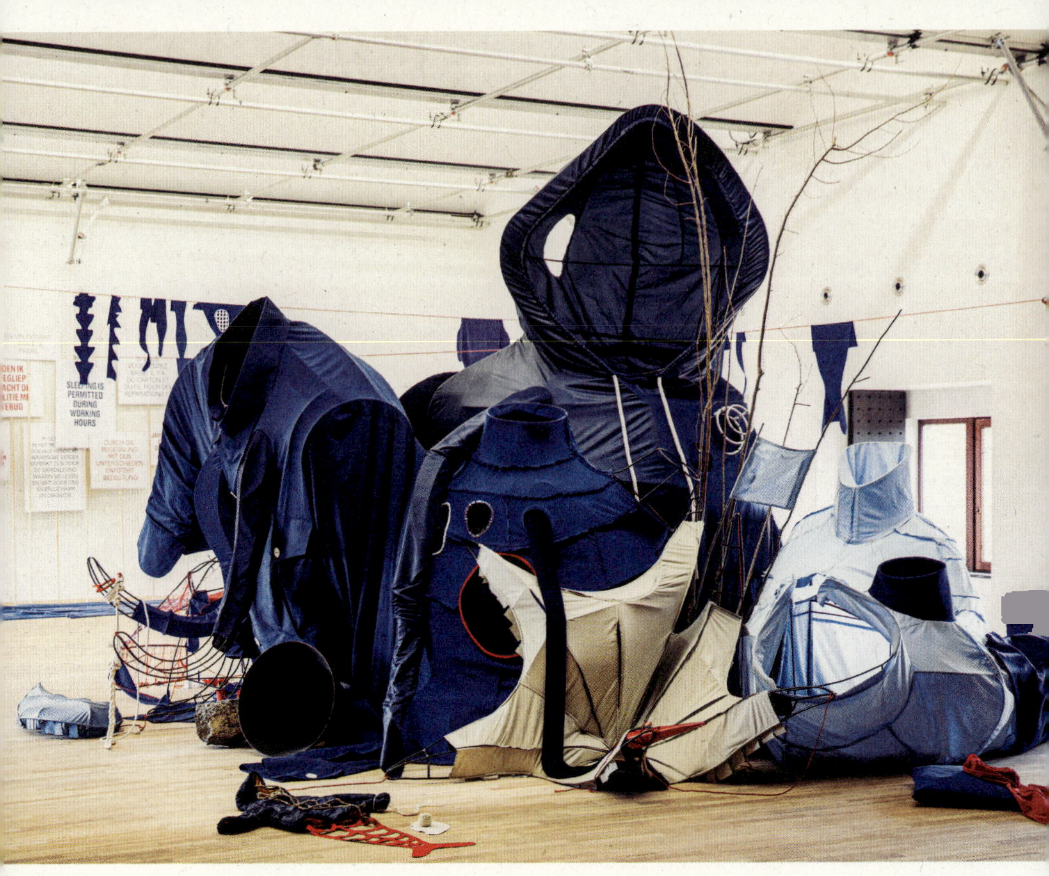



Eva Koťátková, *The Machine for Restoring Empathy* (2019) Installation view, STUK, Leuven, Belgium

## VENUES
⟁ Friedericianum
⟁ Bootsverleih Ahoi

## LUMBUNG INTER-LOKAL
○ Britto Arts Trust
○ FAFSWAG
○ Fondation Festival sur le Niger
○ Gudskul
○ INLAND
○ Instituto de Artivismo Hannah Arendt (INSTAR)

○ Jatiwangi art Factory
○ Más Arte Más Acción (MAMA)
○ Project Art Works
○ The Question of Funding
○ Trampoline House
○ Wajukuu Art Project
○ ZK/U – Center for Art and Urbanistics

# OFF-BIENNALE BUDAPEST

OFF-Biennale Budapest imagines and prefigures a playground and a Transnational Museum of Roma Contemporary Art.

OFF-Biennale Budapest (OFF) was established as a grassroots endeavor when a group of actors in Hungary's art scene came together to forge civil engagement through contemporary art. Since its founding in 2014, the initiative has existed through three editions and dozens of collaborations. Its activities attempt to establish a novel way of working in the cultural sector that is directed by government mandates: OFF refuses Hungarian state funding and, except for a few partnerships, rarely collaborates with state-run arts institutions.

In Kassel, OFF-Biennale presents two projects and a publication. One of them, a long-term collaborative project with the European Roma Institute for Arts and Culture (ERIAC), showcases artworks in relation to the idea, question, and (im)possibilities of a "RomaMoMA" (Roma Museum of Contemporary Art). How can the uncanonized cultural heritage and contemporary art by artists of Roma origin be presented in an exhibition setting when there has been no systematic attempts or institutions dedicated for this task? How can one define, and should one define, "Roma" and "Roma art," "Roma artist" in this context? In the framework of documenta fifteen the exhibition presents the untold past and the unfolding present through artworks and storytelling. The older and younger generations of artists, their differing artistic positions will be highlighted through an installation method that both constructs and deconstructs the idea of a "RomaMoMA," an imaginary, transnational space for the presentation of artworks.

OFF-Biennale's second contribution plays out in close proximity to the Fulda River as a space that oscillates between the concept of the playground, the junkyard, and the construction site—places of creativity, transgression, refuse, and regeneration. In and around the boathouse AHOI!, the space is being transformed by numerous actors—artists, collectives, architects, children communities—enacting construction, creativity, and the building of social systems.

Just as storytelling offers the possibility to reveal unheard or silenced realities, in contrast to canonized narratives, here it becomes—in the context of a playground—a method to foster free play and construction in a tactical way that understands the world along different correlations. Play not only mimics or symbolizes, but also rewrites and prefigures the ways individuals or communities engage and work with each other, while creating and recreating the social domain, an interlocking web of interactions. Although the projects presented are mostly made from simple (construction or used) materials, they use the power of imagination (from daydreaming to social and ecological utopias), to experiment with models of collaboration and collective action—to explore their possibilities as well as their limitations.

The playground is a space and time that is part of the reality that surrounds it, yet it is independent from it. It is a place for questioning, for rejecting, for risk-taking, for trying out, and for correcting reality with unconventional solutions, auto-telism, and sensitive modes of action, a well-defined area where it's fence—imaginary or concrete—marks out a space for thinking about what could be beyond the horizon.

OFF's projects are accompanied by a publication that examines the many aspects of the notion of "independence" as well as the power of collectivity. It is realized by the editorial platform On the Same Page that was initiated as an experimental publication method under the umbrella of OFF-Biennale Budapest, involving the participants and organizers of its 2021 edition.

Krzysztof Kościuczuk

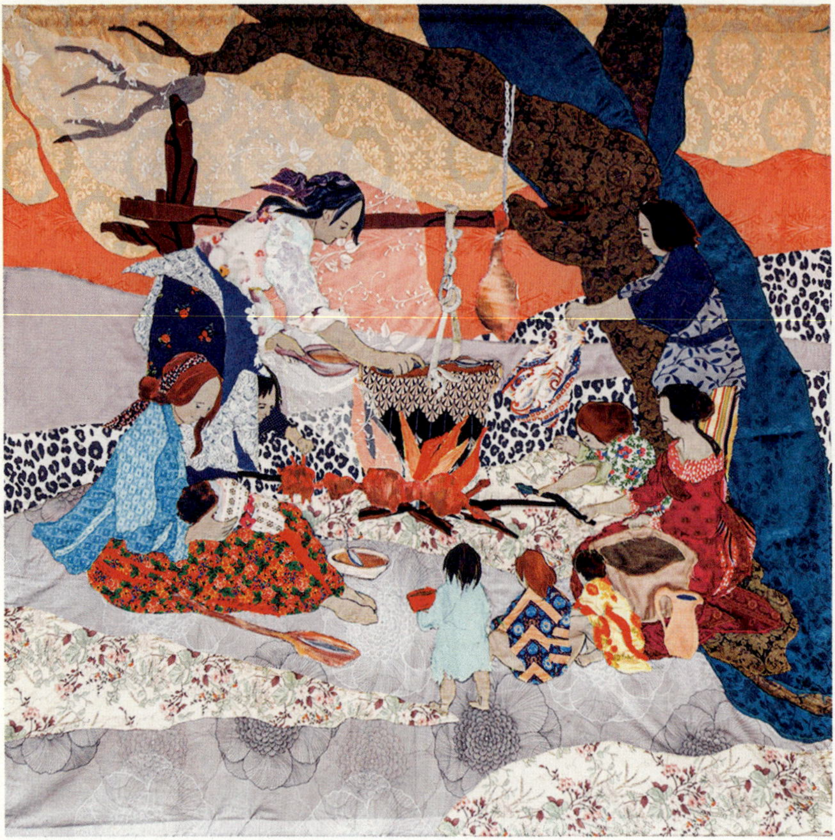

Małgorzata Mirga-Tas, from the series *Out of Egypt* (2021)
Mixed media, dimensions variable

**ONE DAY WE SHALL CELEBRATE AGAIN:**
*RomaMoMA @ documenta fifteen*
**Participating artists:**
Daniel Baker
János Balázs
Robert Gabris
Sead Kazanxhiu
Damian Le Bas
Małgorzata Mirga-Tas
Omara
 (Mara Oláh)
Otto Pankok
Tamás Péli
Selma Selman
Ceija Stojka
**Co-curators:**
Daniel Baker
Ethel Brooks
Tímea Junghaus
Miguel Ángel Vargas

**Curators:**
Hajnalka Somogyi
Eszter Szakács
Katalin Székely (Off-Biennale Budapest)
**Collaborating Institution:**
Eriac (European Roma Institute For Arts And Culture)
**Consultants:**
Eszter György
Angéla Kóczé / Ceu Romani Studies
Anna Lujza Szász
Teri Szücs
**Contributor:**
East Europe Biennial Alliance

**WHAT IFS AND WHY NOTS:**
*OFF-Playground*
**Participating artists:**
Auw (Architecture Uncomfortable Workshop) / Emil Dénes Ghyczy & Lukács Szederkényi
Ádám Kokesch
Eva Koťátková
Ilona Németh
The Randomroutines / Tamás Kaszás & Krisztián Kristóf
Recetas Urbanas
**Curators:**
Nikolett Erőss
Eszter Lázár
Borbála Szalai
Katalin Székely (OFF-Biennale Budapest)

**Collaborating Institution:**
Unterneustädter Schule

**ON THE SAME PAGE**
*(Editorial platform)*
**Editors:**
Rita Kálmán
Lívia Páldi
Katarina Šević

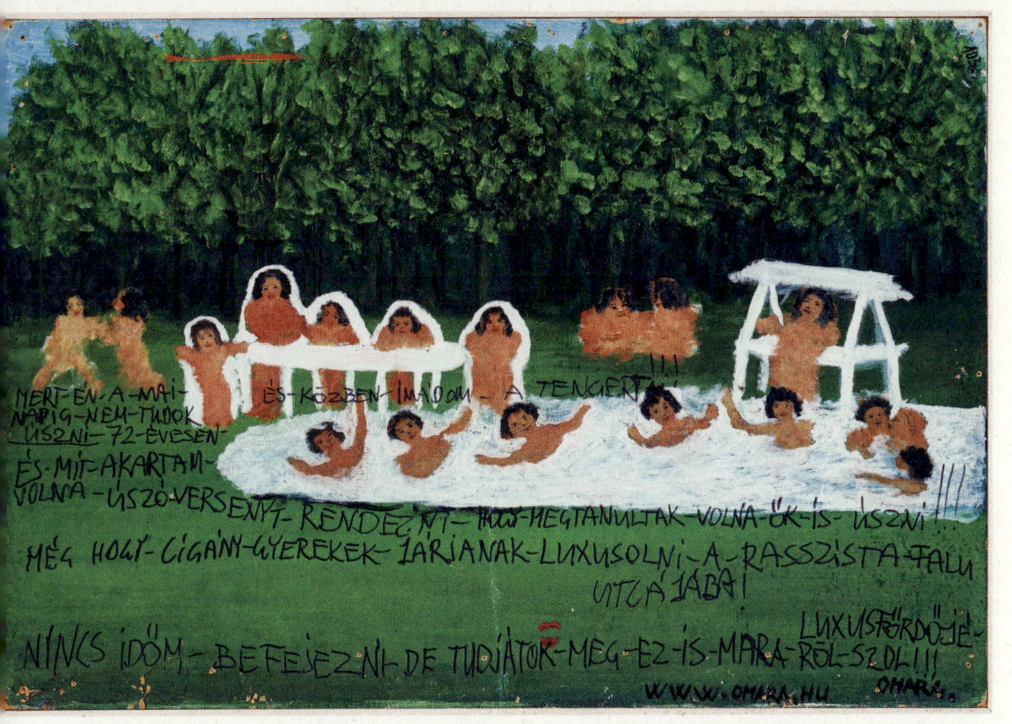


Mara Oláh (Omara), Because I can't swim - at the age of 72 - and I love the sea !!! And what I wanted - to organize a swimming race - that they would have learned to swim !!!" Even the Gypsy children have this luxury - into the street of the racist village! - I have no time to finish - but you should know this is about Mara's luxury bath!!! (2008-2017). Mixed media on wood panel, 70 × 100 cm

# OOK_ [REINAART VANHOE, NEUE BRÜDER-KIRCHE, ESPORA, BPOC FESTIVAL KASSEL, ME_SOBAT, COLORLABOR, GRAANSCHUUR TARWEWIJK, ELAINE W. HO, BARTIRA, WOK THE ROCK, COLLECTIVE, K. FORMAT, TAKE-A-WAY, PLAN B, *DYNAMITAS UNLIMITED* ...]

ook_ have developed the ook_ visitorZentrum, a shrine for collectivism and horizontality.

What is at stake in developing practices that center around making spaces and meeting people? Informal spaces can function as channels to practice being an inhabitant in a social environment. Listening and sharing voices are the main principles guiding the activities of these spaces. This act produces a vocabulary of listening to and appreciating voices.

Making space and meeting people are central to reinaart vanhoe's art. Everyday activities connect vision and plans for how a space is inhabited and activated in practice. In his study of independent cultural spaces and art collectives in Indonesia and China, reinaart refers to his vision of a space as "also space." The meaning of space is flexible, depending on the needs of the context where it is situated. In Rotterdam, the Netherlands, reinaart and his partner, mariëlle verdijk, opened up their house and turned it into ook_huis — a free space for neighbors and friends. To refer to himself, reinaart goes by "ook_". It is also a way to acknowledge collaborations with other people.

For documenta fifteen, ook_ has collaboratively developed ook_visitorZentrum on Weserstraße 26. ook_ consists of various groups of friends, which are also part of the collective's growing name: ook_ [reinaart vanhoe, Neue Brüderkirche, Espora, BPOC Festival Kassel, me_sobat, Colorlabor, graanschuur Tarwewijk, Elaine W. Ho, Bartira, Wok The Rock, COLLECTive, k. format, Take-A-Way, Plan B, *Dynamitas unlimited* ...]. The organization of the space yields more collaborations with different individuals and collectives. To activate the space, the "shrine" concept is appropriated in its literal and metaphorical meanings. In this context, a shrine is divorced from its ascribed meaning as a holy place to host memorabilia and religious relics. The familiarity of the concept is used as a tool and reason to be together with others. The idea of a shrine materializes a space for collectivism and horizontality. It opens up possibilities to problematize the relational positions of the shrine groups, the continuously changing roles of guest and host, in local contexts. Knowledge productions and exchanges are the core activities of the ook_visitorZentrum. Collective intelligence emerges in the process.

Nuraini Juliastuti

*"ook_ members discuss various ideas and share opinions on organizational formats, common ground, and what lumbung means in our context. Together, we watch lumbung konteks, a video program where lumbung members share stories, songs, and tools to get insight into documenta fifteen."—ook_*

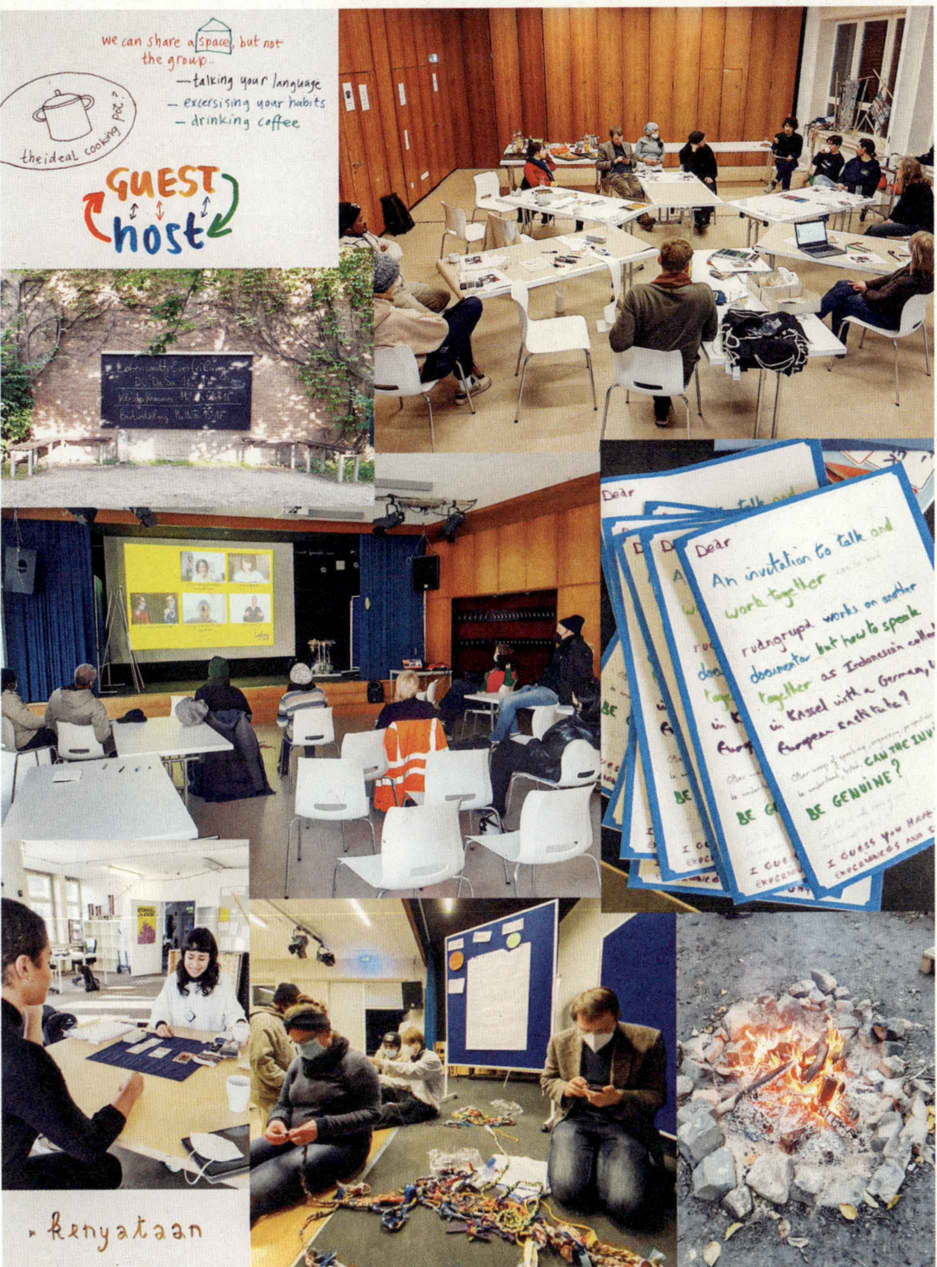




ook_ [reinaart vanhoe, Neue Brüderkirche, Espora, BPOC Festival Kassel, me_sobat, Colorlabor, graanschuur Tarwewijk, Elaine W. Ho, Bartira, Wok The Rock, COLLECTive, k. format, Take-A-Way, Plan B, *Dynamitas unlimited* ...]


**VENUES**
- Ⓡ ruruHaus
- Ⓦ Weserstraße 26

**MINI-MAJELIS**
- ○ ikkibawiKrrr
- ○ Richard Bell
- ○ Taring Padi
- ○ Wakaliga Uganda

*"The acknowledgement of social hegemony carries the ghost of its anti-thesis, social care. Those of us at the margins should consider our desire as central to our lives. Such radical figures in proximity perform the nurturance of queer kinships and care as a pivotal form of labour. A site of resilience, radical pleasure and collective power. At Party Office we play, rest and rave, all of which are denigrated as non-productive actions by the neo-liberal order."*
— *Party Office b2b Fadescha*

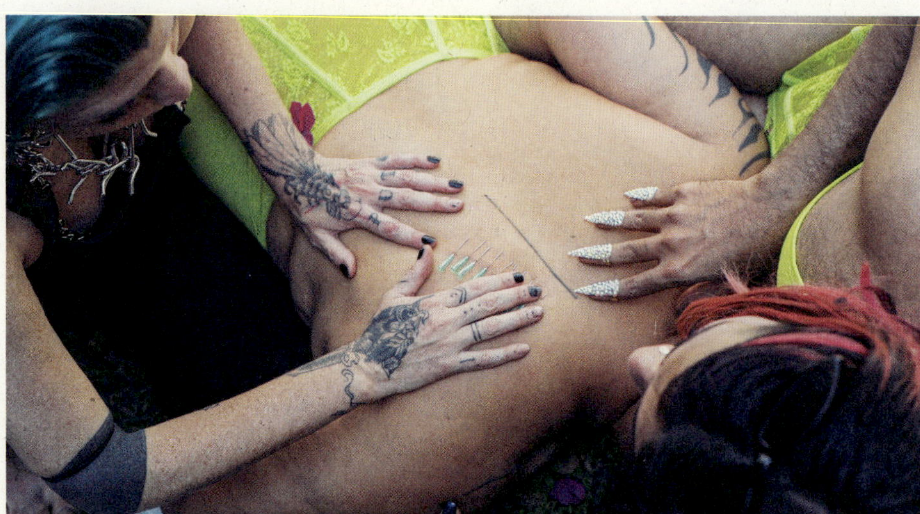

Vidisha-Fadescha,
Qworkaholics Anonymous II (2022)
Two-channel video

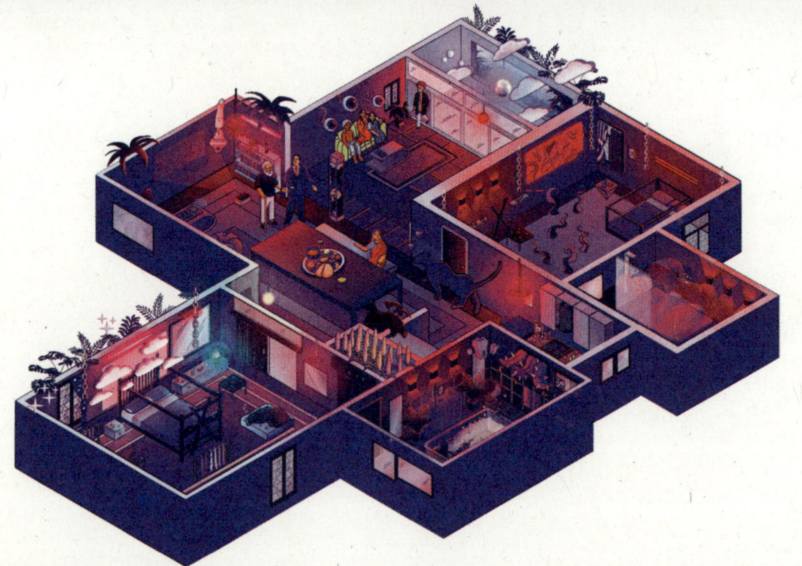

Party Office at New Delhi (2022),
illustration by Jonathan Eden

# PARTY OFFICE B2B FADESCHA

Party Office b2b Fadescha reimagines an inclusive celebration for crip and kink subjectivities, encouraging visitors to play and rest.

Launched in 2020 in a private home in New Delhi, India, Party Office is an independent artist-run initiative aimed at bringing together two different architectural and social concepts: *the party*, referencing a gathering, and also politics; and *the office*, a place of labor. Investigating the commons through trans-national dialogues, fellowship, residency, publications, and parties, it's an attempt to reconfigure public consciousness towards empathetic futures. Framed within this invitation of care is an unapologetically political agenda of creating an inclusive and intersectional, anti-caste, anti-racist, anti-fascist, trans-feminist, queer-crip and kink-celebratory space.

This hospitable space invites conversations and positive acknowledgement and representation, as ways to resist and counter the dominance and subjugation of oppressive power structures towards marginalized communities. Party Office is founded and hosted by artist-curator Vidisha-Fadescha, drawing from their lived social experiences and counter-normative institution building. At the small wine cellar, at WH22, Fadescha's video series "Qworkaholics Anonymous" continues with a two-channel video installation and soundscape, performed by Kinkinella, Shaunak Mahbubani, and Vidisha. The series plays on the format of deaddiction programs like Alcoholics Anonymous, inviting friends, activists, and kinksters to "do nothing" in safe company as a pushback against neoliberal pressures of hyper-productivity.

This satellite iteration of Party Office at Kassel is co-curated with Shaunak Mahbubani, and curatorial advisors Ali Akbar Mehta, Jyotsna, Ramya Patnaik, Joey Cannizzaro, Vidha Saumya, Aru, Amrish Kondurkar, and Abhinit Khanna. At documenta fifteen, Party Office b2b Fadescha draws from the collective's interdisciplinary praxis through the curatorial framework "Queer Time: Kinships & Architecture." The larger wine cellar becomes a multi-functional party space, dungeon, dark room, reading room, public programming space, open to collaborations and community gathering. The project centers on crips and kink subjectivities in acknowledging how disability and deviance have often been excluded from social participation, and to reimagine an inclusive celebration. At their atmospheric site, Party Office b2b Fadescha invites visitors to shake off the burden of self-actualization via productivity imposed by the legacies of the colonial project, and instead seek party, play, pleasure, rest, and rehabilitation.

P

Annie Jael Kwan

VENUE
ⓦ WH22

MINI-MAJELIS
○ Alice Yard
○ Erick Beltrán
○ LE 18
○ MADEYOULOOK
○ Serigrafistas queer

# PINAR ÖĞRENCİ

Pınar Öğrenci's new film *Aşît* is inspired by Stefan Zweig's final novella—a psychological thriller in which chess becomes a survival mechanism in the face of fascism.

Displacement, migration, survival, and resistance are cornerstones of Pınar Öğrenci's documentary-based films and installations. Driving her works are difficult, everyday struggles: the stories she observes, experiences, and documents from different geographies. A personal resonance tinges these narratives: she was forced to move to Berlin from Istanbul, Turkey, as a result of the current regime's stance against Kurdish peace. Persistent is her background in eastern Anatolia: an oppressive geography for non-Muslim and non-Turkish peoples; a place of silenced roots and armed struggle, a sense of constant unsettlement, and normalized mourning.

In earlier works, Öğrenci followed the rarely-told stories of migrating communities around the Mediterranean, the Aegean, and in Berlin. For *Aşît* (2022), her new film for documenta fifteen, Öğrenci returns to her father's hometown, Müküs, within the mountainous region in southern Van. On Turkey's border with Iran, this former capital of the Urartian civilization, and the Armenian Vaspuragan dynasty, today has a dense urban population of mainly Kurdish speaking communities. Müküs is known as Bahçesaray to the Turkish, Moks to Armenians, and Müküs or Miksi to the Kurdish. The town enjoyed a multilingual education and heritage in Armenian, Kurdish, Farsi, and Arabic until 1915.

*Aşît* is inspired by Stefan Zweig's final novella *The Royal Game* (*Schachnovelle*, 1941)—a psychological thriller in which chess becomes a survival mechanism in the face of fascism. Through the tale of a chess game with no winner, Öğrenci's film reconstructs the story of Müküs.

Öğrenci turns to Hayrik Muradyan, an Armenian musician who escaped Van, Turkey in 1918 to hear the impressive landscape of Müküs. She traces everyday survival strategies and cultural facets of the people of Müküs, facing the pressures of state and religion, as enacteed by the police and the mosque, together with the songs Muradyan collected from his homeland. *Aşît*, meaning avalanche and disaster in Kurdish, refers both to the threat of avalanche that disconnects Müküs from the rest of the world and to *"Meds Yegher"* (The Big Disaster) in 1915, when 1.5 million Armenians were deported, killed, or forced to leave Anatolia. The film is also an act of mourning. Sewn handkerchiefs, which she has been using in her recent works, reappear as an installation element; individual and collective symbol of mourning and love.

Övül Ö. Durmuşoğlu

VENUES
◍ Hessisches Landesmuseum

MINI-MAJELIS
○ Hamja Ahsan
○ Jimmie Durham
○ La Intermundial Holobiente
○ Saodat Ismailova

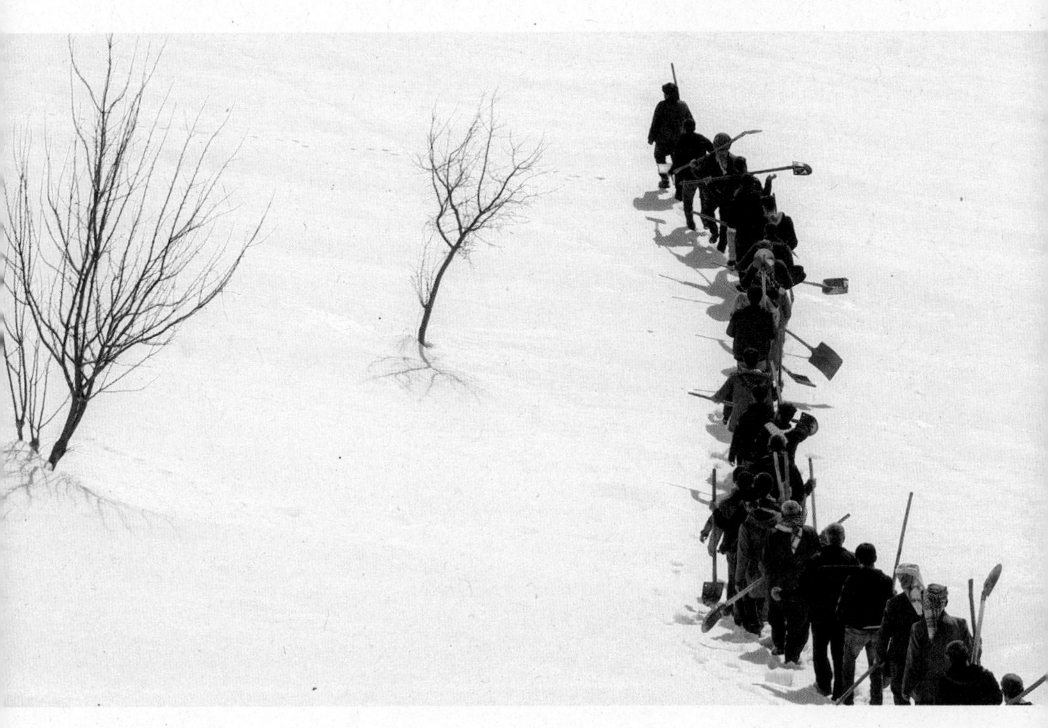

Pınar Öğrenci
Aşıt (Avalanche / Lawine) (2022)
Film still

Pınar Öğrenci

167

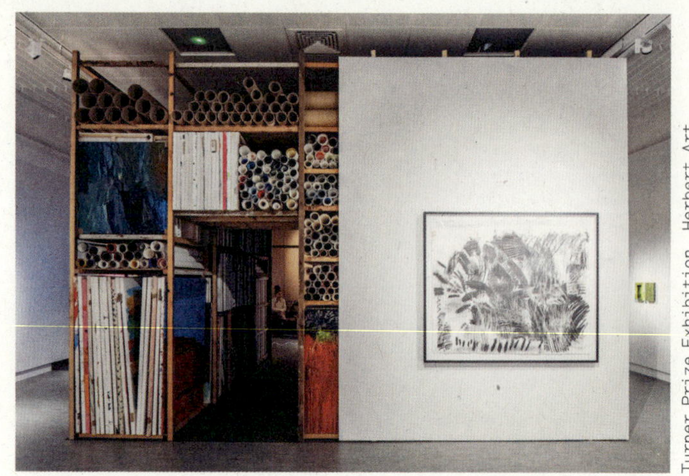

Turner Prize Exhibition, Herbert Art<br>Gallery & Museum, Coventry, UK, 2021

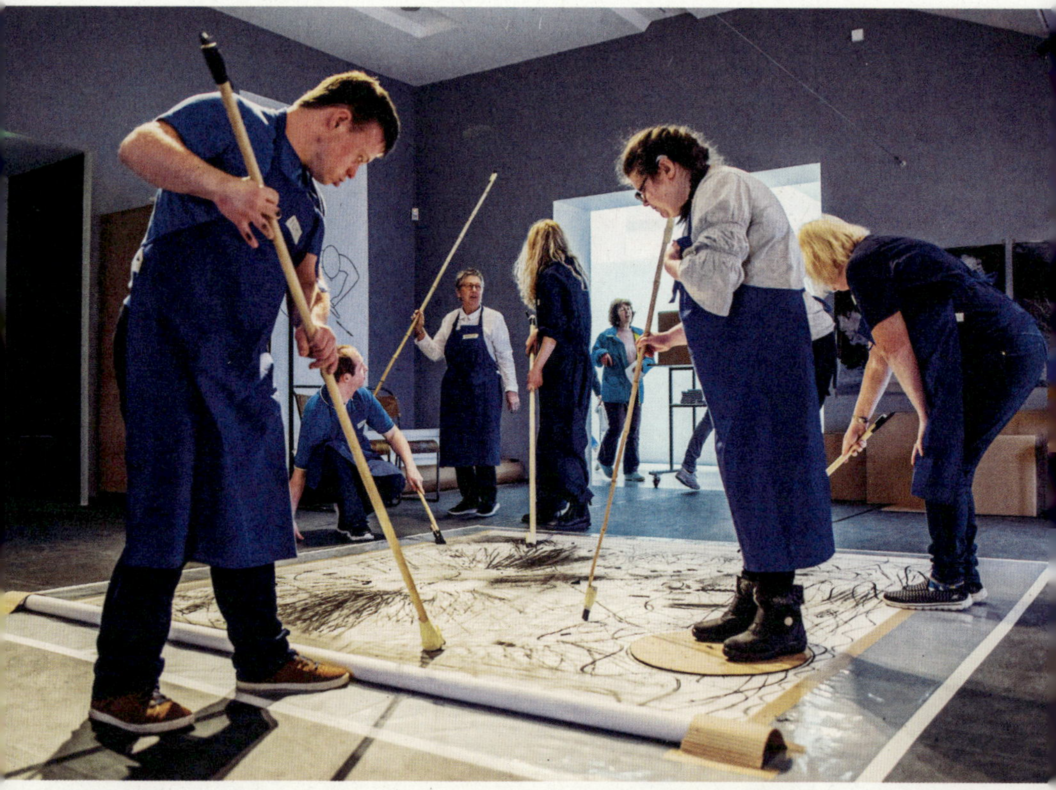

EXPLORERS, Tate Liverpool, UK, 2019

# PROJECT ART WORKS

In studio and exhibition spaces, and through workshops, Project Art Works casts light on the work of people living and working in neuro-diverse ways.

How can we construct an artistic terrain that encourages inclusive forms of mutual support and care? Many values long associated with art-making still contain ableist elements. What do terms such as "productivity", "practice", or "success" mean for those whose lives orient themselves along heterogenous understandings of those terms?

Project Art Works was founded in 1997 in Hastings, UK, by artists Kate Adams and Jonathan Cole in order to explore collaborative creative freedom, visibility, and advocacy alongside people who have complex support needs. Informed directly by experience, the organization is a collective of more than 60 neurodiverse artists, activists, and caregivers. They use a broad set of artistic and holistic practices to realize understanding, representation, and rights for neurominorities.

Project Art Works' contributions to documenta fifteen are oriented around their collaborations with local individuals and groups, the revelations of these interpersonal connections, and the search for universal constants within art and care. An evolving installation at the Fridericianum includes paintings and drawings and recreates their studio environment in Hastings, with rubber flooring and cardboard sheeting on walls; the large archival structure contains artworks and films within its wooden framework. The space becomes a constructed proposition for action, for fundamental human and creative connection, and for change.

The works displayed include an evolving series of large-scale drawings, *cosmologies of care*. These are created through facilitated conversations and encounters within the lumbung, with artists, different participating groups, and audiences in order to articulate the complex networks of relationships and systems that form models of care from around the world, and are shown with a sound installation of voices and environments of neurominorities and caregivers.

A core component of their documenta project is continuously in-the-making, as process. At the Stadtmuseum, the space is used in a hybrid way, as an exhibition and working space. There, workshops with small groups form part of documenta's Meydan program, and provide a welcoming access point for diverse audiences and invited groups—generating new, large-scale, collaboratively-made solar prints and drawings.

The contributions of Project Art Works for documenta fifteen are examples of how to reframe the scope of artmaking by nurturing sustainable everyday practices through the work of people living and working in neurodiverse ways, including their communities of care. More broadly, these practices challenge us all to reconsider art-making in a liberatory way, unconstrained by ableist and other discriminatory forms. In affirming intentionality and creativity, they propose a frame of art-making that can be accessed by all.

Pablo Larios

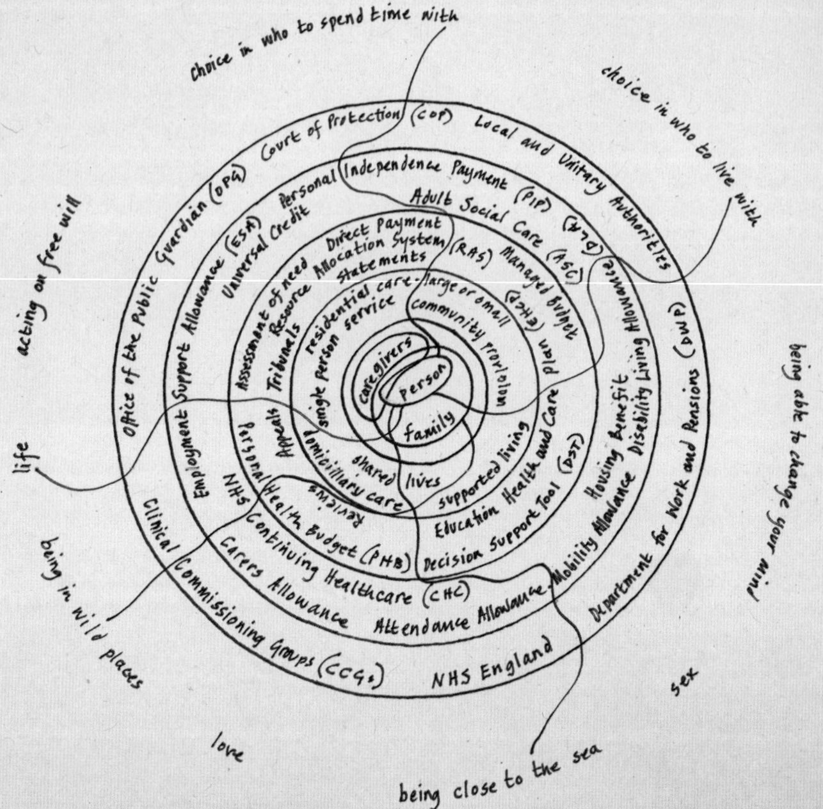

choice in who to spend time with
choice in who to live with
acting on free will
being able to change your mind
life
being in wild places
love
being close to the sea
sex
Court of Protection (COP)
Local and Unitary Authorities
Office of the Public Guardian (OPG)
Personal Independence Payment (PIP)
Employment Support Allowance (ESA)
Universal Credit
Adult Social Care (ASC)
Assessment of need
Direct Payment
Resource Allocation System (RAS)
Managed Budget
Tribunals
Statements
Person
family
caregivers
residential care - large or small
single person service
community provision
Appeals
domiciliary care
shared lives
supported living
plan
Personal Health Budget (PHB)
NHS
Review
Education Health and Care
Decision Support Tool (DST)
Housing Benefit
Disability Living Allowance
Mobility Allowance
Department for Work and Pensions (DWP)
Continuing Healthcare (CHC)
Carers Allowance
Attendance Allowance
Clinical Commissioning Groups (CCGs)
NHS England

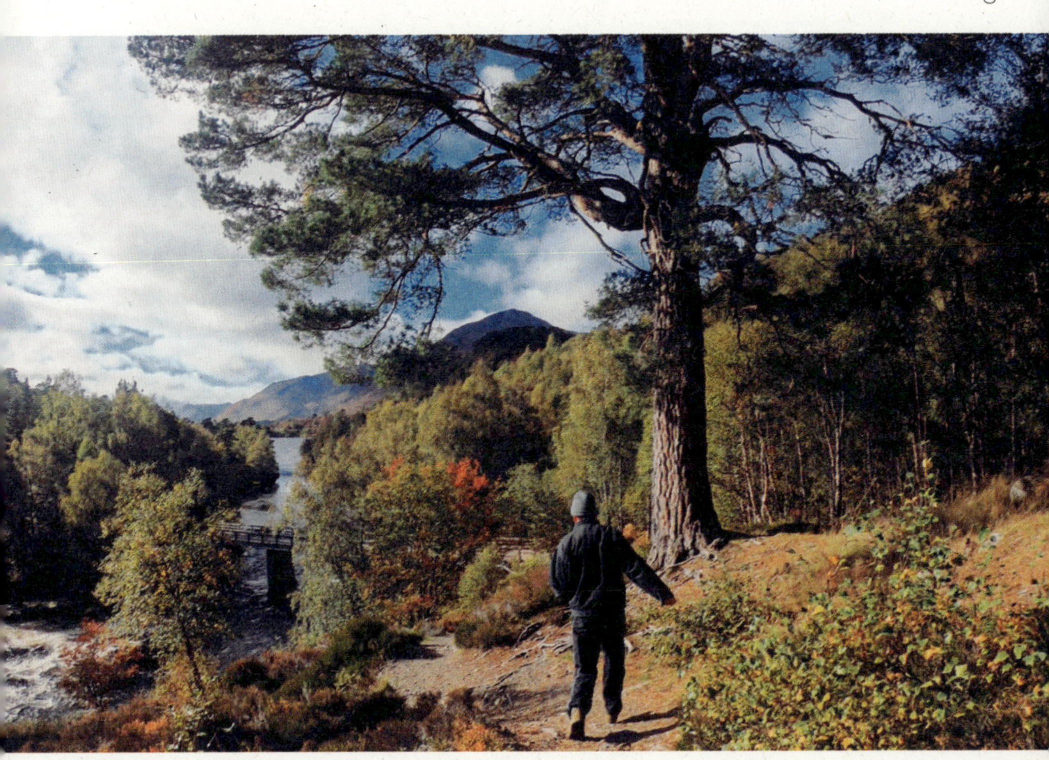

George Smith, *Illuminating the Wilderness* (2018)

# RICHARD BELL

Richard Bell's work bears witness to a long history of anti-colonial struggle—his *Tent Embassy* is an emblem and space for solidarity around the world.

The Aboriginal Tent Embassy celebrated its 50th anniversary in January 2022. The three-day event was organized to honor the strength of Indigenous sovereignty, their care for country, and ongoing Black resistance against the Australian settler colony through warriors past, present, and generations to come.

It has been 50 long years of resistance since First Nations activists set up camp under a beach umbrella in front of Parliament House in Canberra, Australia. At a time of global anticolonial struggle and Black Power, the Australian state could not reject Indigenous demands for land rights and reparations without facing mass opposition. Since 1972, the Tent Embassy has inspired camps across the continent, established at frontier land struggles that evolve with each new generation of activists.

Richard Bell's *Tent Embassy* (2013–ongoing) is a part of this legacy. Bell is from the Kamilaroi, Kooma, Jiman, and Goreng Goreng nations. His project for documenta fifteen features the humble tent that has traveled many exhibitions, this time in Friedrichsplatz. *Tent Embassy* seeks to facilitate cultural sharing, political discourse, and solidarity with struggles around the world. All talks are recorded and uploaded online for anyone to access. Along with lumbung artists, members and Europe-based speakers, Bell invites Digi Youth Arts—a Meanjin-based (Brisbane) organization—to contribute. Led by young Indigenous slam poets, rappers, dancers, filmmakers, and visual artists, it cultivates and amplifies Aboriginal and Torres Strait Islander youth stories and leadership through arts practices.

Bell's protest and text paintings from the 1970s and 1980s are on display alongside a new iteration of his Duchampian urinal, now attached to colorful, shiny, metallic balloons (alluding to a Jeff Koons-led shiny art movement). *Metronome* features a continuously counting sign— recalling the Union Square *Metronome* in New York City— which shows the debt owed to Aboriginal people by the Australian government from 1901 (the date of Federation) to present. If the original *Metronome* is an obscure digital hourglass that attempts to show time "draining," Bell's new *Metronome* ticks away to algorithmically calculate the unfinished business of colonization through commercial rents, residential rents, parking fees, and other costs. When I spoke to Bell by phone, he said: "we know that they owe us more than they can ever repay."

Carol Que

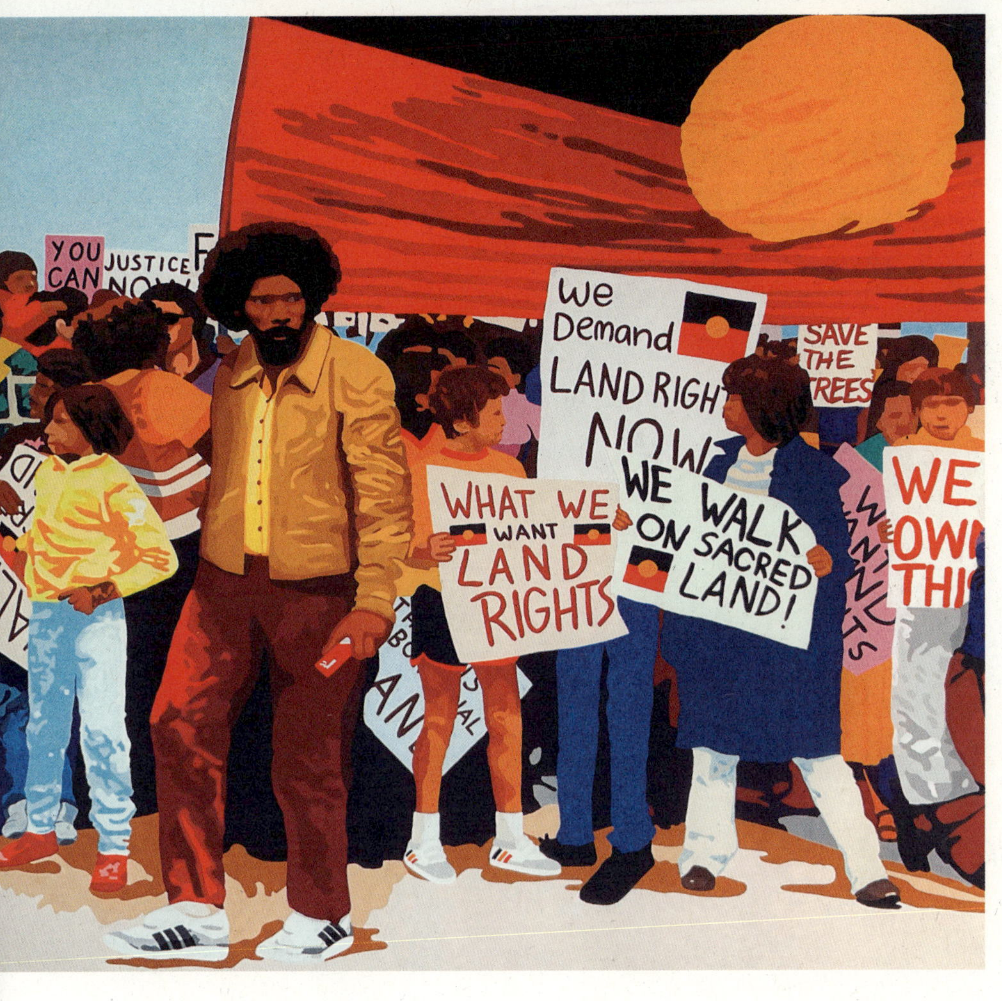


Richard Bell
Sol (2021)
Acrylic on canvas
2 × 2 m



Richard Bell

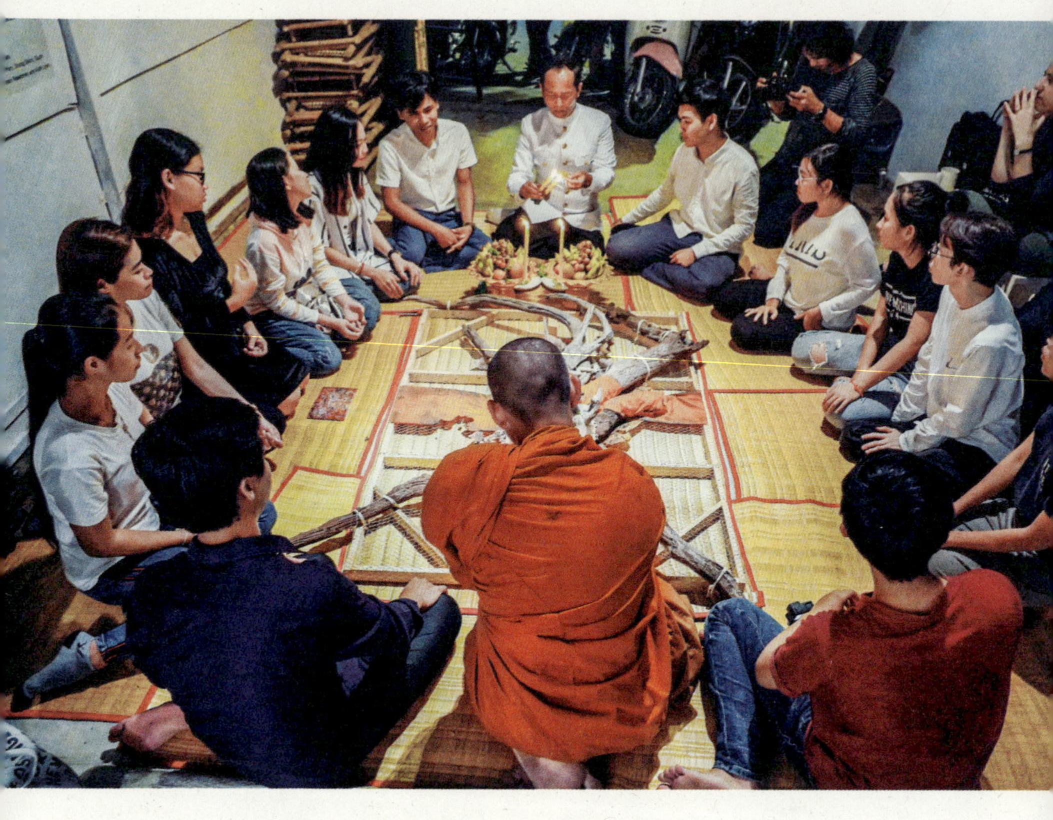

A Bangvil Popil ritual with a sculptural work by Chap Vichet, *The Sadness of Loss* (2019)

# SA SA ART PROJECTS



Set up by artist collective Stiev Selapak in 2010, Sa Sa Art Projects is an artist-run initiative based in Phnom Penh, Cambodia, known for their experimental and relational approach. Their main goals are clear-minded: first, to support young Cambodian artists in their creative practice and critical thinking; and, second, to build stronger communities through facilitating and instigating shared cultural and artistic experiences that are lacking in Cambodia. By community, they mean a new generation of artists and art audiences who can support the arts long-term—internationally, though first and foremost in Cambodia, where the specter of genocide and intergenerational trauma after authoritarian and corrupt states (from the 1970s on) still looms.

Sa Sa's project for documenta fifteen is titled *Dar Lean* (2022), the name of a Cambodian ritual undertaken after the rice harvest season. During Dar Lean, farmers return to share food, exchange ideas, rest, and reflect with one another, whilst celebrating and paying their respects to the lands and waters. Sa Sa wants to keep Dar Lean's spirit of strengthening solidarity alive in two physical sites between Phnom Penh and Kassel; the project is an attempt to facilitate an art ekosistem between Cambodia and the world.

With documenta fifteen funds, a community studio has been set up in Phnom Penh, in order to practically address the lack of accessible working spaces for local artists and offering pragmatic support and enrichment for artists and art collectives who are at the stage of forming and defining their purpose. The space facilitates exchange and collaboration with regional and international guests, including other lumbung artists.

In Kassel, meanwhile, Sa Sa is working with Sandershaus, a warehouse space-turned-multi-function community space, hostel, and temporary accommodation for refugees, many of whom co-organize events and programs there. People from all over the world—from different cultures and class backgrounds—stay at this hostel, where there is additionally a dynamic extended community of queer and trans performers. In conjunction with documenta fifteen, Dorf22—a collective of associations and groups including farmers, workers, students, and architects—has built a flexible architectural structure within Sandershaus. Similar to the residencies Sa Sa hosts, where visiting artists are encouraged to offer something to the Phnom Penh community, Sa Sa is learning from, co-designing and offering a series of engaging events and programs to Sandershaus, the broader Kassel community as well as Cambodian communities in Germany. Their spirit of engagement is to be open and fluid, to listen to local needs so as to not predetermine or override agency from the beginning; whilst still remaining true to their principles in building and leaving behind an infrastructure.

Carol Que



MINI-MAJELIS
O Amol K Patil
O BOLOHO
O Cao Minghao & Chen Jianjun
O Chang En-Man

# SADA [REGROUP]

Sada [regroup] presents films from a selection of artists who came together through Sada in Baghdad from 2010-2015, and who have now contributed films from Iraq, France, Turkey, and the US.

Sada, meaning "echo" in Arabic, was conceived as Sada for Iraqi Art by the Baghdad-born Rijin Sahakian. Sahakian set up the initiative, which ran from 2011 to 2015, in order to support Baghdad-based artists facing the damage done to the contemporary art infrastructure in Iraq after cycles of war, destruction, sanctions, and continual political insecurity.

Their meeting space was first a rented classroom on the riverbank, and later an art studio run in the Karrada district of Baghdad. In these intimate spaces, artists would meet and participate in a virtually- and physically-convened education and production program of seminars, discussion, and workshops. Sahakian used a network of resources from the local context, region, and further afield to provide space of critical thinking and making. As she suggests, "Sada harnessed relational and digital networks that could be accessed by those who were creating through this transformative period of Iraq's (and the world's) conditions for living."

For documenta fifteen, Sahakian invited former participants of Sada to produce video work reflecting on their practice and where they are today. The participating artists are Sajjad Abbas, Bassim Al Shaker, Layth Kareem, Ali Eyal, Raed Mutar, Sarah Munaf and Sahakian herself. The videos have been compiled into an anthology film to screen at and beyond the 100 days for the Kassel show. This particular form was chosen to produce a visualization of Iraqi from artists who were committed to working through the aftermath of American-led wars and occupation. The participants raise important questions as to how artists survive in the aftermath of US-led wars and occupation, with minimal supportive infrastructures, inclusion in regional and critical dialogues, or opportunities for the development of their practice.

Accessibility to the international art ekosistem has become dependent on graduating from elite art schools, having a practice that speaks to the international art language and current debates and being conversant in English. This system often requires artists to address the exoticness of their ethnicity, and offer themselves as "authentic voices." What Sada highlights is the profound loss incurred when artists working in Baghdad are shut out of this complex, networked art ekosistem in a site that remains both starkly relevant for the world, historically and culturally.

Tina Sherwell



MINI-MAJELIS
- Another Roadmap Africa Cluster (ARAC)
- Archives des luttes des femmes en Algérie
- Asia Art Archive
- Centre d'art Waza
- El Warcha
- Graziela Kunsch
- Keleketla! Library
- Komîna Fîlm a Rojava
- Siwa plateforme - L'Economat at Redeyef
- The Black Archives

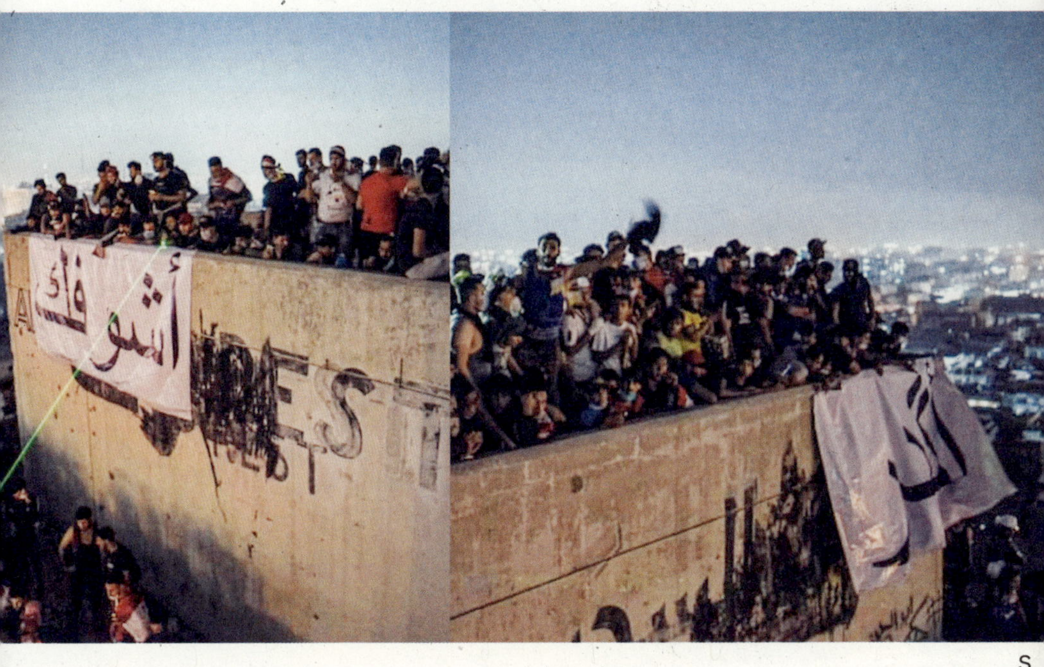




Protesters atop a building in Baghdad, Iraq, face the fortified Green Zone. Film still by Sajjad Abbas, 2022

*"Sada was created in 2010 to support young artists residing in the enduring capital of Baghdad, rather than use its position as a site of macabre curiosity or to pretend at a rebirth through artmaking. Wars haven't stopped Iraqis from making art, they simply cut Iraqis out of what the rest of the world wanted to look at."*
*– Rijin Sahakian, Sada [regroup]*

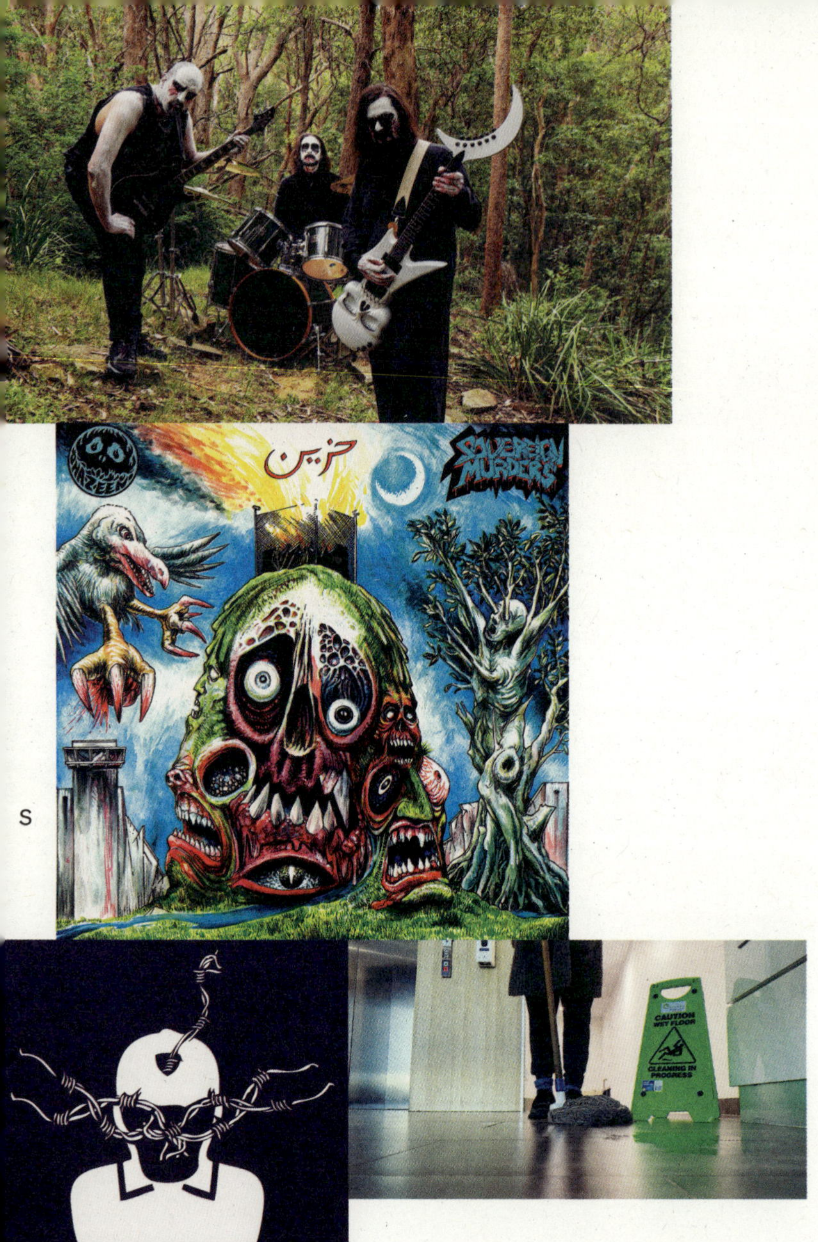



S

Members of Hazeen performing in the
Australian bush landscape
from left: Safdar Ahmed, Can
Yalcinkaya, Kazem Kazemi

Safdar Ahmed, Album cover art for Hazeen's
debut record, Sovereign Murders (2022)
Watercolor on paper

Graphic from the zine Alien
Citizen (2022) by Safdar Ahmed
and Susie Nelson

Miream Salameh, Cleaning In
Progress (2022) video still

VENUE
Ⓢ Stadtmuseum Kassel

MINI-MAJELIS
О Another Roadmap Africa
 Cluster (ARAC)
О Cinema Caravan and Takashi
 Kuribayashi
О Kiri Dalena
О Nguyen Trinh Thi

# SAFDAR AHMED

Safdar Ahmed and collaborators present a video, vinyl record, and zine addressing citizenship, displacement, and the weaponization of borders.

Safdar Ahmed is a visual artist, musician, and community activist based in Sydney, Australia. Born in Liverpool, UK, a site of rich migration histories, to an Indian Muslim father and British white mother, he moved as a child with the family to Australia. His aesthetic and political agendas are expansive, transnational, and reparative. His interests range from Sufi art and poetic traditions, drawing, and performance, to youth subcultures such as DIY zines, comics, and heavy metal. He approaches these with a deep empathy for the refugee community suffering under the racist conditions of Australian border incarceration, prolonged instability, and lack of safety, which lead to medical and psychological harm. His documentary graphic novel, *Still Alive* (2021), is based on his experiences working with refugee communities in the Villawood detention center and in Western Sydney through his not-for-profit initiative, Refugee Art Project.

Ahmed's practice challenges the conventional limitations of storytelling to offer a compelling, cathartic, and effective witness to the outrages suffered by those oppressed by xenophobic immigration systems. At documenta fifteen, with Irani refugee musician Kazem Kazemi, cinematographer Alia Ardon, artists Can Yalcinkaya and Kian Dayani, and members of Refugee Art Project, Ahmed presents *Border Farce-Sovereign Murders-Alien Citizen* (2022). It is a three-part work—a two-channel video installation, a vinyl record, and zine— interrogating citizenship, the politics of representation, and the weaponization of borders.

The video installation takes documentary footage of Kazemi's traumatic experience at the Manus detention camp which resulted in his evacuation to Brisbane, where due to the Australian government, he remains stateless. This footage is combined with discordant audio-visuality inspired by Hazeen, the death metal band formed by Ahmed and Kazemi. Hazeen recuperates black metal and its theatrical corpse make-up and rawness—a genre synonymous with European white supremacy—and channels it into an antagonistic and anguished anti-racist exhortation. Accompanying this is a series of short films made by women associated with Refugee Art Project, screened in partnership with Cinema Caravan and Takashi Kuribayashi. This project invites the viewer to join those who have peered into the abyss at "unspeakable" acts left out of narratives of trauma and human rights violations, and whose anger and courage provide a critical resource for change.

Annie Jael Kwan

S

# SAODAT ISMAILOVA

Inspired by such references as the number 40, and shapeshifting mythical beings from Central Asian cultures, Saodat Ismailova's work combines film, performance, and the environment. Ismailova has invited 18 artists from Kazakhstan, Kyrgyzstan, Tajikistan, and Uzbekistan, showing as DAVRA, who work in music, clay sculpture, and film.

In Central Asian cultures, *chilltan* are shapeshifters that take the form of young or elderly women, animals, such as snakes, birds, or tigers, animate or inanimate parts of nature, and even natural phenomena like wind or clouds. Existing on the fringes of Islam and the crossroads of ancient beliefs, primal myths, and animism, *chilltan* are guardians of knowledge and keepers of spiritual diversity. The word *chilltan* derives from Persian and means "40 bodies," or "40 beings" of no specific gender.

Playing out throughout a sequence of interconnected rooms in the basement of the Fridericianum, *Chilltan* is a labyrinthine work by Saodat Ismailova that combines film, performance, and environment to invoke the spirits of those beings. In an adjacent space, Ismailova invited 18 artists from Kazakhstan, Kyrgyzstan, Tajikistan and Uzbekistan, working as DAVRA, to enact works involving, amongst others, music, clay sculpture, and film. The succession of spaces draws the visitor in to meander through arrangements of traditional materials and historical accounts: sheets of silk cloth, artisanal Uzbek mattresses, and texts of shamanic pleas.

*Chilltan* speaks of a multitude of entities, but also, as the artist puts it, of "unity and continuity." Recurrent in the work is the presence of the number 40 which holds a significance across cultures, one of them being the period of what is considered the most excruciatingly hot sequence of days in Central Asia, during which life grinds to a halt. In Kassel, Ismailova choreographed an opposite situation, 40 days being the duration of public events organized by the female artists in DAVRA, which take place as part of the work. The artist's practice interweaves and blurs modern time with mythical one, stillness with motion, death with life. Ismailova explored this motif in her debut feature film *40 Days of Silence* (2014), and performance *Qyrq Qyz* (2018), a mythical tale of 40 warrior girls who defend their land from invaders led by the daughter of a tribal ruler. A filmmaker and artist, living between Paris, France, and Tashkent, Uzbekistan, Ismailova pursues an essentially archaeological practice, unearthing layers of time their accumulation across regions, challenging not only the "post-Soviet condition" and geographical divide between what came to be considered East and West (from a European perspective), but its temporal aspect.

Krzysztof Kościuczuk

VENUE
Fridericianum

MINI-MAJELIS
○ Hamja Ahsan
○ Jimmie Durham
○ La Intermundial Holobiente
○ Pınar Öğrenci

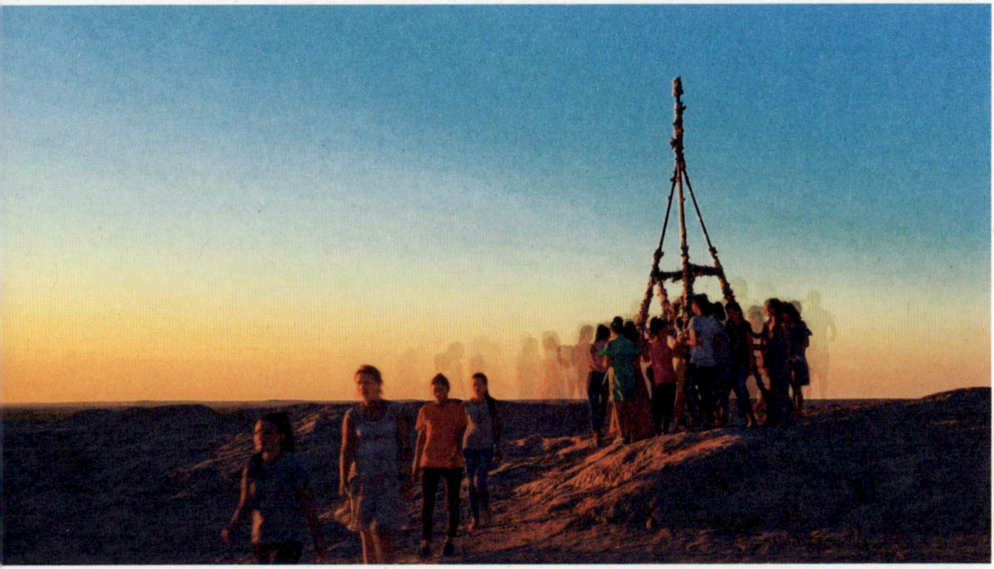

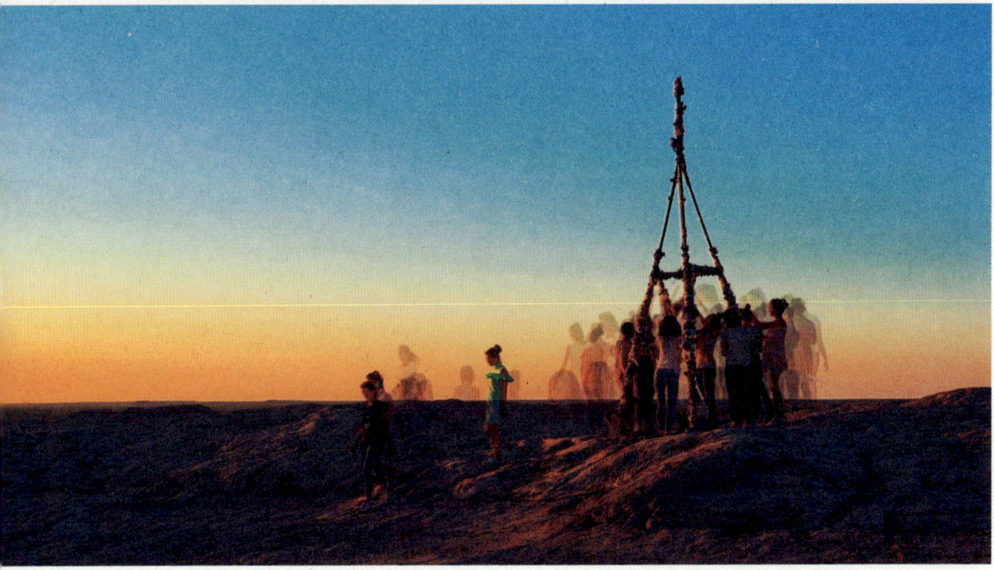

*Chillpiq* (2018)
Video stills

Saodat Ismailova

181

S

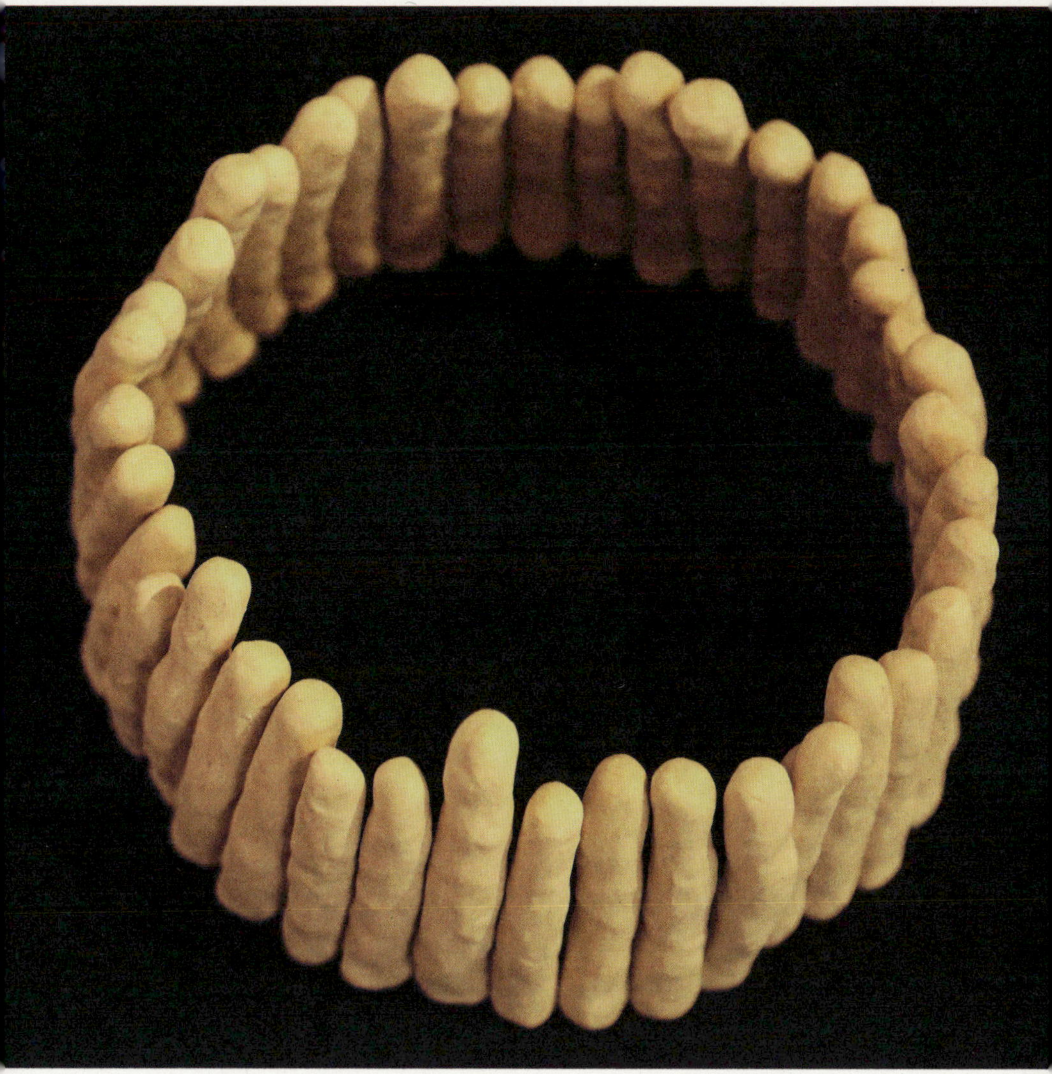

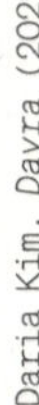



Daria Kim, Davra (2022)

Saodat Ismailova

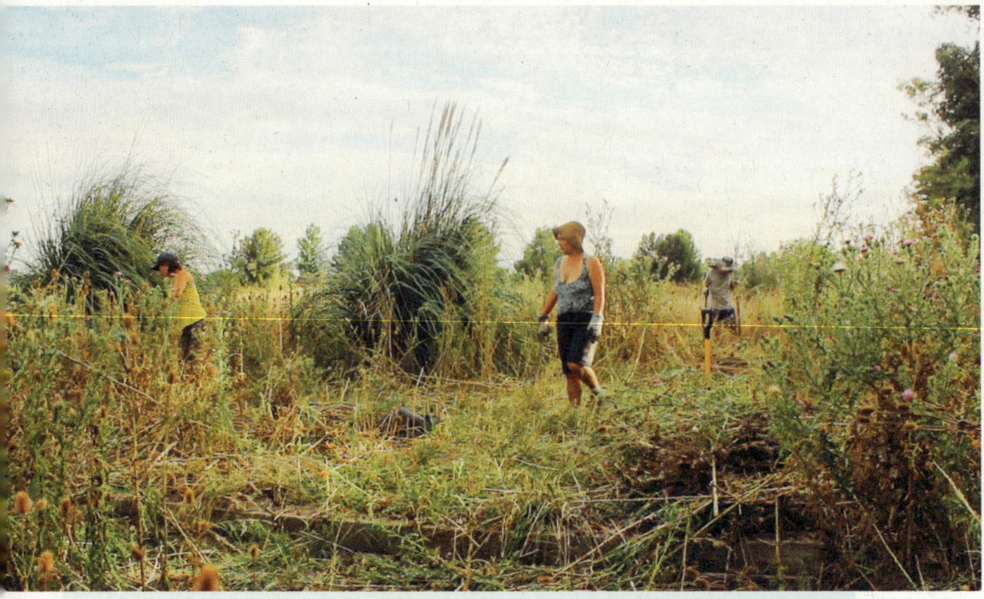

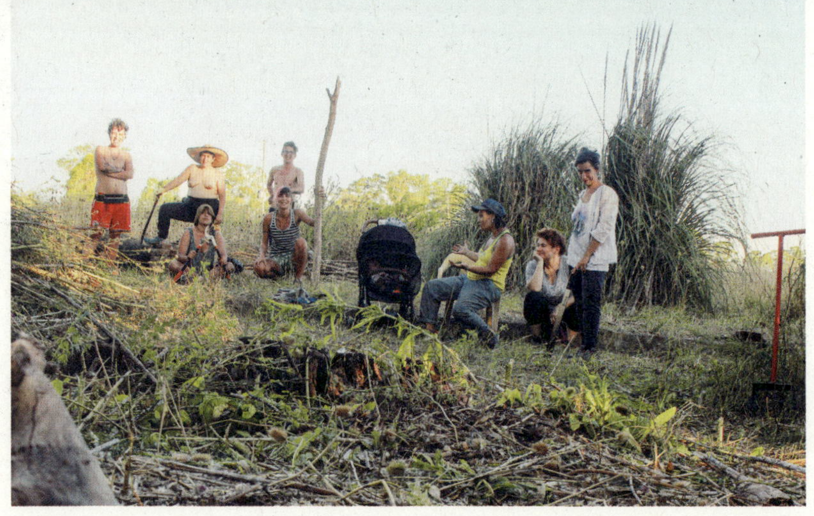



Preparing the ground for the *Rancho cuis*

Weeding the *Rancho cuis*, January 2022

# SERIGRAFISTAS QUEER

Serigrafistas queer's project connects social protest with spending
time together, continuing their
preoccupation with collective
care, learning, and sharing.

Serigrafistas queer was born in 2007 through social protest, LGBTIQ+, and feminist marches, catalyzed by Argentina's 2001 economic crisis. The self-defined "non-group" carves out queer ways of being in the world, working with artisanal silkscreen making and the co-creation of slogans, creating assemblies and printing slogans in the field during demonstrations.

Serigrafistas queer's mutating self-definition ensures radical openness, while allowing continuous reinvention, broadening their struggles beyond identity politics. Its work with silkscreen printing is marked by attention to bodily pleasure and limits, and to modes of mutual care. The group was involved with Radio Rancho Fuego Abierto—a radio station set up during the 2018 protests urging decriminalization of abortion in Argentina—and in 2019, they launched their first editorial project, *Papel Cuis,* with the publication of Karina Pinterelli's poetry collection *Me quedé en Karina* (I Stayed in Karina).

*Rancho Cuis* (2022), Serigrafistas queer's project for documenta fifteen, continues their preoccupation with collective care, learning, and sharing. *Rancho* is slang for precarious, generally rural, living spaces, and *ranchear* is the verb that is used to describe their habitation. Argentinian social protest has semantically modified these terms. In 2018, for example, protesters would *ranchear*, or spend time together, in makeshift shelters while awaiting the results of congressional debates. *Ranchear,* then, means attending to each other without expectation of any final product.

*Rancho Cuis* is manifested through different interventions. The first is a construction project taking place in a rural area outside of Buenos Aires. (The word "cuis" is derived from *kuir*, which means "queer" in Spanish, and is a homophone of *cuis*, an Argentinian rodent.) The second is practical and economic: place-making activities through collective learning and intersectional healing with local organizations and collectives working on issues from gender violence to land rights.

The third aspect is editorial, translating the experiences of *Rancho Cuis* in Argentina to a smaller iteration in Kassel, built behind Sandershaus, its form and function evolving during the 100-day event in response to the activities and needs generated through inhabiting the space. Apart from hosting the non-group's archives, the ranch's construction will continue to evolve based on the interactions between members of Serigrafistas queer and visitors, using the materials generated through silk-screen printing and other spontaneous activities. In this way, to *"ranchear cuis,"* constructing a collective space, becomes synonymous with inhabiting it together.

Ferdiansyah Thajib

VENUE
● Sandershaus

MINI-MAJELIS
○ Alice Yard
○ Erick Beltrán
○ LE 18
○ MADEYOULOOK
○ Party Office b2b Fadescha

# SIWA PLATEFORME – L'ECONOMAT AT REDEYEF

Through a collective proposal of interventions, installations, images, drawings, and performances, Siwa plateforme's work bridges the Fridericianum and their base in Tunisia.

Conceived as a nomadic program for exchange between artists and thinkers from Tunis, Tunisia, Baghdad, Iraq, and Paris, France, Siwa platforme has taken root in the mountainous region of Gafsa, Tunisia. Redeyef, in one of the world's largest phosphate basins, remains one of the most marginalized towns in Tunisia. Its inhabitants are mainly miners and unemployed youth, with a strong trade unionist tradition. Precarious living conditions contributed to a spirit of revolt that gained momentum in 2008, anticipating the worldwide uprisings of 2011.

Composed of Yagoutha Belgacem, Arafat Sadallah, Jean-Pierre Han, and Chems Zitouni, since 2011 the group has worked with artists from France and Tunisia, and the inhabitants of Redeyef. Through a collaborative renovation of L'Économat, the mining settlement's colonial general warehouse, they turned it into a laboratory for activities, breathing life into possible common futures. Through a collective proposal of interventions, installations, images, drawings, and performances, their work for documenta fifteen bridges the Fridericianum and the Économat in Redeyef.

Haythem Zakaria's installation draws a topography of the luminous desert landscape, while Mohammed Znaidi tells stories of the desert. Radio transmitters broadcast recordings of inhabitants of Redeyef narrating a scorching desire to burn national borders. In a sound installation *Nantes – Redeyef* (2022), Guellaa, a rapper from the region, recounts his perilous journey over the Mediterranean to France.

While the musician Loup Uberto records and transfigures the traditions of song and poetry from Redeyef, Okacha Ben Salah, a young filmmaker, paints a filmic portrait of the town. Yagoutha Belgacem and Marianne Dautrey propose a visual montage of the archives of the ten years of Siwa in Redeyef and make audible the voice of the choreographer-dancer Imen Smaoui, who speaks of the freedom of the bodies of the people of Redeyef and their relationship to the space of the desert. Paintings close to concrete art, made by the inhabitants of Redeyef, collected by Jean-Michel Diaz, form the bed of another thorny Redeyef story, facing the photographs of Fakhri El Ghezal. Hamouda Jarrar recounts the story of his famous grandfather, El Hedi Ben Salem, who grew up in Redeyef and worked with German filmmaker Rainer W. Fassbinder. Muntasser, spokesperson for the youth of Redeyef, is present in Kassel as a kind of ambassador.

Stories—and ways of telling these stories— form the material bridge between Redeyef and Kassel, built by Yagoutha and her curatorial team. Bypassing tenacious global frontiers, Siwa challenges inhabitants of Redeyef to host the hospitable space created at documenta fifteen.

Joachim Ben Yakoub

VENUE
 Fridericianum

MINI-MAJELIS
- Another Roadmap Africa Cluster (ARAC)
- Archives des luttes des femmes en Algérie
- Asia Art Archive
- Centre d'art Waza
- El Warcha
- Graziela Kunsch
- Keleketla! Library
- Komîna Fîlm a Rojava
- Sada [regroup]
- The Black Archives

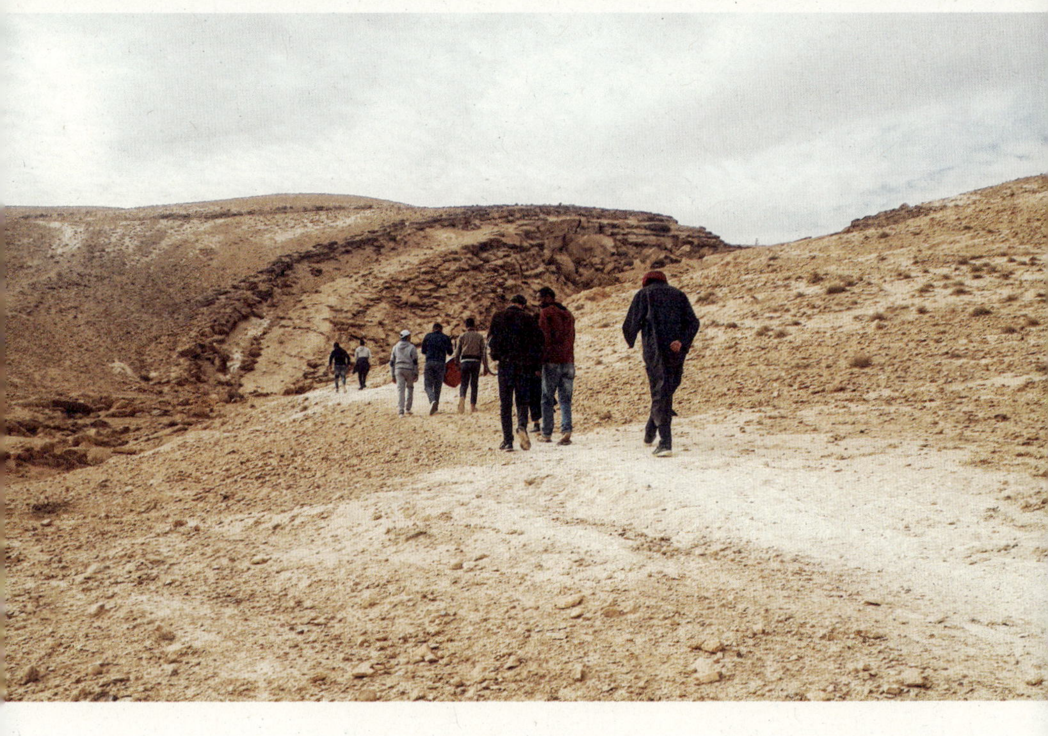



"*Redeyef in October 2021. This is a group walk in the desert surrounding the town. Redeyef was founded in beginning of twentieth century by French colonisers as a phosphate mining town. The majority of workers were nomadic people from the region. The desert is essential to understanding life here; we connot conceive of it without the influence of two elements: desert and phosphate mines.*"—Siwa plateforme, 2022

Group walk during residency of Loup Uberto in Redeyef, Tunisia, October 2021

Siwa plateforme - L'Economat at Redeyef

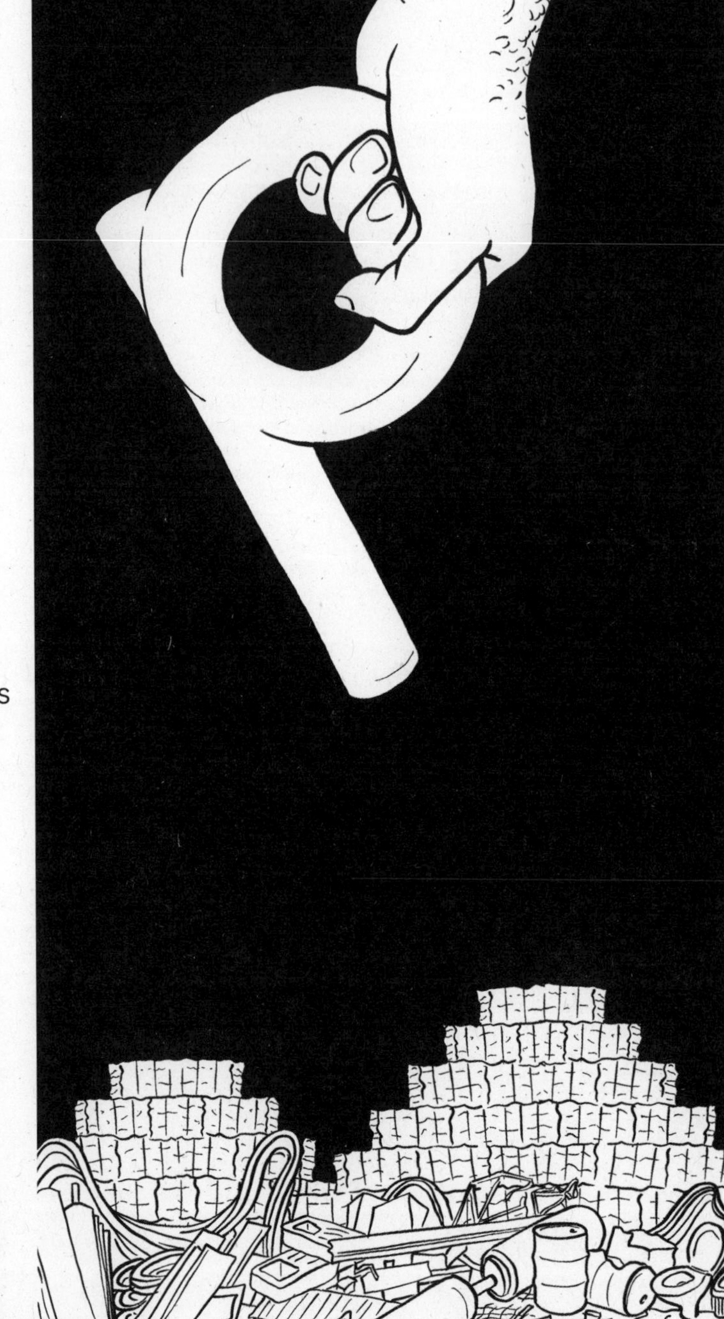

s

# SOURABH PHADKE

In Kassel, the architect
Sourabh Phadke has devised
an infrastructure to support
renewable exhibition-making.

Sourabh Phadke is an architect, but it was through working as a schoolteacher that his practice took shape: while teaching science, ecology, and social studies to students aged three to 16, he noted a discrepancy between the spaces he worked within and the pedagogy he taught. Ever since, he has focused on designing environments and objects that communicate and embody hyper-local, ecologically aware knowledge systems. Such thinking is influenced by Indigenous building traditions, which are often celebratory, ontological, and even spiritual.

In Kassel, Phadke is devising a renewable and proactive infrastructure for large-scale exhibition-making—which, at this time of extended crisis and increasing scarcity, needs to be radically restyled. His work for documenta fifteen is on the life-cycles of materials used in building exhibition spaces. In a reimagined material cycle of wood, plastic, and other building materials, Phadke has enabled a system of exchange between an existing Kassel material ekosistem—such as government cleaning and recycling services, design teams, for-profit organizations, and groups working with waste and junk—and the documenta one. Both feed into each other. If a building is being torn down in Kassel, the wood and other materials can be made available to the documenta team and artists, who can likewise procure specific items sustainably.

It's Phadke's vision that spaces function not only as venues, but also as sites designed for the production of knowledge. He has taken on the toilets, too—spaces he sees as having political potential. Together with students at the Kunsthochschule in Kassel, he is building and designing the toilets, which will be compostable, with a friendly interface, as sites for artistic intervention. There, he will do a three-month-long module on low-cost technologies, ecological sanitation and localized design.

ruangrupa member Iswanto Hartono describes Phadke as "a mediator and translator" working between the documenta community and their desired material, to unite them in a durable, ecologically sustainable fashion. He is working with individual artists to help them realize their projects, too. Phadke is a ceramic artist himself and is making terracotta water bottles for visitors. He views the 100 days of the exhibition as a time period in which material is both produced and recycled. For this, Phadke puts into use his unique ability to intuit relations among climate, politics and people, and transform these into informed, always-living enterprises.

Skye Arundhati Thomas

S

VENUE
- Fridericianum
- Hiroshima-Ufer (Karlsaue)
- Hübner areal
- Nordstadtpark

MINI-MAJELIS
- Atis Rezistans | Ghetto Biennale
- Marwa Arsanios
- yasmine eid-sabbagh
- *foundationClass*collective



"

# SUBVERSIVE FILM

Subversive Film presents a film program of twenty films that, for four decades, have been safeguarded in Tokyo by a solidarity network, as well as a film about the archive.

When Beirut, Lebanon was besieged by the Israeli army in 1982, a flourishing environment for political artistic practices in the Palestinian revolution collapsed. A growing archive of internationalist militant cinema since 1968 was seized and later abandoned in a secret military store. The cinema research and production collective Subversive Film investigates ways of retracing and re-distributing this lost archive of silenced revolutionary images.

Always in movement in between Ramallah, Palestine, and Brussels, Belgium, the collective's Reem Shilleh and Mohanad Yaqubi restore the equally besieged relations of transnational solidarity between different liberation struggles by instituting archival practices anew. Whether reissuing militant images or texts in their raw form in new publications, or curating screening cycles, Subversive Film not only holds space for the unearthed archival material to speak for itself, but again facilitates the circulation of seized material and its unresolved narratives, aesthetics and politics.

For documenta fifteen, Subversive Film has curated a cinematic program around the screening of a recently restored film, shedding light on the overlooked and (until now) still-undocumented anti-imperialist solidarity relations between Japan and Palestine.

After meeting in Tokyo with Masao Adachi, acclaimed director of different experimental agit-prop films and former member of the Japanese Red Army, disbanded in 1988, Subversive Film was entrusted with a collection of 16mm films and U-matic tapes, dozens of posters, and a full wall library safeguarded by a Japanese solidarity group in Tokyo. The material, considered either lost or unknown to the public, was sent to Japan in several waves from 1967 to 1982. The centerpiece of

Subversive Film's presentation during documenta fifteen is a speculative documentary collectively made by British, Italian, German, Palestinian, Egyptian, Iraqi, and Japanese filmmakers. The imperfect aura of the film is witness to the changing political attitude of the internationalist solidarity movement that took center stage during the long 1960s.

In Kassel, the solidarity relations between Tokyo, Palestine, and the world unfold in a nomadic film program around different disassembled fragments of the restored film, interlaced with a live symposium. With this open invitation in ways of facilitating assembly through forms of assemblage, re-assemblage and montage of a restored film, Subversive Film proposes to collectively reflect on possible processes of unearthing, restoring and momentary disclosure of the imperfect archives of transnational militant cinema. By bringing back into circulation these moving images, they all the while carefully reactivate present-day solidarity constellations, reflecting the lively utopia of a worldwide liberation movement.

Joachim Ben Yakoub

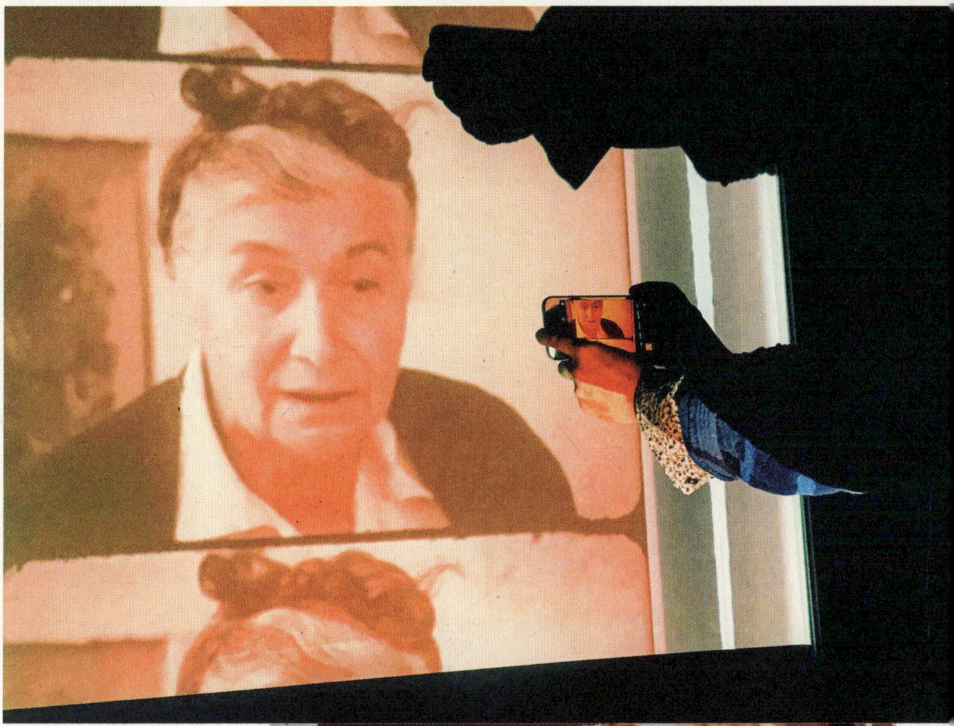

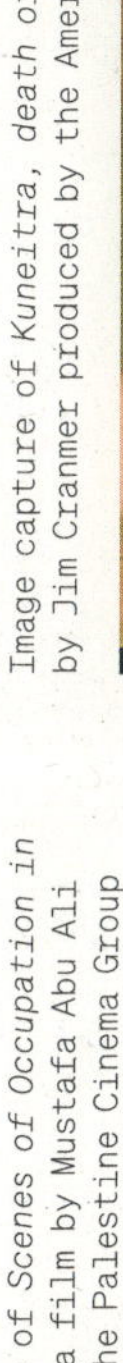



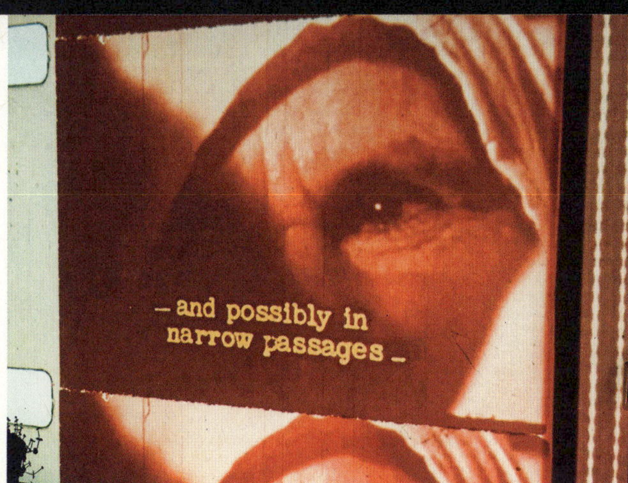



Image capture of Scenes of Occupation in
Gaza (1973), a film by Mustafa Abu Ali
produced by the Palestine Cinema Group

**VENUES**
- Ⓗ Hübner areal
- ⑥ Gloria-Kino

**MINI-MAJELIS**
- ○ Arts Collaboratory
- ○ Black Quantum Futurism
- ○ Chimurenga
- ○ Jumana Emil Abboud
- ○ Nino Bulling
- ○ Agus Nur Amal PMTOH

Subversive Film

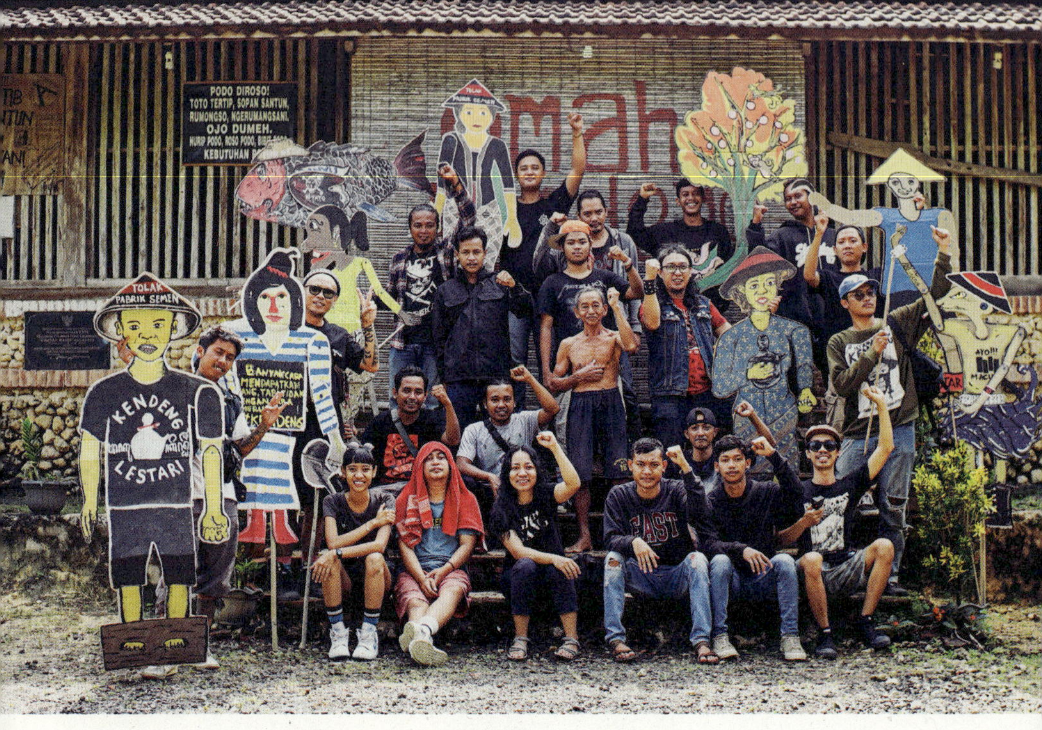


PODO DIROSO!
TOTO TERTIP, SOPAN SANTUN,
RUMONGSO, NGERUMANGSANI,
OJO DUMEH,
NURIP PODO, ROSO PODO,
KEBUTUHAN
KENDENG LESTARI
TOLAK PABRIK SEMEN

# TARING PADI



Alongside workshops with communities around the world, Taring Padi show new and old banners, woodcut posters, and *wayang kardus* that convey socio-political issues.

Taring Padi is a collective of artists and activists founded in Yogyakarta, Indonesia, in 1998: a critical juncture in the nation's history, during which public dissatisfaction with the administration, economic collapse, and allegations of political corruption triggered nationwide protests and violent, often ethnically targeted, riots. These mass actions culminated in the resignation of then-president Suharto and the end of his three-decade-long New Order Regime, signaling the beginning of Indonesia's Reformation era.

The majority of Taring Padi's founding members were art students, galvanized by the political concerns of the time, from Yogyakarta's Indonesian Institute of the Arts, joined gradually by students and activists from other disciplines, universities, and cities. Taring Padi can be translated as "fangs of rice," referring to the sharp tips of unhusked rice. As Indonesia's staple food, rice conjures up its farmers and the working class whose interests the collective aims to serve. Moreover, the rice "fangs," which can prick careless fingers, are constant reminders to sharpen one's mind.

Motivated by these guiding principles, Taring Padi's primary approach is collaborative and politically conscious: they organize workshops with community groups in and beyond Indonesia to make life-sized *wayang kardus* (cardboard puppets), woodcut posters, and large banners, measuring as wide as 8 meters, and other objects that are then mobilized in protests, carnivals, and musical performances. Through satirical iconography and concise, conspicuous text, these artistic materials communicate incisive political messages regarding local grievances and concerns.

For documenta fifteen, Taring Padi has continued to practice their three core principles—organize, educate, and agitate—under the theme of *"Bara Solidaritas: Sekarang Mereka, Besok Kita"* (Flame of Solidarity: First they came for them, then they came for us). Through workshops with various communities—such as urban, migrant, and street artist groups, and schools—in Germany, Indonesia, the Netherlands, and Australia, they have collaboratively created a variety of new artworks that convey local socio-political issues. At the Hallenbad, Taring Padi present more than 100 artifacts, including banners, woodcut posters, and *wayang kardus* from the past 22 years of their practice.

Wong Binghao

VENUES
- C&A Façade
- Hallenbad Ost
- Rondell

MINI-MAJELIS
- ikkibawiKrrr
- ook_
- Richard Bell
- Wakaliga Uganda

Taring Padi, *Sekarang Mereka, Besok Kita* (Today they've come for them, tomorrow they come for us) (2021)
Acrylic on canvas
8 × 5 m

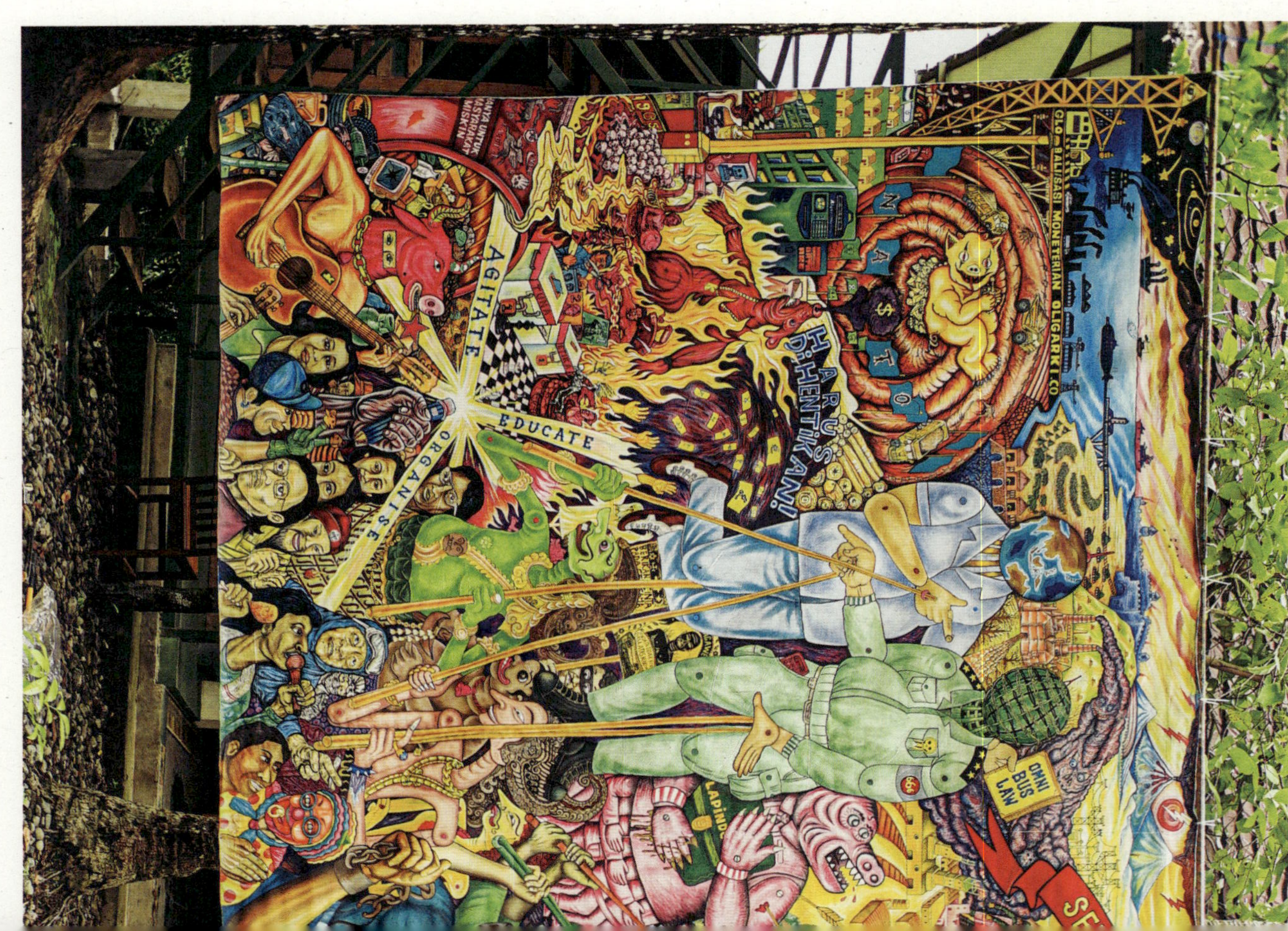

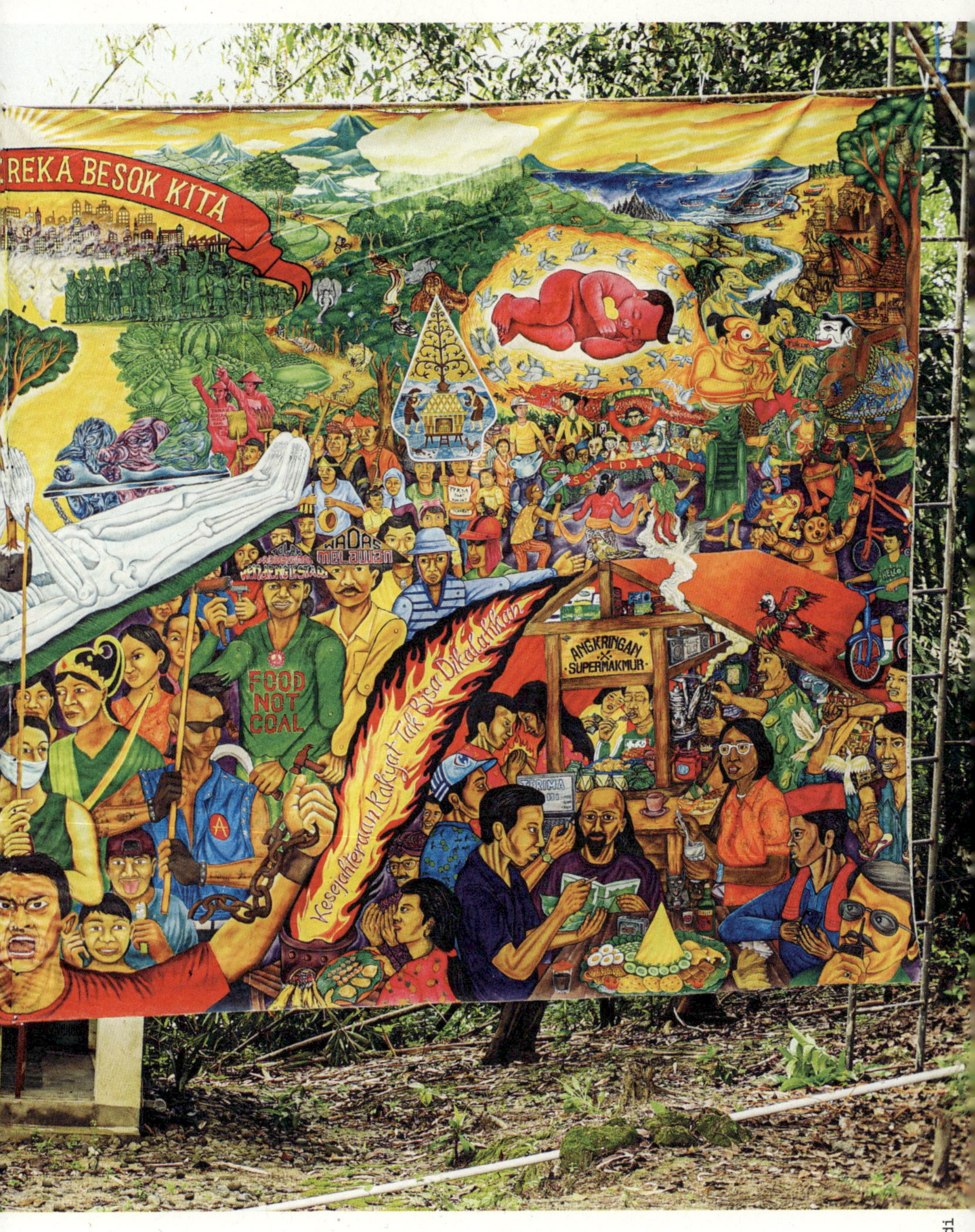
REKA BESOK KITA
FOOD NOT COAL
SOLIDARITY
Kesejahteraan Rakyat Tak Bisa Dikalahkan
ANGKRINGAN SUPERMAKMUR
MADAS MELAWAN

# THE BLACK ARCHIVES

The Black Archives show how storytelling and archiving are vehicles
for Black resistance.

A new generation of Black activists, artists and researchers, and those of Color, have brought into visibility the enduring coloniality as well as the afterlives of slavery in contemporary Dutch society, where race continues to determine the opportunities afforded to its members. Global movements such as Black Lives Matter and #RhodesMustFall certainly gave force to their activism; yet, many Dutch and non-Dutch Black intellectuals who previously fought structural racism and the silencing of slavery's legacies did not enjoy the same visibility. In agreement with theorist Frantz Fanon's observation that coloniza-tion distorts and disfigures the pasts of oppressed people, The Black Archives aims to counter such negation of historicity and humanity. To this end, they gather silenced histories of struggle, neglected heritages, and the legacies of the Surinamese and African diaspora in the Netherlands and beyond.

At their site in Amsterdam East, The Black Archives hosts a unique collection of more than ten thousand books, documents, photographs, audio-visual material, and artifacts. These focus in particular on Black and non-Western histories, and the history of transnational solidarity movements of the oppressed that are not taught in schools or narrated as part of institutional public history.

Sharing stories and political discourse is an important part of The Black Archives' practice, as they aim to keep their collection accessible to (Black) resistance and solidarity movements. Their public programming and exhibitions emphasize affective connections to the archival material to foster the close bonds necessary for solidarity. For documenta fifteen, The Black Archives demonstrate how they both collect and enact resistance. They are replicating a section of their book collection as well as parts of their exhibitions *Facing Blackness* (2022) and *Black and Revolutionary: The Story of Hermine and Otto Huiswoud* (2018). The latter reveals the hidden history of the Huiswouds' courageous fight against colonialism, racism, and economic inequality, which they uncovered in their own collection. Their installation serves as the basis for conversation, for sharing materials and for raising awareness around issues of decolonization, intersectionality, and anti-racism. Material can be copied, and donations are accepted. The Black Archives continue to build a community of activists with whom to reconstitute a collective memory and fight for human rights.

Carine Zaayman, Chiara De Cesari,
Nuraini Juliastuti

VENUE
Fridericianum

MINI-MAJELIS
- Another Roadmap Africa Cluster (ARAC)
- Archives des luttes des femmes en Algérie
- Asia Art Archive
- Centre d'art Waza
- El Warcha
- Graziela Kunsch
- Keleketla! Library
- Komîna Fîlm a Rojava
- Sada [regroup]
- Siwa plateforme - L'Economat at Redeyef

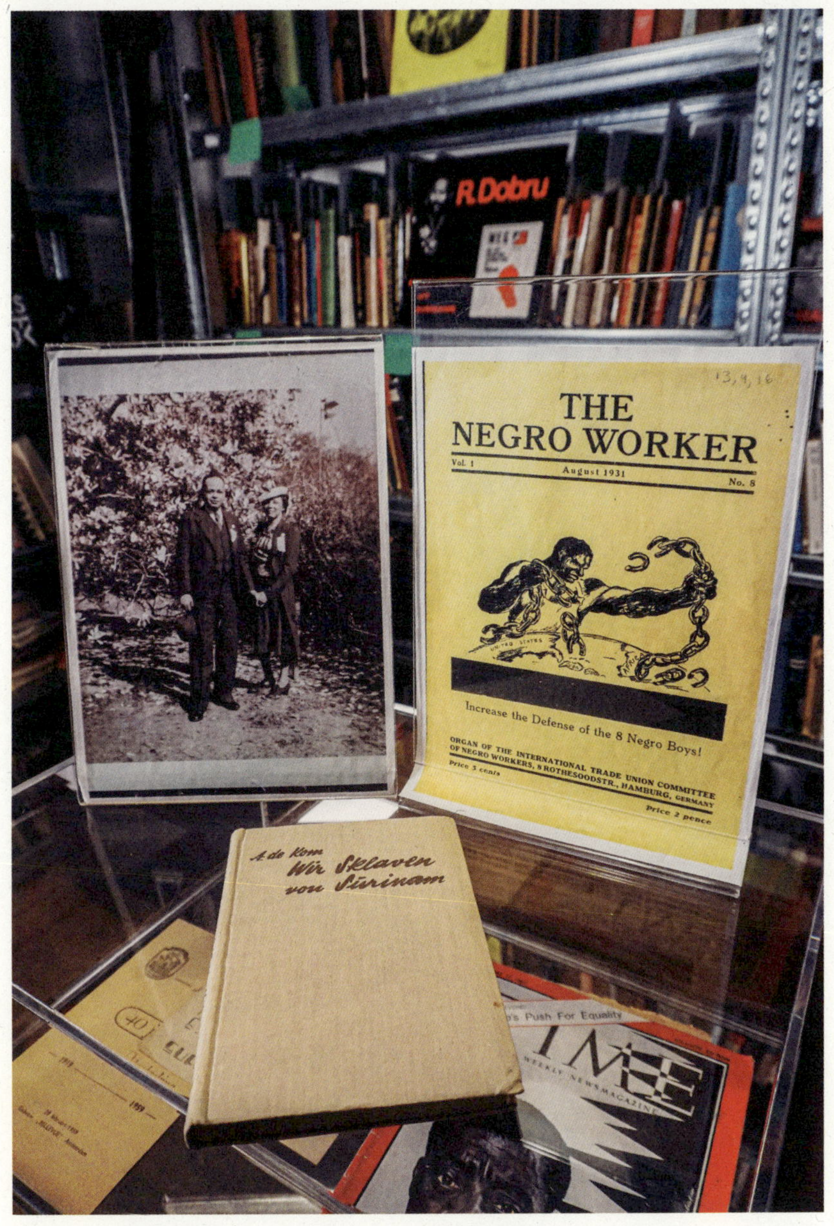


*The Black Archives explores radical international solidarity movements and its leaders, such as the Black communists Hermine and Otto Huiswoud with their publications. The German translation of* We Slaves of Surinam *by another Surinamese anti-colonial thinker, Anton de Kom, also reflects how various histories intersect.*

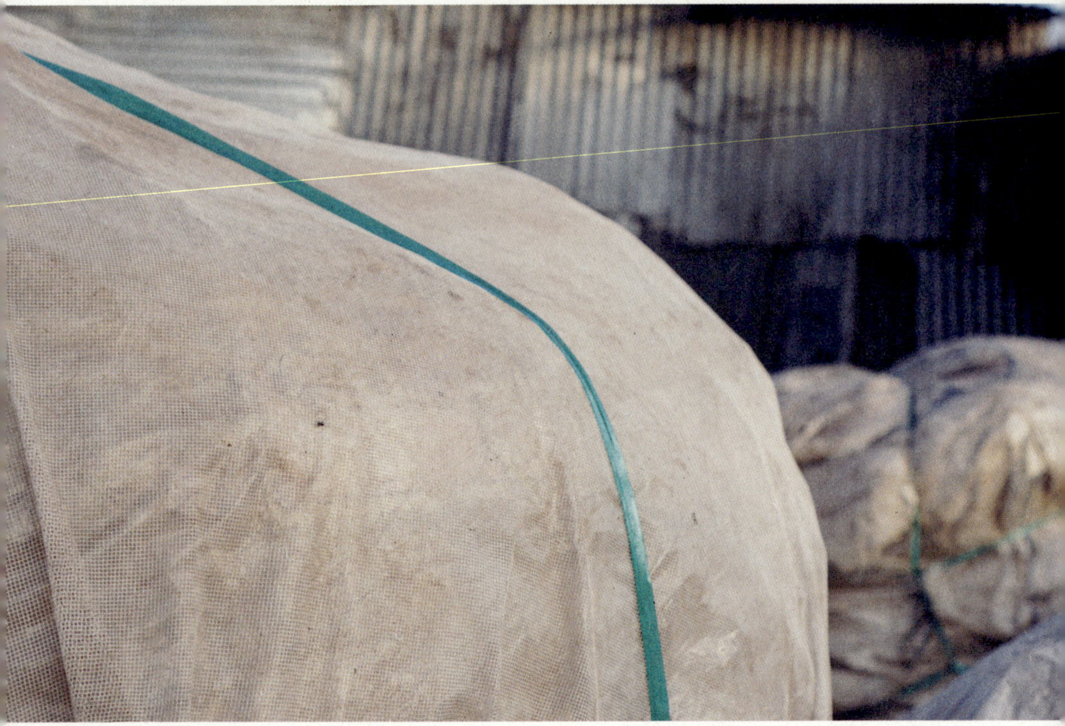

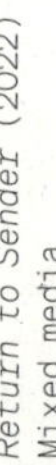

*"Just because the cost is passed on doesn't mean it's not being paid"*—The Nest Collective



VENUE
🄚 Karlswiese (Karlsaue)

MINI-MAJELIS
O Baan Noorg Collaborative
  Arts and Culture
O Dan Perjovschi
O Fehras Publishing Practices
O Nhà Sàn Collective

# THE NEST COLLECTIVE

The Nest Collective makes an architectural intervention: a multimedia installation that imitates a dystopian waste landscape.

For the past decade, the Nest Collective has been a beacon of cultural production in East Africa. Representing a brand of African urban sensibilities, The Nest often engages evolving struggles within African cities and the heightened consciousness of African urban centers as symbols of diversities, recognizing the tensions that come with acknolwedging or celebrating these layered diffrences. As hubs for the reorganization of Black consciousness, contemporary African cities—and their potential—are indisputably central to the collective's vision.

For documenta fifteen, some of the collective's site-specific presentations extend beyond urban perspectives and situate the expressions within a universal way of being related to Blackness. Emphasis on Black fantasies, and on speculative futures, is almost instinctive. But these expressions, in their examination of historical realities, are recalibrations of defective representation of racial identities, especially for people of African descent.

Recurring visual patterns in The Nest's efforts denounce significant negative aspects of urbanization in Kenya and, by extension, across Africa. Such critically relentless energy thrives in their imposing architectural intervention: a multimedia installation that summons the actualities of dystopian waste landscapes. *Return to Sender* (2021/2022) is a work of visual activism whose dominating element is hundreds of bound bales (condensed packages of used clothing), a statement on reversing the global movement and storage of give/throw-away garments and textiles. Not only does this installation, which resembles a dumpsite in front of the Orangerie, upset and disenchant; with its grotesque display of waste, and taking up space as a symbol of massive overconsumption, it also highlights the massive environmental impact of movement of unwanted objects from industrialized to less industrialized nations. This work will be accompanied by thematic ambient sound playing outside the installation, to be heard from all angles.

Still, the totality of this collective's productions offers both approval and disapproval to norms, igniting conversations on new frontiers for Black existences. *Return To Sender - Delivery Details* (2022) is a companion piece that explores the context of the mountain of litter which may only be visiting Kassel public space for 100 days, but is a current unending reality in Kenya and many African countries. To be screened inside the hollow installation, the video contemplates this difficult scenario through different contributors and viewpoints. There are those of history, unpacking the interconnections between the passing macroeconomic decisions made along pristine Global North corridors, and the daily micro realities on the crowded sidewalks at home. There are the eyes of celebration, giving deserved flowers to those who work hard to eke livings out of sustainability labour they did not choose. They look through the eyes of grief, considering the deliberate destructions of ambitious African maker-cultures, and the deaths of African dreams, all for second hand clothing trade to flourish almost by accident. These polarities are acknowledged, as is the dissonance of living within the resulting incompatibilities, leading to reflections on what futures may be made from within them. No doubt, all presentations are deliberately flavored by challenges original to the East African context, and a full engagement with The Nest would be inconclusive unless the complexities thereof are extracted, processed, and demystified, manifesting as everyday gestures, as residues of urban legends, or as improvised language.

Enos Nyamor

# THE QUESTION OF FUNDING

The Question of Funding invites Kassel-based activists, and a Gaza artist group, to share perspectives around funding and the ethics of survival.

The Question of Funding (QoF) is a collective of cultural producers and community thinkers focusing on cultural economy in Palestine. QoF poses critical questions around donor culture in Palestine and the rest of the world. In the late 1990s, the institutional form of the NGO became a hegemonic model for art spaces in Palestine. This model reflects the growing power of funding mechanisms in the contemporary economy. The concept of funding is used to reimagine alternative institutional structures and economic models which are based on justice and solidarity principles.

QoF is situated within communities that practice diverse economies and communal funding systems. They function as a collection of tools to govern the relations between community members and to mobilize collective strengths. Grant-makers operate through the creation of funding systems which are based more on professionalization and regimes of accountability.

Funding becomes a foreign word. It downplays the resilient capacities of the social environment. In QoF practices, funding is perceived as part of technologies for dealing with a sense of crises. Their works are directed to invert the funding mechanism and design a just ekosistem through connecting different economic localities. QoF creates and introduces the use of Dayra, a blockchain currency, as an economical and technological system. Dayra derives from an Arabic word which means "a circle" and "circulating". Central to this is the thought that individuals and collectives are entangled in the structures of everyday funds. Unlike a normal currency, Dayra starts with zero. The value adds up according to how people circulate resources in the community. Dayra serves as an affirmative critique and action to reconnecting with various forms and scales of resources.

For documenta fifteen, QoF activates a space where they invite Kassel based activists and collectives to share perspectives around funding and ethics of survival. In addition QoF has extended an invitation to one of the oldest artist collectives in Palestine; Eltiqa'—an artist group in Gaza. It aims to show how the questions of funding, speculative art markets, and solidarity are intertwined in daily attempts to exist. Another component of QoF's works is a harvest of their work around questions of economy. The series is written for both adults and children. Taking economy as the main discourse of the series, the publications serve as an act to make economy as an open domain and study subject accessible to many.

Nuraini Juliastuti

VENUE
Ⓦ WH22

LUMBUNG INTER-LOKAL
O Britto Arts Trust
O FAFSWAG
O Fondation Festival sur le Niger
O Gudskul
O INLAND
O Instituto de Artivismo Hannah Arendt (INSTAR)
O Jatiwangi art Factory
O Más Arte Más Acción (MAMA)
O OFF-Biennale Budapest
O Project Art Works
O Trampoline House
O Wajukuu Art Project
O ZK/U - Center for Art and Urbanistics

Question of Funding, *Under the fig tree meeting* (2020)
Notes on A3 paper

*Eltiqa' group is a collective of artists who have been working together for the last twenty years in Gaza City. It is founded by seven artists: Mohammed Al Hawajri, Mohamed Abusal, Dina Matar, Rauf Alajouri, Raed Issa, Mohammed Dabous, and Sohail Salem. Each has their individual art artistic practice, along with the platform for younger artists they have created.*

*The group formed slowly while working at the Palestinian Red Crescent Society in Gaza as resident artists and arts educators from 2002–2007. After the loss of the studios at PRCS and amid an absence of cultural infrastructure in Gaza, the Eltiqa' group were compelled to create their studies and art space. In 2009, and after the war on Gaza (2008–2009) the group succeeded in establishing an artist-run space in an old house on Omar Al Moukhtar St., a major street in Gaza city. The group*

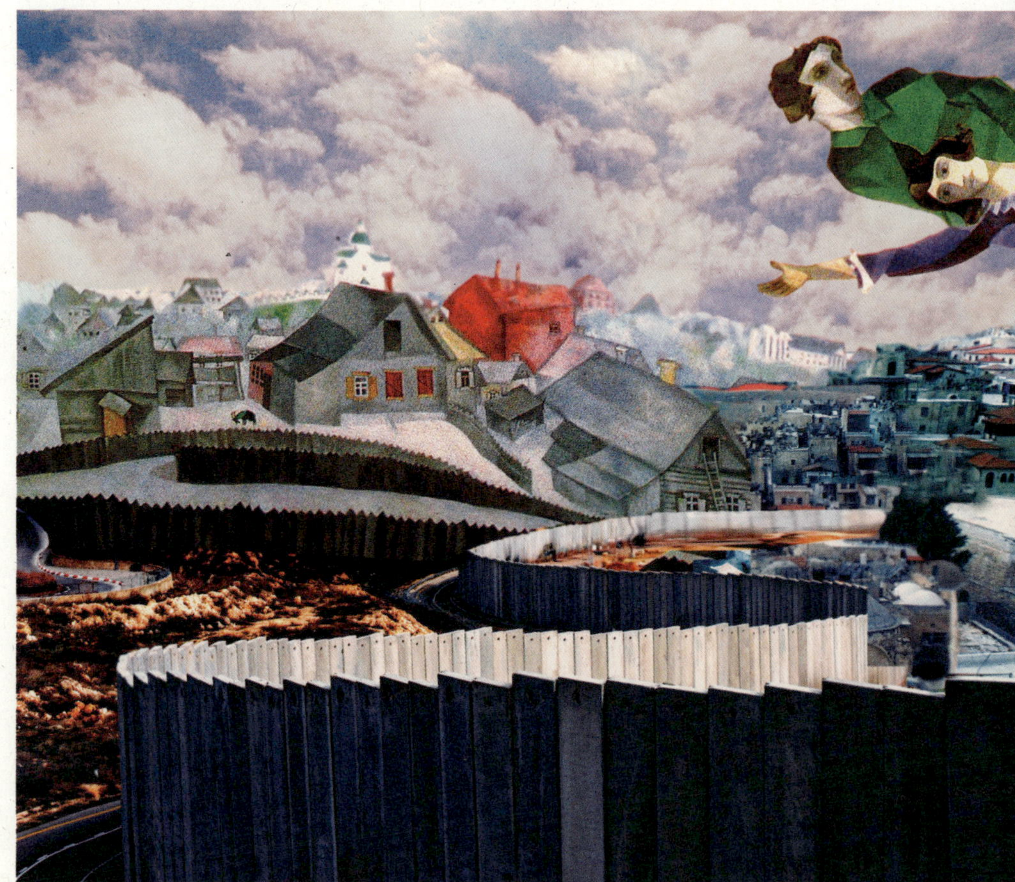

supports young and emergent artists, exchange knowledge and
provide education, practical training, and resources for artists in
Gaza, as well as mediating dialogue around the arts. Their 200-m2
space consists of a gallery, work studios, events area, a library, and
a workshop for engraving and printmaking. The group provides
us with an economical and cultural model that has managed to
overcome the hardships of living and working in a besieged territory
for more that 15 years, managing to work between individual
practice and collective structures.— Adele Jarrar

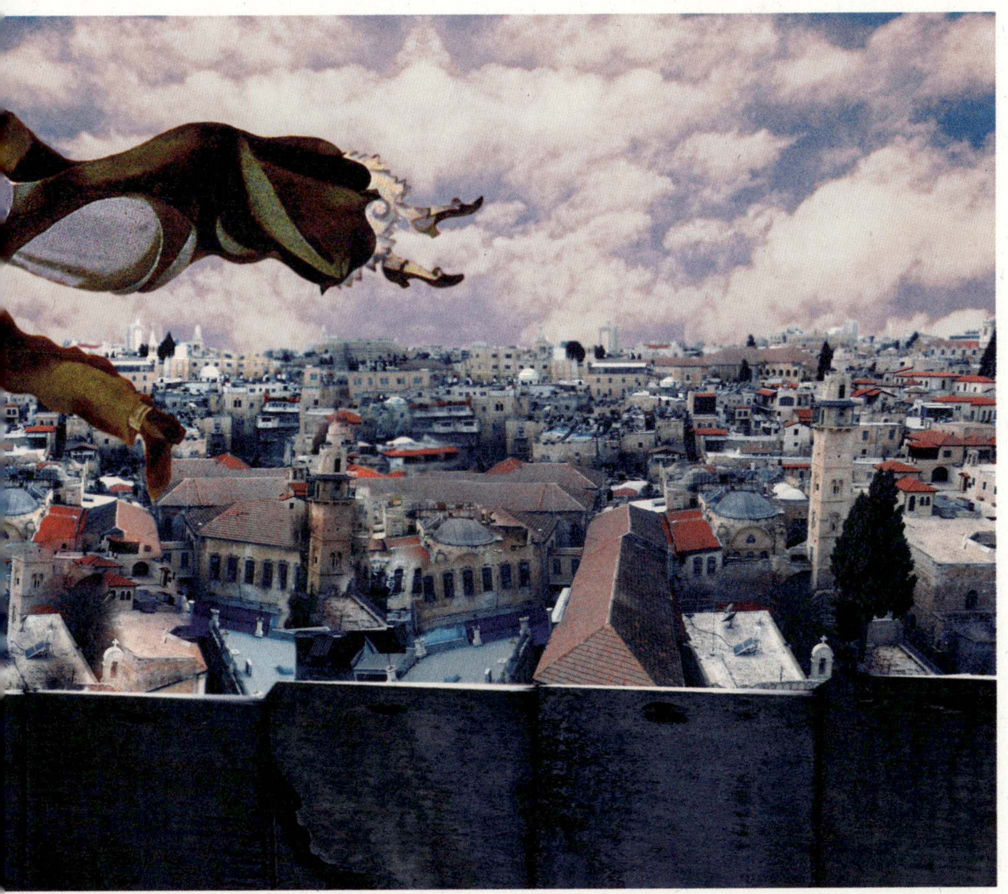

Mohammad Al Hawajri, Above the City (2013)<br>Digital art, print on photo paper

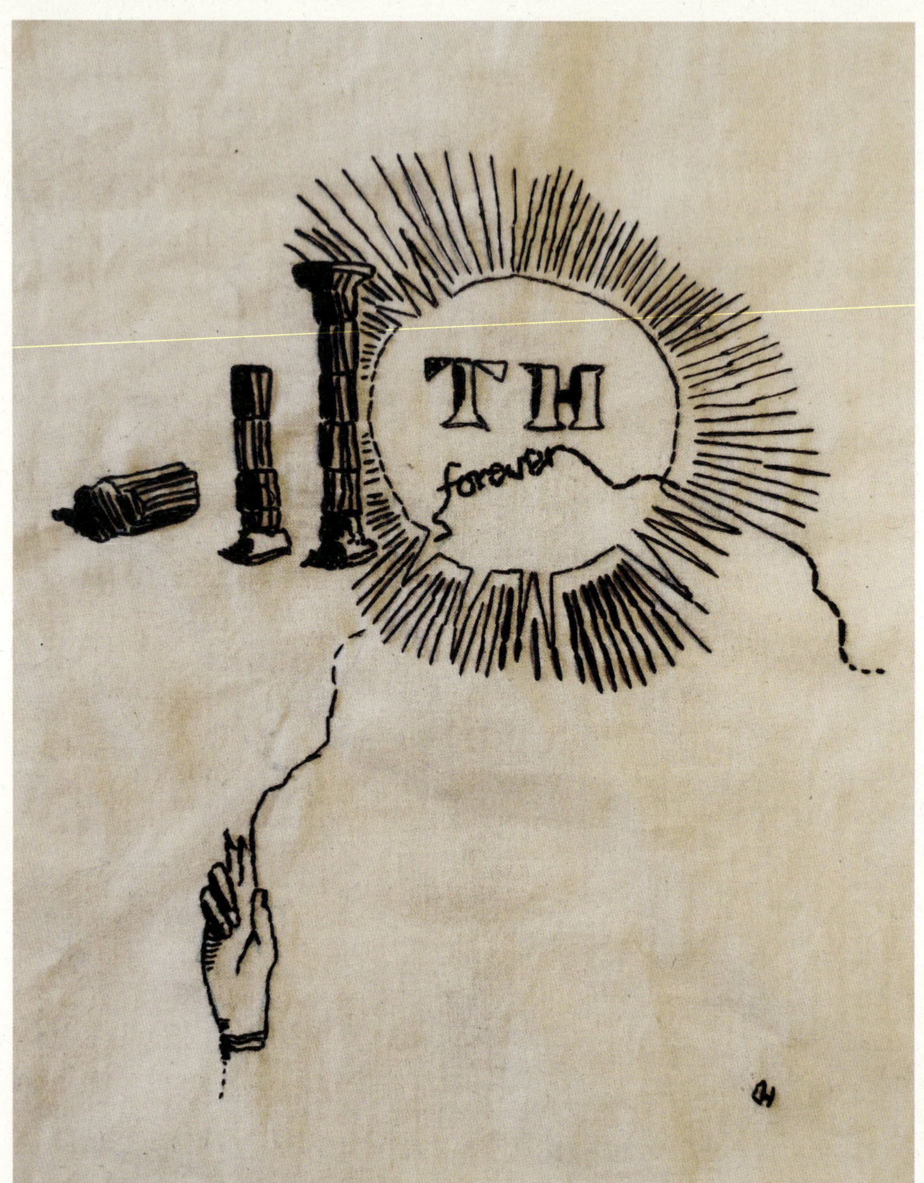




Joachim Hamou
*TH Forever* (2019)
Embroidery

# TRAMPOLINE HOUSE

In Copenhagen, Denmark, the Trampoline House emerged to give space and advocacy to those facing a rigid asylum system. In Kassel, their contribution includes works by a group of invited collaborators, ranging from a theater workshop put on by displaced people, fashion-show style performances, and a creative writing workshop.

The Trampoline House emerged more than a decade ago in Copenhagen, Denmark, where the state places asylum seekers in remote camps far from the rest of the population, amid a political discourse in which asylum seekers are demonized. This results in physical and existential isolation for asylum seekers and their children.

Against this debilitating isolation the Trampoline House—a sanctuary where people with and without papers can meet beyond the confines of camps—is crucial. It offers everything from legal advice and language courses to women's clubs and dinners and dancing; a break from the struggles of a rigid asylum system. Today, a lack of funding has turned the daily gathering place into a weekly edition, Weekend Trampoline House.

Trampoline House's contribution to documenta fifteen—*Castle in Kassel*—hints at the physical and metaphorical representation of territorial power and the exercise of ownership. Physically, the "castle" is a territory marked by a circle of chalk on the floor. Inside the circle, there is a public program of performances, debates, and screening of artworks that puts into perspective the Danish asylum system and

attitudes towards refugees and migrants. The castle also represents the unbreakable prison, or what Shakira Kasigwa Mukamusoni, one of the artists invited by Trampoline House, calls "the chain"—a representation of the invisible shackles of the asylum system and its intangible policies. Through a theater workshop with asylum-seekers, rejected asylum-seekers, and refugee youth, the participants write and perform sketches about life in the Danish asylum system from a youth perspective. Other contributions by Trampoline House include designer Dady de Maximo Mwicira-Mitalis, who uses fashion for the purpose of activism and social justice. Outfits are presented by the participants as models at a fashion show-style performance. A creative writing workshop facilitated by Jean Claude Mangomba examines the criminalization of asylum seekers and a retracing of the rights lost in an unjust and discriminatory system.

*Castle in Kassel* is not merely site-specific. With its walls easily erased, the castle presents its own antidote to a discriminatory system, tied together through live streaming and documentation to convey Trampoline House's vital role.

Farhiya Khalid

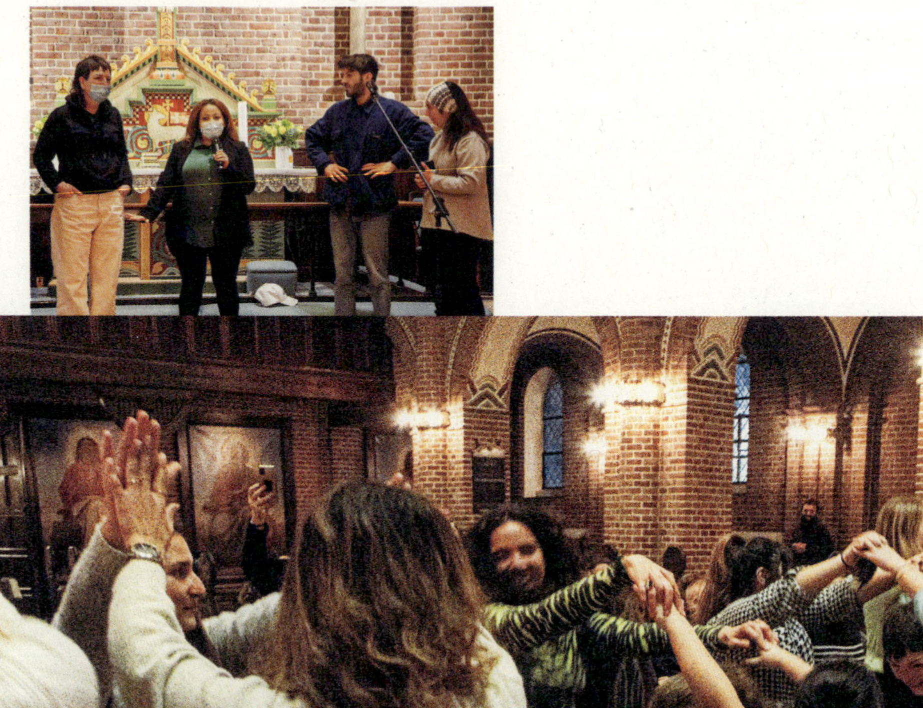

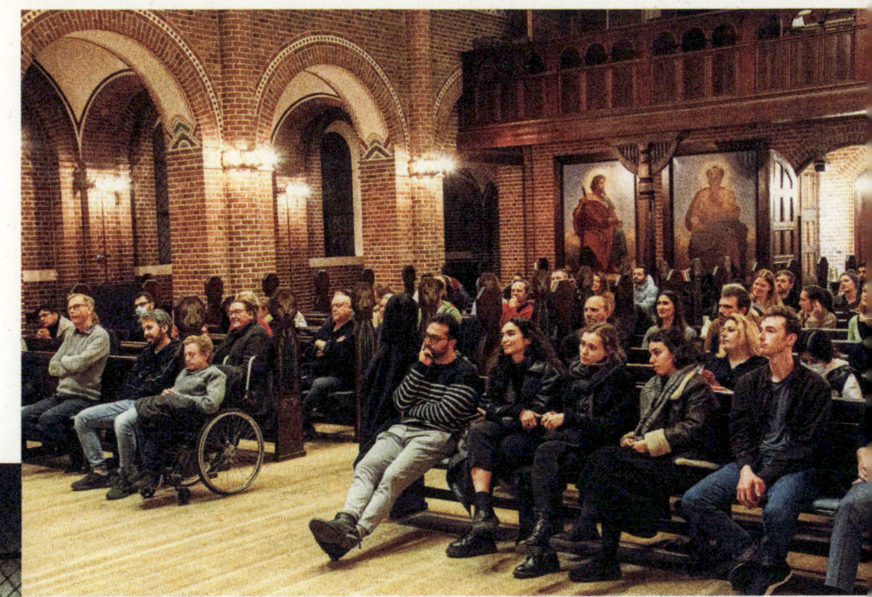

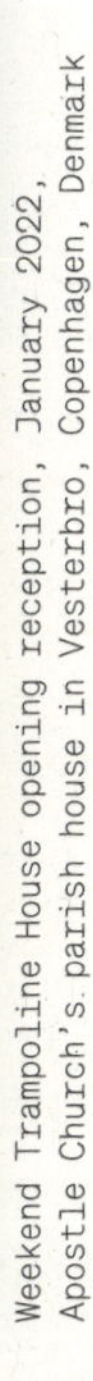

Weekend Trampoline House opening reception, January 2022, Apostle Church's parish house in Vesterbro, Copenhagen, Denmark

**TRAMPOLINE HOUSE'S DOCUMENTA FIFTEEN TEAM ARE**

Carlota Mir
Christine Mbabazi
Dady de Maximo
 Mwicira-Mitali
Helene Grøn
Hannah Lutz
Jean Claude Mangomba
Joachim Hamou
Khalid Albaih
Morten Goll
Muhannad Al Ulaby
Paul Farah Cox
Sara Albarani
Shakira Kasigwa
 Mukamusoni
Tommaso Daverio.

**FORMER MEMBERS OF THE DOCUMENTA TEAM:**

Fedaa Sultan
Nyari Yomdo
Tone Olaf Nielsen
Yong Sun Gullach

# WAJUKUU ART PROJECT

Wajukuu Art Project's architectural installation at the documenta Halle is a tunnel inspired by both Maasai traditional housing and the informal aesthetics of slums.

Almost ten kilometers east of Nairobi, Kenya's central business district, the tarmac road splinters into dirt roads of black volcanic soil. Encircled by factories and warehouses, a canopy of roofs is Lunga Lunga, one of Nairobi's most densely populated slums and home to the Wajukuu Art Project. Nails fix corrugated sheets to poles, low-intensity electric cables slither between iron sheet walls, improvised bridges are two poles rolled across the adjacent Ngong' River, children's games involve leaping across sanitation trenches. A vigorous informality enshrouds Lunga Lunga.

Tenacity highlights Wajukuu's approach to art and life, inserting art as the base and everything else as a superstructure. The reality of constant economic difficulties seeps through the expressive intentions in Wajukuu's socially conscious project. The collective's participation in lumbung, *Killing Fear of the Unknown,* culminates with a sustainability project, in which Wajukuu will secure a permanent project space, financially empower members, and share insight and techniques in woodwork workshops.

Aesthetic values nurtured by Wajukuu are organic extensions of the improvised functionalities, both culturally and socially, in their community. Objects of value and shelters reflect cultural attitudes and accessibility to materials. Lunga Lunga is an intersection, a mirror of the cultural diversity in Kenya, but also the clash between urbanization and heritage. Wajukuu's project anchors on conservation and reinvention of cultural heritage, both aspects evident in a folklore publication collaborating with senior storytellers and a site-specific intervention.

Wajukuu's architectural installation at the Documenta Halle is a tunnel simulation inspired by the Maasai *Manyatta* (traditional housing for the Maasai People of East Africa) and the informal aesthetics in the slums. Visitors enter the tunnel, wander into darker, coded space to experience multimedia expressions by Wajukuu-affiliated artists. Apart from a documentary, Wajukuu presents delicately refined objects, including a sculpture of a pedaled knife sharpener.

The intricacies activated by Wajukuu Art Project, as a collective and as individual artists, converge in the ever-evolving conditions in its actual environs. Every other year, fires raze sections of the slum, bulldozers flatten shelters. Wajukuu's library was part of a recent demolition. These misfortunes permeate creative consciousness, yet also catalyze imaginative energy and solidarity.

Enos Nyamor

INVITED PARTICIPANTS
Lawrence (Shabu) Mwangi
Ngugi Waweru
Josphat Kimathi
Joseph Waweru
Freshia Njeri
Joseph Ndung'u
Lazarus Tumbuti
Charles Muthumbi Githinji
Paul Irungu
Victor Chege Gatugi
Wambui Ngombo
Emmaus Kimani

VENUE
◎ documenta Halle

LUMBUNG INTER-LOKAL
O Britto Arts Trust
O FAFSWAG
O Fondation Festival sur le Niger
O Gudskul
O INLAND
O Instituto de Artivismo Hannah Arendt (INSTAR)
O Jatiwangi art Factory
O Más Arte Más Acción (MAMA)
O OFF-Biennale Budapest
O Project Art Works
O The Question of Funding
O Trampoline House
O ZK/U – Centre for Art and Urbanistics

Wajukuu Art Project, *wakija kwetu ndio wata tujua*, three-day art and music festival, platform for small scale economical activities in the community, kids' competitions, and art talks
Nairobi, Kenya, December 2021

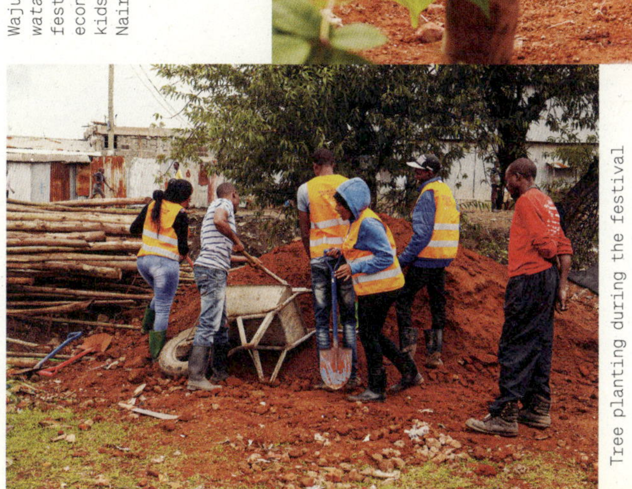

Tree planting during the festival

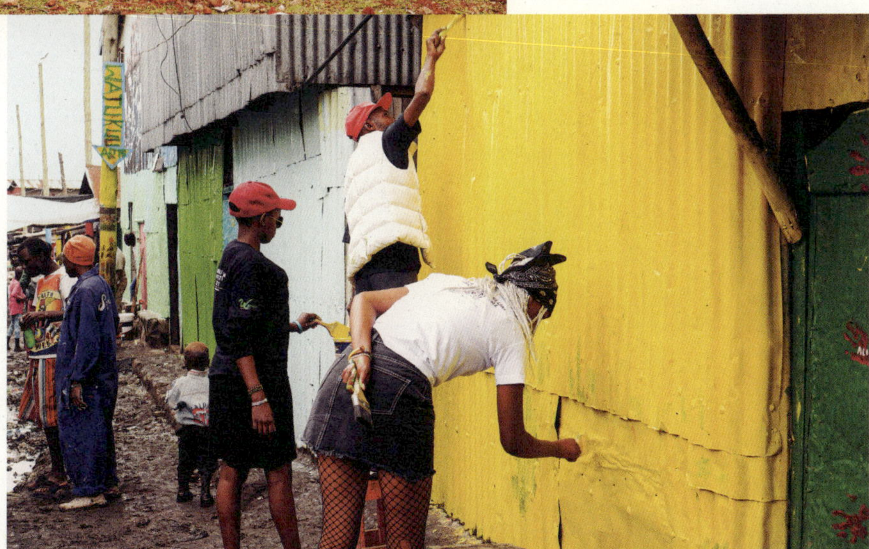

Street painting

Wajukuu Art Project

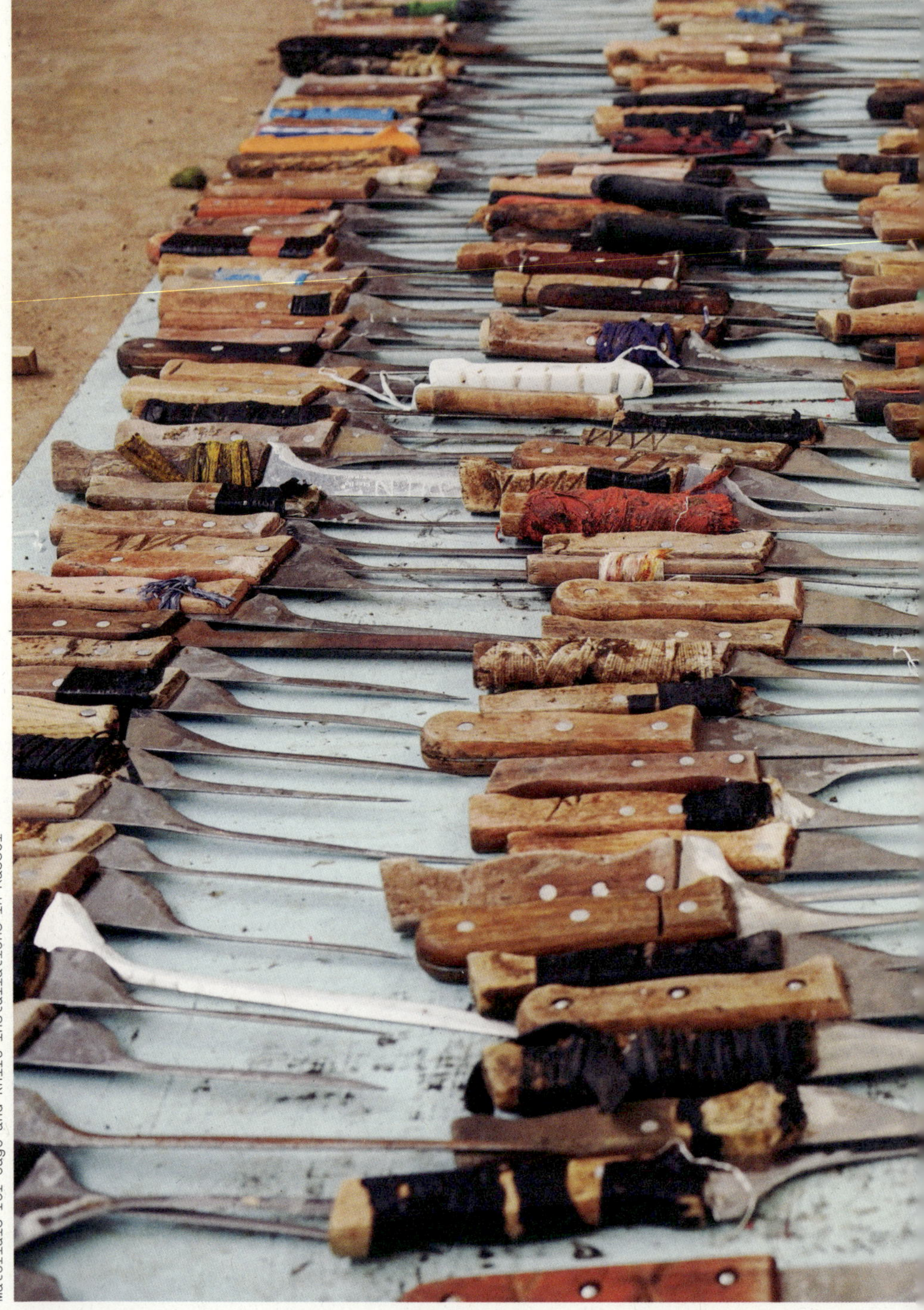

Materials for cage and knife installations in Kassel

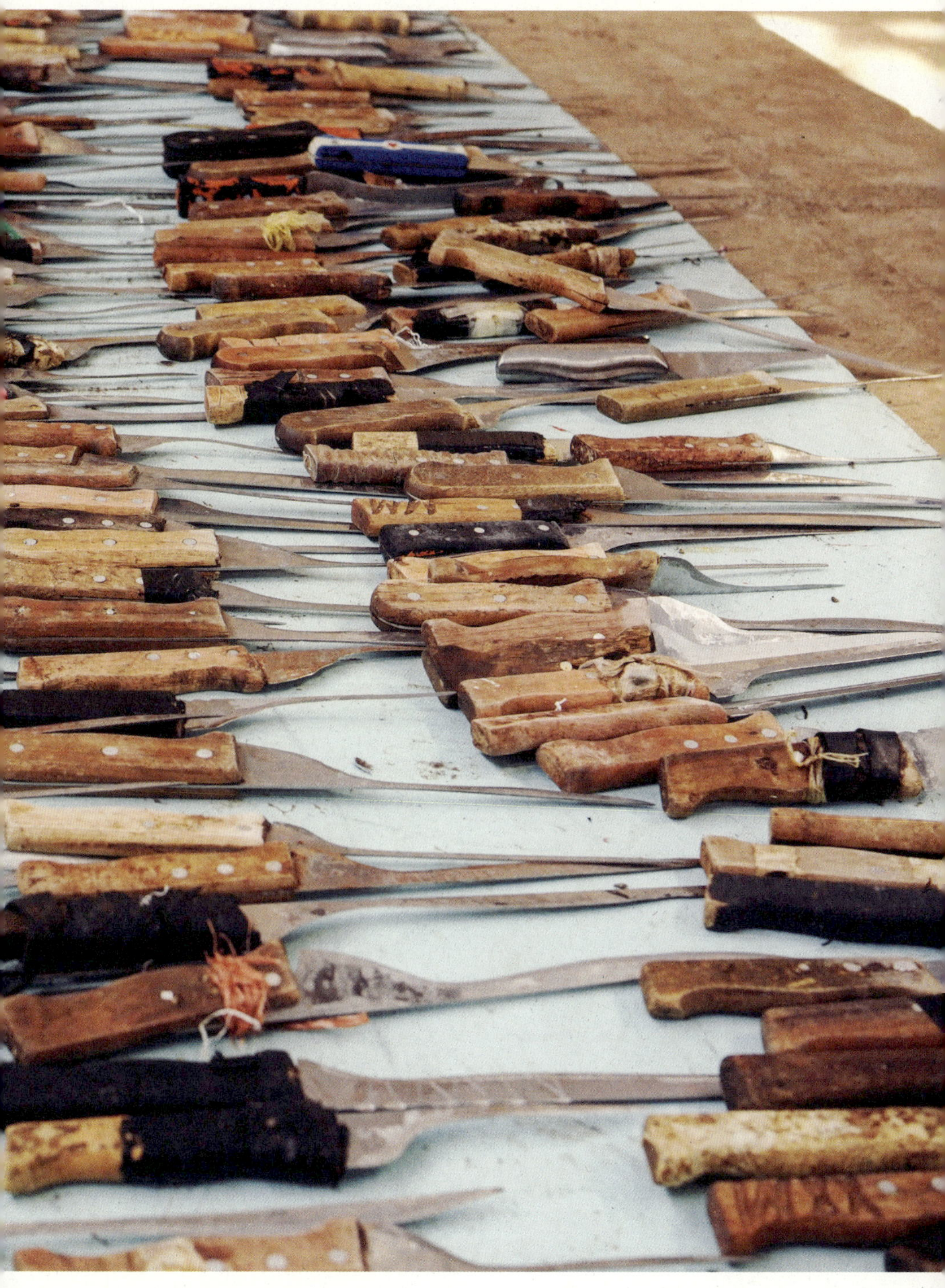

*Football Kommando*, 2022
In this Wakaliga Uganda story about human trafficking, a German football player and his wife search for their missing son. Movie produced in Wakaliga by Nabwana Isaac in collaboration with documenta fifteen.

# WAKALIGA UGANDA

A.K. Kaiza visits the legendary film studio Wakaliga Uganda, named after the neighborhood in Kampala. The studio's films are made collectively with people from mechanics to fruit vendors. Their work elevates everyday experience for the greater good.

The studio cannot be more underwhelming; it could not be more authentic.

The 10 x 15 m inner dirt courtyard is strewn with the bare, skeletal chassis that make the cars and helicopters in the iconic films. In the flat, floodplains fringing Kampala city in Uganda, where the air outside reeks with the putrescence of waste in stagnant water runnels, the big sign saying "Wakaliwood" stands like a Dadaist celebration of the bathetic.

It is here that such classics as *Who Killed Captain Alex?* (2010), *Kapitano* (2016) and *Bad Black* (2016) were made. When it started in 2005, Wakaliga Uganda was a new idea. Nearly two decades later, it remains a new idea. Which is ironic, because Wakaliga Uganda—properly known as Ramon Production Studios—has been making films as if a hundred years of filmmaking had not happened.

"Movies were meant to be entertaining," say founder and director Isaac Godfrey Geoffrey Nabwana and his co-founder Harriet Nakasujja. "These days, movies are boring. They say, the angle is not good, the light is not good, the sound is not good. But sometimes life is not straightforward and people making movies want to make life straightforward."

Nabwana is an inveterate conversationalist with a conspiratorial twinkle in the eye, and a riveting storyteller whose mantra seems to be a list of cinematic don'ts:

*"I don't premier my movies." "We make movies for entertainment. We are not the Ministry of Education." "We don't make movies for judges, which is why we don't go for festivals." "Our filmmakers don't come for salaries; they come to be stars."*

The biggest don't of all is that they operate without much of a budget. For films made on 200 US dollars a pop, Wakaliga's offerings punch way above their financial weight. But how is it even possible that films made without money can so move the cinematic world?

The secret—if such it is—lies in the social systems that make it possible. Known in the local lingua as *Bulungi Bwa'nsi* (good of the land), the collective spirit by which individuals freely sacrifice, for the greater good without expectation of material reward, is itself the making of Wakaliga Uganda.

By this philosophy, social, class and educational lines are erased and a community spirit becomes the guiding principle. Although he is the founder and director, Nabwana does not claim sole ownership of the films. He may come up with some of the ideas, but the "script" is collectively written as each crew and caste member brings ideas to create the film—collective authorship. They will take as pay what comes up but its not what brings them here. There is an open-door policy. Anyone that walks in is considered, and often, cast. The philosophy eschews rank. In the billing, there is no star system. Everyone, even "main characters", dies in the movies. No plot device is deployed to maintain an aristocracy of character.

And then beyond that too. Famous the world over, Wakaliga Uganda still measures its success

VENUE
*documenta* Halle

MINI-MAJELIS
O ikkibawiKrrr
O ook_
O Richard Bell
O Taring Padi

by how well the slums in the city receive its offerings.
Nabwana tells with pride the story of a cinema nearly
burnt to the ground by an irate mob of 400 who
sat waiting for him to finish editing a film they had
advertised on a megaphone, as affirmation that what
they did mattered.

The raffia and canvas cinemas are as symbolic
to Wakaliga Uganda as red carpets are to other filmic
"woods"; they are the fare of slum dwellers.

The collective spirit builds resilience, and in
the past two decades, Kampala's slums have become
important sites for music and cinema revolutions,
and have attracted state persecution. The key is the
collective spirit that sees ghetto creatives sacrifice
without pay to build art movements.

It is the elevation of the everyday man and
woman to heroic status; here, the garage mechanic
is the props master; a fruit and vegetable vendor in
the week, might become a crew head at the studio;
there is the music stall owner, the salon hair-dresser
who address studio hands Behind them is a network
of families and family friends who come to Wakaliga
Uganda because a trusted uncle works there. The process belongs in this network. The pay-off? Belonging
in fraternity and giving their neighborhood pride.

"For me film is friendship," Nabwana says.
"It is brotherhood."

The privileges that ring-fence postcolonial
city elite also erect rules, but as Nabwana says, those
rules disempower filmmakers. "People who have
gone through film school bring many rules. They are
shy; they fear to make mistakes. They become slaves
of papers. They say a camera should be on a tripod?
For me a camera should shake; Hollywood stars don't
die in movies, for me a main character should die. We
don't expect to have only one central star in a movie."

A.K. Kaiza

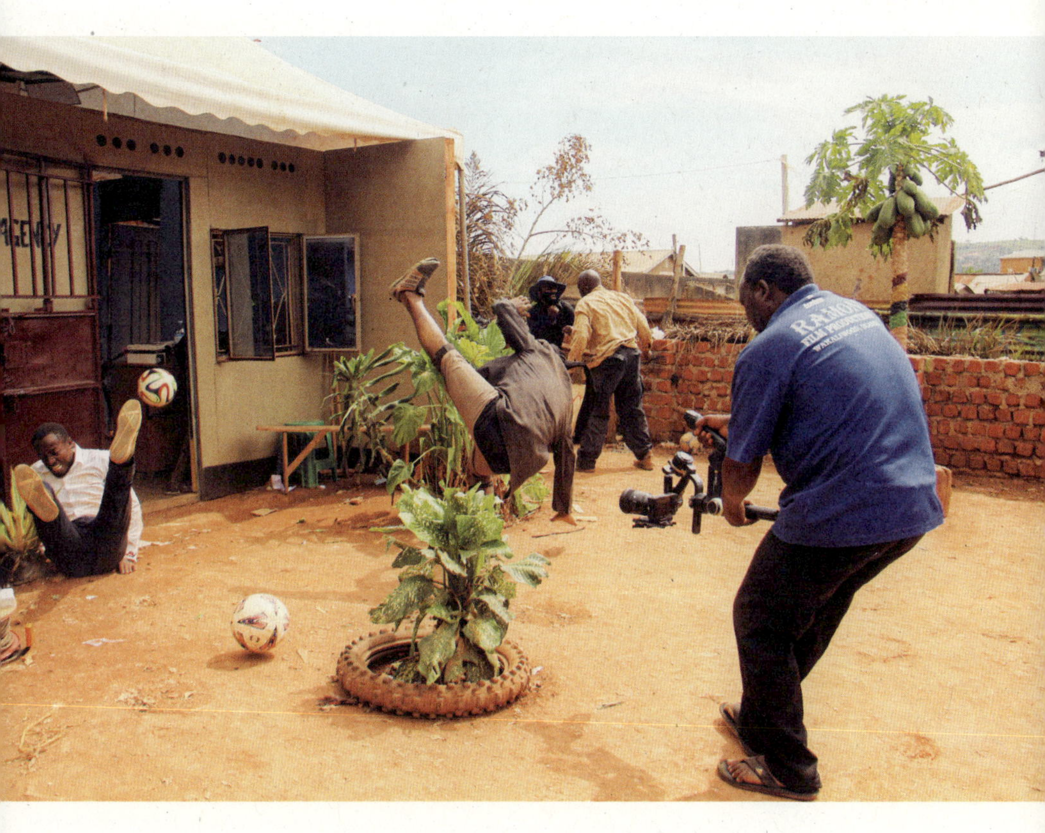

On the set of *FOOTBALL KOMMANDO*.
"Ruminiger attacks the Tiger base,
shoots Tiger mafias with balls to save
his wife", December 2021.
Wakaliga, Kampala, Uganda

# YASMINE EID-SABBAGH

yasmine eid-sabbagh's work explores the impossibilities of
representation. It departs from
photography collections assembled
in collaboration with inhabitants
of Burj al-Shamali, a Palestinian
refugee camp near Tyr, Lebanon.

What can communities who do not possess their own archive achieve through the process of collaboratively building a collection? How can such a photography collection be constituted in a way that does not reproduce the violence of national and colonial archives? These are some of the questions that yasmine eid-sabbagh, together with residents of Burj al-Shamali, brings to Kassel. Displaced to the south of Lebanon, Burj al-Shamali's inhabitants were forced to leave historic Palestine and the territories that became the state of Israel in 1948. Despite their right of return being sanctioned by the UN, they have been prevented from going home. For many it is the fourth generation who live in segregated areas such as Burj al-Shamali, caught between perma-nence and impermanence as their status remains unresolved, reliving the trauma of dispossession.

During her stay in Burj al-Shamali from 2006 to 2011, eid-sabbagh, along with inhabitants of the camp, gathered digital surrogates of their collection's personal photographs, and also engaged (from 2001 onwards) a group of young camp residents to produce their own images. This collaborative process enacts a mode of collecting that is informal, bottom-up, impromptu, creative, socially responsive, and has a built-in reflexive, self-critical mechanism to think through notions of archival agency, authority, and circulation.

For Hamada al-Joumah, who has ac-companied the project for some time, building this collection enables individuals to narrate Palestinian lives and histories of the camp differently. Photography, in his words, is a medium through which to contemplate life. The process produces a collective space of creativity and self-reflection, as well as a sense of trust, where individual positions can be expressed and co-exist. Rather than an end in itself, the collection is a means to engage in a negotiation in which the refugee condition can be reflected upon in different terms.

Due to its process of creation, this digital re-pository reveals profound affective and emotional layers that shift in response to the conversations and the settings in which the photographs are encountered. In its instantiation in Kassel, the project is concurrent with a collective editorial process activating the archive, and public events which leading to a sound installation. The work brings to light people's obstinate resistance to the negation of historicity as operated by coloniality, which, in Europe especially, is so often obscured from view.

Carine Zaayman, Chiara De Cesari,
Nuraini Juliastuti

VENUE
Hafenstraße 76

MINI-MAJELIS
O Atis Rezistans | Ghetto
  Biennale
O Marwa Arsanios
O Sourabh Phadke
O *foundationClass*collective

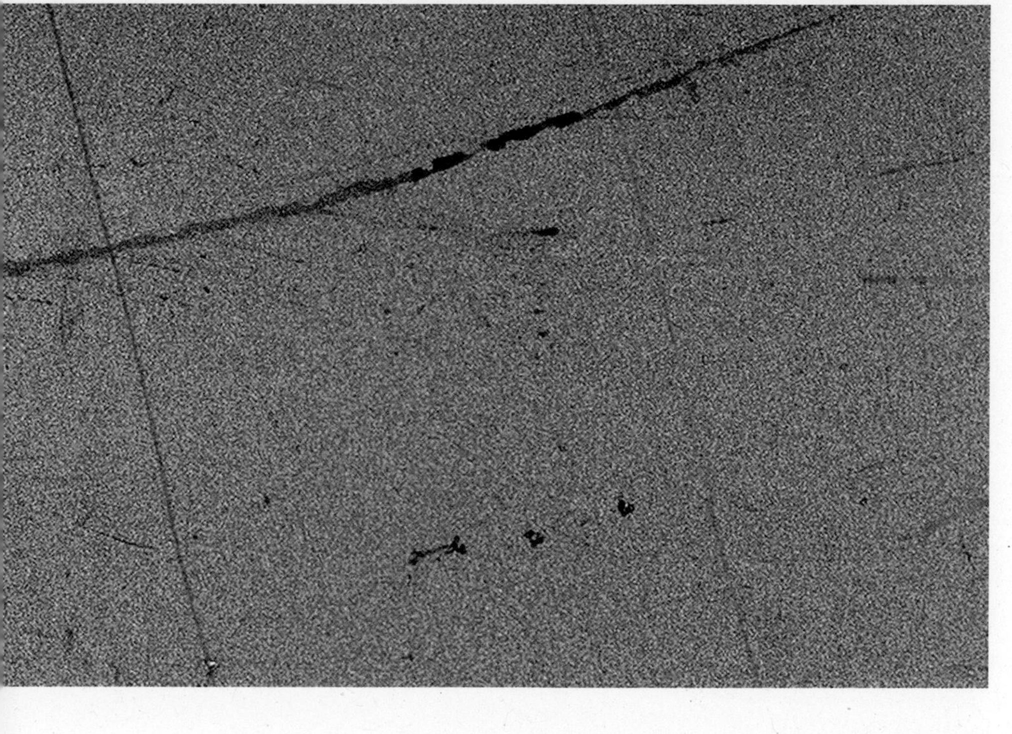



Y

yasmine eid-sabbagh

Two details from the project
*Beeholder – Beecoin* (2019)
Display with continuously collected
data from beehive

Overhead view of beehive

**VENUES**
- Hiroshima-Ufer (Karlsaue)
- ruruHaus

**LUMBUNG INTER-LOKAL**
- O Britto Arts Trust
- O FAFSWAG
- O Fondation Festival sur le Niger
- O Gudskul
- O INLAND
- O Instituto de Artivismo Hannah Arendt (INSTAR)
- O Jatiwangi art Factory
- O Más Arte Más Acción (MAMA)
- O Project Art Works
- O The Question of Funding
- O Trampoline House
- O Wajukuu Art Project
- O OFF Biennale

# ZK/U – CENTER FOR ART AND URBANISTICS

ZK/U works at the intersection of architecture, urbanism, and social issues. They are manually pulling a ship from Berlin to Kassel.

For many years, Berlin , Germany was a place of temporary use, affordable housing, and abundant space. All this has radically changed. In no other major German city have rents risen so sharply—in the last five years alone, by 42 percent. New social inequalities are emerging, and urban open space is shrinking.

ZK/U – Center for Art and Urbanistics was founded in 2012 when three members of the artists collective KUNSTrePUBLIK, Matthias Einhoff, Philip Horst, and Harry Sachs, moved into an abandoned freight station in Berlin's Moabit neighborhood. A former industrial and working-class district, the area—once bordering the Berlin Wall—has been the site of several historical ruptures. Fittingly, ZK/U translates global discourses onto the city, architecture, social issues and ecology into local terms. ZK/U proposes alternative models for neighborhood empowerment and participation—often in exchange with other artists and worldwide.

In the wake of an extension of the ZK/U building, the main wooden roof was removed and became the starting point for ZK/U's first documenta project, *Citizenship* (2022). The roof was turned upside down and became a boat. Being launched in early June, it now travels from Berlin-Moabit to Kassel without the use of fossil fuels—collecting muscular energy and renewable sources. During the approximately seven-week journey, the *Citizenship* affords a gaze at German landscapes and communities via the Elbe-Havel Canal, Mittelland Canal, Weser, and Fulda. Workshops, debates, and performances with local and lumbung communities outline new perspectives on distribution of wealth, energy, and time. Installed on the Fulda riverbanks in Kassel, the boat once again is turned upside down to become a community structure that hosts artifacts and rituals from the trip, and opens a dialogue with citizens from Kassel.

At the conjunction of artistic creation, urban activism, crypto-economic design and beekeeping, the second documenta contribution, *Beeholder - Beecoin*, stands out in the field of block-chain-based practices. Operating as a Distributed Autonomous Organizations (DAO), Beecoin is an art project dedicated to the improvement of the living conditions of bees. Following a first iteration developed in 2019 it represents a cutting-edge, locally grounded experiment participating in the recent emergence of a variety of artistic endeavors, pioneering alternative paths for the future development of decentralized applications (dapps) for common good.

Visitors can participate by becoming active members of the network, and as part of the project, more than 15 beekeepers from Kassel act as mediators. Members—bees as well as visitors—can decide upon proposals that promote non-human-agent well being. As with many other projects in the blockchain world, *Beeholder - Beecoin* is speculative at its core, projecting a radically disruptive future socio-technical development.

Ralf Schlüter

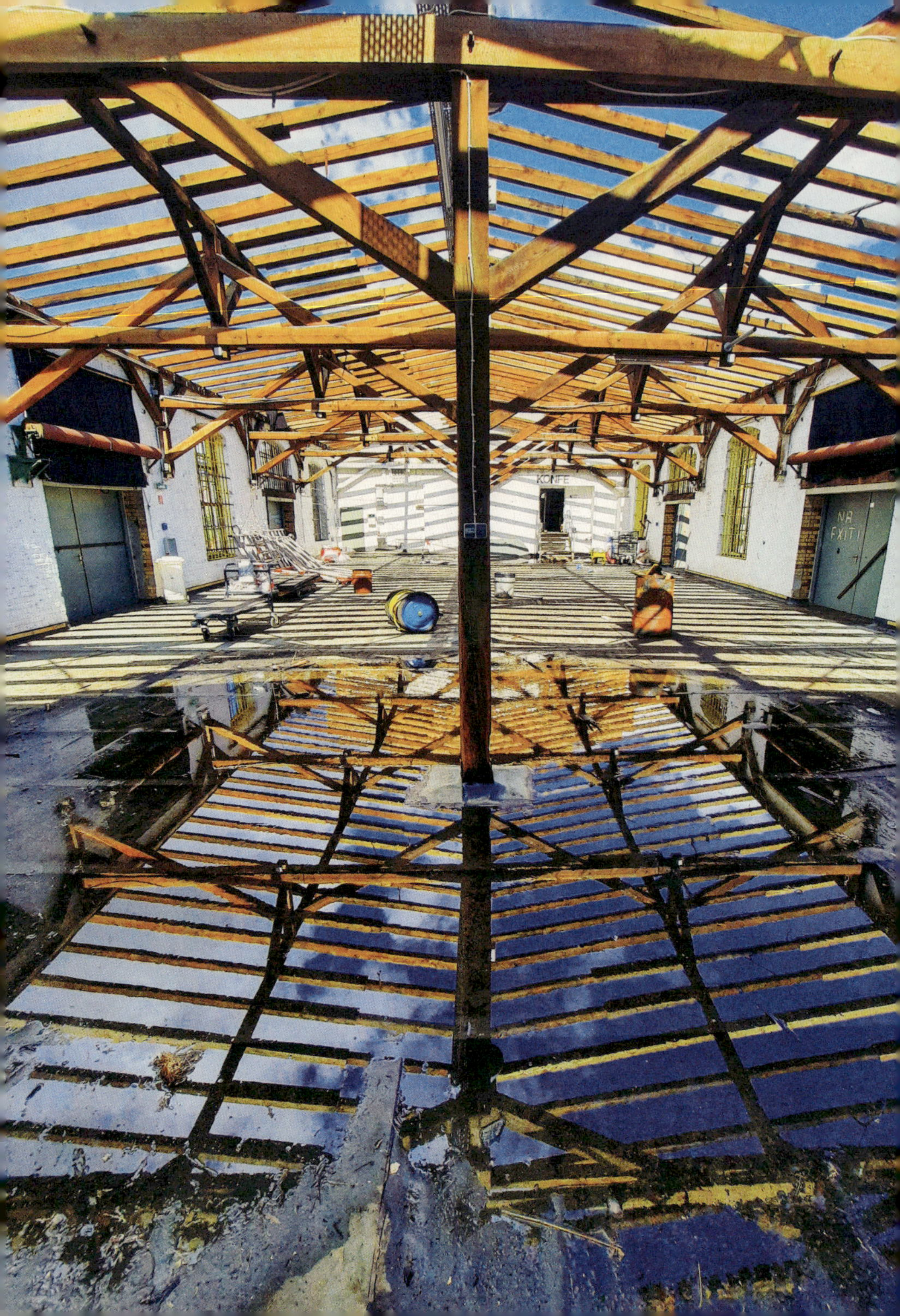

KONFE
NA
EXIT

ROUTE CITIZENSHIP
START : BERLIN
ZIEL : KASSEL
STRECKE : 602,5 Km
STOPS : 48

HANNOVER
WOLFSBURG
o BRAUNSCHWEIG
MINDEN
BRANDEN BURG
ZK/U BERLIN
MUSEUMSINSEL

HANN MÜNDEN
d15 KASSEL



Left: View of the roof
truss before demolition

ZK/U team after transporting roof truss

The roof truss after dismantling

ZK/U headquarters in an old goods
station, Berlin-Moabit

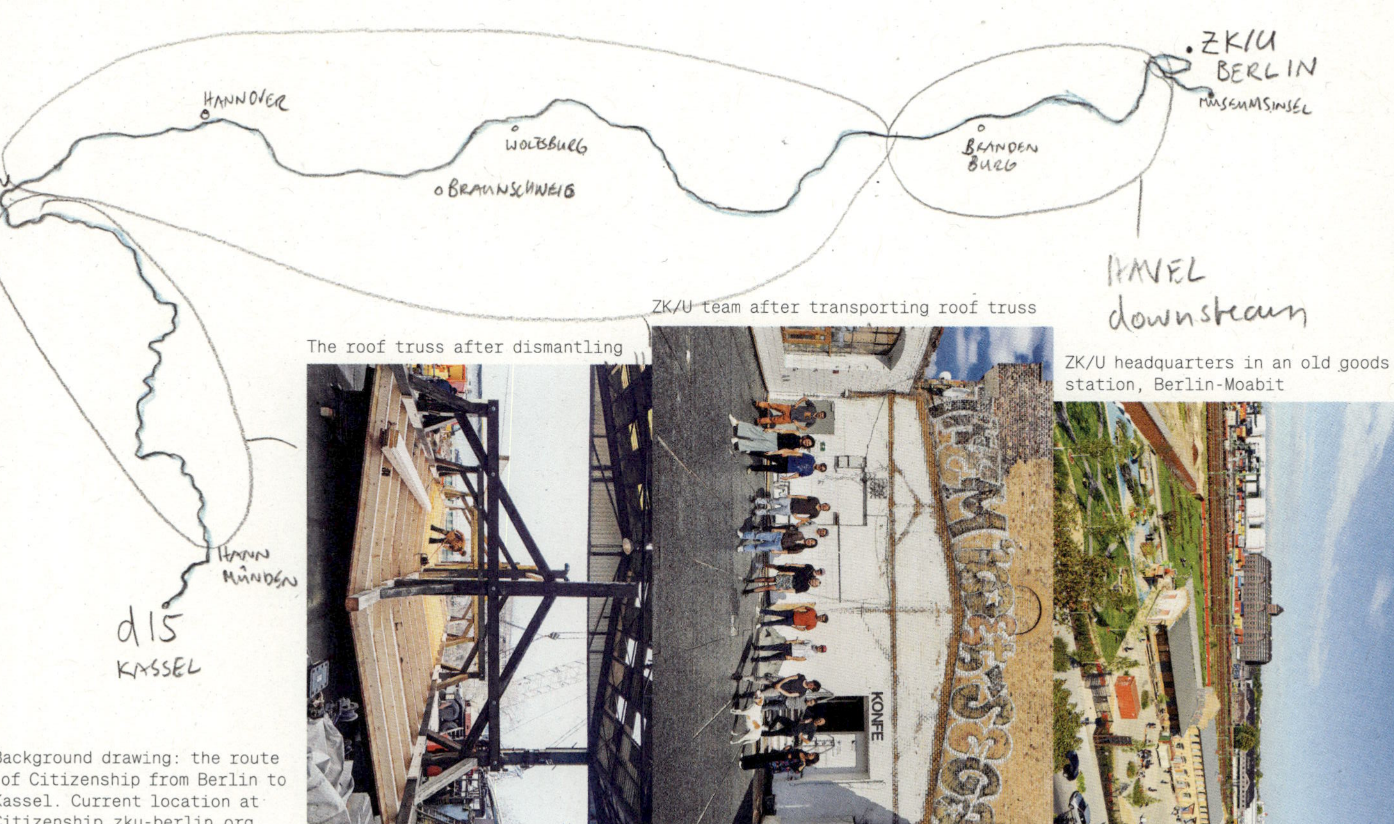

Background drawing: the route
of Citizenship from Berlin to
Kassel. Current location at
Citizenship.zku-berlin.org



ZK/U – Center for Art and Urbanistics

# INVITED PARTICIPANTS

The following is a list of documenta fifteen lumbung members and lumbung artists as well as their invited participants. For the most up-to-date list of participants, as well as acknowledgements, please refer to our website at documenta-fifteen.de

***FOUNDATIONCLASS***
 **COLLECTIVE**
Abiye Okujagu
Ali Kaaf
Anwar Al Atrash
Bora Yediel
Cẩm-Anh Lương
Carolyn Amora Bosco
Fadi Aljabour
Hatef Soltani
Katharina Kersten
Krishan Rajapakshe
Miriam Schickler
Mohamad Halbouni
Nadira Husain
Nour Yassin
Susan Azizi
Ulf Aminde
Vera Varlamova
Yemisi Babatola

**AMOL K PATIL**
Das Rollschuhmagazin
Parul Sinha
Poonam Jain
Sachin Kondalkar
Saviya Lopes
Vinit Dharia
YALGAAR Sanskrutik
 Manch
Yogesh Barve

**ANOTHER ROADMAP AFRICA**
 **CLUSTER (ARAC)**
Andrea Thal
Cedrick Nzolo
Christian Nyampeta
Jean Kamba
Lineo Segoete
Patrick Mudekereza
Puleng Plessie
Quadri Oluwasegun
Rana El Nemr
Rangoato Hlasane
Sari Middernacht
Zachary Rosen

**ARTS COLLABORATORY**
**Arts Collaboratory**
 **School hosting team**
Adrian Milpa Jimar
Alex Rubuela
Álvaro Castillo
Ana Milena Garzón
Andrés Villalobos

**Arts Collaboratory**
 **members and ekosistems**
Binita Shrestha
Darina Kaparovaa
Dasha Chernysheva
Diego Teo
Geral Faun
Jazael Olguinzapata
Juan Jaramillo
Juan Mena
Luciana Fleischman
Macarena Hernández
Malika Umarova
Marat Raiymkulov
Maria R. Collado
Mario Morales
Michelle Coffey
Omar
Sally Mizrachi
Sandro Brito
Sari Denisse
Stefania Acevedo
Syafiatudina
Waysatta
Yamir Castillo
Yanireth Jiménez

**ASIA ART ARCHIVE**
Carol Choi
Charlotte Mui
Christopher K. Ho
Chương-Đài Võ
Debby Tsui
Gabrielle Chan
John Tain
Leah Lam
Lydia Lam
Özge Ersoy
Pallavi Arora
Rebecca Tso
Samantha Chao
Samira Bose
Sneha Ragavan
Susanna Chung
**Featuring materials**
 **from the archives of:**
Jyoti Bhatt
Karla Sachse
Lawan Jirasuradej
Lee Wen
loans from the
 Department of
 Painting, Faculty
 of Fine Arts, M.S.
 University of Baroda

Museum of Art &
 Photography, Bangalore
Nilima Sheikh
Nitaya Ueareeworakul
Phaptawan Suwannakudt
Ray Langenbach
Womanifesto

**BAAN NOORG**
 **COLLABORATIVE ARTS**
 **AND CULTURE**
Alfred Banze
Christine Falk
Dangchanok Pongdam
Jiradej Meemalai
Krittaporn Mahaweerarat
Lo Shih-Tung
Pakchira Chartpanyawut
Pornpilai Meemalai
Timothy Liam Morgan

**BRITTO ARTS TRUST**
Abdur Rab
AKM Maynul Islam
Alok Raj Bongshi
Arpita Singha Lopa
Ashim Halder Sagor
Azizee Fawmi Khan
ColorKubes, Kassel &
 Britto's Mural Team
Emdadul Hoque Topu
Emran Sohel
Farah Naz Moon
Fareha Zeba
Farhana Ferdausi
Imran Hossain Piplu
Jewel A Rob
Jinnatun Jannat
Kabir Ahmed Masum
 Chisty
Kazi Sydul Karim
Khushi Kabir
Lutfun Nahar
Mahbubur Rahman
MD. Aminul Islam
Md. Hanif Pappu
Md. Khairul Alam
MD. Rakibul Anwar
Mehedi Hasan
Milton Anwar
Mohosin Kabir
Nijhum Zannatun Nahar
RA Kajol
Reetu Sattar

S.M.Saha Anisuzzaman
 Faroque
Safiha Hossain
Saidul Haque Juise
Salahuddin Khan Srabon
Sarah Jabin
Sayed Fida Hossain
Shahriar Shaon
Shimul Datta
Shimul Saha
Shishir Bhattacherjee
Shree Tapan Chandra
Tarun Ghosh
Tayeba Begum Lipi
Trishna Paul
Yasmin Jahan

**CENTRE D'ART WAZA**
AGATHON KAKUSA
Bodil Furu
Bram Goots
Cecile Mwepu
Chadrack Kakule
Chriss Kabongo
Christelle Ntanga
Christian Nyampeta
Damien Kahambwe
Denise Maheho
Feza Kayungu
Guellord Mbolela
IIunga Kangalele Richar
Jean-Guy Mbopey
Jeanne IIunga
Joseph Kasau
Kabala Mwana Mbuyi Adam
Kabulo Kazadi Richard
Kazadi Kapenda Richard
Leon Verbeek
Lubange Wa Kangalele
Lumbwe Kafwana Laurent
Lumuna Ndala
Mamán Kisimba
Maya Van Leemput
Michel Kasongo
Mwewa Kasongo
Nadine Pena
Naomie Monga Masengo
Nontobeko Ntombel
Olivier Bwihangane
Patrick Mudekereza
Pierre Kahenga
Prodige Makonga
Raphael Salumu
Rene Ngombe
Richard Mbuyu

Rita Mukebo
Samuel Luenberger
Sari Middernacht
Stephane Kabila
Tresor Makonga
Veronique Poverello

**CHANG EN-MAN**
Han-Fang Wang
Shueh Ching Lu
Ting Tsou

**CHIMURENGA**
Akin Adesokan
Bianca Van Rooi
Bogani Kona
Chantal Bouw
Graeme Arendse
Mamadou Diallo
Moses Marz
Nomaliqhwa Hadebe
Ntone Edjabe
Pura Lavisa

**CINEMA CARAVAN AND
TAKASHI KURIBAYASHI**
Akira Okura
Eikou Haraguchi
Eisuke Ogawa
Gen Nagashima
Kazuaki Komiya
Mickey Varot
Masaya Fantasista
Michinori Maru
Mizuki Nishimura
Naoito
Rai Shizuno
Satoru Segi
Takashi Kuribayashi
Tatsuya Sano

**EL WARCHA**
Aziz Aissaoui
Aziz Romdhani
Benjamin Perrot
Chiraz Guellela
Marlene Halbgewachs
Naomi Nantois Meadow
Radhouane Boudhraa
Selma Kossentini

**FEHRAS PUBLISHING
PRACTICES**
Kenan Darwich
Omar Nicolas
Sami Rustom

**JIMMIE DURHAM & A
STICK IN THE FOREST BY
THE SIDE OF THE ROAD**
Bev Koski
Elisa Strinna
Hamza Badran
Iain Chambers
Joen Vedel

Jone Kvie
Maria Thereza Alves
Wilma Lukatsch

**JUMANA EMIL ABBOUD**
Anna Sherbany
Issa Freij
Lydia Antoniou
Mounya Elbakay
Sourabh Phadke
Yasmine Haj

**LA INTERMUNDIAL
HOLOBIENTE**
Anahí Rayen Mariluán
Carla Grunauer
Claudia Fontes
Erica Bohm
Gabriela Cabezón
  Cámara
Graciela Carnevale
Guadalupe Lucero
Guadalupe Miles
Gustavo Ibarra
Hector (Chino) Soria
Ingrid Bleynat
Isabel Mendoza
Juan Mendoza
Karina Mendoza
Leticia Obeid
Lucas Di Pascuale
Lucio Capece
Luis Sagasti
Noelia Billi
Pablo Martín Ruiz
Paula Fleisner
Ral Veroni
Reynaldo Jiménez
Sergio Raimondi
Sol Rébora
Susana Villalba
The ten thousand
  things
Tulio De Sagastizábal
Virgini Buitrón
Weavers of the Tewok
  Cultural Centre

**LE 18**
Francesca Masoero
Laila Hida
Nadir Bouhmouch
Soumeya Ait Ahmed
Curatorial / AD
  contributors
Abdellah Hassak
Ahmed Bennys
Ahmed Bouanani
Amine Lahrach
Archives Bouanani
  Collective
Assia Djebar
Audi George Bajalia
AWAL
Benjamin Verhoeven

Caravane Tighmert
Carlos Perez Marin
Contributing Artists
Elisa Zorzi
Farida Benlyazid
Firas Hamdan
Grocco
Hadia Gana
Imane Zoubai
Jumana Emil Abboud
Khadija El Abyad
Le Brouillon
Louisa Aarrass
Mamans Douées
M'barek Bouhchichi
Meriem Benmhamed
Mohamed Oubenaal
Montasser Drissi
Mounir Rahmouni
Nabil Himich
Nassim Azarzar
QANAT
Reem Shadid
Rim Mejdi
Sara Frikech
Shayma Nader
Sofia Fahli
Teckchbila
Touda Bouanani
Troupe Asnimer
Troupe Cheikh Hammou
Untitled Duo
Yasmine Benabdallah
Yassine Rachidi
Zakia Kadiri

**MARWA ARSANIOS**
Joanna Dammour and
  the AUB Geological
  Museum
Jowe Harfouche
Katrin Ebersohn
Magda Nammour and
  the Bibliotheque
  Orientale in
  Beirut
Marie Nour Hechaime
Mazen Hachem
Mohamed Blakah
Nadim Choufi
Nagham Darwich
Nancy Nasserdine

**MÁS ARTE MÁS ACCIÓN
 (MAMA)**
**MAMA TEAM**
Alejandra Rojas
Carmenza Rojas
Fernando Arias
Jonathan Colin
Paola Pérez
Rossana Alarcón
**MAMA Ecosystem.
  Artists/
  Collaborators**

Ailie Rutherford
Alejandro Castillejo
Ana Milena Garzón
Ariane Andereggen
Atelier Van Lieshout
David Paredes
Elkin Calderón
Enrique Murillo
Fausto Moreno
Fernando Serrano
Gregorio Gómez
Jhon Esteban Lasso
Karina Angulo
Kathrin Wildner
Manuel David Riascos
María Andrade
Osneyder Valoy
Sina Ribak
Stefan Peters
Ted Gaier
Teresa Feldmann
Velia Vidal
Yaisa Mariam
  Rodríguez
Yuli Correa

**NGUYEN TRINH THI**
Jamie Maxtone Graham
Lê Quang Minh
Lê Thuận Uyên
Nguyễn Xuân Sơn
Phạm Chí Khánh
Phạm Hoàng Gia Khang
Uông Thanh Ngọc

**NINO BULLING**
Aisha Franz
Aki Hassan
Ansgar Lorenz
Bea Kittelmann
Bilge Emir
Chiny Udeani
Eva Gräbeldinger
Eva Müller
Ilknur Kocer
Jiaqi Hou
Jo Rüßmann
Joseph Kai
Jul Gordon
Malika Teßmann
Malwine Stauss
Marc Hennes
Marijpol
Martin Keziah Vella
Michel Esselbrügge
Mloukhiyyé Al-Fil
Natyada Tawonsri
Nour Hifaoui
Nygel Panasco
Romy Matar
Sheree Domingo
Stefanie Leinhos
Tinet Elmgren
Ulrike Steinke

## OFF-BIENNALE BUDAPEST

Ádám Kokesch
Angéla Kóczé
Anna Lujza Szász
Architecture Uncomfort-
  able Workshop (Emil
  Dénes Ghyczy & Lukács
  Szederkényi)
Borbála Szalai
Ceija Stojka
Damian Le Bas
Dr.-Ing. Florian
  Bellin-Harder /
  Fachgebiet Land-
  schaftsbau, Land-
  schaftsmanagement
  und Vegetationsent-
  wicklung
East Europe Biennial
  Alliance
Eszter György
Eszter Szakács
Eszter Lázár
Ethel Brooks
European Roma Institute
  for Arts and Culture
  (ERIAC)
Eva Koťátková
Hajnalka Somogyi
Ilona Németh
János Balázs
K&K Stauden
Katalin Székely
Małgorzata MirgaTas
Manolo Gomez
Mara (Omara) Oláh
Marián Ravasz
Maximilian Mechsner
Miguel Ángel Vargas
Nikolett Erőss
On the Same Page (Rita
  KÁLMÁN, Lívia PÁLDI,
  Katarina ŠEVIĆ)
Otto Pankok
Prof. Dr.-Ing. Stefan
  Körner / Fachgebiet
  Landschaftsbau, Land-
  schaftsmanagement und
  Vegetationsentwick-
  lung
Recetas Urbanas Santi
  Cirugeda, Alice
  Attout
Robert Gabris
Sead Kazanxhiu
Selma Selman
Tamás Péli
Teri Szücs
The Randomroutines
  (Tamás KASZÁS,
  Krisztián KRISTÓF)
Timea Junghaus
Unterneustädter Schule
  (Kerstin Schwabe-
  Matic, Klaus Kurtz)

## OOK_ [REINAART VANHOE, NEUE BRÜDERKIRCHE, ESPORA, BPOC FESTIVAL KASSEL, COLORLABOR, LUMBUNG_TARWEWIJK, ELAINE W. HO, BARTIRA, WOK THE ROCK, COLLECTIVE, K. FORMAT …]

Almu
Ana Maria Vallejo
Ana Vera
Angeliki Diakrousi
Araby Yakoub Ibrahim
BPOC Festival Kassel
Camilo Vega
Carl-Schomburg-Schule,
  Kassel
Carolin Angulo Hammes
Christian Reber
Coco Rufer
Cristina Cochior
Dalia Velandi
Deborah Manavi -
  Partizipative
  Tanzforschung zum
  Common Ground
Diakonisches Werk
  Region Kassel
Divine Impact Church
  of God
Donata Clemens
Essbare Stadt e.V.
Estefanía
Ev. Hoffnungskirchen-
  gemeinde
Familienbildungsstätte
  Sternschnuppe
Flora Saß
Florian Cramer
Friederike Spieker
Friedrich Carl von
  Uckro
Goethe-Gymnasium
  Kassel
Hannah Koerner
Hannan El Mikdam-
  Lasslop
Ingo Nitsche
Institut Sozialwesen
  der Universität
  Kassel
Islamisches Zentrum
  Kassel
Jan Wortmann
Jana Faßbender
Jens Redemann
Josefina Dux
Judith Leijdekkers
Jugendarbeit Wesertor
  der Stadt Kassel
Julia Kopylova
Kassel Kunsthoch-
  schule's Performance
  and Multidisciplinary
  Class in collabora-

tion with Class for
Performance and Time
Based Media from the
Berlin University of
the Arts
Khalat Khalaf Khalil
Kita Sonnenhang
Kulturzentrum
  Schlachthof gGmbH
Luca Marie Tüshaus
mariëlle verdijk
Matin Abbas
Mayra Alejandra
  Schultheis
Meike Stricker
Merlind Sauerland
Niklas Holzhauer
Nisa e.V.
Norgard Kröger
Ole Handschug
Palaver Rhababa
Pauline Brämer
Philipp Colorado
Philipp Firmbach
Pris Roos
Rahila Sahebdel
Rana Matloub
Rieneke de Vries
Rosalío Ochoa Saavedra
Rui Reis
Sabine Dühring
Sara Hamadeh
Sascha Nelle
Selma El Mikdam-Lasslop
Silvio Lorusso
Simon Browne
social sculpture lab
  e.V.
Sophie Stein, Kassel
Stadtteilzentrum
  Wesertor
Stefan Nadolny
Stefan Roser
Stefany Karghoti
Suchee Simonti
Tamara Drath
Teferi Mekonen
Tilman Evers
Tomi Hilsee
Unterneustädter
  Grundschule
Wad Maback
Walter-Lübcke-Schule
Zemenu Tenagne Zeleke
Zoë Cochia
and others…

## PARTY OFFICE B2B FADESCHA

Abhinit Khanna
Ada Navarro
After Party Collective
Ali Akbar Mehta
Aliens for Uncertain
  Futures

Amrish Kondurkar
Aru
Aum
Caitlin Adams
Constanza Pina
Joey Cannizzaro
Jyotsna
Kinkinella
Maria Jorge Medina
Ramya Patnaik
Shaunak Mahbubani
Vidha Saumya
Vidisha-Fadescha

## PINAR ÖĞRENCI

Ayşe Dorak
Didare İşleyen
Neşe Polat
Nuriye İşleyen

## PROJECT ART WORKS

Aida Ashall
Amy Fenton
Andrew Cooper
Annie Rose Walter
Annis Joslin
Carl Sexton
Charlie Thomas
Charlotte Hanlon
Charlotte Stephens
Christopher Tite
Claire Matthews
Connor Ashley
Darryl Spencer
David Geall
Dion Downes
Eden Kötting
Esther Springett
Gabriella Rapisarda
Gemma Evans
George Smith
Georgie Scott
Helen Carlton
Holli Macnamara
India O'Sullivan
Jack Goldsmith
Jessica Courtney
  Bennett
Jo Goldman
Johnny Caroll Pell
Kate Adams
Katie Taylor
Leila Mcmillan
Luise Newham
Lucy Jenion
Luke Bebb
Magda Pata
Marion Willis
Mark Daniels
Martin Swan
Maya Shapiro Steen
Michelle Roberts
Nathalie Dance
Neville Jermyn
Oliver Crowther

Patricia Finnegan
Paul Colley
Peter Quinnell
Phoebe Ellen Prebble
Sam Smith
Sara Dare
Sarah Dunn
Sarah T
Sean Ormonde
Sharif Persaud
Siddharth Gadiyar
Stanley Elis
Thomas Lepora
Tim Corrigan
Wendy Routley
Will Shepherd

## RICHARD BELL
Digi Youth Arts

## SADA [REGROUP]
Ali Eyal
Bassim al Shaker
Laith K. Daer
Raed Motar
Rijin Sahakian
Sajjad Abbas
Sarah Munaf

## SAFDAR AHMED
Alia Ardon
Can Yalçınkaya
Kazem Kazemi
Miream Salameh
MN (identity is
  concealed for
  reasons of privacy)
TABZ A (identity
  is concealed for
  reasons of privacy)
Zeinab Mir

## SIWA PLATEFORME
   - L'ECONOMAT AT
   REDEYEF
Abdelhamid Mansouri
Aicha Mansouri
Ali Dhahri
Atef Maatallah
Fakhri El Ghazel
Farid Yahyaoui
Fatima Machouch
Francois Tanguy
Hamouda Jarrar
Haytham Zakaria
Haythem Ben Bousaha
Houcine Chraiti
Houcine Ezzedini
Imen Smaoui
Jean Michel Diaz
Jean Pierre Han
Laid Bouoni
Lassad Beldi
Laurence Chable
Loup Uberto

Malek Bouaoni
Marianne Dautrey
Marwan Akrouti
Matheiu Lontanaza
Mohamed Amin Ezzedini
Mohamed Labidi
Mohamed Znaidi
Mouna Belhouchet
Muntasser Kramti
Nadia Tazi
Noura Ben Ali
Okacha Ben Salah
Rai Uno
Rochdy Machouch
Saad Tabbabi
Salah Znaidi
Salim Ben Mohamed
Samir Ben Boubaker
Sophie Bessis

## SUBVERSIVE FILM
Aoe Tanami
Baker Sharqawi
Don Catchlove
Ghaleb Shaath
Ismail Shammout
Iwanami Productions
Jack Madvo
Jim Cranmer
Khaled Siddik
Monica Maurer
Mustafa Abu Ali
Riuychi Hirokawa
Sabih Al Zoohiri
Sami Salamoni
Samir Nimr
Samir R. Hissen
SHIRAK
T. Maki
Tom Hollyman
Victor Haddad
Wakamatsu Productions

## THE QUESTION OF
   FUNDING
Adele Jarrar
Amany Khalifa
Dena Matter
Fayrouz Sharqawi
Martin Heller
Mohammad Hawajri
Mohammad Abu Sal
Noor Abed
Raed Issa
Raoof Alajouri
Rayya Badran
Siwar Kraitm
Yazan Khalili

## ZK/U – CENTER FOR ART
   AND URBANISTICS
### ZK/U Team
Anita Rind
Dennis Lindenau
Elisa Georgi
Harry Sachs
Lars Hayer
Matthias Einhoff
Miodrag Kuc
Philip Horst
Tirdad Zolghadr

### Fussballaballa
David Zabel
Henning Beste
Janis Feneberg
Jessie
Klaus Wiese
Max Winkler
Mustafa Gündar
Robin Pach
Sabine Pach
Samuel Rettenmaier
Tom Zölzer

### Beecoin
Clemens Gruber
Curvelabs
Erik Bordeleau
Hiveeyes
Lars Neckel
Max Hampshire
Nascent
Paul Seidler
Steph Holltrieu
Steve Rogenstein

### Citizenship
Alberto Stievanin
Alexa Kreissl
Alexander Callsen
Alexander Römer
Alina Schwörer
Andrea Chudack
Andrea Goetzke
Arda Yelda
Arda Yeldan
Arved Schultze
Axel Loytved
Barbara Bernsmeier
Benjamin Menzel
Bernd Schulz
Brennstoff Efoy
Cecilia Andersson
Daniel Seiple
Danijela Pivašević-
  Tenner
David Becker
Feeda Sultan
Feliks Oldewage
Felix Kremer
Florian Dietrich
Florian Sprenger
Folke Köbberling

Frank Jimin Hopp
Frederick Becker
Georg Scherlin
Gergely Laszlo
Gob Squad
Hajo Toppius
Holz Jordan
Institut für
  Architekturbezogene
  Kunst TU
  Braunschweig
Ilja Borgböhmer
Jan Körbes
Jan van Esch
Janis Barner
Jonas Hohmann
Jozef van der Heijden
Junhen Zhang
Katharina Laura Kunz
Klara Adam
Lars Straehler-Pohl
Lea Grönholdt
Lea Schleiffenbaum
Lea Søvsø
Leo Busch
Madeleine Madej
Manuel Strube
Marie Salcedo Horn
Markus Shimizu
Markus Zimmermann
Martina Pozzan
Matthias Kremsreiter
Max Jeromin
Mecki Pääda
Michael Meister
Michael Zwingmann
Michael Herzog
Min Kyung Kim
Nelli David
Nelly Choné
Olesia Vitiuk
Olesia Voss
Pablo Santacana Lopez
Paul Keßler
Redwane Jabal
Reiko Kanazawa
Rene Shenouda
Roland Castringius
Roland Gaber
Sascha Schneider
Schneider TM
Seb Birch
Sina Ahlers
Sina Heffner
Sonja Sommer
Svenja Simone Schulte
Tobias Opialla
Tomoko Nakasato
Verena Seibt
Viviane Tabach
Yong Sun Gullach

# KASSEL

KULTURZENTRUM SCHLACHTHOF
UNI KASSEL
FULDATALSTRAßE
KASSEL HBF
AM STERN
KURT-WOLTERS-STR.
KÖNIGS PLATZ
OBERE KÖNIGS STR.
FRIEDRICHS PL.
STEINWEG
WESERSTRAße
FULDA
SCHARNHORSTRAße
DRESDENER STRAße
PLATZ DER DT. EINHEIT
FRANKFURTER STR.
KÜCHENGRABEN
AUEDAMM
FULDA
SANDERSHÄUSER STRAße
LEIPZIGER STRAße
LEIPZIGER STRAße
LILIENTHALSTRAße
HOLLÄNDISCHE STRAße
83

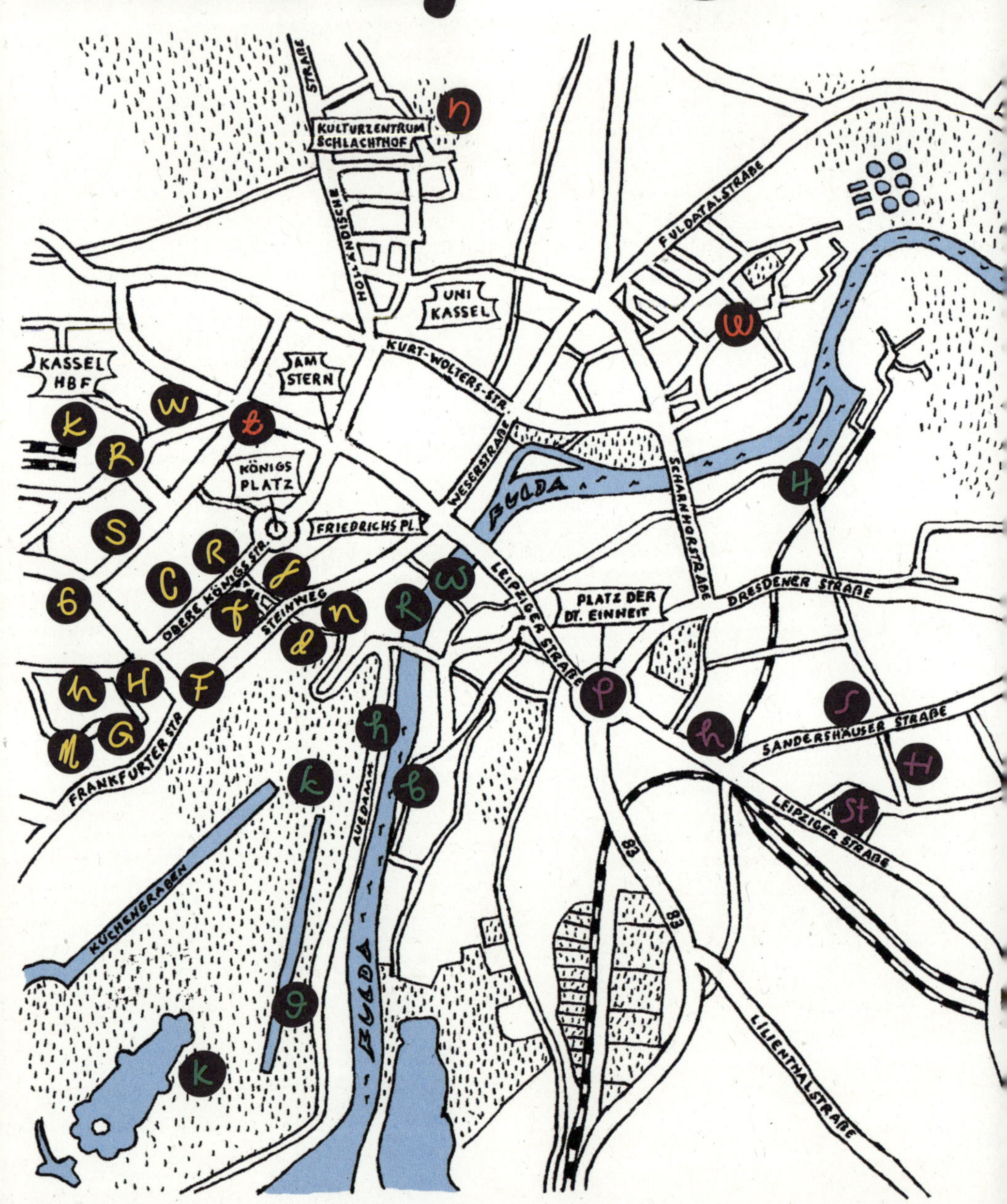

# VENUES

documenta fifteen does not regard Kassel as an exhibition venue. Rather, the city is understood as an ekosistem: a network of social contexts in which documenta emerges and grows. This continual evolution brings together traces of Kassel—as a former seat of the principality, and today's culturally diverse city. Both are in evidence, as is Kassel as an industrial area that was later subjected to massive destruction during World War II, and that housed the armaments industry (and still does).

documenta fifteen is being held in sites with historical and social associations in order to place them in new contexts. Its focuses include the Mitte district of Kassel, with its many museum buildings; the Fulda River, a formerly important artery and waterway; and the industrial district of Bettenhausen. In these sites, the structures of colonialism and Western dominance are made visible in order to enable the design of new social models. documenta fifteen sees itself as part of the Kassel ekosistem, to which partners and artists belong, and as part of the inter-lokal—a network of the localities where the lumbung members and lumbung artists work. Some of them also place projects at public sites in the city, rather than at clearly marked exhibition sites. Visitors are invited to discover them.

## MITTE

- C&A Façade
- documenta Halle
- Frankfurter Straße / Fünffensterstraße (Underpass)
- Fridericianum
- Friedrichsplatz
- Gloria-Kino
- Grimmwelt Kassel
- Hessisches Landesmuseum
- Hotel Hessenland
- KAZimKuBa
- Museum for Sepulchral Culture
- Museum of Natural History Ottoneum
- Rainer-Dierichs-Platz
- ruruHaus
- Stadtmuseum Kassel
- WH22

## FULDA

- Bootsverleih Ahoi
- Walter-Lübcke-Brücke
- Greenhouse (Karlsaue)
- Hafenstraße 76
- Hiroshima-Ufer (Karlsaue)
- Karlswiese (Karlsaue)
- Compost heap (Karlsaue)
- Rondell

## BETTENHAUSEN

- Hallenbad Ost
- Hübner areal
- Platz der Deutschen Einheit (Underpass)
- Sandershaus
- St. Kunigundis

## NORDSTADT

- Nordstadtpark
- Weserstraße 26
- Trafohaus

# MITTE

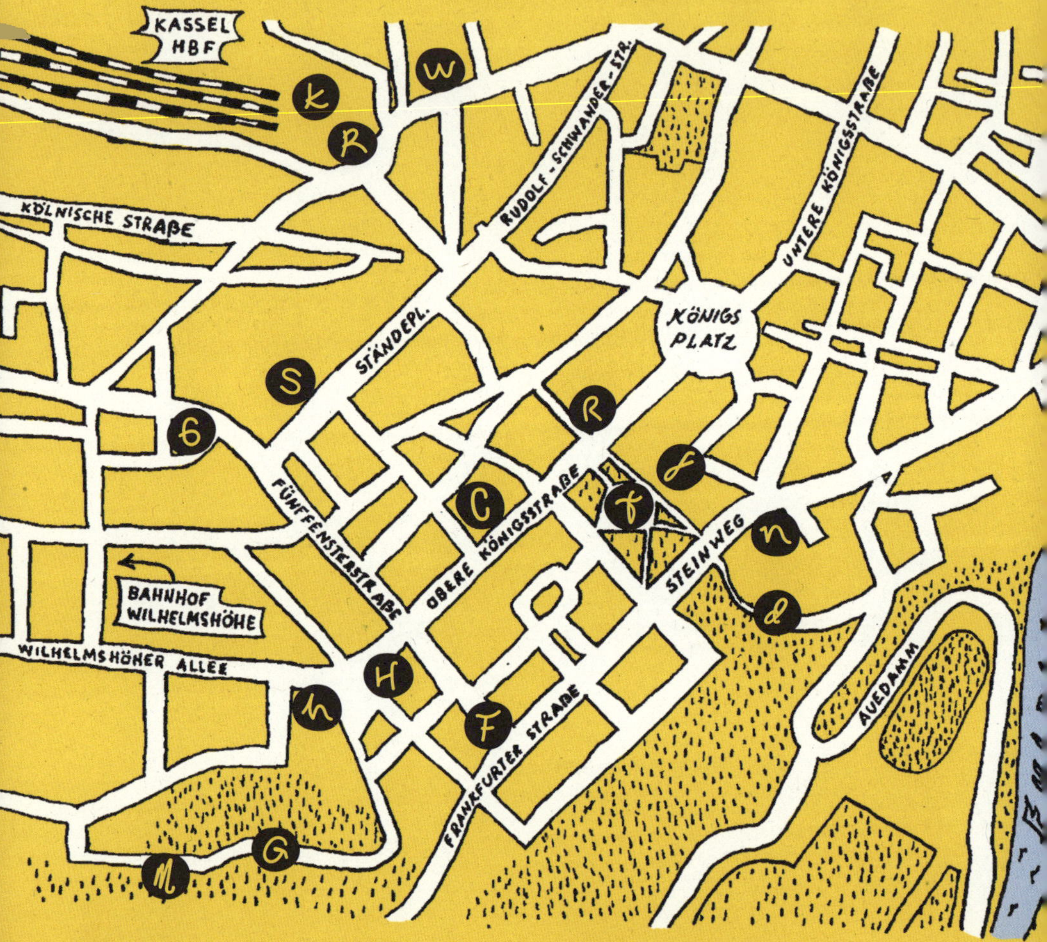



C&A Façade
documenta Halle
Frankfurter Straße / Fünffensterstraße (Underpass)
Fridericianum
Friedrichsplatz
Gloria-Kino
Grimmwelt Kassel
Hessisches Landesmuseum
Hotel Hessenland
KAZimKuBa
Museum for Sepulchral Culture
Museum of Natural History Ottoneum
Rainer-Dierichs-Platz
ruruHaus
Stadtmuseum Kassel
WH22

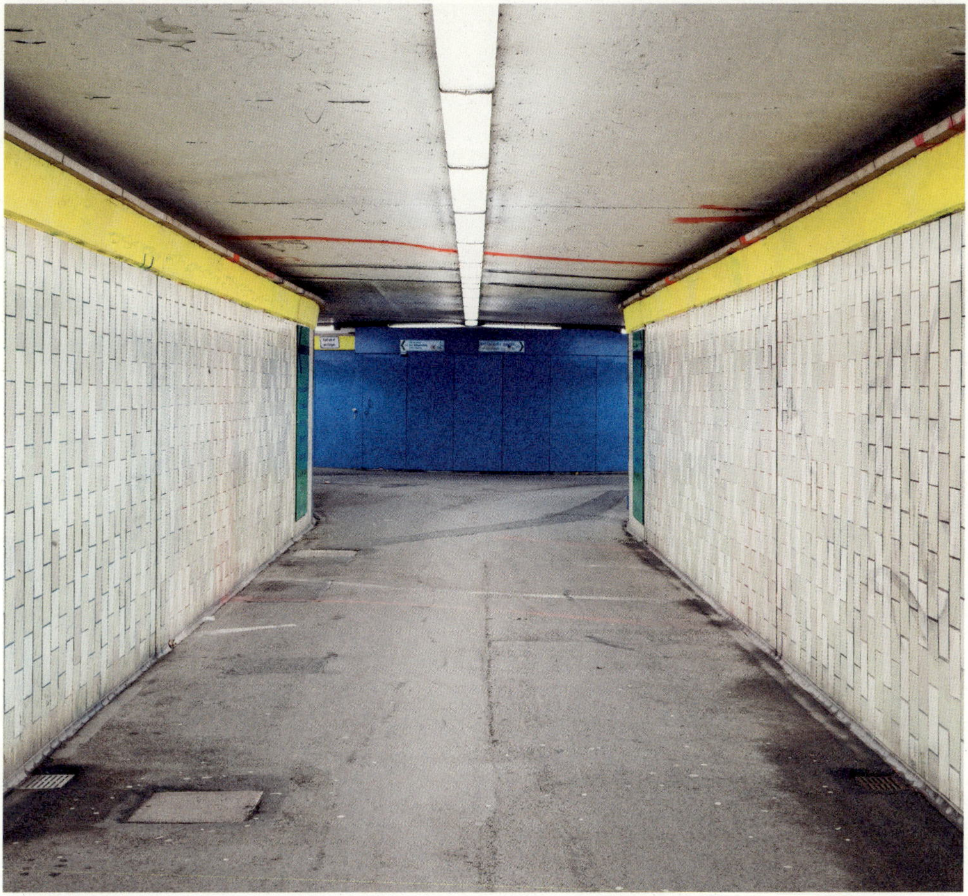

# Ⓕ Frankfurter Straße / Fünffensterstraße (Underpass)

Typical of the postwar period: beginning in the
1950s, in order to create more space for cars,
pedestrian zones were banished underground.
The underpass where Fünffensterstrasse and
Frankfurter Strasse merge is a good example of the
misguided urban planning of that era. It resulted
in a dreariness that is not made more beautiful
by colorful tiles—but, at least, the tunnel, which
is illuminated at night, offers a place safe from
street traffic. Black Quantum Futurism, from
Philadelphia, USA, is using the pipes of the underpass for a sound installation, and have created a
room in which visitors can leave spoken messages.

LUMBUNG ARTISTS &
LUMBUNG MEMBERS
Black Quantum Futurism

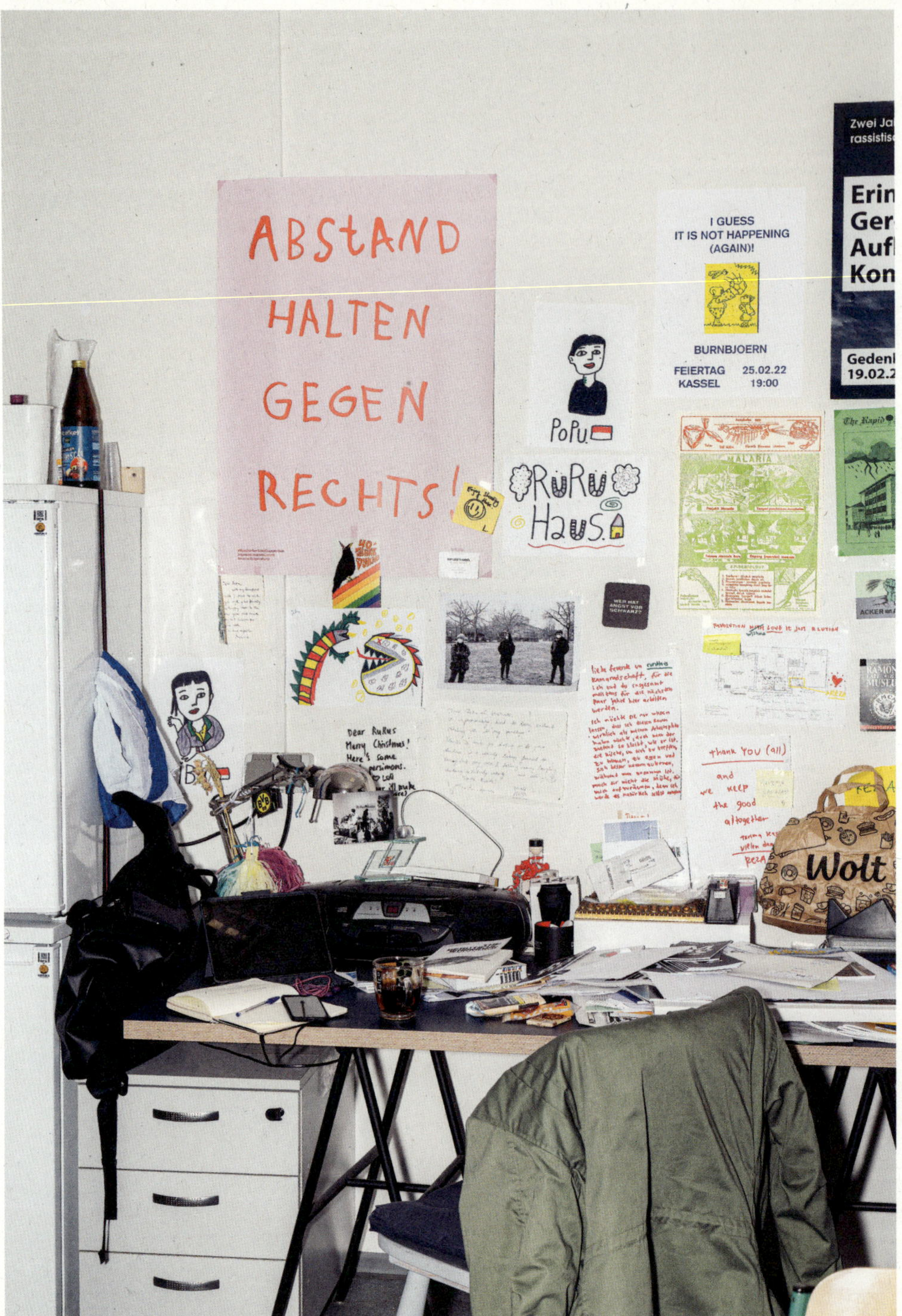

ABSTAND
HALTEN
GEGEN
RECHTS!

PoPu

RuRu
HauS.

I GUESS
IT IS NOT HAPPENING
(AGAIN)!

BURNBJOERN
FEIERTAG    25.02.22
KASSEL      19:00

Zwei Ja
rassistisc

Erin
Ger
Auf
Kon

Gedenk
19.02.2

Dear RuRus
Merry Christmas!
Here's some
persimons.

thank YOU (all)
and
we KEEP
the good
altogether

Wolt

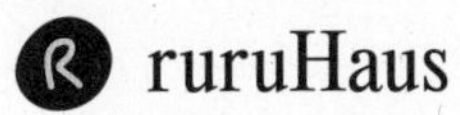

# ruruHaus
Obere Königsstraße 43

The ruruHaus is the heart of documenta fifteen. Here you can experience the practice of lumbung. Even before the opening, a constant coming and going reigned in the building, a sum of many conversations, Zoom meetings, cooking sessions, and brainstorming bouts. The ruruHaus is the "living room" of documenta fifteen. Its current concept, thought up by ruangrupa, comes together and can be experienced here. Because of the political and societal situation in Indonesia, in the early 2000s, ruangrupa transformed private living rooms into public spaces so that it could dedicate itself to the practice of art there. In Kassel, they are continuing that history by other means—and of course they need more than one living room for that. They are using the department store at the corner of Treppenstrasse and Obere Königsstrasse that opened in 1950, has a view of the Fridericianum and Friedrichsplatz, and most recently housed a sports arena but has been vacant since 2018.

In the ruruHaus, visitors can familiarize themselves with how ruangrupa works and how it understands art. It pays to learn a few new terms: For example, "lumbung" is the Indonesian word for a rice barn for communal use in which the excess harvest is stored for the benefit of the community. It also defines the artistic practice of ruangrupa, which is based on the principle of collectivity, on the idea of shared resources. That is why they bring together local ekosistems in the ruruHaus that are formed of people, materials, and other living organisms. They include, for example, artistic, sociocultural, and environmental initiatives or other networks. One central element of this is nongkrong (Indonesian for "hanging out", meaning unforced togetherness and socializing). It stands for openness, common ground, and the exchange of resources.

Thus, the ruruHaus is a place on the move. It is a meeting place with a welcome area, a café, and an arena that offers the opportunity for gatherings, for example at symposia, workshops, or discussions. The documenta ticket office and two bookshops are also located here.

The Arts Collaboratory, a network of twenty-five organizations from Asia, Africa, Latin America, and the Middle East, is running a newspaper, a collective workshop space, and a newsroom at the ruruHaus. The ZK/U – Center for Art and Urbanistics, from Berlin, Germany, will house a project about bees here. The collective ook_ connects its own ook_visitorZentrum at Weserstrasse 26 with the official visitor center of documenta fifteen through an installation.

LUMBUNG ARTISTS &
LUMBUNG MEMBERS
Arts Collaboratory
Hamja Ahsan
ook_ [reinaart vanhoe, Neue
Brüderkirche, Espora, BPOC
Festival Kassel, me_sobat,
Colorlabor, graanschuur
Tarwewijk, Elaine W. Ho,
Bartira, Wok The Rock,
COLLECTive, k. format,
Take-A-Way, Plan B, Dynamitas
unlimited ...]
ZK/U - Center for Art and
Urbanistics

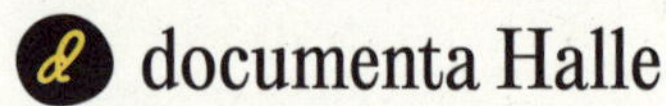 documenta Halle

`Du-Ry-Str. 1`

Flat roof, steel beams, and a glass façade: the documenta Halle by Jourdan & Müller architects is typical of sober 1990s architectural style. In 1992, it was built for documenta 9, curated by Jan Hoet, as the exhibition's first building of its own, in a postmodern-constructivist mode, and conceived as a kind of "bridge" from the Staatstheater to the Karlsaue. In documenta fifteen, it is rather an exception: visitors will otherwise only rarely find the likes of its large, empty space with white walls in the tradition of European museums, built to present static artworks. The documenta Halle is being used in unusual ways by the participating collectives: the nonprofit artists' initiative Baan Noorg Collaborative Arts and Culture, from the province of Ratchaburi in Thailand, contributes a three-part project here. It includes an installation with a livestream dedicated to the dairy business in Germany and Thailand, a shadow-puppet theater, and a skateboard ramp that is being made available to Kassel's skater scene. Community-based Wajukuu Art Project from the Mukuru slum in Nairobi, Kenya, is presenting works by its members and a documentary film. The Instituto de Artivismo Hannah Arendt (INSTAR) from Havana, Cuba, is organizing a series of ten exhibitions with artists from Cuba that produce a counter-narrative of Cuban art and history. Britto Arts Trust is a collective from Dhaka, Bangladesh, that concentrates on nutritional policies and communities suffering the effects of industrialization. They take on issues related to environmental changes as well as to foods that, only a few years ago, were typical of certain regions of their homeland but are now at risk of disappearing. The lumbung Press is also located there: a print workshop where artists and collectives can print and bind their publications.

LUMBUNG ARTISTS &
LUMBUNG MEMBERS
Baan Noorg Collaborative Arts
and Culture
Britto Arts Trust
Hamja Ahsan
Instituto de Artivismo Hannah
Arendt (INSTAR)
lumbung Press
Wajukuu Art Project
Wakaliga Uganda

 Rainer-Dierichs-Platz

When the Wilhelmshöhe train station opened in 1991, it overtook Kassel's central station in importance. The central station is now largely used as an exhibition venue and cultural center. On its large plaza, named after publisher Rainer Dierichs, who died in 2007, the city erected the sculpture *Man Walking to the Sky*, which Jonathan Borofsky showed at documenta 9 in 1992.

With his work on Rainer-Dierichs-Platz, Dan Perjovschi alludes to his work *Horizontal Newspaper*, on which he has been working since 2010 in his hometown of Sibiu, Romania. Belonging, community, and the future are themes that Perjovschi addresses time and again. *Horizontal Newspaper* is continually updated here during documenta fifteen.

LUMBUNG ARTISTS &
LUMBUNG MEMBERS
Dan Perjovschi

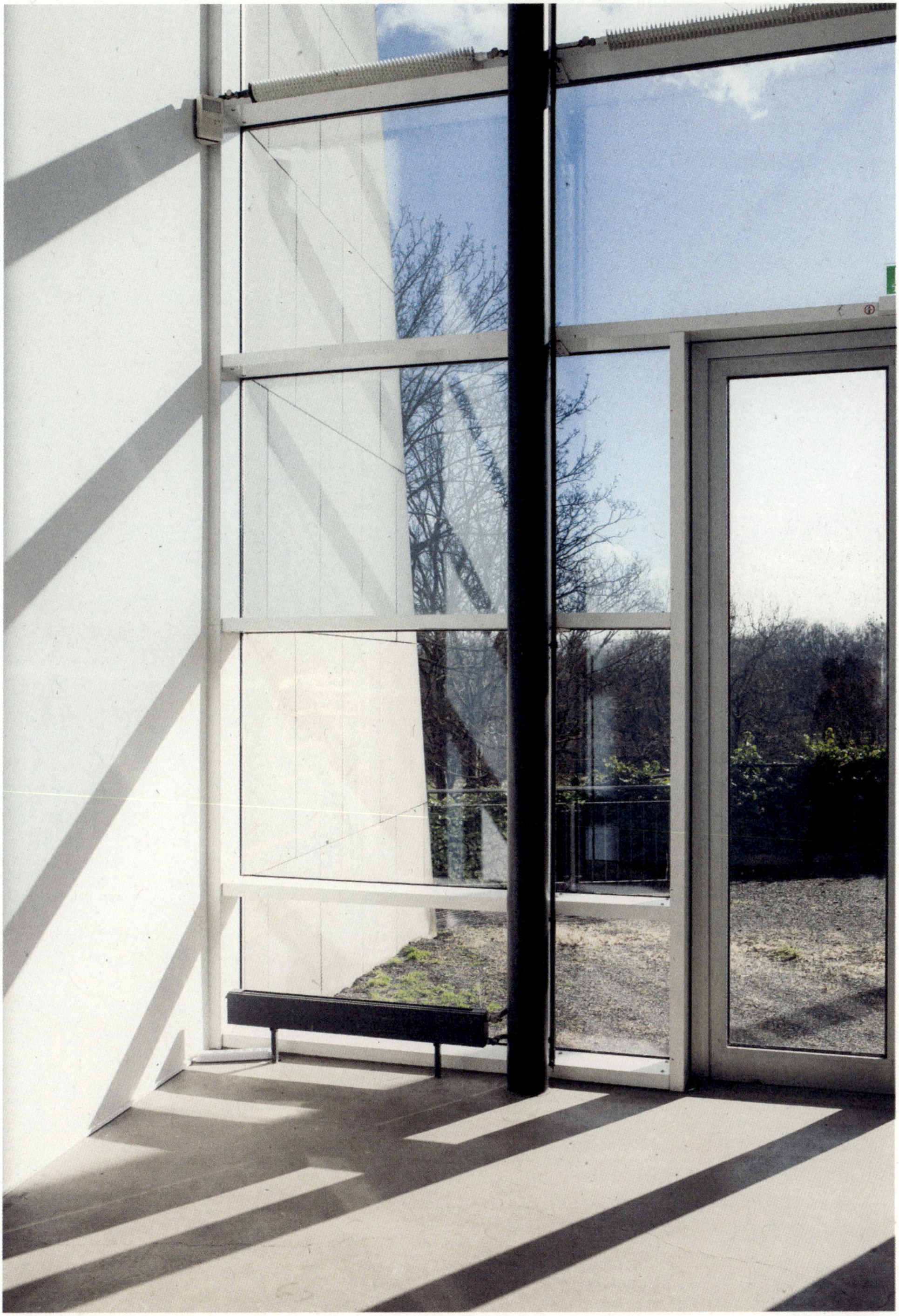

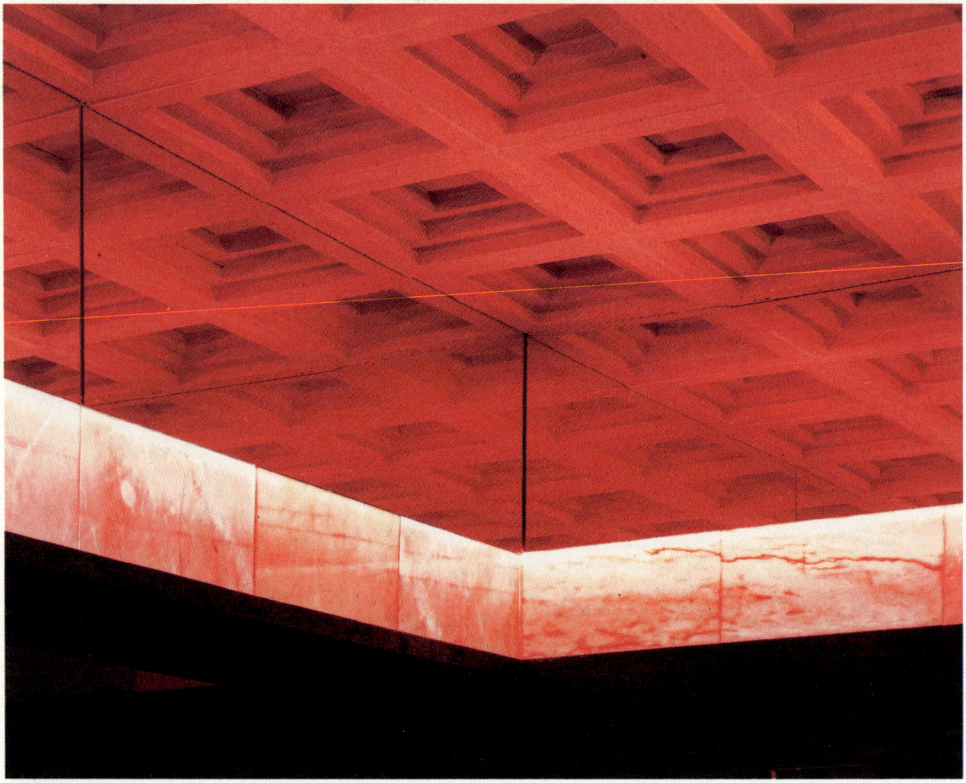

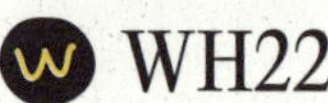

# WH22

Werner-Hilpert-Straße 22

Werner-Hilpert-Strasse 22 is famous in Kassel. The building complex's Club A.R.M. and Lolita Bar were important nightlife spots. Only the Lolita Bar is still in business today—and its beer garden in the courtyard is open during the 100 days. The building was built in the nineteenth century as the headquarters of Gundelach wine shop.

The Question of Funding has set up a gallery space with art by artists and a collective from Palestine, and is also working on developing its own currency. Alice Yard, from Trinidad and Tobago, and LE 18, from Marrakesh, Morocco, are also represented in the WH22. Here, too, Alice Yard hosts a residency program for 100 days. Nhà Sàn Collective is inviting people to a traditional Vietnamese sauna, and Party Office b2b Fadescha is organizing its own club evenings and concerts with DJs, producing inclusive, intersectional, trans-feminist, and queer-crip spaces.

LUMBUNG ARTISTS &
LUMBUNG MEMBERS
Alice Yard
Hamja Ahsan
LE 18
Nhà Sàn Collective
Party Office b2b Fadescha
The Question of Funding

# C&A Façade

Obere Königsstraße 35

The lot where the C&A clothing shop has stood since 1960 was the site of one of the most elegant townhouses in Kassel until World War II. The Palais Waitz von Eschen was built from 1770 onward as a stately city palace and—like much of the city center—was destroyed by the Allied forces' largest bombing raid, on October 22, 1943. A balustrade with fountains was all that survived, and in 1955, the German Federal Post Office built a large sorting office there that functioned as a temporary post office during the first documenta. When the C&A was built, the balustrade and fountains disappeared as well. A simple, unornamented façade now blends in with the cityscape—typical of the monotony of West Germany's rebuilt inner cities after wartime destruction. A monument in front of the building recalls its former glory and the reason the square is called Opernplatz (Opera Square): it is dedicated to Louis Spohr, the court's *kapellmeister* in the nineteenth century and a composer for the Kassel Opera. Today, people wait for the streetcar in front of it. Like many German companies, C&A profited under National Socialism from the seizure of Jewish assets and from forced labor; the company was also criticized for poor working conditions in its global textile production. Today, it participates in the campaign *Aktiv gegen Kinderarbeit* (Active against Child Labor) and is said to be the world's largest buyer of organic cotton. documenta fifteen is using the building's façade. Taring Padi is displaying a large-format painted banner here. Street protests, woodcut workshops, art carnivals, and exhibitions in unexpected places are just some aspects of the Indonesian collective's practice.

LUMBUNG ARTISTS &
LUMBUNG MEMBERS
Taring Padi

# KAZimKuBa

Rainer-Dierichs-Platz 1

In the former accommodations of the Bahnhofsmission, seven members of the Association of German Architects founded KAZimKuBa (Kasseler Architekturzentrum im Kulturbahnhof) in 1998. The goal of the association is to draw attention to urban design and architecture. During the 100 days, a group of people connected to Jimmie Durham, who died in November 2021, is exhibiting under the name A Stick in the Forest by the Side of the Road. The US-born artist, poet, and writer, who lived between Berlin, Germany and Naples, Italy, became internationally known in the 1980s for objects and sculptures made of materials such as stone, animal skulls and bones, and wood carvings, and was a strong advocate of Indigenous rights. A Stick in the Forest by the Side of the Road consists of friends and acquaintances of the artist. The group members' works respond to histories and memories, and develop (among other projects) a collection of stories and dishes using recipes and ingredients from the Kassel region.

LUMBUNG ARTISTS &
LUMBUNG MEMBERS
Jimmie Durham & A Stick in the
Forest by the Side of the Road

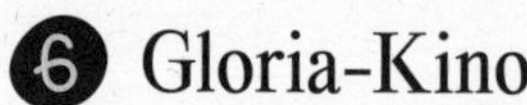 # Gloria-Kino



The Gloria-Kino is one of the few arthouse cinemas for independent film in Kassel. The cinema, which opened in 1954, has preserved the character of its 1950s architecture, even though parts of the present interior design date from the 1980s. The Gloria-Kino is a place where collectives such as Subversive Film and Komîna Fîlm a Rojava are presenting film festivals. Under the title *lumbung Film*, a series of films and videos by lumbung members and lumbung artists are shown across the 100 days.

LUMBUNG ARTISTS &
LUMBUNG MEMBERS
Komîna Fîlm a Rojava
lumbung Film
Subversive Film

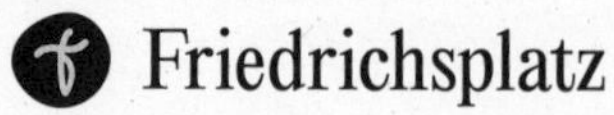 # Friedrichsplatz

This square, which was laid out in the eighteenth century and is named after Landgrave Friedrich II, is a place of condensed history. It is still one of Germany's largest inner-city public squares, in which the monumental pomp of the Wilhelmine era is inscribed just as much as the parades of the Nazi era and the destruction and reconstruction of the Second World War and its aftermath. Several documenta artists have left their traces here: Joseph Beuys planted the first oaks of his *7000 Eichen* (1982) in front of the Fridericianum; Walter De Maria's *Erdkilometer* (1977) sinks deep into the earth on this square; the laser-light sculpture *Laserscape Kassel* (1977) by Horst H. Baumann spans the city from here to the Bergpark Wilhelmshöhe; the *Rahmenbau* (1977) by Haus-Rucker-Co forms a window onto the landscape of the Karlsaue. This year, on Friedrichsplatz, Richard Bell's *Tent Embassy*, which has been traveling the world since 2013, is a note of resistance against colonial power. A digital sign mounted on the façade of the Fridericianum displays the amount that the Australian government owes First Nations groups from 1901 to the present.

In addition, the documenta food market has set up its food trucks and cargo bikes here. The gastronomic offer is based on sustainably and organically grown food from the region.

LUMBUNG ARTISTS &
LUMBUNG MEMBERS
Richard Bell

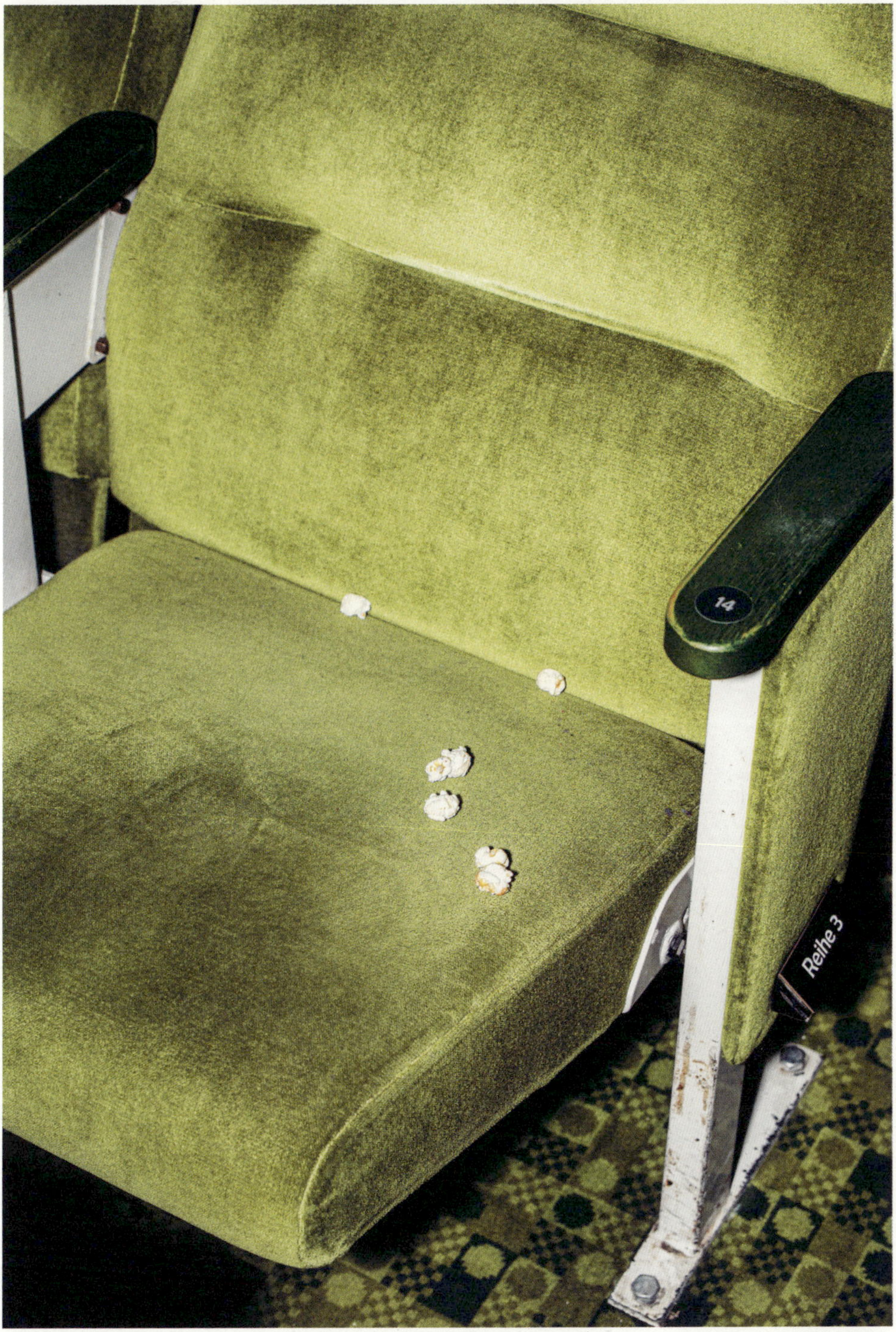

14
Reihe 3

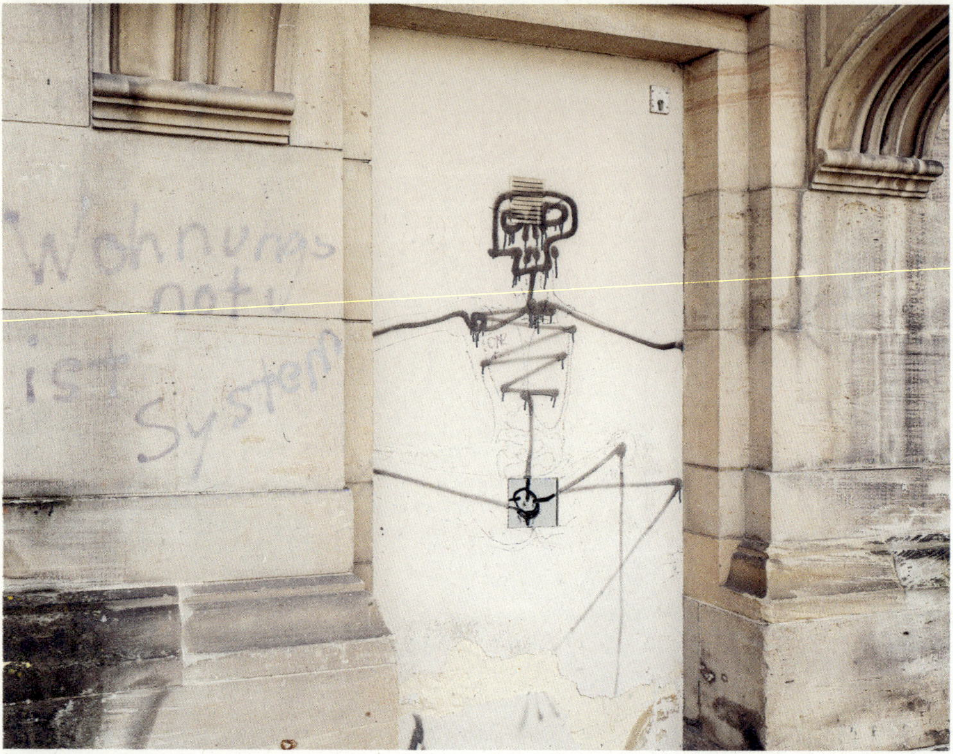

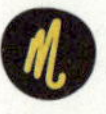

# Museum for Sepulchral Culture
## Weinbergstraße 25–27

Kassel has an unusual institution in the Museum
for Sepulchral Culture, which explores the culture
of dying, mourning, remembering, and burying. Its
permanent exhibition presents exhibits of sepulchral culture, primarily in the German-speaking
world, from the Middle Ages to the present. As if
descending into a crypt, on the lower floor visitors
encounter coffins, hearses, clothing, and jewelry
for funerals, gravestones, and tomb sculptures.
For documenta fifteen, the Mexican artist Erick
Beltrán, who lives and works in Barcelona, Spain,
addresses the power mechanisms that define, eval-
uate, classify, reproduce, and disseminate images
and discourses. Together with a local research
group, he addresses the question "What is power?"
and presents the results in the form of a large-format installation with prints and sculptures.

LUMBUNG ARTISTS &
LUMBUNG MEMBERS
Erick Beltrán
Hamja Ahsan

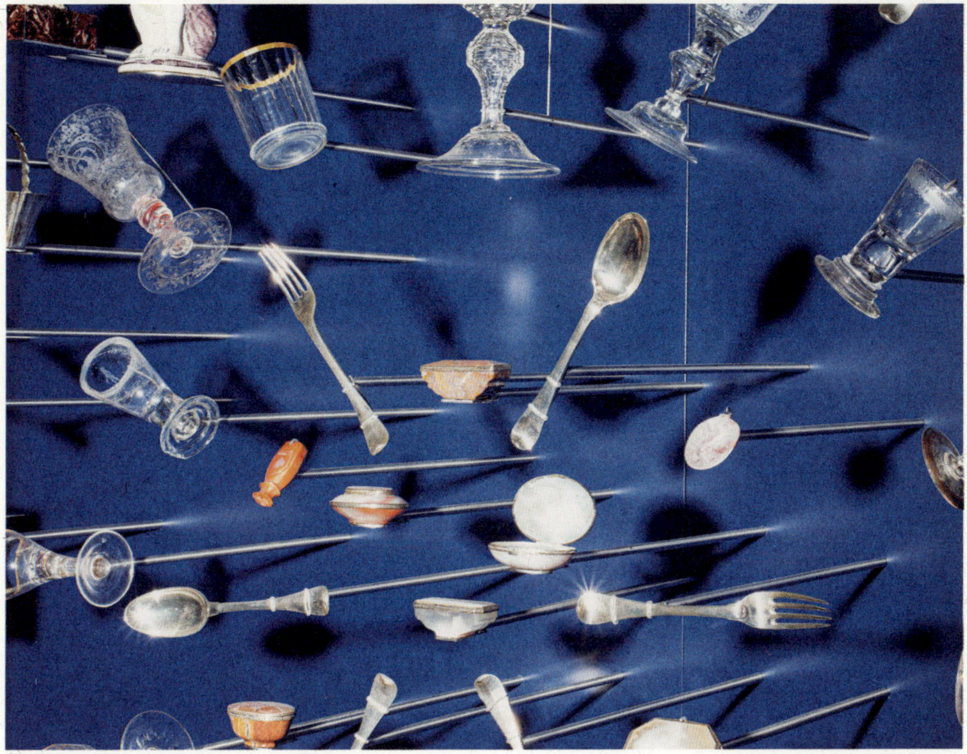

## Stadtmuseum Kassel

Ständeplatz 16

After a 2015 reopening, the Stadtmuseum is now a modern museum in the historical building of the Kulturhaus on Ständeplatz. The focus of its permanent exhibition is the evolution of the city from the eighteenth century to the twentieth. The early history of the first settlements and the flooding catastrophes on the Fulda River are presented on a large table display. The history of migration in Kassel is mentioned only in passing.

documenta fifteen is showing artists who consider issues of representation and practice. For example, Project Art Works of Hastings, UK, is based on the recognition of neurological diversity and works with artists and makers with complex support needs. They are creating works of art and holding workshops in the Stadtmuseum, and exhibiting in the Fridericianum. The FAFSWAG collective, from Aotearoa/New Zealand, was founded in 2013 with the idea of questioning the lack of representation of queer, Indigenous people. It is presenting an archive of their own works. The Nhà Sàn Collective, from Hanoi, Vietnam, is working on building a residence for queer people, and Safdar Ahmed and collaborators present a video installation, zine, and vinyl record based on the lived experiences of refugees.

LUMBUNG ARTISTS &
LUMBUNG MEMBERS
FAFSWAG
Nhà Sàn Collective
Project Art Works
Safdar Ahmed

 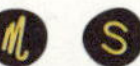

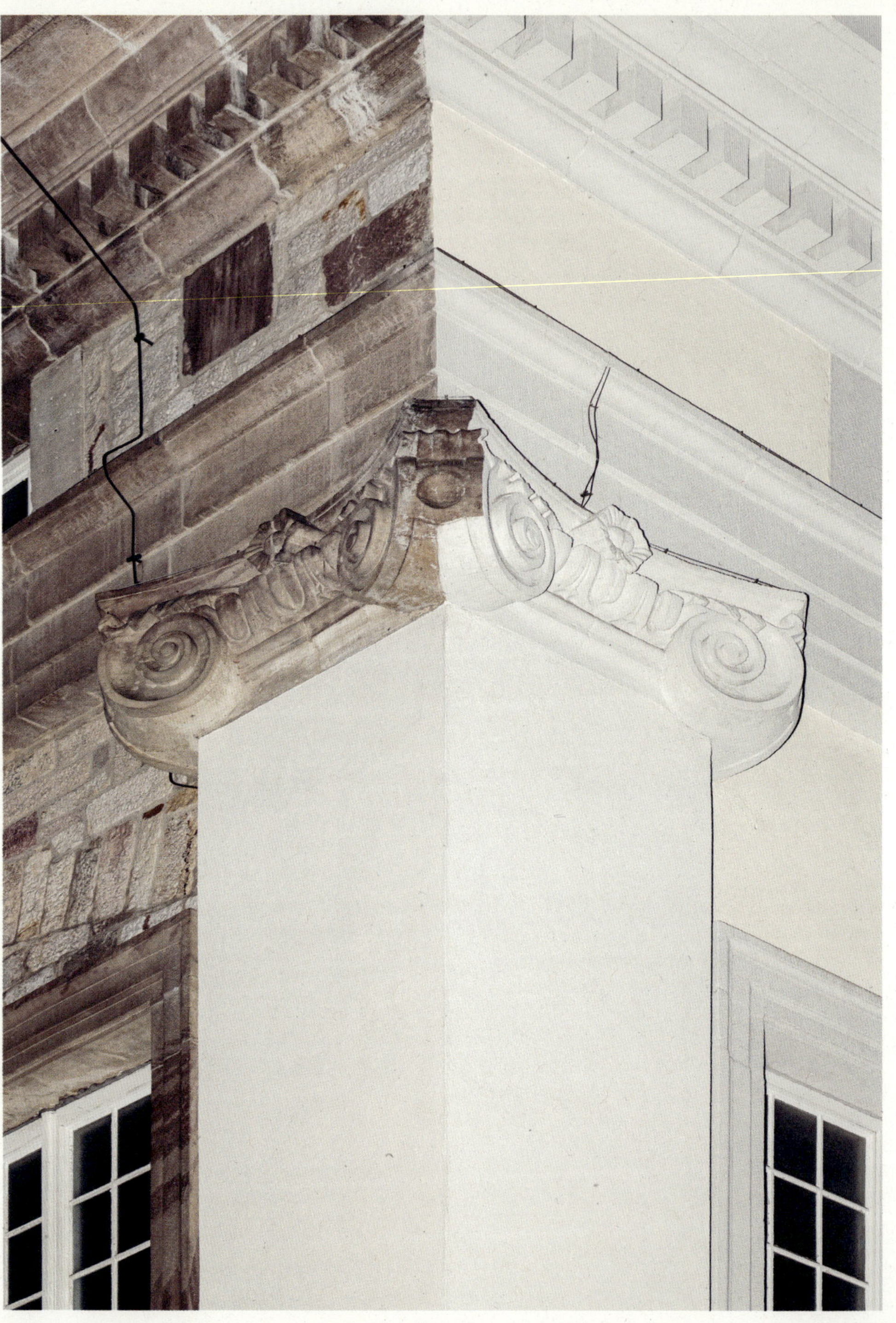

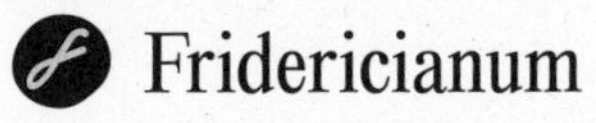

# Fridericianum

`Friedrichsplatz 18`

The Museum Fridericianum is closely interconnected with the development of the European Enlightenment idea of the museum. It opened in 1779 to provide public access to the collections of the Landgraves of Hesse. When princely collections were transferred to public ownership, the bourgeoisie adopted art as a medium for reflection, for prestige, and interpretative authority. Only in the postwar period was the Fridericianum used exclusively for exhibitions. The first edition of documenta in 1955 restricted itself entirely to the Museum Fridericianum. The building has since then repeatedly been the focus of documenta, and has therefore come to be considered the main building of documenta.

ruangrupa, the artistic team and the artists occupying Fridericianum see it as a lumbung. lumbung is a practice of sharing but also a form of architecture which usually stores the harvest. It is simultaneously a domestic place and a social and gathering space for all. The Fridericianum is a place that becomes that warm and dynamic space, rather than a cold museum space. The former exhibition building has become the FRIDSKUL (Fridericianum as school) and is being used by the FRIDSKUL artists and collectives to use and show different models of horizontal education which is rooted in life. The group of artist collectives have been meeting periodically and collectively deciding on the use of the rotunda which has come to be the FRIDSKUL library. They see their relationships as neighbors and will host and collaborate with each other on various programs. The host is the Gudskul collective from Indonesia, of which ruangrupa is a founding member. Gudskul is running workshops and seminars, and knowledge-market events as well as karaoke nights with other collectives. A dormitory and a kitchen have been installed in the ground floor of the building so that the participating artists and students can sleep in the Fridericianum during the hundred days. At the Fridericianum, OFF-Biennale Budapest imagines a Transnational Museum of Roma Contemporary Art. The ground floor houses the RURUKIDS: an initiative founded by ruangrupa in 2010 to enable artists to work with children and teenagers. An evolving installation here includes paintings and drawings recreating the Hastings, UK, studio environment of Project Art Works. Dan Perjovschi draws on the columns of the Fridericianum, representing central themes of documenta fifteen. Another focus in the Fridericianum is on archives, as The Black Archives, the Asia Art Archive, and the Archives des luttes des femmes en Algérie show what archival practices become when they are tied to protest and community.

 # Museum of Natural History Ottoneum

Steinweg 2

On the tour through the Museum of Natural History Ottoneum, you will find out about the human understanding of nature and see several exhibits that are famous in this city, such as the so-called "Goethe Elephant." In Goethe's day, an elephant did indeed live in the landgrave's menagerie in the Karlsaue, and it died in an unfortunate fall. The Ottoneum is even older: it was the first permanent theater building in Germany in the early seventeenth century. Today, its museum also serves as a platform for discussions of the protection and preservation of the environment.

The Korean visual research collective ikkibawiKrrr sought out this place because it is dedicated to the diverse connections between plants and human beings, civilization and natural phenomena, colonialism and ecology. The Korean word *ikkibawi* means a rock with moss growing on it; *Krrr* is an onomatopoetic word. In its installation, the collective works with seaweed, which, especially during the war, was used in many ways: for example, for food but also to produce weapons. INLAND, by contrast, brings together actors from agricultural, social, and cultural fields.



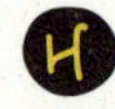 # Hotel Hessenland

Obere Königsstraße 2

The Hotel Hessenland was designed by Paul Bode, the brother of documenta's founder, Arnold Bode, for a bombed-out lot destroyed in the war next to the Hugenottenhaus in the city center. Its unadorned green façade conceals an example of 1950s architecture that is listed on the historical register, with an elegant lobby featuring a spiral staircase and a ballroom that in its heyday provided space for around 800 people. The ballroom has not been used since the 1990s; the hotel (including a room with the original furniture from the 1950s) stood vacant for about a year until documenta fifteen brought it back to life. The hotel is a guesthouse for artists, and the ballroom is an exhibition venue showing MADEYOULOOK—an interdisciplinary artists' collaboration from Johannesburg, South Africa. With their works they seek to provide decolonial perspectives on land, and are presenting a floor installation of around 100 m$^2$ based on texts and images, as well as a sound installation.

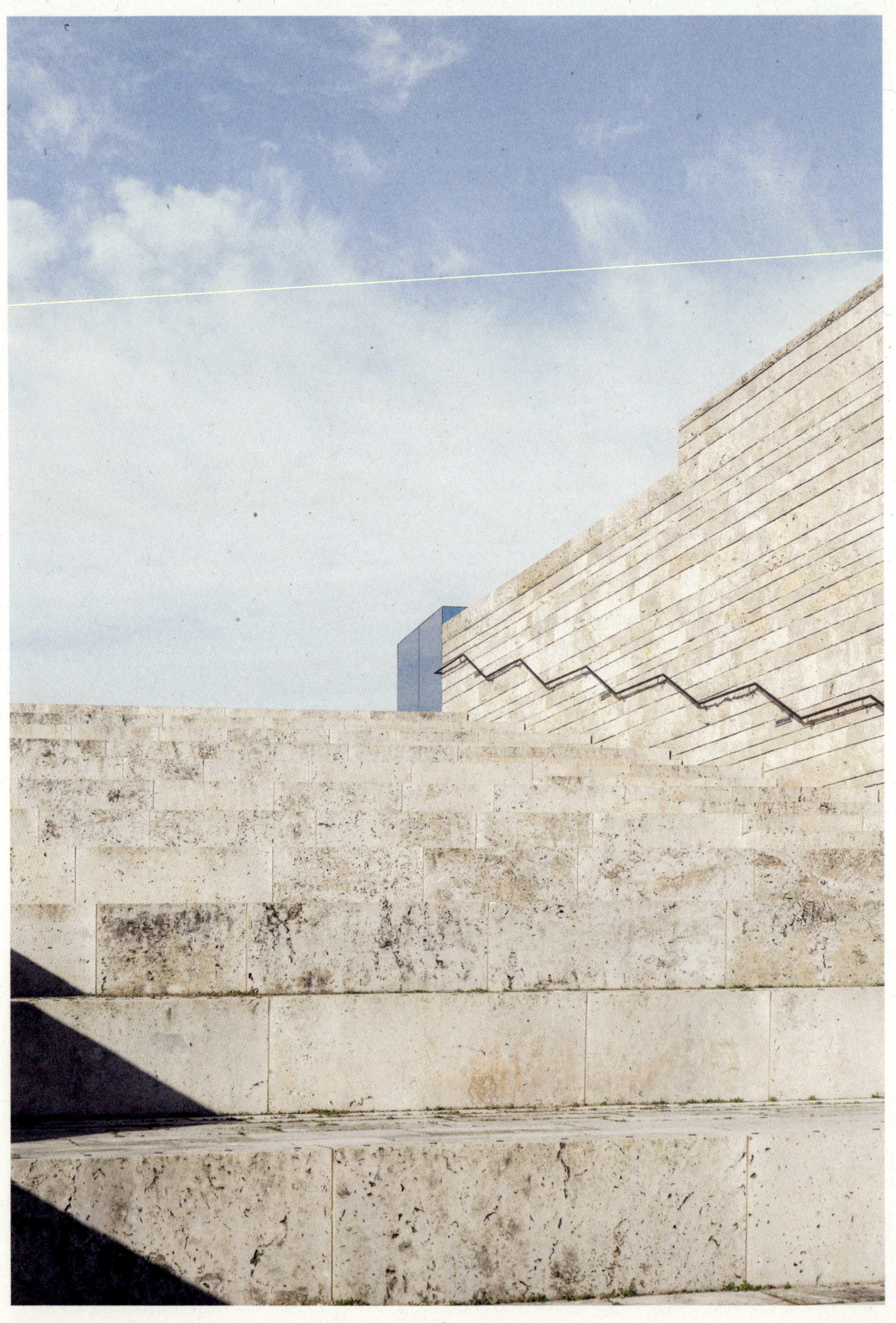

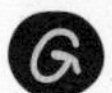 # Grimmwelt Kassel

Weinbergstraße 21

Grimmwelt Kassel is a place where the beautiful and the horrible coexist, as in German fairy tales. Our assessment of the linguists and folklorists Jacob and Wilhelm Grimm can no longer remain entirely unchanged, because of anti-Semitic statements in their diaries and letters. The site also triggers ambivalent emotions: The building opened in 2015 on the Weinberg, a hill in the center of the city, on the ruins of Henschel Villa, which was destroyed in the 1930s. The firm Henschel & Sohn manufactured locomotives and armaments in both world wars and was an important supplier to the Nazi regime.

Grimmwelt Kassel explicitly understands itself not as a museum but rather as an exhibition venue or walk-in sculpture.

In Grimmwelt, you can see the work by the artist Agus Nur Amal PMTOH. He presents both videos and installations created with things found in everyday life. These objects reflect his practices as a storyteller and are lent color by narrative, musical performances based on a Sundanese life principle. Also here, Jumana Emil Abboud presents several artworks related to variations of folkloric and contemporary stories around water springs.

 # Hessisches Landesmuseum

Brüder-Grimm-Platz 5

In contrast to the nearby inner city, this historicist building, inaugurated in 1913 for the city's millennial jubilee, survived World War II almost undamaged. In the postwar period, the museum housed a famous collection of Flemish and Dutch Old Masters, before reopening in November 2016 after extensive conversion and renovation work.

Since then, it has been dedicated to the history of Hesse. From prehistory and early history to exhibits on the landgraves and the everyday culture of the present, the development of the region is abundantly presented.

On the first floor, Berlin-based artist Pınar Öğrenci shows a film and an installation of hand-sewn paper tissues produced by women who suffered from the Turkish-Kurdish conflict. The artist, who had to leave her homeland in 2015, deals with conditions of oppression and exclusion in her father's village, Moks, in Van, Turkey. In the heraldry room above FAFSWAG installations, screenings, and a digital sculpture. The visitor is also invited to a video game dedicated to the queer, non-white body and the expressive and body-emphasizing dance movements of voguing.

LUMBUNG ARTISTS &
LUMBUNG MEMBERS
Agus Nur Amal PMTOH
Alice Yard
Hamja Ahsan
Jumana Emil Abboud

LUMBUNG ARTISTS &
LUMBUNG MEMBERS
FAFSWAG
Pınar Öğrenci

# FULDA

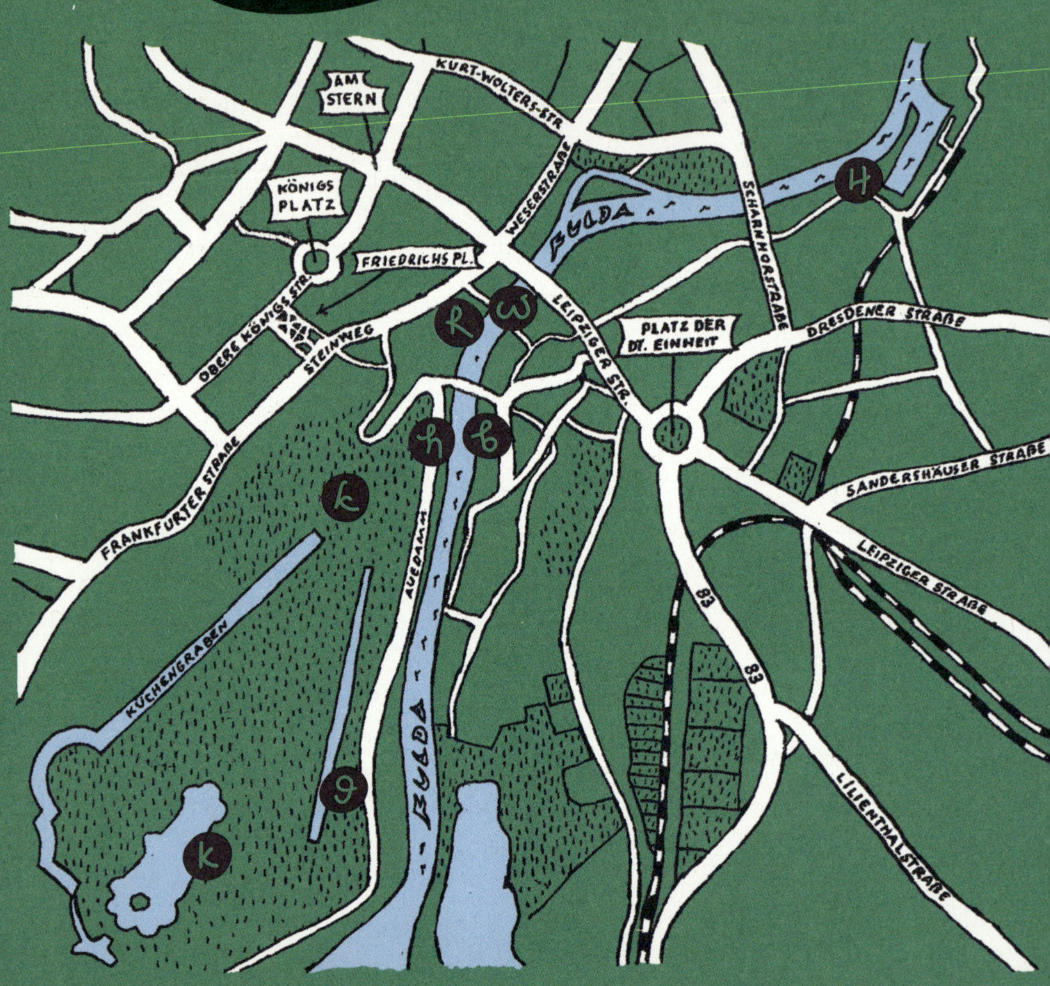



- Bootsverleih Ahoi
- Walter-Lübcke-Brücke
- Greenhouse (Karlsaue)
- Hafenstraße 76
- Hiroshima-Ufer (Karlsaue)
- Karlswiese (Karlsaue)
- Compost heap (Karlsaue)
- Rondell

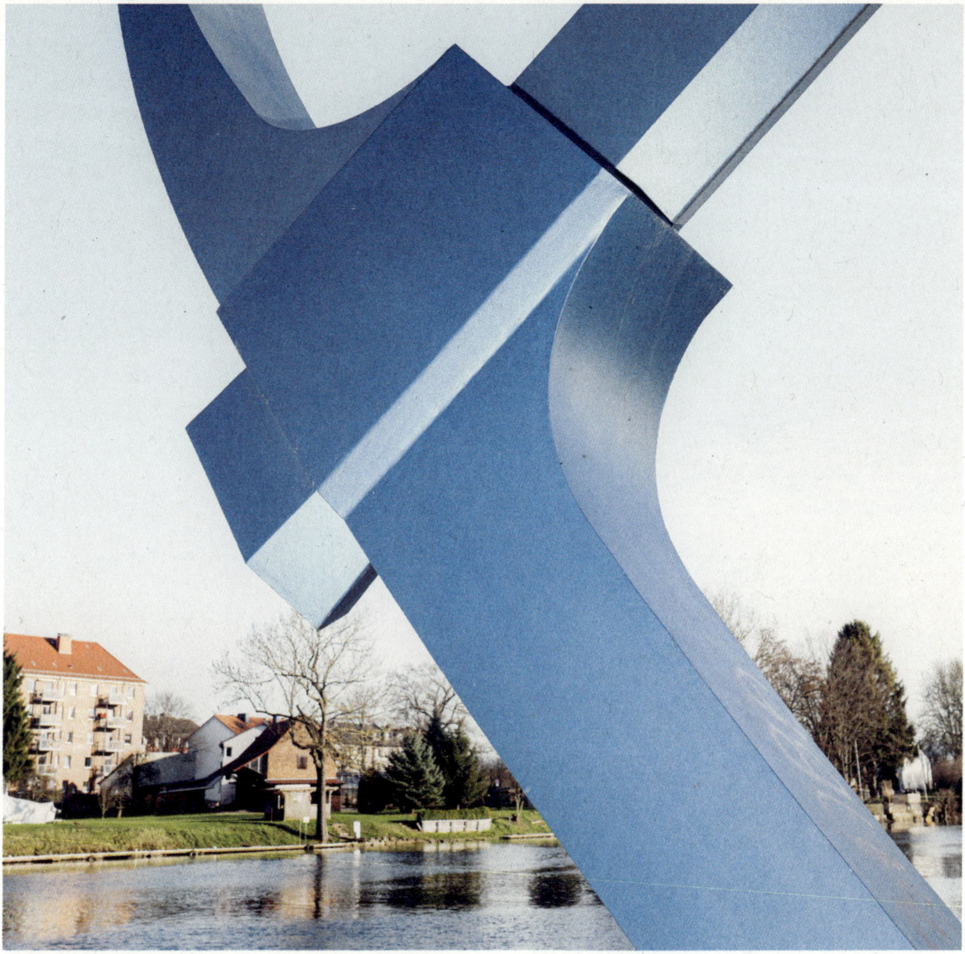

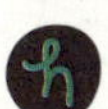

# Hiroshima-Ufer (Karlsaue)

August 6, 2022, is the 77th anniversary of the dropping of the atomic bomb on the Japanese city of Hiroshima. Because there has traditionally been a memorial for this day on the Fulda-Ufer, the section where Claes Oldenburg's 1982 steel sculpture *Spitzhacke* (Pickaxe) stands, which can be seen from afar, was renamed Hiroshima-Ufer several years ago. During documenta fifteen, the boat *Citizenship*, built from a dismantled roof truss by the ZK/U – Center for Art and Urbanistics in Berlin, Germany, will dock here, having been brought from Berlin to Kassel with muscle power and the aid of renewable energy. At various moorings, artists seek exchange with local communities in workshops, debates, and performances.

LUMBUNG ARTISTS &
LUMBUNG MEMBERS
Sourabh Phadke
ZK/U – Center for Art and
Urbanistics

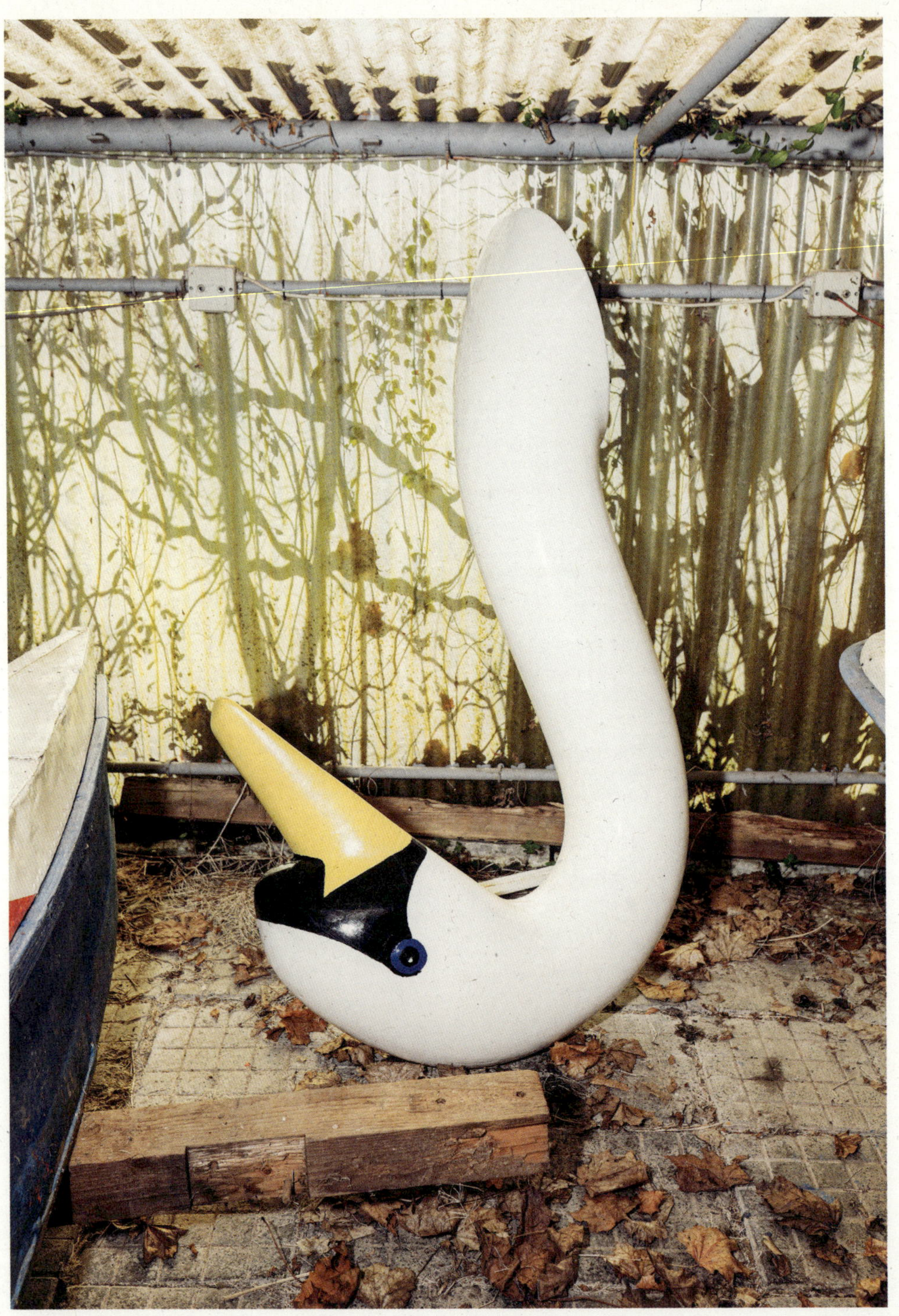

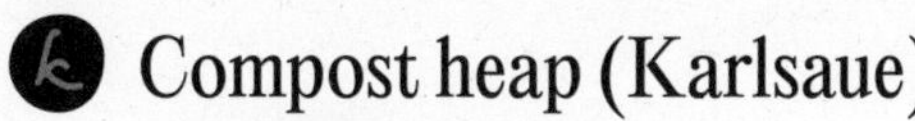# Compost heap (Karlsaue)

Coordinates:
51.298472, 9.493083

Near the Greenhouse in the Karlsaue is a compost heap used by the landscape gardeners of the Museumslandschaft Hessen Kassel (MHK). The interdisciplinary artists La Intermundial Holobiente are using it as a point of departure for a work being created *in situ*, in cooperation with students. The aim is to find inspiration for their own artworks from the site where a scaffold is standing. In a feral area that escapes human design, La Intermundial Holobiente has designed a space for reading, writing, discussion, and contemplation based on their own interpretation of lumbung.

LUMBUNG ARTISTS &
LUMBUNG MEMBERS
La Intermundial Holobiente

# Bootsverleih Ahoi

Blücherstraße 22A

In 1950, Theo Kissler founded a boathouse on the banks of the Fulda. After many changes, the Bootsverleih Ahoi has been a meeting place for anyone who wants to have an outing on the water since 2015. For documenta fifteen, OFF-Biennale Budapest transforms part of the grounds into an imaginary playground where people can construct new models for society, together with a collaboration with Kassel's Unterneustädter Schule, which takes over the bridge afterward. Moreover, there is a multipart project by the artist Chang En-Man that tells the story of imperialism in terms of the "migration" of a certain species of snail. The artist addresses the history of the Paiwan Indigenous people of Taiwan. Her contribution is a two-part installation: a boat, and a newly constructed waiting room for the boat rental agency.

LUMBUNG ARTISTS &
LUMBUNG MEMBERS
Chang En-Man
OFF-Biennale Budapest

# Walter-Lübcke-Brücke

This bridge for pedestrians and cyclists, which connects the districts of Mitte and Unterneustadt, was renamed only about a year ago after Walter Lübcke, the district president of Kassel, who was murdered by right-wing extremists in 2019. In renaming the bridge, the city was also responding to the controversy around the Nazi past of its former mayor, Karl Branner, after whom the structure was named in 2000.

Here, the Nhà Sàn Collective addresses the agricultural and artistic culture of its homeland, Vietnam, and its representation of queer people; they are showing a rug work on the bridge. Here, too, Black Quantum Futurism's installation, resembling a water clock, serves as a hub for memories, and as a stage.

LUMBUNG ARTISTS &
LUMBUNG MEMBERS
Black Quantum Futurism
Nhà Sàn Collective



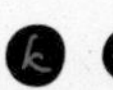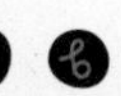

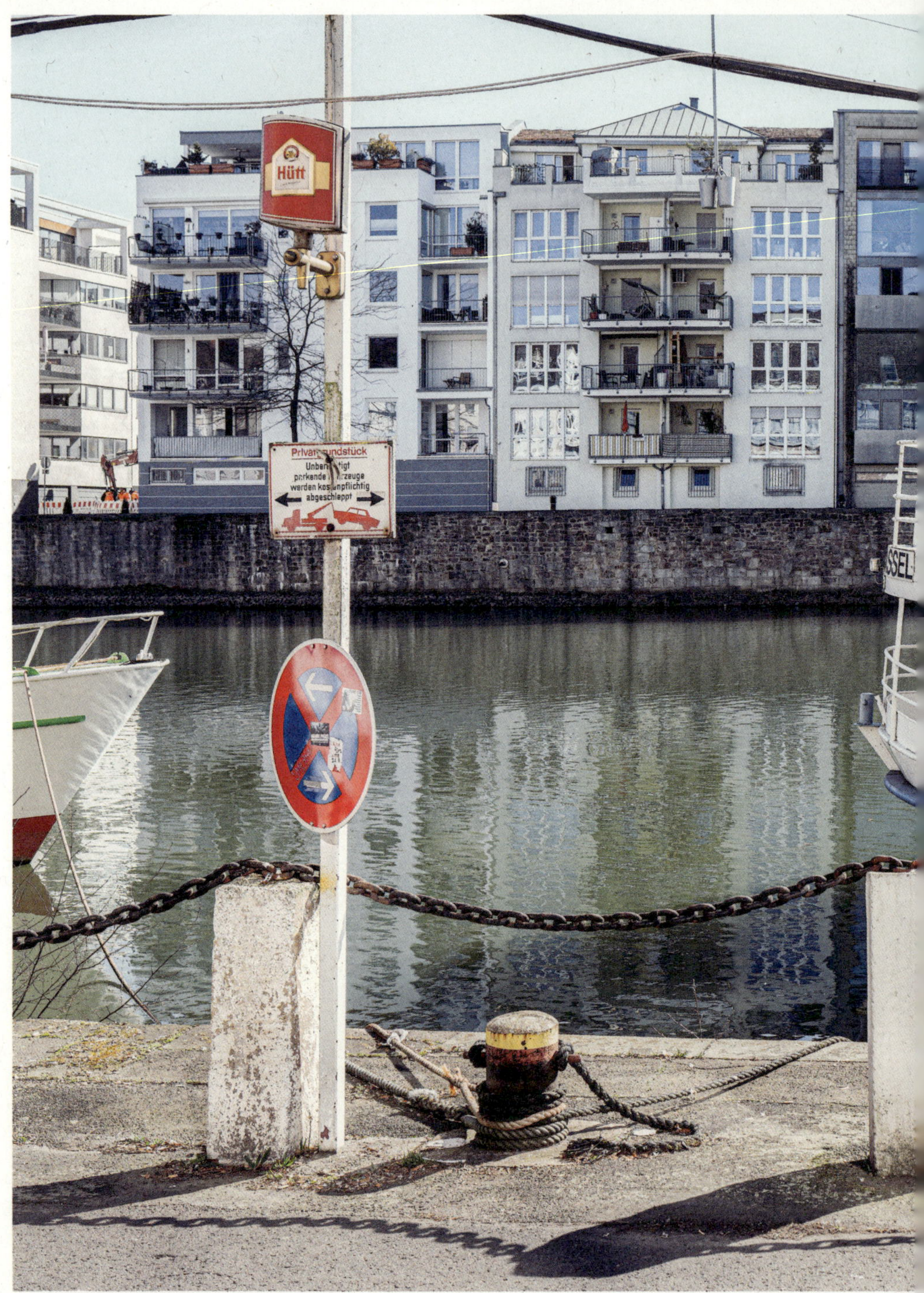
Hütt
Privatgrundstück
Unberechtigt
parkende Fahrzeuge
werden kostenpflichtig
abgeschleppt
SSEL

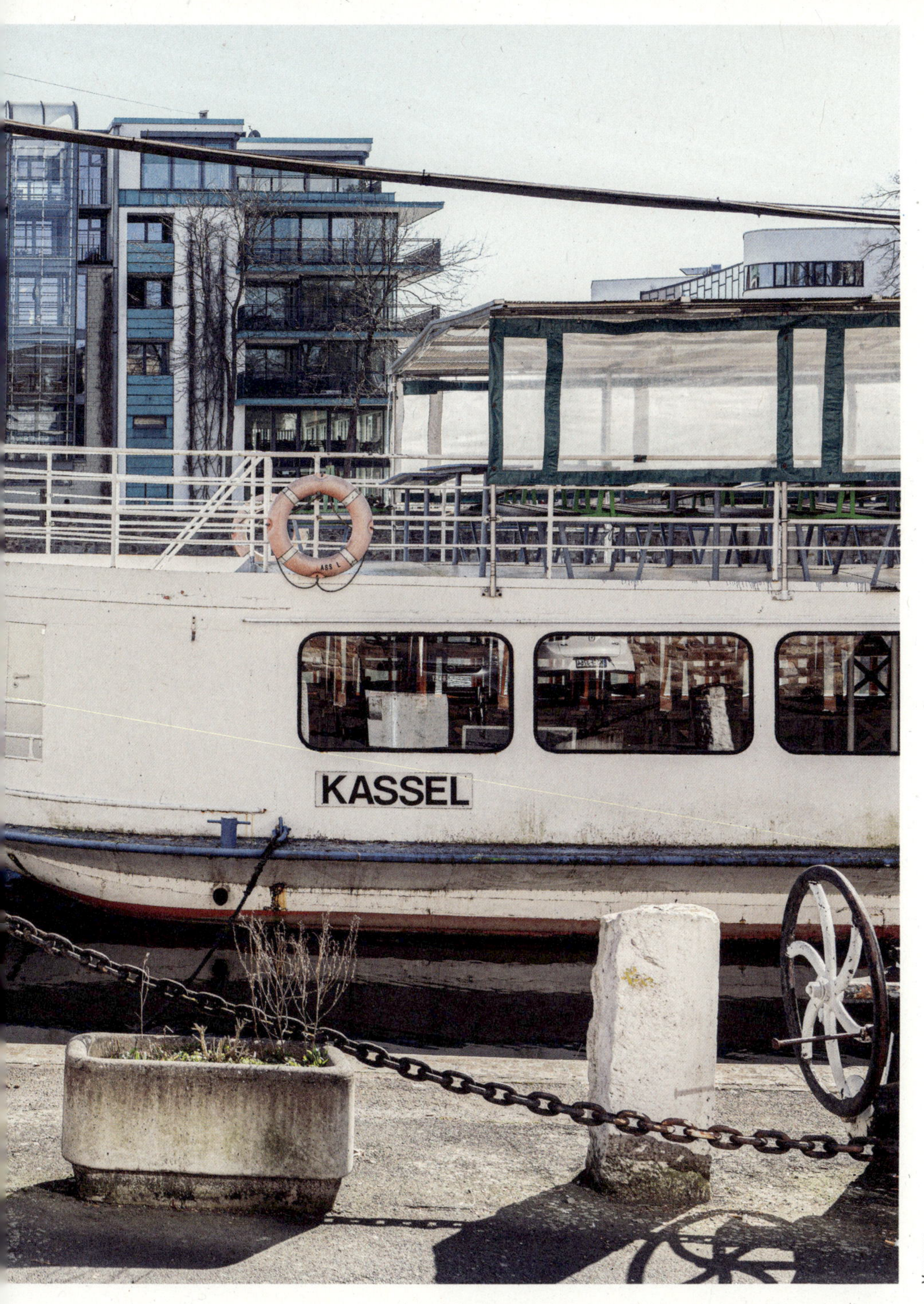
KASSEL

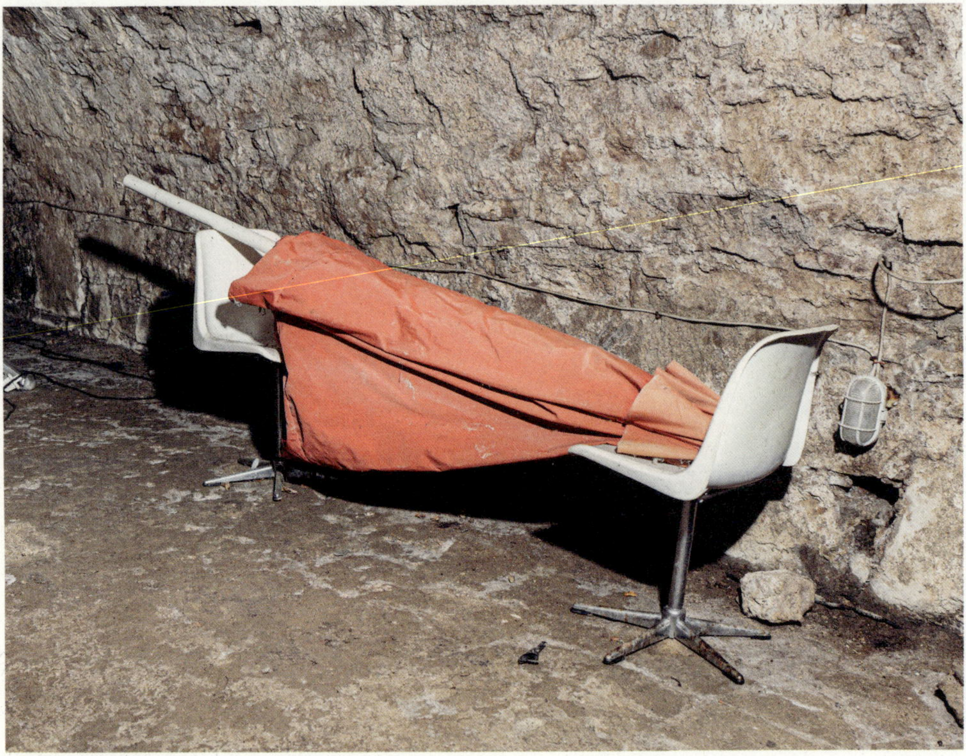

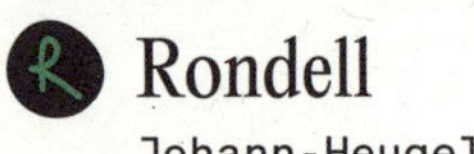

# Rondell

Johann-Heugel-Weg

Firewalls are important today to protect the critical—digital—infrastructure of cities and countries. Once people needed defensive walls of thick stones to deter enemies. The Rondell, built in 1523 in Unterneustadt on the Fulda, was a defensive tower that formed part of the old fortifications of the city. Landgrave Friedrich II had the largest parts of it removed in the eighteenth century. The 15-meter-high domed space, with its nearly 10-meter-thick walls, can only be entered via a floating metal footbridge. Since the year 2000, there has been a beer garden in the Rondell; one room inside the Rondell serves as an exhibition space.

The Hanoi, Vietnam-based filmmaker and artist Nguyen Trinh Thi works with the multi-layered relationships between image, sound, and space. Her documenta fifteen project is based on an autobiographical novel that describes conditions in detention camps. The artist shows scenes in which prisoners go through the forest and harvest chilis to recall home; she combines sound images with memories, landscapes, and stories.

LUMBUNG ARTISTS &
LUMBUNG MEMBERS
Black Quantum Futurism
Nguyen Trinh Thi
Taring Padi

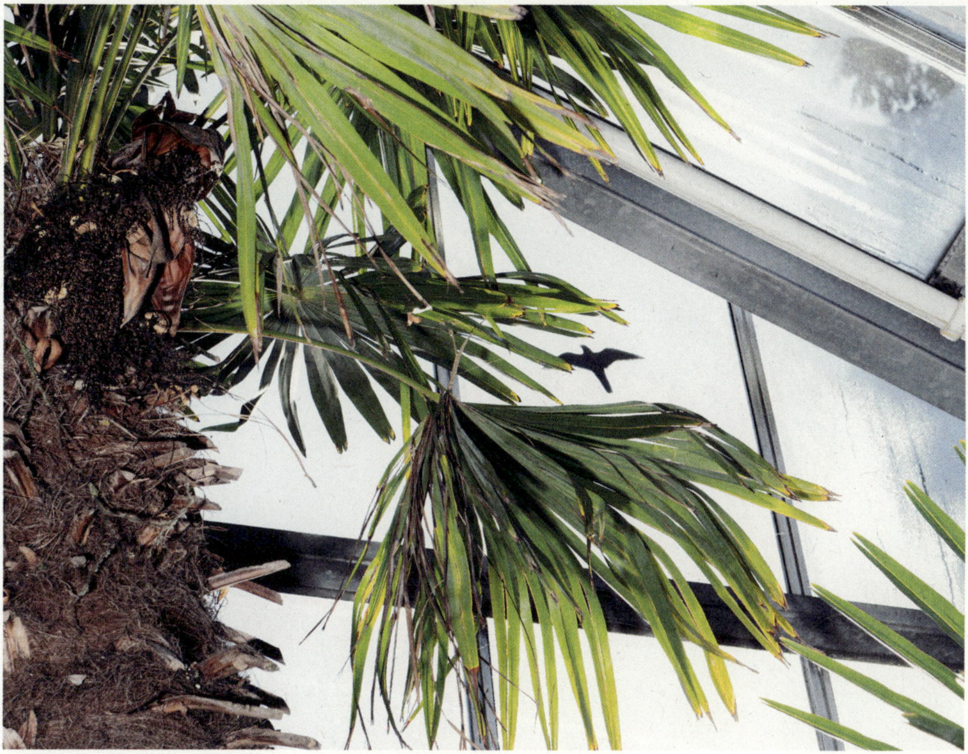

 # Greenhouse (Karlsaue)

Coordinates:
51.300310, 9.498459

Thinking about climate change and other environmental themes is occurring in an interdisciplinary way and in many places in the world: Más Arte Más Acción (MAMA) brings artists, scientists, activists, and writers together on Colombia's Pacific Coast to dedicate themselves to this subject. Thematizing environmental and socio-political problems, MAMA is showing in the Greenhouse, in the depot of the management of the Staatspark Karlsaue. Their installation includes a sound collage, tree trunks, and salvaged wood from HessenForst.

LUMBUNG ARTISTS &
LUMBUNG MEMBERS
Más Arte Más Acción (MAMA)

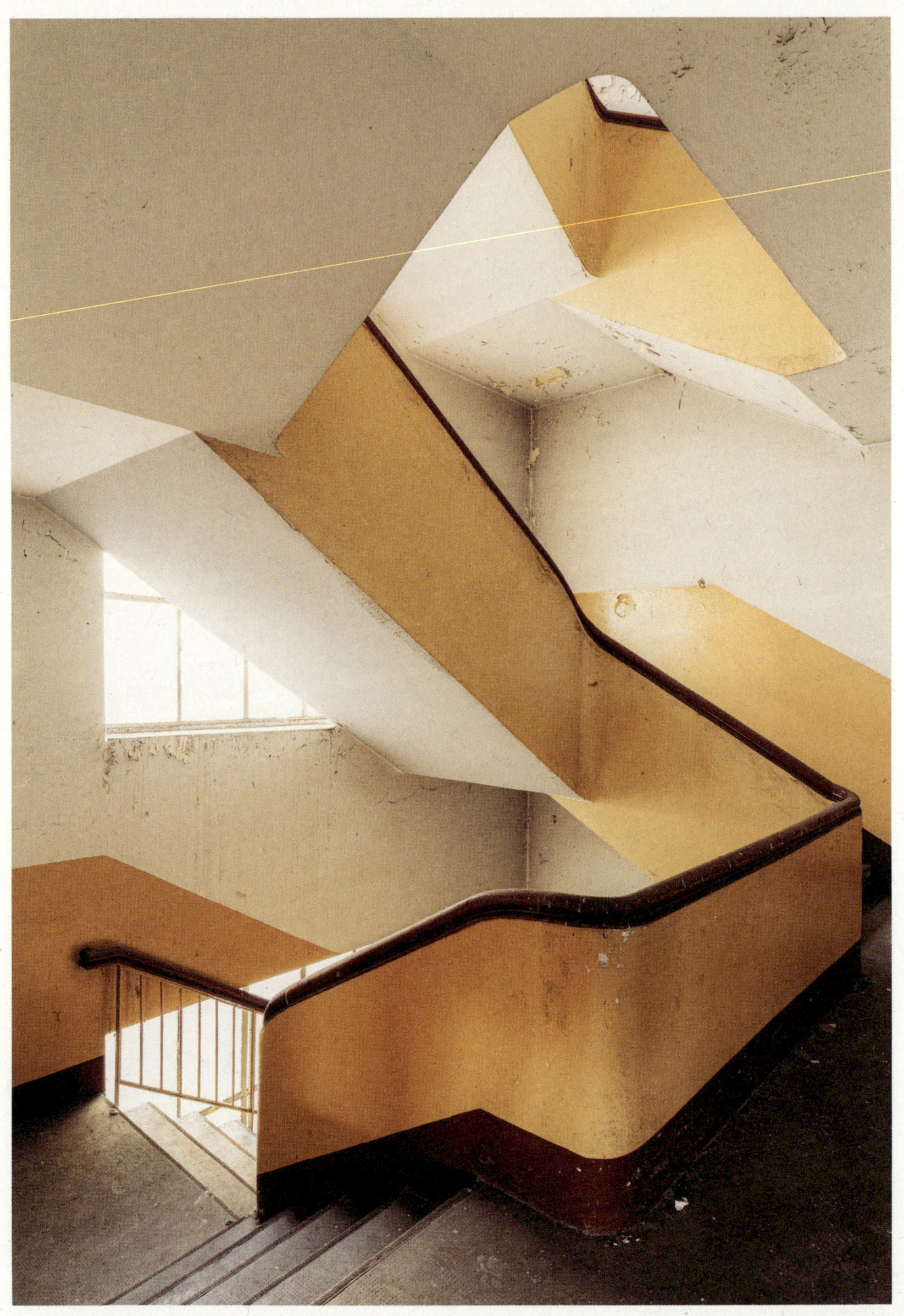

 Kassel / Fulda

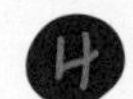# Karlswiese (Karlsaue)

The large Karlswiese in front of the Orangerie is the heart of the 125-hectare Karlsaue state park. The baroque Auepark, named after its patron Landgrave Karl von Hessen-Kassel, has been an important exhibition venue for documenta for many years. It was also the site of the 1955 Federal Garden Show, during which Arnold Bode conceived his first documenta. This year, Cinema Caravan and Takashi Kuribayashi are also present in the park with mosquito tents, an herbal sauna, and an open-air cinema. The collective uses the caravan as a model of a community in which individuals retain their autonomy, yet grow together with others to form a community.

The Nest Collective from Nairobi, Kenya, draw attention to the transport of garbage, e-waste and textiles to the countries of the Global South, which contribute to the destruction of the environment and the economy there, with *Return to Sender*, a walk-in installation made of garbage. In addition, Cao Minghao & Chen Jianjun from Chengdu in China, who work on the current socio-ecological realities and the human-nature relationship, erect a nomadic yak tent here.



# Hafenstraße 76

Kassel did indeed once have a port that was used for goods traffic. During World War II and thereafter, it flourished again. Since 1977, the harbor has been home to the local yacht club. That has made many of the old industrial buildings superfluous. For example, the multistory complex at Hafenstrasse 76, built in 1907, stands empty. The Berlin collective Fehras Publishing Practices is working on its fictional photo novel *Borrowed Faces* here. It is about three women who visit the archives during the Cold War era. An installation shows these archives as if they were real today. An installation and a film shot in Lebanon about common property, land rights, and land use are shown by the artist Marwa Arsanios of Beirut, Lebanon. The opportunities for converting real estate into common property and issues of land ownership and property are essential parts of her artistic work. Here, too, the graphic artist Nino Bulling presents selected drawings from a publication that takes a gender-fluid perspective on issues such as climate change, hand-painted on silk, and *foundationClass*collective activates the ground floor as a community space.

Teachers and students come together in the CAMP notes on education network. They work on new ways of mediating in the fields of art, art history, and cultural education. The CAMP workspace in the courtyard forms the basis for the Arts Educators in Residence, where fellows develop new ideas and working methods. The collective Composting Knowledge develops its projects together with local initiatives.

# BETZEN HAUSEN

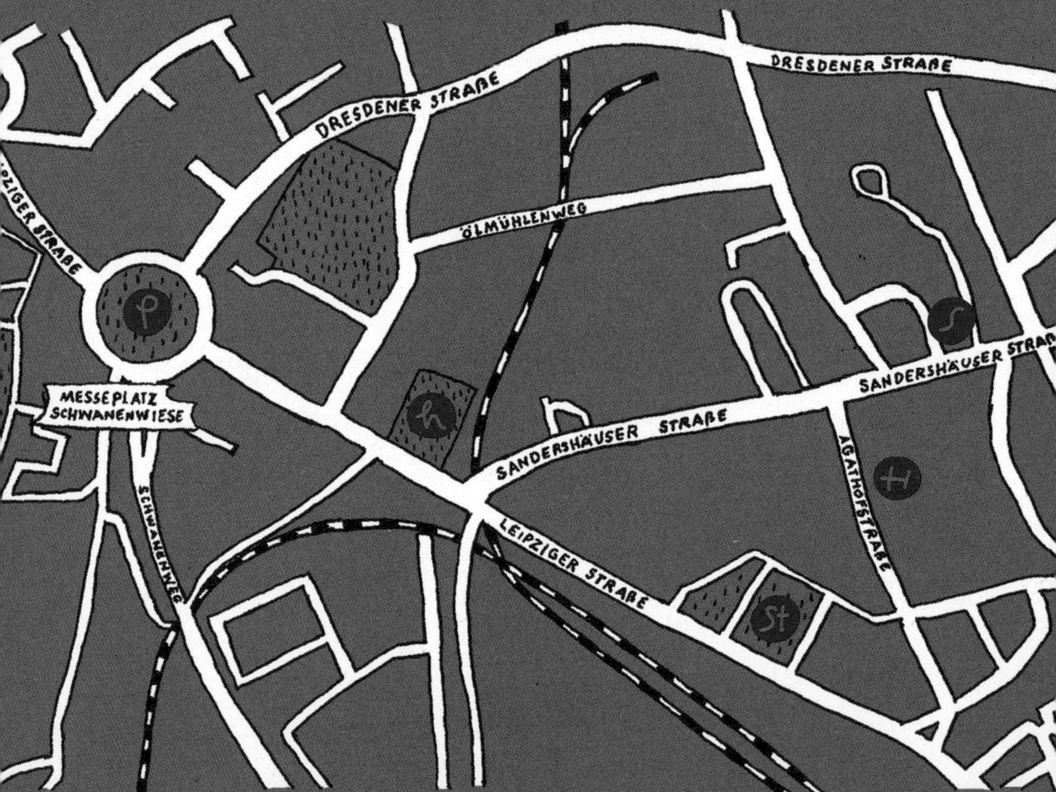


- Hallenbad Ost
- Hübner areal
- Platz der Deutschen Einheit (Underpass)
- Sandershaus
- St. Kunigundis

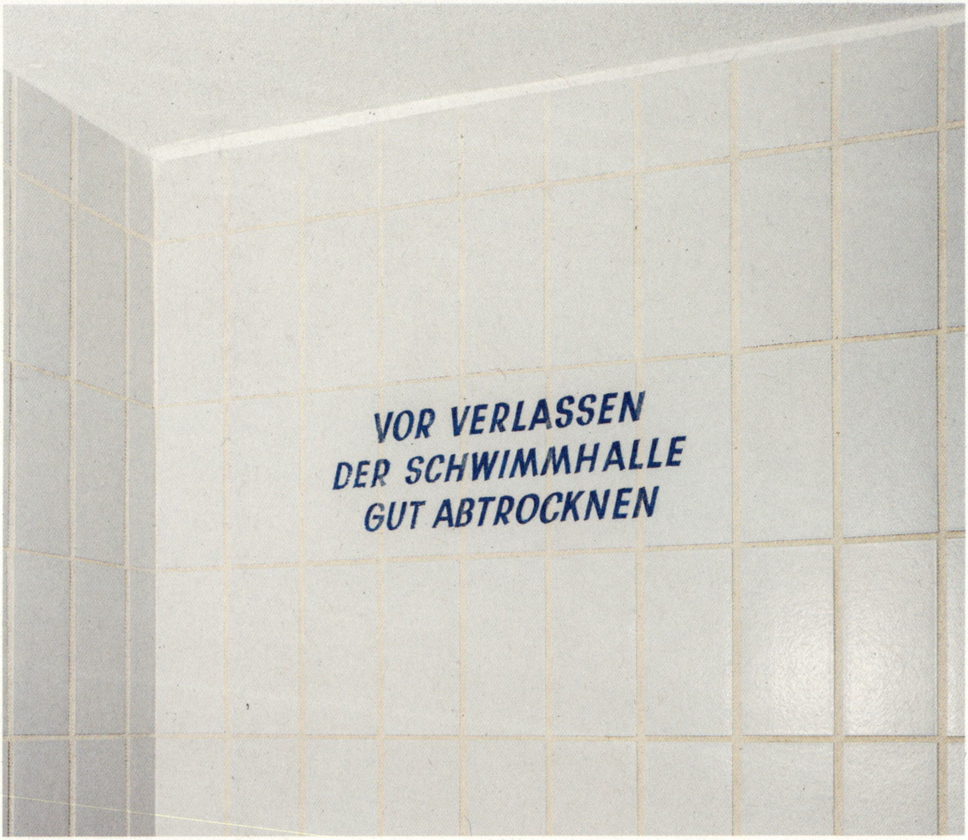

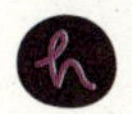



# Hallenbad Ost
## Leipziger Straße 99

The city's long-time residents still remember swimming outings to the Hallenbad Ost. But operations ceased in 2009, and the building stood empty for nearly ten years and was almost demolished. Today the indoor swimming pool, which was built in 1929, is one of the few buildings in Kassel in the Bauhaus style. It has since been listed on the historical register and represents an architectural highlight in the industrial district of Bettenhausen; it is being used for a documenta exhibition for the first time. On 600 m², the Indonesian collective Taring Padi is presenting its archive. The group is informed by working-class experiences and regards organization, education, and agitation as its primary tasks. With large-format banners, woodcut posters, and *wayang kardus* (life-sized cardboard puppets), Taring Padi is showing artworks from twenty-two periods in a retrospective.

LUMBUNG ARTISTS &
LUMBUNG MEMBERS
Taring Padi

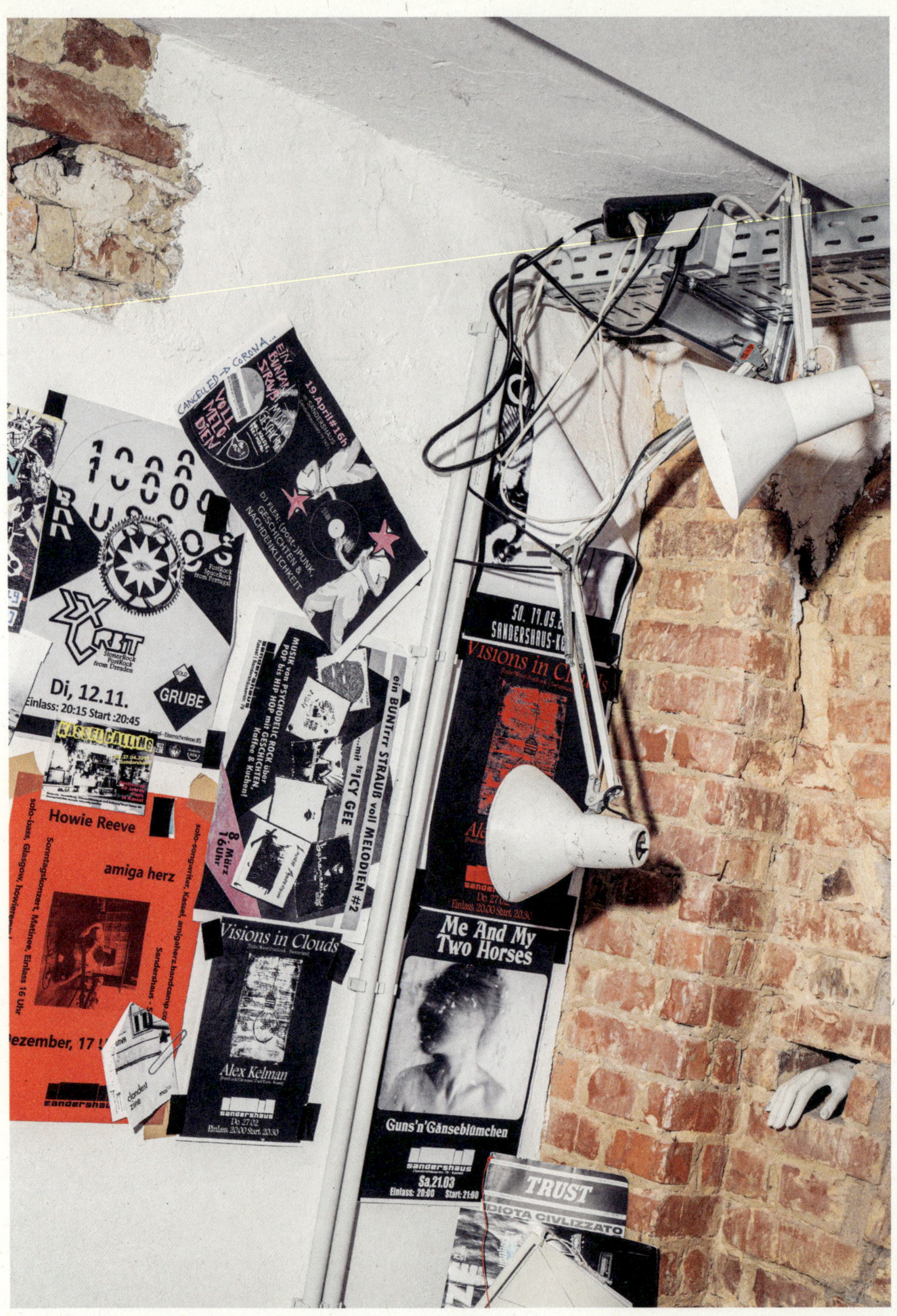

EIN BUNTER STRAU
VOLL MELO DIEN
19. April #16h
CANCELLED — CORONA...
DJ FLEN, IDOAL-)PUNK,
GESCHICHTEN &
NACHDENKLICHKEIT
10000 RUSSOS
Di, 12.11.
Einlass: 20:15 Start :20:45
GRUBE
Howie Reeve
amiga herz
Dezember, 17
Visions in Clouds
Alex Kelman
ein BUNTrrr STRAUB voll MELODIEN #2
mit ICY GEE
8. März
16 Uhr
Musik von PSYCHDELIC
POP bis HIP HOP mit GESCHICHTEN,
Kaffee & Kuchen!
SO. 17.05.
SANDERSHAUS-KO
Visions in Clouds
Me And My
Two Horses
Guns'n'Gänseblümchen
Sa.21.03
Einlass: 20:00  Start: 21:00
TRUST
DIOTA CIVLIZZATO

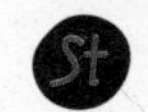 # Sandershaus

Sandershäuser Str. 79

Against the backdrop of an empty industrial factory and large vacant lots in the district of Bettenhausen, the Sandershaus opened in 2017 as the city's first hostel. The Sandershaus is, however, more than that: it is a place for culture and the art of sustainable handiwork such as repair cafés, and the upcycling movement. The team shows its hospitality by operating not only a bar, a restaurant, and a hostel but also the Amal, a housing for refugees. Serigrafistas queer have set up a rural meeting place outside of the Haferkakaofabrik that they use as a gathering space: in Argentina they make prints for LGBTIQ+. Also present are Sa Sa Art Projects, and Trampoline House, which furthers its ongoing work supporting refugees.

# St. Kunigundis

Leipziger Str. 145

St. Kunigundis Roman Catholic Church, completed in 1927 in the district of Bettenhausen, is thought to be the first church built in Germany with prestressed concrete and is therefore listed on the historic register. The building survived World War II practically undamaged. Today, however, the church is in need of renovation, but has been abandoned by the diocese. The group Atis Rezistans | Ghetto Biennale from Haiti is using the location. In the interior of the church, the artists are installing mixed-media sculptures.

LUMBUNG ARTISTS &
LUMBUNG MEMBERS
Serigrafistas queer
Trampoline House

LUMBUNG ARTISTS &
LUMBUNG MEMBERS
Atis Rezistans | Ghetto
Biennale

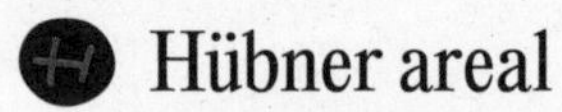

# Hübner areal
## Agathofstraße 15

One central site in the Kassel district of Bettenhausen, which is being used by documenta for the first time this year, is the grounds that the Hübner company—which is a major builder of parts for buses and trains—only recently vacated. The company's move left space for a collaborative exhibition, the works in which influence one another. Fondation Festival sur le Niger, from Mali, which has initiated a world-famous festival in its homeland and explores hospitality and other central traditions of Malian culture, are bringing processions, concerts, theater, films, and (other) contemporary art to the areal. BOLOHO, from Guangzhou, China, is shooting and streaming a sitcom in the cafeteria. Trampoline House, which advocates migrants' rights in Copenhagen, Denmark, are symbolically bringing their project to Kassel in a Brechtian chalk circle to present a public program that questions the Danish system of asylum. Amol K Patil, from New Delhi, India, is creating an installation from, among other things, a stage with kinetic sand, performers who skate for 100 days, a hologram, a screening, and several objects.

Additionally, the Jatiwangi art Factory is presenting installations of roof tiles and bricks. This joint project by the Indonesian collective is also enlivening the exhibition hall with musical performances and performative events, including a coffee tasting, conferences, and discussions.

LUMBUNG ARTISTS &
LUMBUNG MEMBERS
Amol K Patil
BOLOHO
FAFSWAG
Fondation Festival sur le Niger
Hamja Ahsan
Jatiwangi art Factory
Kiri Dalena
Project Art Works
Sa Sa Art Projects
Sourabh Phadke
Subversive Film
Trampoline House

# Platz der Deutschen Einheit (Underpass)

After the fall of the Berlin Wall, Kassel became the geographical center of the Federal Republic of Germany, and so it is only logical that the city should have a Square of German Unity (Platz der Deutschen Einheit). It is, however, not its most beautiful public square but rather an enormous, busy traffic circle—a relic of Kassel's past as a "car-friendly city." For documenta fifteen, the activists from Denmark's Trampoline House are using the pedestrian underpass on the south side of the square for a sound installation.

LUMBUNG ARTISTS &
LUMBUNG MEMBERS
Trampoline House

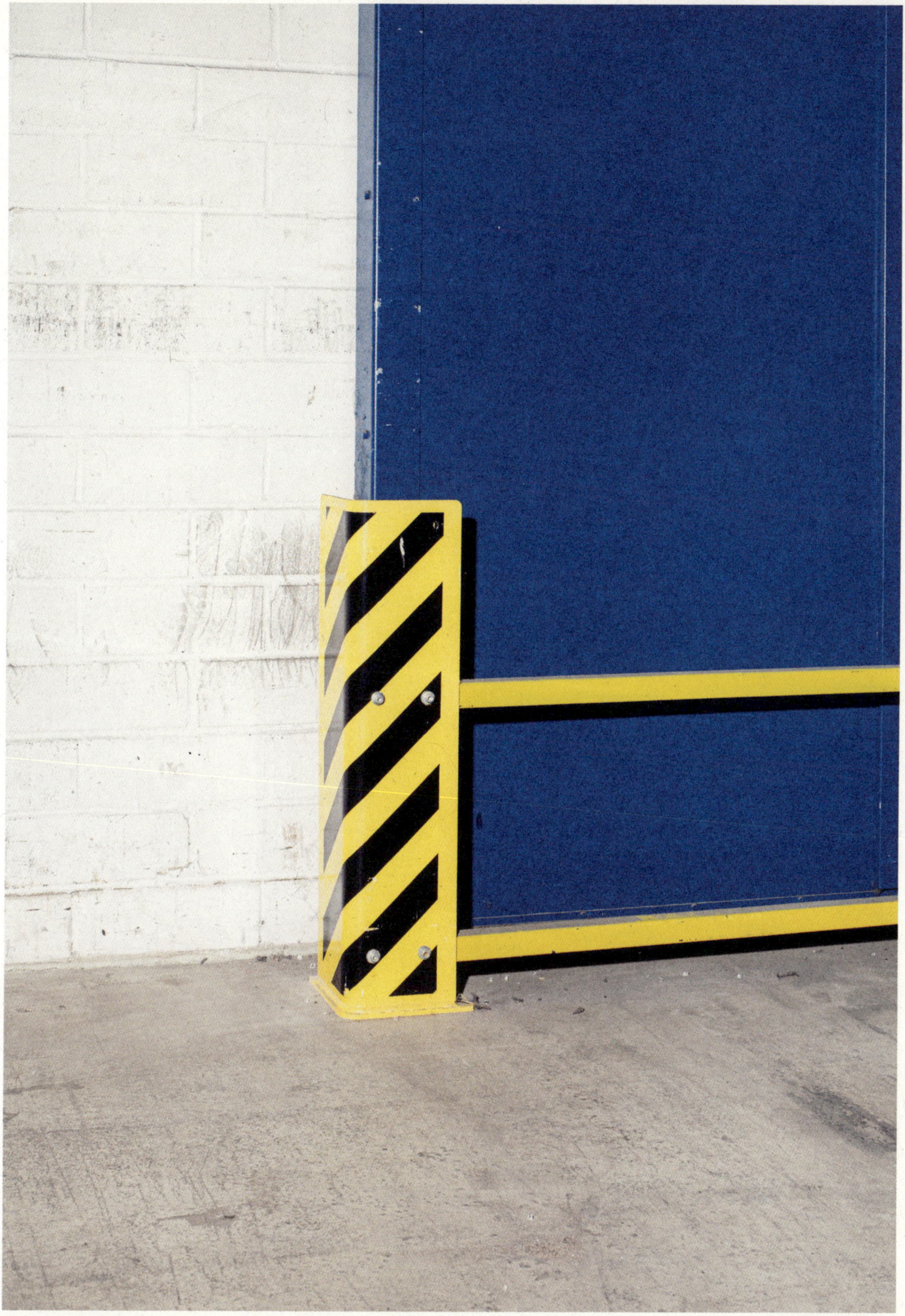

Venues / Hübner areal / Platz der Deutschen Einheit (Underpass)

# NORDSTADT

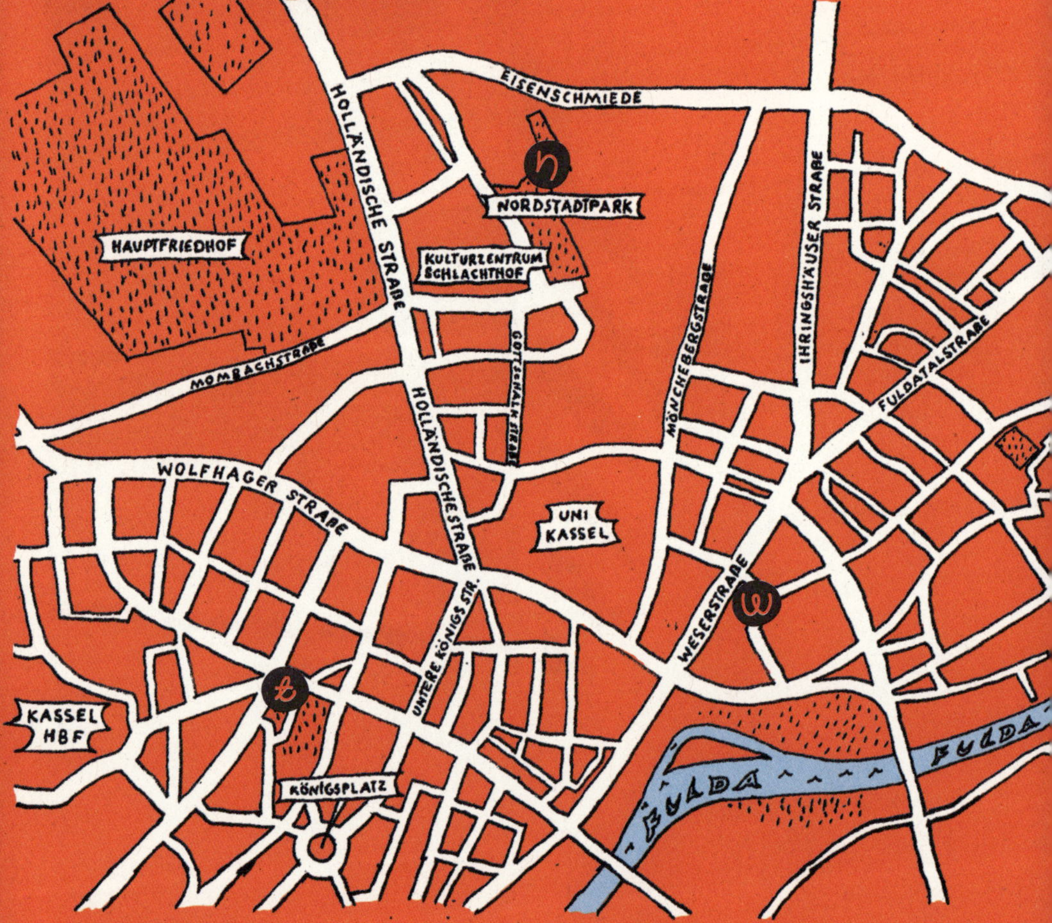


 η Nordstadtpark
ω Weserstraße 26
ℓ Trafohaus

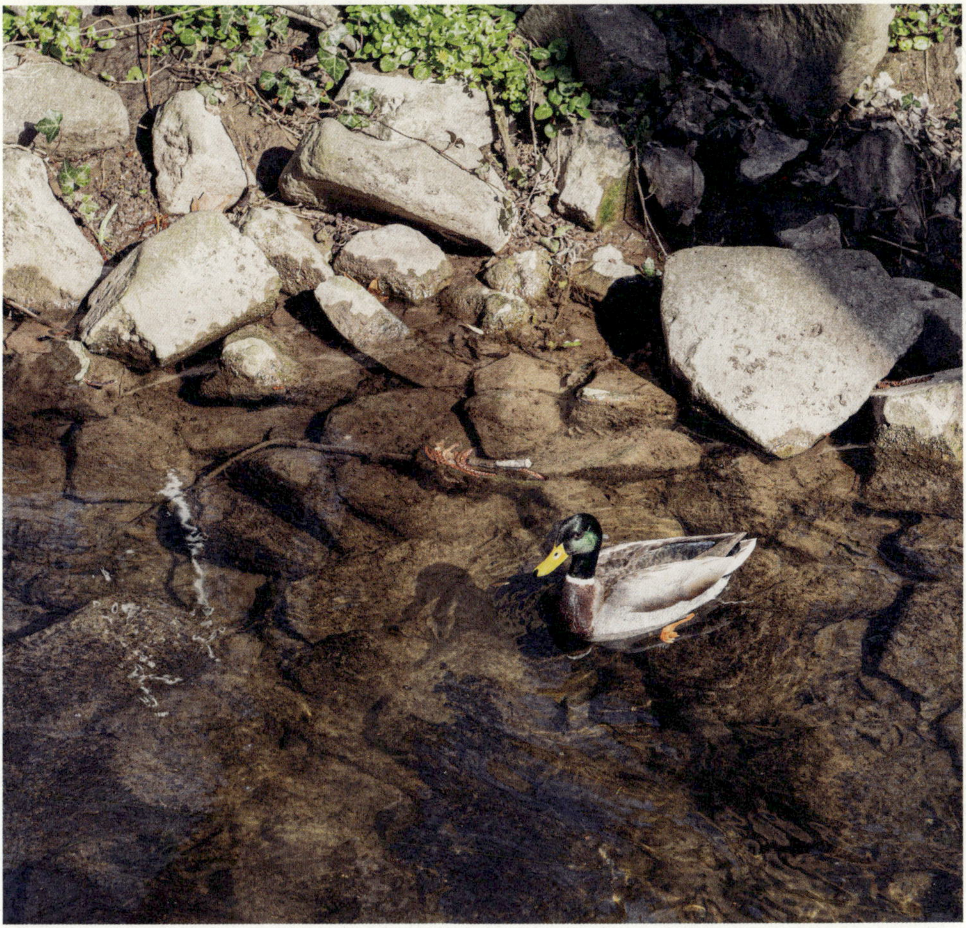

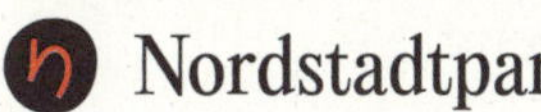

# Nordstadtpark

Kassel is almost more park than city. The greenery in the Nordstadt district of Kassel lies on the Ahne, a tributary of the Fulda, in the immediate vicinity of the university campus and the Kulturzentrum Schlachthof. The Nordstadtpark is particularly famous for music and a free open-air music festival. documenta fifteen is offering a summer stage: Sourabh Phadke designed a podium here for Jumana Emil Abboud that is made of clay and other sustainable materials and extends over the Ahne. Water and the right to water in the Palestinian territories is a theme of Emil Abboud's work. The stage is regularly used for performances and an open-air cinema during documenta fifteen.

LUMBUNG ARTISTS &
LUMBUNG MEMBERS
Jumana Emil Abboud
Sourabh Phadke

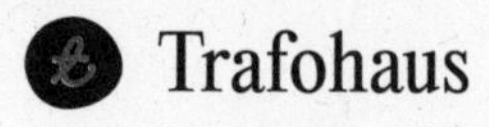

# ⓦ Weserstraße 26

The Neue Brüderkirche was built in 1971; it
is one of the most unusual sacred buildings of
postwar modernism in Kassel. A spire was part
of the original design, but it was cut to save
money for developmental projects. Since 2012,
the Neue Brüderkirche has served as a church
for vespers. During documenta fifteen, ook_ has
collaboratively developed ook_visitorZentrum
on Weserstrasse 26. ook_ consists of various
groups of friends, which are also part of the artists
still growing name: ook_ [reinaart vanhoe, Neue
Brüderkirche, Espora, BPOC Festival Kassel,
me_sobat, Colorlabor, graanschuur Tarwewijk,
Elaine W. Ho, Bartira, Wok The Rock,
COLLECTive, k. format, Take-A-Way, Plan B,
*Dynamitas unlimited* ...]. Here, the group offers
workshops for other collectives and visitors. Many
things can be produced here, from house altars to
self-printed magazines.

# ⓣ Trafohaus
## Lutherstraße 2

What the Trafohaus (Transformer Station) on
Lutherplatz once did is now done by a small box
next to it: transforming electricity. The white
building lies between districts; it has been used as
a kiosk, a telephone booth, and a post office. Since
the early 1990s, it has also hosted exhibitions. For
documenta fifteen. The worldwide network Arts
Collaboratory is also using the Trafohaus—as a
newsroom, radio station, rooftop garden, and site
of a theater performance.

Texts by Max Kühlem

LUMBUNG ARTISTS &
LUMBUNG MEMBERS
ook_ [reinaart vanhoe, Neue
Brüderkirche, Espora, BPOC
Festival Kassel, me_sobat,
Colorlabor, graanschuur
Tarwewijk, Elaine W. Ho,
Bartira, Wok The Rock,
COLLECTive, k. format,
Take-A-Way, Plan B,
*Dynamitas unlimited* ...]

LUMBUNG ARTISTS &
LUMBUNG MEMBERS
Alice Yard
Arts Collaboratory

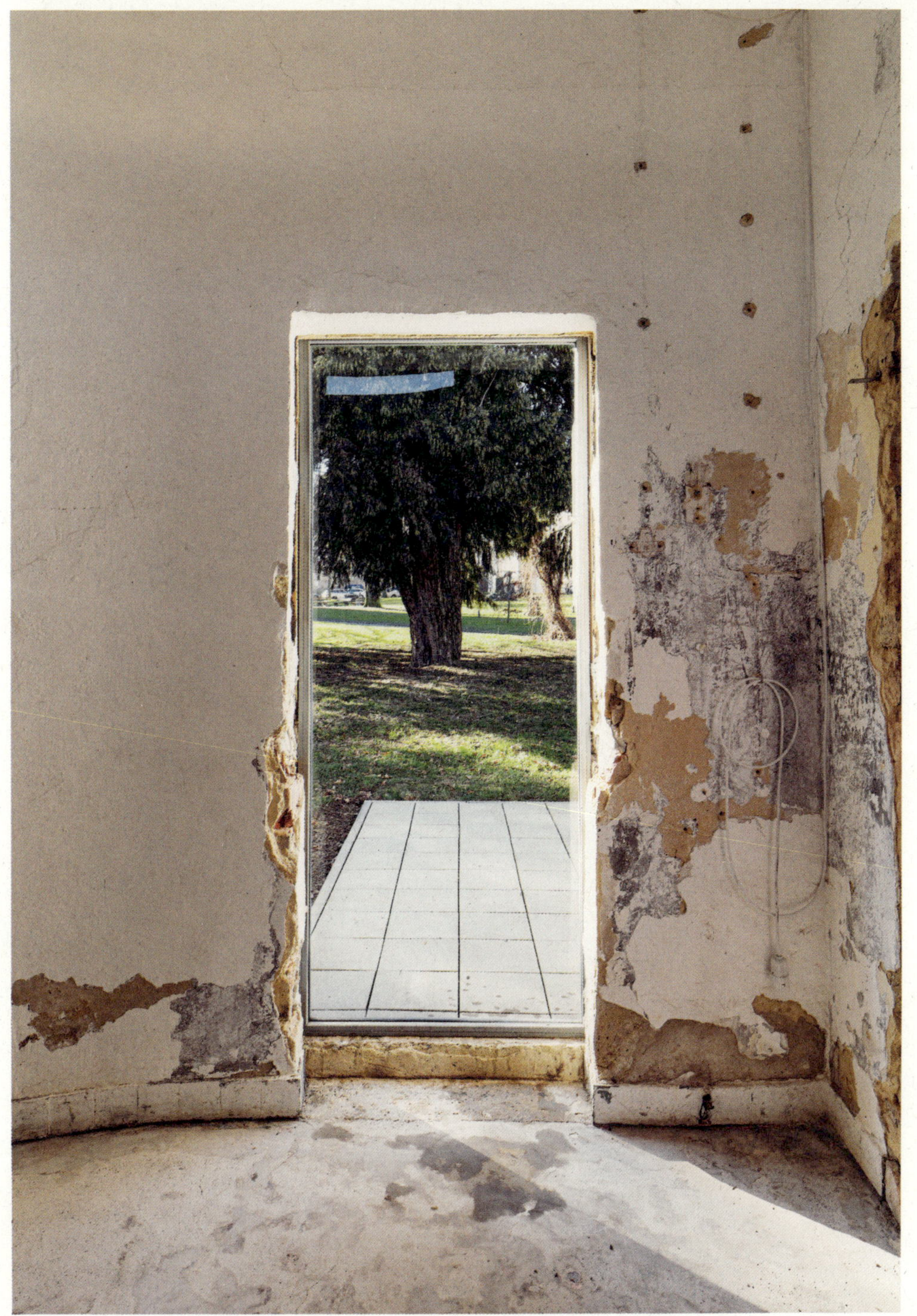

# SUSTAINABILITY & ACCESSIBILITY

# LESS ENVIRONMENTALLY HARMFUL AND SOCIALLY FAIR

Sustainability at documenta fifteen begins with a question: In light of the alarming consequences of climate change worldwide, how can a globally oriented art exhibition that attracts visitors from all over the world and lasts 100 days be less harmful to the environment and at the same time economically and socially fair? And in the process, how can it not only do justice to the artistic directorship's concept based on resource sharing and participation, but also carry out its responsibility as a multiplier?

To answer this question documenta has worked with competent partners: together with Prof. Dr. Christian Herzig and Kristina Gruber, Justus-Liebig-Universität Giesen/Universität Kassel, it worked out a strategy for the sustainable organization and planning of the art exhibition that considers all the fields of its action with the goal of achieving as many practical improvements as possible. This was then realized with countless likeminded people.

## THIS BOOK

Sustainability at documenta fifteen therefore also begins with this book: working with Hatje Cantz, a concept was developed for the four main publications involved printing on paper certified with the Blue Angel ecolabel at a printer located less than 150 kilometers away with an adjacent binder in order to avoid long transportation routes as well as licensed editions for independent publishers in the areas from which the artists come. The possibility of on-demand reprinting and e-book variants were considered. This not only reduces $CO_2$ considerably but also allows smaller publishing houses to participate.

## PROVISIONS AND MERCHANDISE

documenta fifteen has worked with Kassel Marketing to create food offerings that are as ecological, regional, and low-waste as possible, for example, at the café in the ruruHaus or the food market on Friedrichsplatz. For the merchandise, sustainably produced licensed products were developed with regional suppliers, from the organic beer from the medium-size Hütt-Brauerei in Baunatal to the organic-certified "seed confetti" of a small startup in Kassel and the seat cushions of virgin wool from Habbishaw carpet manufacturer in the small village of Rückersfeld in northern Hesse.

## MOBILITY AND ENERGY

More environmentally friendly mobility was also introduced, for example, by cooperating with Volkswagen AG in the area of e-mobility and with the Kasseler Verkehrs- und Versorgungs-GmbH and the Kasseler Verkehrs-Gesellschaft AG to include public transportation with the ticket to documenta fifteen. Regional green energy is being used, for example.

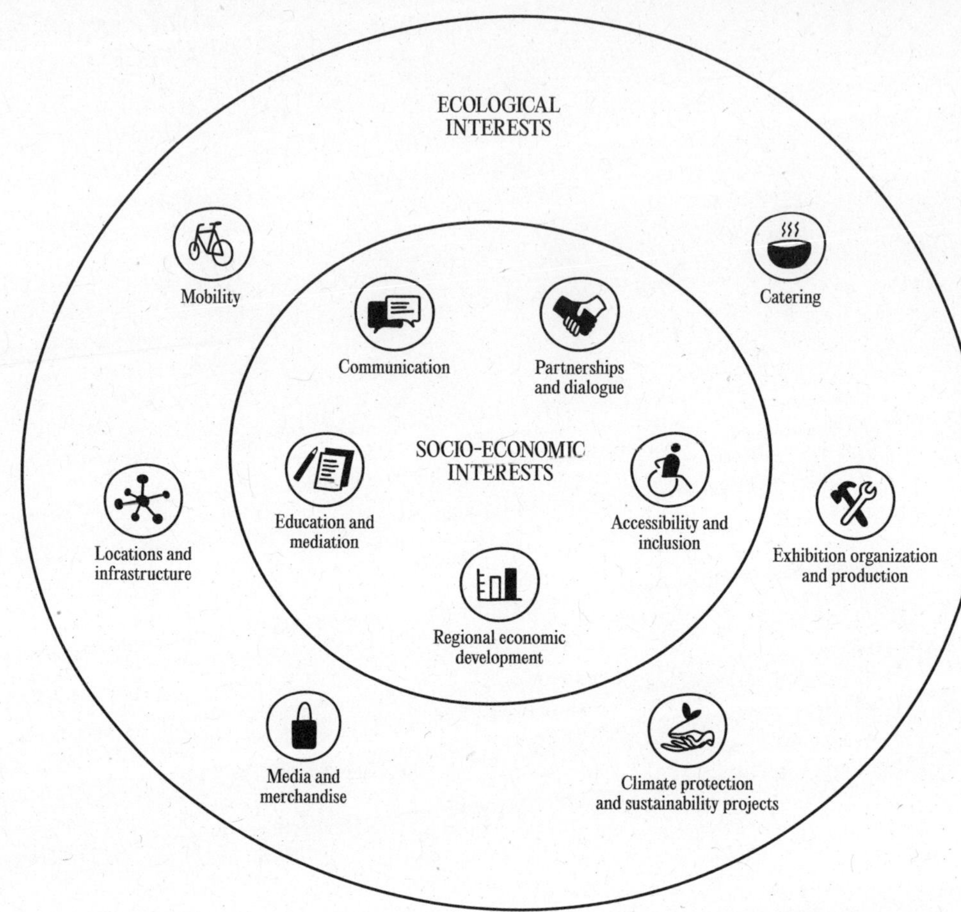


## THE EXHIBITION

The organization and production of the exhibition are based on ideas of circular economy, that is to say, recycled, recyclable, or used materials and objects are employed whenever possible. In parallel, documenta fifteen is working to build a comprehensive and practical network of collectives and initiatives in the field of art and culture that is concerned with the distribution and reuse of materials and exchanging knowledge about this. Action Network Sustainability in Culture and Media (Aktionsnetzwerk Nachhaltigkeit in Kultur und Medien) is funded by the Federal Government Commissioner for Culture and Media. In general, all investment decisions focus on reuse, not just on producing from sustainable perspectives. Another example: the welcome center at the ruruHaus, operated in cooperation with the Sparkassen-Finanzgruppe, is based on these principles.

Among other things, the bookstores located there—the Hofbuchhandlung Vietor and the Buchhandlung Walther König—are using a shelving system developed by Jochem Jourdan, the architect of the documenta Halle, for a bookstore in Düsseldorf that is no longer in business. The owner of Hatje Cantz Publishing had placed it in storage and is making it available to documenta fifteen.

COOPERATION PROJECTS
In order to actively support ideas of sustainability, one Euro from each documenta fifteen ticket sold supports sustainability projects in Indonesia and the Kassel region. On Sumatra it goes to the Sustainable Village Project in cooperation with the EFForTS collaborative research center of Georg-August-Universität Göttingen and the University of Jambi in Indonesia to improve the ecology of palm oil and rubber plantations working with the artists' collective Rumah Budaya Sikukeluang. In the Reinhardswald forest, together with the state enterprise HessenForst, open areas caused by bark beetles, storms, and drought are being reforested. At the Offene Schule Waldau, a cooperative project of Kasseler Wohnungsbaugesellschaft GWG, school associations, and the Smart City model project has purchased a plant container that uses as much as 90 percent less water and energy than usual. It can be used by students, teachers, and neighbors to grow lettuces and herbs.

PARTICIPATION
Another aspect of sustainability is enabling partic-ipation by as broad a public as possible. In order to encourage encounters, exchange, and the involve-ment of many people from different backgrounds, documenta fifteen is implementing a series of measures to improve accessibility of its website, infrastructure, and education program. For exam-ple, the website offers information in easy-to-read language and a higher-contrast design. In addition to taking into account low-threshold paths and access, break rooms have been created in the exhibition and the guidance system offers planning assistance for your visit.

The educational offerings of documenta fifteen have been conceived to be as accessible as possible. In addition to the exhibition tours Walks and Stories in many languages, including German Sign Language, International Sign, and Easy Language, tours with descriptive multisensory content are also planned.

The development and implementation of measures to remove barriers at documenta fifteen have integrated diverse voices from local and international networks. They include the lumbung member Project Art Works, which has initiated encounters between the staff of documenta fifteen and neurodiverse communities in Kassel and environs, a collaboration with berlinklusion, and initiatives from Kassel and the city's expert advisory boards.

LEARNING FOR THE FUTURE
documenta fifteen is accompanied by an online survey of visitors on issues of sustainability. In addition, selected, relevant areas of action are assessed ecologically. The results of the survey will be used to refine the concept and to design the areas of action and measures, above all with an eye to the next edition of documenta.

With support from its shareholders, the State of Hesse, the City of Kassel, and the German Federal Cultural Foundation, the documenta und Museum Fridericianum gGmbH has set off on a journey with many partners and an eye to the theme of sustainability and has introduced a long-term learning process that is intended to emanate beyond documenta fifteen to all the areas of the gGmbH's activities and future documenta exhibitions.

Sabine Schormann,
Philipp Greguhn

# VISITOR INFORMATION

documenta fifteen takes place in
Kassel from June 18 - September 25,
2022. Regular opening hours are
10 am-8 pm daily. Event times may
vary.

TICKETS
The following tickets are available and valid
for all documenta fifteen locations during the
exhibition period.

tickets@documenta.de
www.documenta-fifteen.de/tickets
Ticket hotline +49 30 84108908
(daily from 10 a.m. to 4 p.m.)

Day ticket 27 Euro /
reduced* 19 Euro
        (valid on a day of your choice)

2-day ticket 45 Euro /
reduced* 32 Euro
        (valid on two consecutive days, the first of
which can be chosen freely)

Season ticket 129 Euro /
reduced* 104 Euro
        (valid for the entire exhibition period)

Season ticket - Print@Home
125 Euro / reduced* 100 Euro
        (valid for the entire exhibition period)

Evening ticket 12 Euro /
reduced* 8 Euro
        (valid on a day of your choice from 5 to 8 pm)

School class ticket 7 Euro
        (per pupil or teacher)

Family ticket 60 Euro
        (valid on a day of your choice for up to two
adults with up to three children up to and including
the age of 18)

Solidarity ticket 27 Euro
        (Make a gesture and donate a solidary ticket,
which can be used as a free ticket by another
person)

Free admission
        Children up to and including twelve years of
age and users of a solidarity ticket.

With every ticket purchase, you automatically
donate 1 Euro to sustainable projects in Germany
and Indonesia. You can find more information at:
www.documenta-fifteen.de/en/substainability

The tickets (except the season ticket) entitle you to
use public transport in the KasselPlus tariff area.
Visitors can use public transport free of charge
until the end of operation on the day for which the
ticket is valid. Season ticket holders can purchase
discounted MultiTickets during the exhibition
period.

* Pupils, students, trainees, recipients of
basic social security benefits (e.g. ALG II or
supplementary pension benefits), persons
in the Federal Volunteer Service or FSJ,
refugees, and people in the asylum process
as well as people with severe disabilities
(from 50%) receive reduced admission upon
presentation of appropriate documentation.
People with severe disabilities who are
dependent on an accompanying person
may take this accompanying person into
the exhibition free of charge. Proof must
be presented at the ticket inspection. The
*Teilhabecard Kassel* can replace the corre-
sponding official proof. It is only accepted
in conjunction with a valid identification
document.

GROUP OFFERS AND PACKAGES

Up to 15 people can participate in an exhibition tour.

Please note that group offers do not include admission tickets. These can be purchased separately via the webshop, the advance booking offices or our box offices. Packages for groups can also be booked via our webshop. The booking here requires a minimum of eight working days in advance.

www.documenta-fifteen.de/gruppen

WALKS AND STORIES

Exhibition walk with the art mediators sobat-sobat: Explore the exhibition on foot or seated. You will share stories and talk to each other in different places. You can find an overview of all offers on the website under "exhibition walks".

www.documenta-fifteen.de/
ausstellungsrundgaenge

`Booking and Services`
tickets@documenta.de

`Bootsverleih Ahoi`
Walk from Ahoi Boat Rentals to Hallenbad Ost

`documenta Halle`
Walk from Friedrichsplatz via the documenta Halle to Karlsaue

`Fridericianum`
Walk from Friedrichsplatz to the Fridericianum

`Grimmwelt Kassel`
Walk from Grimmwelt Kassel via Museum for Sepulchral Culture to Karlsaue

`Hafenstraße 76`
Walk through Hafenstrasse 76

`Hübner areal`
Walk from Hübner-Areal to the Sandershaus Hostel

`ruruHaus`
Walk from ruruHaus via Friedrichsplatz to the Natural History Museum in the Ottoneum

`WH22`
Walk from WH22 via Trafohaus to ruruHaus

`ruruHaus TALK`
Sitting down: Talk in the ruruHaus

`Early & Late`
Walk from Friedrichsplatz to documenta fifteen's outside locations
Early 8 – 10 am
Late 8 – 10 pm, 8.30 – 10.30 pm, 9 – 11 pm

MEYDAN – PUBLIC PROGRAM

The Meydan Public Program of documenta fifteen encompasses various forms of social gathering. Taking place every other weekend of the month through the 100 days of the exhibition, Meydan occurs in different areas in the city that are home to local initiatives in the Kassel ekosistem.

During this period, designated nongkrong spaces in various spaces across Kassel will function as living rooms: community spaces that accommodate conversation for initiating collaborations in a casual atmosphere that is intimate, warm, and relaxing. This includes foods, drinks, hospitality, and various programs organized by the community in specific space for three weekends during Meydan.

```
Meydan #1
July 8 - 10, 2022
Area: Mitte & Fulda
```
With readings, creative workshops and discussion panels, the focus this weekend will be on the meeting of more than 20 independent, international publishers. In addition, an open-air music festival is being hosted by Festival sur le Niger, RRREC Fest, and Cinema Caravan and Takashi Kuribayashi, as well as a variety program of food, music, films, and talks.

```
Meydan #2
August 12 - 14, 2022
Area: Nordstadt
```
Organized and hosted in collaboration with Kulturzentrum Schlachthof, a street festival and an education program take place, together with events in other locations in the Nordstadt area

```
Meydan #3
September 9 - 11, 2022
Area: Bettenhausen
```
A Harvest Festival—including the lumbung Film festival, music events, talks, and workshops on sustainability and artistic alternative institution-building—are taking place around Sandershaus and Hübner areal.

ACCESSIBILITY

All venues and activities are made as accessible as possible. Here you will find a selection of our barrier-free activities for groups. Booking deadline: four weeks in advance.

A selection of our accessible offers for groups can be found on the website under Accessibility. Booking deadline is four weeks in advance.

Accessible and multilingual public offers take place regularly. Individual booking via www.documenta-fifteen.de

Accessibility advice: accessibility@documenta.de

GENERAL INFORMATION

welcome@documenta.de
www.documenta-fifteen.de

NEWSLETTER

www.documenta-fifteen.de/newsletter

COVID-19 REGULATIONS

The health of our visitors is very important to us. For this reason, documenta fifteen pursues a safety and hygiene concept that is constantly adapted to meet current developments and regulations.

As soon as there are any changes to these regulations, you will find the latest version on our website under the menu item "Visit".

www.documenta-fifteen.de/covid-19

# ENG〰GEMENT

ON THE WAY TOGETHER
An undertaking such as documenta
fifteen cannot be realized without the commitment of countless
international and national partners from business, society,
the media, politics, social and
non-profit sectors, art and
culture, and science. Our heart-
felt thanks go to these supporters for joining us on the road
to documenta fifteen, first and
foremost to our main partners,
the Sparkassen-Finanzgruppe and
Volkswagen AG, as well as the
Goethe-Institut, which has supported our lumbung network.

This goes for our shareholders,
the City of Kassel and the State
of Hesse, our Supervisory Board,
as well as the German Federal
Cultural Foundation, who accompanied our journey with advice
and support and never let the
operating funds run out.

# ORGANIZERS

### ORGANIZER

documenta und Museum
Fridericianum gGmbH
Friedrichsplatz 18
D-34117 Kassel
T +49 561 707270
F +49 561 7072739
office@documenta.de
www.documenta.de

### SHAREHOLDERS

Land Hessen
Stadt Kassel

### CHIEF EXECUTIVE OFFICER

Dr. Sabine Schormann

### AUTHORIZED SIGNATORY

Andreas Brandenstein

### SUPERVISORY BOARD

**Christian Geselle**
Oberbürgermeister, Kassel
Vorsitzender

**Angela Dorn**
Staatsministerin, Wiesbaden
Stellvertretende Vorsitzende

**Axel Wintermeyer**
Staatsminister, Wiesbaden

**Mark Weinmeister**
Regierungspräsident, Kassel

**Dr. Martin J. Worms**
Staatssekretär, Wiesbaden

**Karin Müller**
Abgeordnete des Hessischen
Landtags, Wiesbaden

**Dr. Rabani Alekuzei**
Stadtverordneter, Kassel

**Markus Leitschuh**
Stadtverordneter, Kassel

**Gernot Rönz**
Stadtverordneter, Kassel

**Dr. Susanne Völker**
Kulturdezernentin, Kassel

documenta and Museum Fridericianum gGmbH
is a nonprofit company supported and jointly
financed by the City of Kassel and the State of
Hessen in their capacity as shareholders, with
financial support from the Federal Cultural
Foundation.

Funded by the
German Federal
Cultural Foundation

Funded by the
Federal Government Commissioner
for Culture and the Media

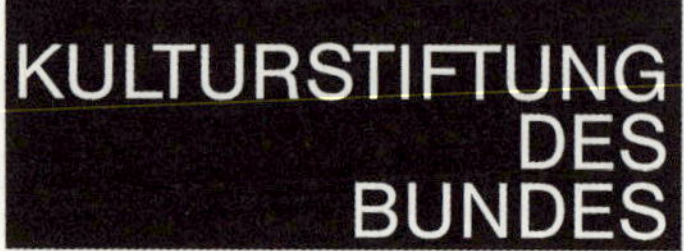


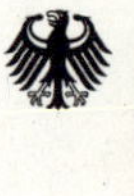


The German Federal Cultural Foundation is one of the largest publicly funded cultural foundations in Europe. With an annual budget of 35 million euros financed by the Federal Government Commissioner for Culture and the Media (BKM), the Foundation has funded some 4000 projects of contemporary culture since it was established by the German federal government in March 2002. It is a civil-law foundation with headquarters in Halle an der Saale, Germany.

The primary task of the German Federal Cultural Foundation is to promote innovative programs and projects in an international context. Cultural exchange and cross-border collaboration are central to its funding activities. General Project Funding allocates up to ten million euros per year to support a discretionary number of projects in all artistic fields. The Foundation also offers Program-Based Funding to support larger-scale cultural projects on issues of societal significance, e.g. climate change, digitalization, structural transformation, diversity, and superregional and international collaboration. By granting funding for multiple years at a time, the Foundation provides outstanding cultural institutions and internationally renowned festivals with a high degree of planning security. The documenta in Kassel is one of the select group of "cultural beacons".

The German Federal Cultural Foundation is funded by the Federal Government Commissioner for Culture and the Media upon the resolution of the German Bundestag.

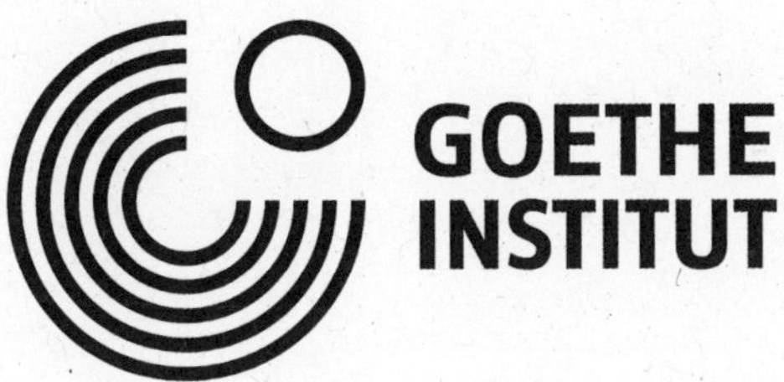



As a partner of documenta fifteen, the Goethe-Institut supports the development of the lumbung network. This includes the online discussion series lumbung calling and lumbung konteks as well as lumbung meetings and events in cooperation with the Goethe-Institutes abroad. Our commitment to the lumbung idea is also expressed in the support for the book publication *majalah lumbung* and for the website lumbung.space (https://lumbung.space/), which serves as a place for the lumbung members and participating artists to exchange ideas.

The Goethe-Institut is the cultural institute of the Federal Republic of Germany with a global reach. It promotes knowledge of the German language abroad and fosters international cultural cooperation. It conveys a comprehensive image of Germany by providing information about cultural, social and political life. Its cultural and educational programs encourage intercultural dialogue and enable cultural involvement. They strengthen the development of structures in civil society and foster worldwide mobility.

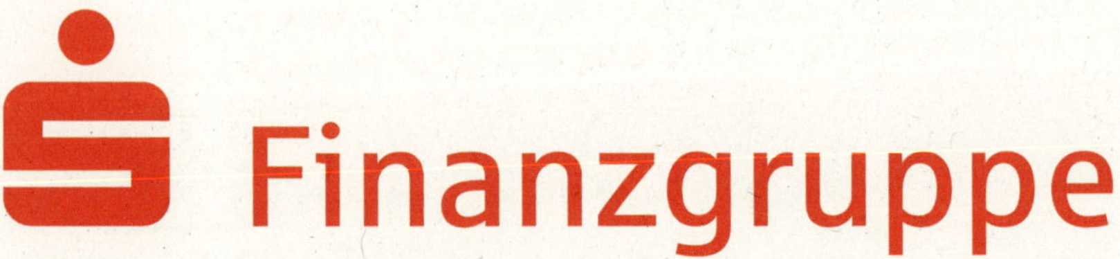


The 367 Savings Banks and their affiliated partners in the Savings Banks Finance Group are on hand to provide lifelong support to people throughout Germany.

As public financial institutions with regional roots, the Savings Banks and their affiliated partners are committed to serving the public interest nationwide. The Savings Banks see it as their duty to facilitate both economic and social participation for everyone. This commitment has been embedded in the concept of Savings Banks for over 200 years.

Art and culture sponsoring plays a key role in the organisation's CSR activities: the Savings Banks Finance Group has been Germany's largest non-government sponsor in this sphere for many years.

Art and culture broaden horizons, foster imagination and promote mutual understanding. This two-way communication is one of the cornerstones of an open and diverse society. In its sponsorship work, the Saving Banks Finance Group seeks to make cultural experiences accessible to as many people as possible.

documenta fifteen is sponsored by the Sparkassen- und Giroverband Hessen-Thüringen, the Sparkassen-Kulturstiftung Hessen-Thüringen, Kasseler Sparkasse, Helaba, DekaBank, SV SparkassenVersicherung, and the Savings Banks Cultural Fund of the German Savings Banks Association.

# VOLKSWAGEN

## AKTIENGESELLSCHAFT

Acting as documenta's lead partner for the fifth time, Volkswagen proudly supports the world's leading exhibition for contemporary art. We dedicate our efforts to help documenta fifteen meeting their ecological goals: new e-mobility solutions and advanced charging infrastructure provide visitors with resource saving options to reach exhibition venues. And we remain actively involved when our technology aids to realize selected artworks and practical support is being lent by trainees from our Kassel plant.

Volkswagen's Cultural Engagement is led by the vision to open the world of culture and the arts for as many people as possible. As a premiere, documenta will be able to use 14,000 Volkswagen Art4All tickets to invite young students from the Kassel region, enabling the young generation to engage with the art of their time.

We would like to wish documenta fifteen and the involved artists a wide-ranging recognition of their work and a vivid discourse with the audience.

# Funders

AC/E
ACCIÓN CULTURAL
ESPAÑOLA

文化庁
Agency for Cultural Affairs, Government of Japan

A
O M
D M
O

ARTS COUNCIL
NEW ZEALAND TOI AOTEAROA
creative nz

Australian Government
Australia
Council
for the Arts

BAGRI
FOUNDATION

Botschaft der
Argentinischen Republik
in der Bundesrepublik Deutschland

Botschaft
der Bundesrepublik Deutschland
Dhaka

Botschaft
der Bundesrepublik Deutschland
Jakarta

Botschaft
der Bundesrepublik Deutschland
Kampala

Botschaft
der Bundesrepublik Deutschland
Nairobi

Botschaft
der Bundesrepublik Deutschland
Port-au-Prince

Botschaft
der Bundesrepublik Deutschland
Port-Of-Spain

Embassy
of the Republic of Indonesia
Berlin

Consulate General
Republic of Indonesia
Frankfurt

We are Family
CTBC BANK
中國信託銀行

STICHTING
DOEN
NATIONALE
POSTCODE LOTERIJ

FANAK FUND
YOUR ART ECHOES THROUGHOUT THE WORLD

GREEN FAMILY
FOUNDATION

IASPIS
Konstnärsnämnden
The Swedish Arts Grants Committee

ifa
Institut für
Auslandsbeziehungen

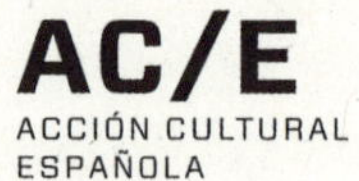

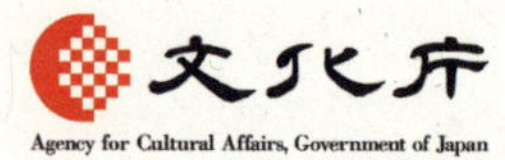

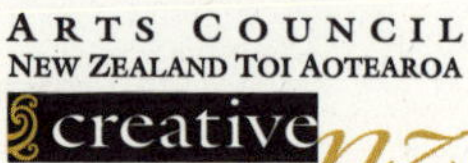

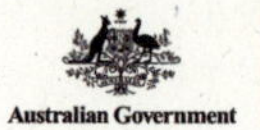

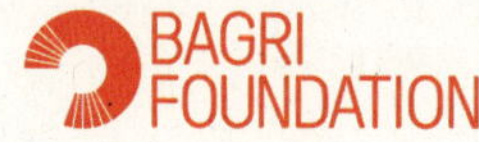

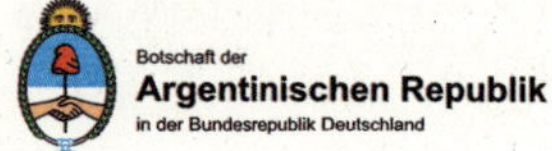

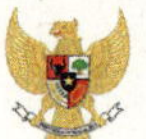

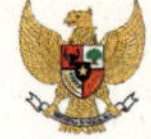

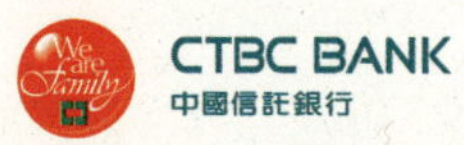

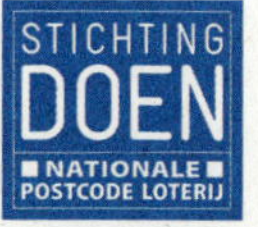

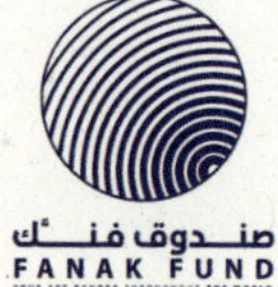

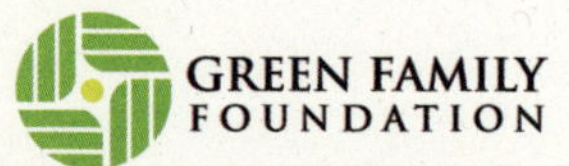

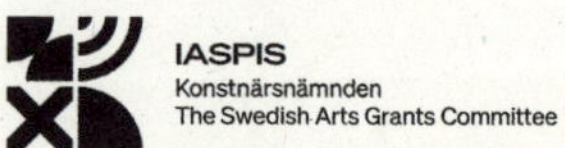

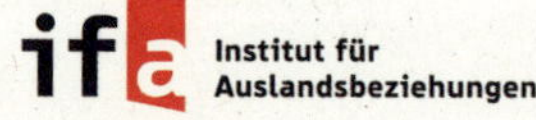

Funders

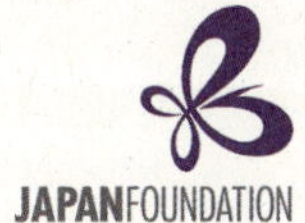
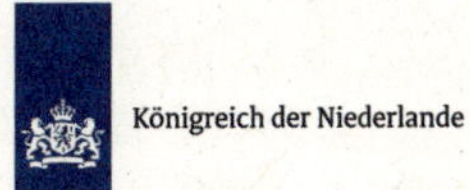

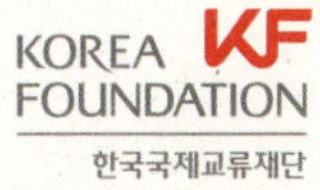
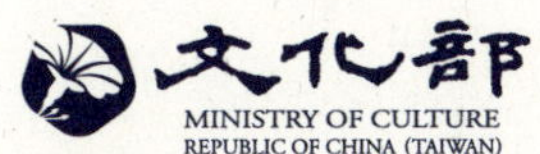
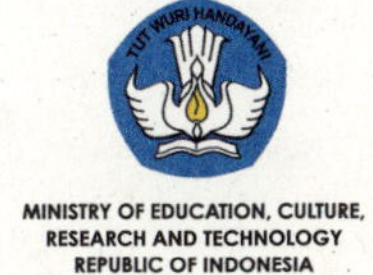

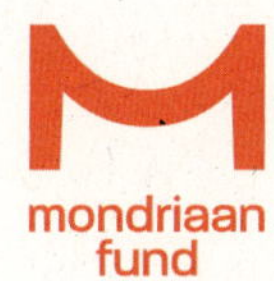
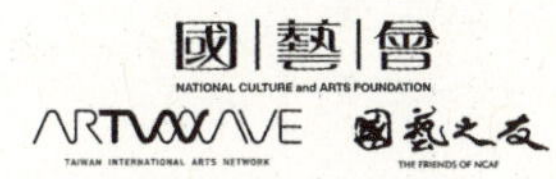
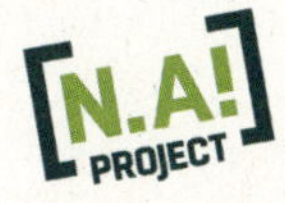

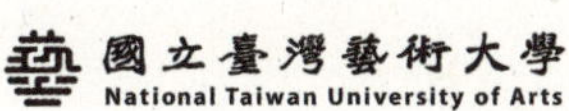
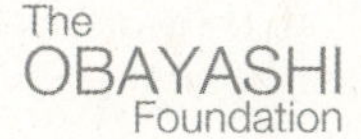
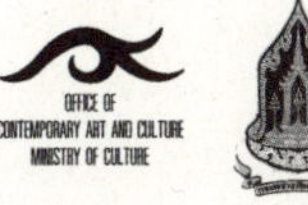

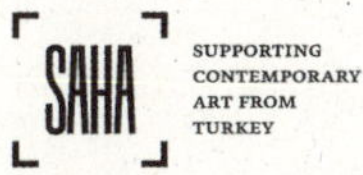
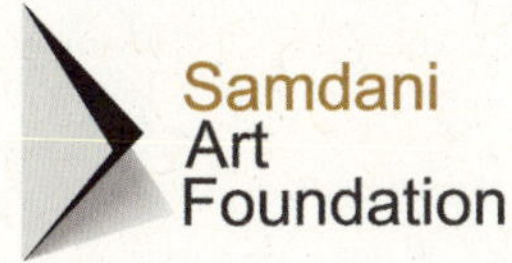

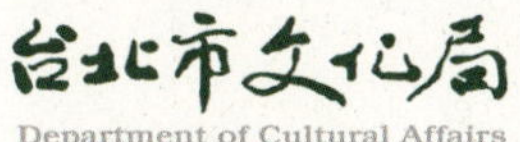

Teiger   Foundation

Contributors

Baunataler Diakonie Kassel e. V.
Bunna Kaffeemanufaktur e. K.
Fachhochschule des Mittelstands
Georg-August-Universität Göttingen
GWG – Gemeinnützige Wohnungsbaugesellschaft
der Stadt Kassel mbH
HessenForst
Hütt-Brauerei Bettenhäuser GmbH & Co. KG
Justus-Liebig Universität Gießen
Kassel Marketing GmbH
Kasseler Verkehrs- und Versorgungs-GmbH
Kunsthaus Göttingen gGmbH
Landfleischerei Koch
Offene Schule Waldau
Regionalmanagement Nordhessen GmbH
Sonett GmbH
Saatgutkonfetti BBS UG (haftungsbeschränkt)
Schlitzer Korn- & Edelobstbrennerei GmbH
soki
Steidl GmbH & Co. OHG
Teppichmanufaktur Habbishaw
Universität Kassel


Corporate Partners

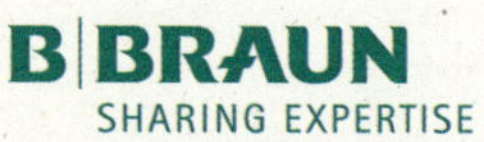

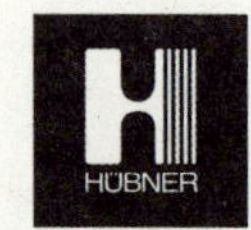

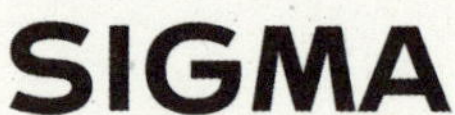

Supporters

August Lücking GmbH & Co. KG
BASTION KUNST e.V.
byon GmbH
Caparol Farben Lacke Bautenschutz GmbH
Druckerei Boxan
Faubel & Co. Nachf. GmbH
FUJIFILM Deutschland
INAPA Deutschland
W. & L. Jordan GmbH
Mathieu Carrière
MOST gartenlandschaften
Orbit Transporturi Internationale
Owsley Brown III
SFC Energy AG
Technisches Hilfswerk Kassel
Thiele & Schwarz
Wendy Lee & Stephen Li and Virginia & Wellington Yee
Westermann Gerüstbau


Friends

Anna & Stefan Schreiter
Irene & Bertrand Jacoberger
Michael Andreae-Jäckering


Media Partners                    Marketing Partners

Asphalt                           STRÖER

# APPendix

documenta fifteen would not have been possible without the extraordinary commitment, passion, perseverance, competence, willingness to compromise and firmness, but above all without the never-ending belief in the success of many people. Therefore, I thank everyone from the bottom of my heart who made this exhibition possible.

Unlike a website, a book has an editorial deadline. In the case of the handbook, this date is May 1, 2022. Unfortunately, changes and requests after printing could not be taken into account, nor could one or the other contributor be included.

For this reason, I would like to expressly refer to our website https://documenta-fifteen.de, which we update regularly. A list of thanks for all those who have supported us so far and will continue to do so even after this book goes to press is available here. There you will also find our sobat-sobat, the friendly companions of our guests, who were unfortunately not yet fully confirmed at the time of going to press.

Now, I wish our guests, our team, and our partners a great deal of joy on the further course of the journey—and I wish the lumbung network that it will continue to grow and flourish even after documenta fifteen.

Sabine Schormann

# DOCUMENTA COMMISSION

MEMBERS

Amar Kanwar
    Artist, filmmaker,
    New Delhi

Charles Esche
    Director of the Van Abbemuseum
    Eindhoven

Elvira Dyangani Ose
    Director MACBA Contemporary
    Art Museum Barcelona

Frances Morris
    Director of Tate Modern
    London

Gabi Ngcobo
    Curatorial Director of Javett
    Art Centre at the University of
    Pretoria (Javett-UP)

Jochen Volz
    Director of the Pinacoteca
    do Estado de São Paulo

Philippe Pirotte
    Professor at Staatliche
    Hochschule für Bildende Künste –
    Städelschule Frankfurt am Main

Ute Meta Bauer
    Founding Director of the NTU
    Centre for Contemporary Art
    Singapore

# DOCUMENTA FIFTEEN TEAM

## ARTISTIC DIRECTION

ruangrupa
Ade Darmawan
Ajeng Nurul Aini
Daniella Fitria Praptono
farid rakun
Indra Ameng
Iswanto Hartono
Julia Sarisetiati
Mirwan Andan
Reza Afisina

Assistant Artistic Direction
Bellina Erby

## ARTISTIC TEAM AND COORDINATION

General Coordinator and Artistic Team
Andrea Linnenkohl

Artistic Team
Ayşe Güleç
Frederikke Hansen
Gertrude Flentge
Lara Khaldi

Assistant to the General Coordinator
Verena Bornmann

Curatorial Coordinator
Chiara Ianeselli

Curatorial Assistants
Cem A.
Gözde Filinta
Jaroslava Tomanová
Jasa McKenzie
Noor Abed
Tyuki Imamura

Coordinator Public Programs
Kasia Wlaszczyk

Assistants Public Programs
David Zabel
Eugene Yiu Nam Cheung
Felipe Steinberg
Kira Goldbourne
Nancy Naser al Deen

Coordinator ruruHaus
Alissa Hälbig

Project Coordinator lumbung
of publishers
Leonhard Flemisch

Travel Department
Veronika Waindzioch

Student Assistant Travel Department
Laura Arico
Philipp Borkiewicz

Office Management
Lisa Pfort

Student Assistant
Robert Semmel

## ACCESSIBILITY AND DIVERSITY

Coordination Accessibility and Diversity
Peter Anhalt

Team Accessibility and Diversity
Bo Melanie Liu
Karoline Köber
Magda Duraj

## EDUCATION AND ART MEDIATION

Head of Education and Art Mediation
Susanne Hesse-Badibanga

Coordination Accessibility and Diversity
Peter Anhalt

Coordination Education and Art
Mediation
Irina Denkmann

Coordination sobat-sobat
Bich Ngoc Luu

Coordination Walks and Stories
(Guided Tours)
Gloria Aino Grzywatz
Jil Hingott

Project Coordination CAMP notes on
education
Katharina Hilgert

Content Management CAMP notes on
education
Lotte Höfert

Editor CAMP notes on education
Raffael Tobias Streicher

Program and Coordination Arts Educators
in Residence
Esther Poppe
Pia Wagner

Sobat-sobat early birds
Andreia Bickenbach
Consuelo Javiera Arévalo-
Ortiz
Flora Saß
Franziska Weygandt
Gudrun Ingratubun
Huizi Yao
Jo Brummack

PARTNERSHIPS AND FUNDING

Head of Partnerships and Funding
Antje Haferkamp

Coordination Partnerships and Funding
Barbara Toopeekoff

Assistant Partnerships and Funding
Eleanor Taylor


PRODUCTION

Head of Production and Technical
Department
Martin Fokken

Deputy Head of Production and Technical
Department – Architectural coordination
Larissa Hüttenhein
Yannis Arvanitis

Coordination Production and Technical
Department
Johannes Choe
Malene Saalmann
Michael Weber
Niki Dimopoulou
Thomas Engelbert

Media Coordination
Ben Brix
Georg Scherlin

Wood Workshop Manager
Lukas Laudage

Coordination Venues
Eric Pries
Erich Weiss
Johannes Schilling
Lydia Antoniou
Ralf Mahr
Torben Röse
Walter Peter

Coordination Lighting
Martin Lange

Head of Restoration
Marlies Peller

Team Restoration
Hannah Backes
Josephine Opitz

Registrars
Feodora Heupel
Robin Vehrs

Office Management Production and
Technical Department
Christina Lindner

Front Desk Production and Technical
Department
Teresa Fichtel

Student Assistants Production and
Technical Department
Hannah Horn
Pauline Brämer
Vicco Agung Saputra

Intern Production and Technical
Department
Baldwin Maslim
Felix Esche


PUBLICATIONS

Managing Editor
Petra Schmidt

Executive Editor
Ralf Schlüter

Editor-at-Large
Pablo Larios

Editor
Sofia Asvestopoulos

Picture Editor
Frauke Schnoor

Artistic Editor
consonni

Student Assistant
Annika Immisch


SECURITY

Safety Advisor
Ralf Rauwolf

Assistant Safety Advisor
Gunter Göring

Head of Guards
Dieter Trümpert

Assistant Head of Guards
Canan Aksu
Kevin Stuhl

DOCUMENTA ARCHIV

Director
Dr. Birgitta Coers

Personal Assistant to the Director and
Administration
Alexandra Winterhoff
Sigrid Heisel-Hennchen

Head of Records, Papers and Media Archive
Saskia Mattern

Cataloguing, Service and Reading Room
André Biribanti
Berlind Schneider
Fynn Grage
Jenny Beringmeier
Karoline Achilles
Lena Küh
Natalie Schmidt
Susanne Rübsamnel
Marcus Freymuth
Mareike Walch

Head of Art Library
Sara Melchior

Art Library Service
Emily Denyer

Documentation
Michael Gärtner

Research
Dr. Sebastian Borkhardt
Martin Groh

Communication and Research
Julius Lehmann

Media and Paper Conservation
Arlett Sauermann
Melissa Köhler

Media archive Student Assistants
Anne Koch
Diana Weber
Kevin Anacker
Lukas Eckhardt
Maximilian Preuss
Paula Hummel

MANAGEMENT
DOCUMENTA AND MUSEUM
FRIDERICIANUM GGMBH

Director General
Chief Executive Officer
Dr. Sabine Schormann

Personal Assistants to the CEO
Joanne Eberlein
Jutta Büsch


FINANCE AND HUMAN
RESOURCES

Finance Director
Authorized Signatory
Andreas Brandenstein

Head of Controlling
Andreas Konradi

Assistant Privacy and Tendering
Matthias Schröder

Financial Accounting
Karin Balzer-Meyer

Head of Human Resources
Brigitte Gabler

Assistants Human and Finance
Resources
Carmen Glahn
Tomke Aljets

Student Assistant Human Resources
Jana Wesemüller


LEGAL AND POLICY ISSUES

Head of legal and Policy Issues
Sustainability Manager
Philipp Greguhn

In-house Counsels
Jan Merten Stey
Max Caspar Gödde

# KASSEL EKOSISTEM

Ekosistem, the Indonesian word for ecosystem, describes collaborative networks through which knowledge, resources, and ideas are exchanged, shared, and networked. The Kassel ecosystem is the local network consisting of Kassel collectives and initiatives that collaborate with documenta fifteen on this basis. This list will be printed at the time of publication, but the network is constantly growing. The up-to-date list can be found on our website: www.documenta-fifteen.de

AG Streetworker
allerleih e.V.
Arnold-Bode-Schule Kassel
Autohaus Autohaus zur Förderung von Kunst und Kultur e.V.
Baunataler Diakonie
Begegnungsstätte amos
Biolandhof Krug
Buchkinder Kassel
Bund Deutscher Architekten BDA im Lande Hessen e.V.
Christine Seefried
Colectivo Espora
ColorLabor
Create a political Player
Das Rollschuhmagazin
dezentrale
Die Kopiloten e.V.
Die Stadtreiniger Kassel
DOCUTOPIA
Dynamo Windrad e.V.
Essbare Stadt e.V.
Feinmechanik Kassel
Film-Shop Kassel
ForstFeldGarten
free entry
Freies Radio Kassel e.V.
Fridays for Future Kassel
Friedensbewegung Kassel
Friedrich-Wöhler-Schule
Gallerie Feiertag
Gärtnerei Fuldaaue
Gemeinnützige Wohnungsbaugesellschaft der Stadt Kassel mbH
Georg-Christoph-Lichtenberg-Schule
Glasdach e.V.
Herderschule Kassel
Hier im Quartier
Hugenottenhaus
Indo Club Night (Insan Larasati et Andara Shastika)
Initiative 6. April
Initiative Schwarze Menschen in Deutschland Bund e.V. - Kassel
Initiativen für Materialkreisläufe
Jüdische Gemeinde Kassel
K&K Stauden
k.format e.V.
Karibu Kassel e.V.
Kassel Marketing GmbH
Kassel postkolonial
Kasseler Dokumentarfilm- und Videofest
Kein Schlussstrich!
Kiosk Miriamstrasse
Klimacamp Kassel
kmmn_practice
Kollektiv eigenklang
Kollektivkultur Kassel
KolorCubes e.V.
Kompost-Kollektiv
Kulturamt der Stadt Kassel
Kulturfabrik Salzmann e.V.
Kulturwerkstatt KARNAK
Kulturzelt
Kulturzentrum Schlachthof e.V.
Kunsthochschule Kassel
Lolita Bar
Lost & Found Records
Materialverteilung Kassel
Minicar Citycar Kassel
Moving School e.V.
Mr. Wilson Skatehalle
Multidimensional Strategies Class 2021 of the Kunsthochschule Kassel
Museumslandschaft Hessen Kassel
Neue Brüderkirche
Neue Brüderkirche Community garden
No One is Illegal
Offene Schule Waldau
Offener Kanal Kassel
Ohrenkratzer e.V.
OMAS GEGEN RECHTS (Regionalgruppe Kassel)
ook_me_sobat
outlet.label
„Raamwerk e.V.
Studio für Kunst, Sozial, Kommerz"
Radio Rasclat
Randfilm e.V.
Reformschule Kassel
RHO Kollektiv
Rotopol
Sandershaus e.V.
Schule Hegelsberg
SHARDS - Fliesen aus Bauschutt
Social Sciences Lab
Solidarische Landwirtschaft für Kassel & Umgebung e.V.
Spielmobil Rote Rübe e.V
Staatstheater Kassel
Stadtteilzentrum Wesertor
Station of Commons
Sticky Frames
Streetbolzer e.V.
Study program in product design at the Kunsthochschule Kassel
tanz*werk kassel e.V.
TERRARISTA TV
The Pawn Broker
The Rapid Publisher
Theaterstübchen
Titus Kassel
TOKONOMA e.V.
Trafohaus
Universität Kassel
Unterneustädter Schule
Urbane Experimente e.V.
Warte für Kunst
ZukunftsDorf22

# IMAGE CREDITS

Cover illustration © Studio 4oo2 for documenta und Museum Fridericianum gGmbH

Flap illustration (front) courtesy Iswanto Hartono

p.8 courtesy Indra Ameng

p.9 courtesy Studio 4oo2

p.10-11 right: courtesy Andrés Villalobos, left: courtesy Daniella F Praptono

p.12 courtesy Ade Darmawan

p.13 courtesy Gudskul

p.14-15 courtesy Daniella F Praptono

p.16 courtesy Abdul Dube

p.17-18 courtesy Nino Bulling

p.19 courtesy Abdul Dube

p.20-21 left: courtesy Dan Perjovschi, right: courtesy Jazael Olguín Zapata

p.22-23 courtesy Tropical Tap Water

p.24-25 courtesy Indra Ameng

p.26-27 left: courtesy Sari Dennise, rechts: courtesy Andrés Villalobos

p.28-29 left: courtesy Andrés Villalobos, right: courtesy Safdar Ahmed

p.30-31 left: courtesy Cem A., right: courtesy krishan rajapakshe / *fC*c

p.32-33 courtesy Angga Cipta

p.34-35 left: Abdul Dube. right: Karte © Stadt Kassel - Vermessung und Geoinformation, Diagram: Iswanto Hartono S.36-37 courtesy Sheree Domingo

p.38.39 left: courtesy Indra Ameng, right: courtesy Daniella F Praptono

p.41 courtesy Nino Bulling

p.43 courtesy Cem A.

p.46 courtesy *foundationClass* collective

p.49 courtesy Agus Nur Amal PMTOH; Photo: 324 FRAME production

p.50 Photo: Nicolas Wefers for documenta und Museum Fridericianum gGmbH

p.52-53 courtesy Alice Yard

p.55 courtesy Amol K Patil

p.56 Photo: Christian Nyampeta / Huye Working Group in ARAC

p.59 © Hichem Merouche / Archives des luttes des femmes en Algérie

p.60 courtesy Arts Collaboratory

p.62-63 © Jazael Olguín Zapata; courtesy Arts Collaboratory

p.65 courtesy Yin Xiuzhen

p.67 © Studio Verve

p.68-69 Jean Claude Saintilus: courtesy Jean Claude Saintilus and Pioneer Works; Photo: Daniel Bradica. Ghetto Biennale: Photo: Lazaros

p.71 courtesy Baan Noorg Collaborative Arts and Culture

p.72-73 Reclamation: Space-Times: courtesy Black Quantum Futurism and Monument Lab and The Village of Arts & Humanities; Photo: Nomieh Jovin. Nonlinear Histories: courtesy Black Quantum Futurism and Manifesta 13 Marseille; Photo: Jean Christophe Let

p.74 courtesy BOLOHO

p.77 courtesy Britto Arts Trust; Photo: Shahriar Shaon

p.78-79 courtesy Britto Arts Trust; Photo: Emdadul Hoque

p.81 Photo: Cao Minghao & Chen Jianjun

p.82 © Prodige Makonga, courtesy Centre d'art Waza

p.85 courtesy Chang En-Man

p.87 courtesy Chimurenga

p.88 courtesy Takashi Kuribayashi

p.91 courtesy Dan Perjovschi

p.92 courtesy El Warcha

p.95 courtesy Erick Beltrán

p.96 courtesy FAFSWAG Arts Collective

p.98-99 courtesy FAFSWAG Arts Collective; Photo: Pati Solomona Tyrell

p.101 courtesy Fehras Publishing Practices and Mosaic Rooms, London; Photo: Noam Gorbat

p.102 courtesy Foundation Festival Sur la Niger. Photo: Kôrè Design

p.104-105 all images: courtesy Foundation Festival Sur la Niger. Photos: Kôrè Design

p.106-107 courtesy Deborah Salles and Graziela Kunsch p.109-111 all images courtesy Gudskul

p.113 courtesy Hamja Ahsan; Graphic Design: Ala Uddin

p.114 Photos: ikkibawiKrrr

p.117 courtesy INLAND

p.118-119 diagram: courtesy INLAND. Cheese tasting: courtesy INLAND; Photo: Marta Goro.

p.120 Photo: INSTAR

p.125-127 all images: courtesy Jatiwangi art Factory

p.128 courtesy Labinac; Photo: Amedeo Benestante

p.130 courtesy Jumana Emil Abboud and Sharjah Art Foundation; Photo: Issa Freij

p.132-133 all images courtesy Jumana Emil Abboud

p.135 courtesy
Keleketla! Library
and 10th Berlin
Biennale. Photo:
Timo Ohler
p.136 courtesy Kiri
Dalena
p.139 courtesy Komîna
Fîlm a Rojava;
Photo: Eli Kocer
p.140 courtesy Tulio
de Sagastizábal
and La Intermundial
Holobiente
p.143 courtesy LE 18
p.144 Photo:
MADEYOULOOK
p.146 courtesy Marwa
Arsanios
p.149 courtesy
Fernando Arias,
Atelier Van Lieshout
and El Honorable
cartel
p.150-151 courtesy
Fernando Arias and
El Honorable cartel
p.153 courtesy Nguyen
Trinh Thi; Photo:
Jamie Maxtone-Graham
p.154 © Tuấn Mami
p.157 courtesy Nino
Bulling
p.158 Eva Koťátková:
courtesy the artist,
Meyer Riegger,
Berlin/Karlsruhe
and hunt kastner,
Prague. Photo:
© Kristof Vrancken /
VG-Bild-Kunst, Bonn
2022
p.160-161 Małgorzata
Mirga-Tas: courtesy
Private collection;
Photo: Maciej
Zaniewski. Mara
Oláh (Omara):
courtesy Everybody
Needs Art and
Longtermhandstand,
Budapest
p.163 courtesy OOK_
[REINAART VANHOE,
NEUE BRÜDERKIRCHE,
ESPORA, BPOC
FESTIVAL KASSEL, ME_
SOBAT, COLORLABOR,
GRAANSCHUUR
TARWEWIJK, ELAINE W.
HO, BARTIRA, WOK THE
ROCK, COLLECTIVE, K.
FORMAT, TAKE-A-WAY,
PLAN B, DYNAMITAS
UNLIMITED, ... ]

p.164 all images
courtesy Vidisha-
Fadescha;
Illustration:
Jonathan Eden
p.167 courtesy Pınar
Öğrenci
p.168 Turner Prize
Exhibition:
courtesy Herbert
Art Gallery &
Museum; Photo: Garry
Jones Photography.
EXPLORERS: © Project
Art Works
p.170-171 © Project
Art Works
p.173 courtesy
Richard Bell and
Milani Gallery,
Brisbane; Photo:
Graeme Auchterlonie
p.174 courtesy Sa Sa
Art Projects; Photo:
Lok Chanmakara
p.177 courtesy Sajjad
Abbas
p.178 all images
courtesy Safdar
Ahmed; Alien
Citizen: © Susie
Nelson / VG Bild-
Kunst Bonn, 2022;
Cleaning In
Progress: courtesy
Miream Salameh
p.181 courtesy Saodat
Ismailova
p.183 courtesy Daria
Kim
p.184 courtesy
Serigrafistas Queer
p.187 Photo: Okacha
Ben Salah
p.188 courtesy
Sourabh Phadke
p.191 Scenes of
Occupation: courtesy
Mustafa Abu Ali
and the Palestine
Cinema Group; Photo:
Subversive Film.
Kuneitra: courtesy
Jim Cranmer and
the American Peace
Committee; Photo:
Subversive Film
p.192 -195 Photos:
Taring Padi
p.197 Photo: The
Black Archives
p.198 courtesy Noel
Kasyoka / The Nest
Collective

p.201 courtesy
Question of Funding
p.202-203 courtesy
Mohammad Al Hawajri
p.204 courtesy
Joachim Hamou
p.206-207 © Britta
Thomsen / Weekend
Trampoline House
p.209 courtesy
Wajukuu Art Project;
Photos: James Wamae
p.210-211 courtesy
Wajukuu Art Project;
Photo: Gitonga James
p.212 courtesy
Wakaliga Uganda
p.215 Photo: Ssempala
Sulaiman
p.217 courtesy
yasmine eid-sabbagh
p.218 © KUNSTrePUBLIK
/ VG Bild-Kunst
Bonn, 2022; Photos:
Victoria Tomaschko
p.220-221 © and
courtesy
KUNSTrePUBLIK /
VG Bild-Kunst Bonn
p.226-265 all map
illustrations:
© Janosch Feiertag
for documenta und
Museum Fridericianum
gGmbH; all photos:
© Nicolas Wefers for
documenta und Museum
Fridericianum gGmbH
p.268 © documenta
und Museum
Fridericianum gGmbH
Flap illustration
(back):©Janosch
Feiertag for
documenta und Museum
Fridericianum gGmbH

# AUTHORS

**A.K. KAIZA** (he/him)
Kaiza is a Ugandan journalist and writer who has been an art and literary critic for over two decades. He has been animator and creator of a children's television program, editor of an arts magazine as well as a literary editor. He is currently working in the field of arts and culture development and research in Uganda and Eastern Africa.

**ALVIN LI** (he/him)
Alvin Li is a curator and writer based in Shanghai, China. He currently serves as Adjunct Curator, Greater China, Supported by the Robert H. N. Ho Family Foundation, at Tate; and a contributing editor of *frieze* magazine.

**ANDREW MAERKLE** (he/him)
Andrew Maerkle is a writer, editor, and translator based in Tokyo, Japan. He teaches in the Graduate School of Global Arts at Tokyo University of the Arts. His book of translations *Kishio Suga: Writings, vol. 1, 1969–1979* was recently published by Skira.

**ANN MBUTI** (she/her)
Ann Mbuti is a freelance writer and cultural publicist. She investigates contemporary art and (pop) cultures with a focus on their potential for social change, new fictions, and alternative narratives. Her book on Black Artists will be published by C.H. Beck in the fall of 2022. Ann Mbuti lives and works in Zurich, Switzerland.

**ANNIE JAEL KWAN** (she/her)
Based in London, UK, Annie Jael Kwan is an independent curator and researcher whose practice is located at the intersection of contemporary art, art history, and cultural activism, with interest in archives, histories, feminist, queer and alternative knowledges, collective practices, and solidarity. She leads the research network Asia-Art-Activism and is the instigator of Asia Forum.

**ASHRAF JAMAL** (he/him)
Ashraf Jamal is the author of *In the World: Essays on Contemporary South African Art* and *Strange Cargo: Essays on Art*. He is also the co-author of *Art in South Africa: The Future Present*, the co-editor of Indian Ocean Studies, and the author of *Predicaments of Culture in South Africa, Love themes for the wilderness*, and the award-winning short fiction, *The Shades*. He is a Research Associate at VIAD, the Visual Identities in Art and Design Research Centre, University of Johannesburg, and a regular contributor to *Art Times* and *ArtThrob*.

**WONG BINGHAO** (they/them)
Wong Binghao is a writer, editor, curator, and currently C-MAP Asia Fellow for the Museum of Modern Art, New York, US. They eclectically constellate and mediate ideas, scenes, and devotions in the hope of more expansive, ethical worlds. Their research focuses on feminist, queer, and transgender studies, pop culture, critical theory, digital cultures, and Southeast Asian studies.

**CAMILO JIMÉNEZ SANTOFIMIO** (he/him)
Camilo Jiménez Santofimio is a Colombian journalist, editor, media manager, and consultant with more than sixteen years of experience in media and cultural organizations. He has developed creative initiatives in journalistic, social, and transmedia projects.

**CARINE ZAAYMAN** (she/her)
Carine Zaayman is an artist, curator and scholar committed to critical engagement with colonial archives and collections, specifically those holding strands of Khoekhoe pasts in South Africa. She is currently a postdoctoral researcher in the Worlding Public Culture project, based at the VU, Amsterdam, the Netherlands, and the Research Center for Material Culture in the Netherlands.

CAROL QUE (she/her)
Carol Que is a Chinese migrant settler living in
Naarm/Melbourne on Kulin Lands. Her writing,
teaching, translating, and organizing is invested
in anticolonial and anti-imperial grassroots
struggles.

CHIARA DE CESARI (she/her)
Chiara De Cesari is Associate Professor in
European Studies and Cultural Studies at the
University of Amsterdam, the Netherlands. Her
research explores how forms of memory, heritage, art, and cultural politics are shifting under
conditions of contemporary globalization, (post)
coloniality and state transformation. Chiara leads
the Dutch Research Council-funded Vidi project
on *Imagining Institutions Otherwise: Art, Politics,
and State Transformation*. She is the author of
*Heritage and the Cultural Struggle for Palestine*
(2019), and co-editor of two key volumes in
memory studies (*European Memory in Populism*,
Routledge, 2019; *Transnational Memory*, de
Gruyter, 2014), and of a special issue of the
International Journal of Heritage Studies on urban
heritage and gentrification (2018).

DAGARA DAKIN (he/him)
Dagara Dakin is an art critic and a curator. He
teaches Aesthetics at Paris 8 University and
African Art history (1960s to the present day)
École normale supérieure Paris-Saclay. He recent-
ly published an article in Shirn Magazine titled
"Emerging from anonymity." He lives and works
in Paris , France.

ENOS NYAMOR (he/him)
Enos Nyamor is an art writer and cultural critic
based in New York, US. He is presently working on
a collection of essays on the textures of new media
art consciousness, as well as post-nationalist
urban experiences across Sub-saharan Africa.

FARHIYA KHALID (she/her)
Farhiya Khalid is a Somali journalist and historian
based in Copenhagen, Denmark. Her work examines ethnic media representation, islamophobia,
and right-wing populist discourse in Danish
media. She is also a board member of the Danish
association Responsible Press. Her recent work
includes "More Than Bricks": a podcast about the
Danish ghetto laws that critically investigates the
legislation and its consequences for immigrant
residents in public housing areas.

FERDIANSYAH THAJIB (he/him)
Ferdiansyah Thajib is currently a Postdoctoral
Fellow at the Leipzig Lab, Leipzig University,
Germany. He is also a member of KUNCI Study
Forum & Collective, a transdisciplinary research
collective in Yogyakarta, Indonesia, which since
its founding in 1999 has been experimenting
with modes of producing and sharing knowledge
through studying together.

HERA CHAN (she/her)
Hera Chan is a cultural worker living in
Amsterdam, the Netherlands, by way of Kowloon,
Hong Kong. Currently, she is working on a series
of essays about artistic practices critical to our
understanding of the global uprisings of 2019, with
a focus on the Milk Tea Alliance.

JOACHIM BEN YAKOUB (he/him)
Joachim Ben Yakoub is a writer, researcher and
lecturer operating on the border of different art
institutions and schools in between Tunis, Tunisia,
and Brussels, Belgium. He is currently experimenting with different rhythms of hosting and sharing
fugitive artistic praxis.

KRZYSZTOF KOŚCIUCZUK (he/him)
Krzysztof Kościuczuk prepares art exhibitions,
writes, and works with institutions engaged in
learning. He had previously worked at, amongst
others, Foksal Gallery Foundation, Warsaw,
Poland; German Center for Art History, Paris,
France; documenta 14, Athens/Kassel. He has
served as Artistic Director of Muzeum Susch,
Switzerland. He lives in Basel, Switzerland.

MARTA FERNÁNDEZ CAMPA (she/her)
Marta Fernández Campa is a researcher and
writer. She has published articles and interviews
on Caribbean literature and visual art in various
anthologies and journals including Callaloo and
Small Axe. She also serves as special projects editor
for the cross-disciplinary and multilingual journal
*Caribbean InTransit*.

MAX KÜHLEM (he/him)
Max Kühlem is active as a freelance cultural
journalist, author, presenter, and songwriter.
His work focuses on North Rhine-Westphalia,
but he also travels to Kassel, where he lived
previously. He writes for daily newspapers such
as *taz*, *Berliner Zeitung*, *Ruhr Nachrichten*,
*Rheinische Post*, magazines like *Rolling Stone*,
*WestfalenSpiegel*, *EIKON*, and online portals such
as *Nachtkritik.de*.

NURAINI JULIASTUTI (she/her)
Nuraini Juliastuti is a trans-local researcher,
focusing on art organizations, alternative cultural
production, and vernacular archiving. Nuraini
co-founded the Kunci Study Forum & Collective
in Yogyakarta, Indonesia. She is a postdoctoral
fellow at the Worlding Public Cultures: The Arts
and Social Innovation, University of Amsterdam,
the Netherlands.

ÖVÜL Ö. DURMUŞOĞLU (she/her)
Övül Ö. Durmuşoğlu is an independent curator,
educator and writer, currently guest professor
and program co-leader in the Graduate School,
UdK Berlin, Germany, and visiting professor
in the HBK Braunschweig, Germany. Övül has
recently co-curated the 3rd Autostrada Biennale
in Kosovo, 12th Survival Kit Festival in Riga,
Latvia, and *Die Balkone: Life, Art, Pandemic
and Proximity* in Berlin (2020-21), with Joanna
Warsza. In the past, she was curator at Steirischer
Herbst; co-curated different sections of 10th,
13th and 14th Istanbul Biennials; and organized
Public Programs for dOCUMENTA (13), among
others. She is co-curator for the 4th edition of the
Autostrada Biennale in 2023.

PABLO LARIOS (he/him)
Pablo Larios is a writer and Editor-At-Large
of Publications for documenta fifteen. Born in
San Pedro Sula, Honduras, he lives in Berlin,
Germany.

RALF SCHLÜTER (he/him)
Ralf Schlüter is Executive Editor Publications of
documenta fifteen and lives in Berlin, Germany.
He is a cultural journalist who writes for magazines and newspapers and is also the author and
host of the podcasts *Zeitgeister* and *Ulysses lesen*.
From 2006 to 2020, he was deputy editor-in-chief
at magazine *Art* in Hamburg, Germany.

RAYYA BADRAN (she/her)
Rayya Badran is a writer, translator, and educator
based in Beirut, Lebanon. Her writings and translations have been featured widely. She has taught
courses on contemporary art and sound studies at
the American University of Beirut since 2014 and
has a bi-monthly show on Radio al Hara.

SKYE ARUNDHATI THOMAS (they/them)
Skye Arundhati Thomas is a writer and editor
based in Goa, India. They write for *The London
Review of Books*, *Artforum*, *frieze*, and others.
They are co-editor of *The White Review*. Their
first book *Remember the Details*, on viral images,
chargesheets, and a brief history of a protest movement, is out now with Floating Opera Press.

TINA SHERWELL (she/her)
Tina Sherwell is an artist, curator, and art historian. She is currently Visiting Professor at NYU
Abu Dhabi, UAE, in the Art and History Program.
She was Head of Contemporary Visual Art and
Birzeit University (2017-2021) prior to which
she was Director of the International Academy
of Art, Palestine (2007-2012, & 2013-2017) and
curator of *Intimate Terrains: Representations
of a Diaspearing Landscape at The Palestinian
Museum* (2019).

# INDEX

# COLOPHON


**HANDBOOK**
documenta fifteen, Kassel
June 18 – September 25, 2022

**Artistic Direction**
ruangrupa
Ade Darmawan
Ajeng Nurul Aini
Daniella Fitria Praptono
farid rakun
Indra Ameng
Iswanto Hartono
Julia Sarisetiati
Mirwan Andan
Reza Afisina

**Artistic Team**
Gertrude Flentge
Ayşe Güleç
Frederikke Hansen
Lara Khaldi
Andrea Linnenkohl

**Managing Editor**
Petra Schmidt

**Executive Editor**
Ralf Schlüter

**Editor-at-Large**
Pablo Larios

**Graphic Design**
Leon Schniewind

**Layout**
Rutger Fuchs Amsterdam

**Photo Editing**
Frauke Schnoor

**Editor**
Sofia Asvestopoulos

**Student Assistant**
Annika Immisch

**Translations**
From German
Steven Lindberg

**Copyediting and Proofreading**
Hannah Young

**Hatje Cantz**
**Editorial Team**
Lincoln Dexter
Nicola von Velsen
**Project Assistance**
Yannick Schütte
**Production**
Thomas Lemaître
**Sales**
Claudia Squara

**Artistic Editor**
consonni
Dina Camorino Bua
María Macía Dávila
María Mur Dean
Marta Alonso-Buenaposada
 del Hoyo
Munts Brunet Navarro

**Lithography**
DruckConcept, Berlin

**Paper**
Inside pages – 100 g/m² Lettura 80 Print
Cover – 270 g/m² Creative Print diamant

**Typefaces**
MBI DCMNT 15 – Fabian Maier-Bode
PP Editorial New – Pangram Pangram
Söhne Mono – Klim Type

**Visual Identity**
Studio 4oo2
Stan Hema
Leon Schniewind

Cover illustration:
© documenta und Museum Fridericianum gGmbH

© 2022 documenta und Museum Fridericianum gGmbH, Hatje Cantz Verlag GmbH and authors

© 2022 for the reproduced works by KUNSTrePUBLIK, Kristof Vrancken, Susie Nelson: VG Bild-Kunst Bonn 2022, the artists and their legal successors

S. 4 – 5, Poem *I Want You to Hear These Words About Jo Ann Yellowbird (Ars Poetica)* by Jimmie Durham. Published in: *Poems That Do Not Go Together*, Wiens Verlag, Berlin und Edition Hansjörg Mayer, London, 2012. Courtesy: Estate Jimmie Durham.
© the publishers and Maria Thereza Alves

Editorial deadline:
May 1 / July 14, 2022

**DOCUMENTA UND MUSEUM FRIDERICIANUM GGMBH**
Friedrichsplatz 18
34117 Kassel
Germany
www.documenta.de

**CEO documenta und Museum Fridericianum gGmbH (Director General)**
Dr. Sabine Schormann

**Print and binding**
Westermann Druck Zwickau GmbH
Crimmitschauer Str. 43
08058 Zwickau
Germany

**Published by**
Hatje Cantz Verlag GmbH
Mommsenstraße 27
10629 Berlin
Germany
www.hatjecantz.de
A Ganske Publishing Group Company

ISBN: 978-3-7757-5281-7 (German)
ISBN: 978-3-7757-5282-4 (English)

Printed in Germany

**The documenta fifteen Handbook is also available as e-Book:**
ISBN: 978-3-7757-5351-7 (German)
ISBN: 978-3-7757-5353-1 (English)